HISTORICAL RECORDS

OF THE

FAMILY OF LESLIE

Printed by R. Clark,

FOR

EDMONSTON & DOUGLAS, EDINBURGH.

LONDON . . . HAMILTON, ADAMS, AND CO.

CAMBRIDGE . MACMILLAN AND CO

DUBLIN . . M'GLASHAN AND GILL.

GLASGOW . . . JAMES MACLEHOSE.

HISTORICAL RECORDS

OF THE

FAMILY OF LESLIE

FROM

1067 TO 1868-9

Collected from Public Records and Authentic Private Sources

BY

COLONEL LESLIE, K.H.

OF BALQUHAIN

VOL. III.

EDINBURGH
EDMONSTON AND DOUGLAS
1869

CONTENTS OF VOL. III.

CHAPTER I.

CHAPTER II.

CHAPTER III.

APPENDIX.

CONTENTS.

CHAPTER I.

SIR GEORGE LESLIE,

FIRST BARON OF BALQUHAIN.

George, First Baron of Balquhain.

THE distinguished family of Balquhain is, as Sir Walter Scott styles it, an ancient and honourable family of an ancient and honourable name. It is descended from Sir George Leslie, fifth son of Sir Andrew de Leslie, sixth Dominus Ejusdem, or of that Ilk, by his wife Mary Abernethy.

Sir George Leslie got the estate of Balquhain, in the Garioch in Aberdeenshire, from his father, and obtained a royal grant of it for his services to Robert Bruce in his wars against Edward II., and in those against Edward Baliol during the minority of David II., from whom, in 1340, he received 1340.
charters of the lands and baronies of Balquhain, Syde, and Braco, which his family have continued to possess for upwards of 500 years. Hence he and his successors received the style and title of Barons of Balquhain, and use supporters to their arms—a privilege allowed only to the oldest barons, and acquired by this family very deservedly for its public services, antiquity, extensive possessions, and the number, rank, and quality of its

CHAP. I.

George, First Baron of Balquhain.

descendants. The Barons of Balquhain were wont to be created knights-bachelors, a dignity then only conferred upon earls and great barons, and many of them held the office of Sheriff-principal, or chief magistrate, of their native county of Aberdeen, which office was intrusted solely to the highest nobility.

The following noble and distinguished families in Scotland, Ireland, France, and Germany, are descended from the family of Balquhain:—

I. The Counts Leslie, in Germany.

II. The Leslies of Pitcaple, from whom are descended the Leslies of Old Craig.

III. The Leslies of Kincraigie.

IV. The Leslies of Wardis, baronets, from whom are descended the Leslies of Warthill, the Leslies of Bucharn, the Leslies of Clisson in France, the Leslies of Dyce, the Leslies of Tarbet in Ireland, and the Leslies of Glasslough, also in Ireland.

V. The Leslies of New Leslie, from whom are descended the Leslies of Kininvie, and the family of Leslie, Earls of Leven.

VI. The Leslies of Crichie, from whom was descended General Sir Alexander Leslie of Auchintoul.

VII. The Leslies of Iden, from whom is descended the family of Tytler of Woodhouselee.

VIII. The Leslies of Cults, from whom was descended John Leslie, Bishop of Ross in the reign of Queen Mary.

Sir George Leslie, first Baron of Balquhain, married Elizabeth Keith, daughter of the Baron of Inverugie, and by her had a son, Hamelin, who succeeded him as second Baron of Balquhain.

1351. Sir George Leslie died in 1351, and was buried in the churchyard of Logydurno.

CHAP. I.

SIR HAMELIN LESLIE,

SECOND BARON OF BALQUHAIN.

Hamelin, Second Baron of Balquhain.

SIR HAMELIN LESLIE, son of Sir George Leslie, first Baron of Balquhain, by his wife Elizabeth Keith of Inverugie, succeeded his father as second Baron of Balquhain in 1351. 1351.

Hamelinus de Leslie had a passport or safe-conduct, for himself and two knights, to go into England as far as the city of Canterbury, with liberty to remain there till the ensuing Michaelmas, and then to return to his own country—dated at Westminster, the 10th November 1362.* 1362.

Sir Hamelin Leslie married Ann Maxwell, daughter of Lord Maxwell of Carlaverock, whose successors became Earls of Nithsdale. By her he had issue—

I. ANDREW, who succeeded as third Baron of Balquhain.

II. A Daughter, married to the Laird of Baldathsche.

Sir Hamelin Leslie died in 1378. 1378.

SIR ANDREW LESLIE,

THIRD BARON OF BALQUHAIN.

Andrew, Third Baron of Balquhain.

SIR ANDREW LESLIE, son of Sir Hamelin Leslie, second Baron of Balquhain, by his wife Ann Maxwell, succeeded his father as third Baron of Balquhain in 1378. 1378.

* *Rotuli Scotiæ*, vol. i. p. 866.

CHAP. I.

Andrew, Third Baron of Balquhain.

Sir Andrew Leslie is documented by an indenture, dated 24th November 1390, between Andrew de Leslie, VIII. Dominus Ejusdem, and Norman Leslie, his son and heir, on the one part, and Andrew de Leslie, Dominus de Syde (third Baron of Balquhain), his cousin, on the other part, relating to the settlement of certain lands; to which indenture Andrew and his son Norman are obliged to procure the confirmation of George de Leslie, Dominus de Rothes, heir of entail to the said Andrew and Norman. By this indenture, Andrew de Leslie of Syde and Balquhain got a grant of £13 : 6 : 8 of annual rent, out of the lands of Leslie and Cushnie, from Sir Andrew de Leslie, Dominus Ejusdem, and his son Norman.*

Sir Andrew Leslie seems to have been a turbulent baron, and of very loose morals. He had a numerous progeny of natural children, from whom many Leslies are descended. The Leslies of Buchanstone, Andrew Leslie of Cortashy, James Leslie in Aberdeen, David Leslie in Meikle Durno, George Leslie in Drumdollo, Andrew Leslie in Pitscurry, and many others, were all descended from, or were natural sons of, Sir Andrew Leslie.

One of these natural sons, Andrew Leslie of Pitscurry, was the cause of a great feud between the Leslies and the Forbeses. He carried off the

* *Retour of Charters*, Signet Library, Edinburgh.

CHAP. I.

Andrew, Third Baron of Balquhain.

daughter of Thomas Bisset of Balhagarty, commonly called the Fair Maid of Kemnay, and married her,—she being at the time betrothed to Sir John Forbes of Druminnor, ancestor of the Lords Forbes, and who was bailie to the Earl of Mar for the lands of Balhagarty. Forbes having gathered together a great number of men, attacked the castle of Balquhain, and took and burned it. This occasioned much bloodshed, for Sir Andrew Leslie raised his friends, vassals, and followers, and pursued the Forbeses into their own country, and, in retaliation, destroyed the house of Sir John Forbes, and devastated a great part of the Forbeses' lands, killing many of the people and burning their houses.

It was probably in consequence of this feud with Sir John Forbes, and because he had also given offence to the Earl of Mar, that Sir Andrew Leslie withdrew from Balquhain, and occupied an old fortress on the almost inaccessible pinnacle of Bennachie, nearly 2000 feet high, and not far from the castle of Balquhain. Having repaired this strong post, he remained there till he made his peace with the Earl of Mar, when he returned to Balquhain; but he still retained the fort on Bennachie as a place of security.

It is said that, during his abode on Bennachie, he made an incursion, accompanied by a large body of retainers, up to Strathdon, and devastated the lands, and carried off the daughter and heiress

CHAP. I.

Andrew, Third Baron of Balquhain.

of the Baron of Cray, chief of the Clan Allan, and who was called the Fair Maid of Strathdon ; others say that the lady he carried off was a daughter of Sir James Stewart of Inveravon, also called the Fair Maid of Strathdon. It seems certain that by one or other of these ladies he had a natural son, Malcolm, to whom he gave the lands of Cults, and whose great-great-grandson was John Leslie, Bishop of Ross in the reign of Queen Mary.

Sir Andrew Leslie was Master of the Horse under Alexander Stewart, Earl of Mar, and was one of his chief commanders at the battle of Harlaw, fought against Donald, Lord of the Isles,
1411. 24th July 1411, about two miles from the castle of Balquhain. In this desperate action Sir Andrew Leslie lost six sons, in commemoration of whom a cross was erected on the field of battle and called Leslie's Cross.

On account of another feud with the Forbeses, Sir Andrew Leslie again withdrew to his fortress on Bennachie, and a force was brought against him under the Sheriff of Angus. Sir Andrew Leslie, having assembled his friends and vassals, came down from his stronghold, and gave battle to his opponents at Braco, about two miles from
1420. Bennachie, 22d January 1420. In the heat of the action, his wife, Isabel Mortimer, came and threw herself between the combatants, entreating them to stop the carnage. But her efforts were vain. Sir Andrew Leslie was slain, and many of

Andrew, Third Baron of Balquhain.

his vassals fell with him. His widow erected a chaplainry near the spot where he was buried, and appointed a chaplain, and bequeathed an annual rent for the priest in all time coming, to pray for his soul. Patrick Ogilvie, of Ogilvie of Granden, with consent of his father, Alexander Ogilvie, Sheriff of Forfar, also granted an annuity of ten merks forth of the lands of Strathalva in the sheriffdom of Banff, which failing, from the baronies of Owchtirous and Essy in the sheriffdom of Forfar, to a chaplain performing divine service in the chapel of the blessed Virgin Mary of the Garioch, for the soul of Sir Andrew Leslie, knight.*

This chapel, after the Reformation, about 1620, was converted into a parish church, and now gives the name to the parish of Chapel of Garioch, formerly called Logydurno. 1620.

Sir Andrew Leslie married Isabel Mortimer, daughter of Bernard Mortimer of Craigievar, and by her had—

I. William, his successor.

II. Alexander, married to Margaret Leslie, daughter of David de Leslie, IX. Dominus Ejusdem, from whom she received the barony of Leslie in the Garioch, from which her husband derived the style and title of Leslie of Leslie, or of that Ilk.

III. A Daughter, married to Glaster of Glack.

IV. A Daughter, married to Munroe of Foulis.

V. A Daughter, married to Raynold Cheyne of Straloch.

* *Registrum Episcopatus Aberdonensis*, vol. i. p. 222.

CHAP. I.

Andrew, Third Baron of Balquhain.

Sir Andrew Leslie, third Baron of Balquhain, was slain, as has been narrated, at Braco, 22d January 1420, and was succeeded by his eldest son, Sir William Leslie, fourth Baron of Balquhain.

The Battle of Harlaw.

Fought 28th July 1411.

Near this you'll see where famed Harlaw was fought,
When curst rebellion direful mischief wrought;
Here dreaded Donald from the Isles came down,
Fired with ambition, to attack the crown:
Deep, cunning, artful, he, by various wiles,
Indeed the chieftain of the Western Isles.
Here Mar resolved the rebel force to try,
To tame his prowess, or, attempting, die.

The gallant Fraser, Baron of Philorth,
Of well-known courage and undoubted worth;
The Keiths and Forbeses, in bright array,
By him were joined upon that dreadful day;
Angus, high-sheriff, joined them, with the rest
Of Airly's sons, in manly armour drest;
From Aberdeen two hundred warriors came,
All clad in steel, and not unknown to fame:
Brave Provost Davidson led this chosen band,
And bold Hugh Rose held next the sub-command.
Mar led the centre—the wings extend at large;
All keen advance, in order to the charge;
The noble Keith joined Forbes in the van,
Who led his friends and bravest of his clan;
Drum and the Leiths, and Leslies of Balquhain,
Upon the left the gallant Gordons join.

The signal given, loud pipes and trumpets sound;
The direful charge the neighbouring hills resound.

First Keith and Forbes to the battle flew;
The brave example all the rest pursue.

Andrew, Third Baron of Balquhain.

Like wolves rapacious, these daring foes engage ;
Scots rush on Scots, soon all was blood and rage.
The brave Maclean fought on Macdonald's right ;
He, like the mountain bear, maintained the fight ;
Though wounded, sorely pressed, and bathed in blood,
He kept his ground, and made his party good ;
Still used to conquer, and unknown to yield,
Hopes still to gain the glory of the field.

At last the Leslies, bordering on the Don,
Fired by their chief, who led his warriors on,
First pierced the ranks, then broke Macdonald's horse,
And brought the foe to own superior force ;
Then Drum's proud baron, on a dapple grey,
Spoke to the Keith, and pointed out the prey;
Then as the savage tiger scours the plain,
They force their way o'er mountains of the slain.
Now rushing forward, with a well-aimed thrust
Drum stretched the gallant hero in the dust.

Donald, enraged, called out to all,
"Revenge Maclean ! or bravely by him fall.
Let it not now, my gallant friends, be said,
That we, for courage famed, like cowards fled."
The yielding islanders at these words now turn,
Then onward rush, where combats fiercely burn.
Maclachlan and his clansmen fresh pursue,
And kindle all the rage of war anew ;
Though lost their chief, not unrevenged they mourn,
But wound for wound, and blow for blow return.

Six of the bravest Leslies pressed the plain,
While round these warriors lay whole heaps of slain.
Gordons and Forbeses promiscuous fall,
Death and destruction seemed to threaten all ;
Through studded targets spears were forceful driven,
At every blow sad mortal wounds were given.
Bravely they mock all quarter foes can give,
Their leader killed, they think it mean to live.

CHAP. I.

William, Fourth Baron of Balquhain.

SIR WILLIAM LESLIE,

FOURTH BARON OF BALQUHAIN.

Sir William Leslie, eldest son of Sir Andrew Leslie, third Baron of Balquhain, by his wife Isabel Mortimer of Craigievar, succeeded as fourth Baron of Balquhain, on the death of his
1420. father, 22d January 1420.

Sir William Leslie was esteemed a man of great prudence and valour, and he received the honour of knighthood at the coronation of King
1424. James I., 1st April 1424.

Willelmus de Leslie de Syde (Balquhain) is a witness to a charter granted by Alexander de Seton, Lord Gordon, to William Forbes of Kin-
1432. aldie, dated 30th June 1432.

Alexander Stewart, Earl of Mar and Lord of the Garioch, granted to William Leslie of Bal-
See App. No. I. quhain a charter of the lands of Selby and Lochtillok, in the district of the Garioch, in the county of Aberdeen, dated at Kildrummy, 10th
1433. December 1433.

Sir William Leslie was one of the principal officers and commanders under Alexander, Earl of Huntly, at the battle of Brechin, fought, 18th
1452. May 1452, against the Earl of Crawford, who was in arms against King James II., to avenge the death of his confederate, the Earl of Douglas. In reward of his services and undaunted bravery,

CHAP. I.

William, Fourth Baron of Balquhain.

the Earl of Huntly bestowed on Sir William Leslie the lands of Kincraigie in Mar, and Avochie in Strathbogie, in lieu of which lands, King James II. granted to the Earl of Huntly the lordships of Badenoch, Lochaber, and other lands.

Sir William Leslie was bailie to the Queen for the regality of the Garioch, as is shown by the following charter :—

"Be it maide kende til al men by thir present lettris me Wilyame of Leslie of Balquhane knycht bailze til our Souerane Lade the Quene of the regality of the Garvyach til have giffin heritabil state and possessioun til Jonn of Winton of the Andate of half the landis of Drumdurnoch with the pertinentis lyande within the forsaide regalite efter the fourme and the effect of our Souerane Lordis the Knyngis breves dereckyt thar upon til me—and this til al that effeyris I mak it knowin be thir my present lettris. In the witnes of the quhilkes til thir my present lettris I haf set to my sele at Wardris this xxiij dae of the month of Maij the yer of our Lord ane thousand four hundredth fyftie and thre yeris befor thir witnes 1453.
Jorg of Lesley, Malcome Mortimar, with utheris sundrie."*

Sir William Leslie was one of the jury in the assize held before Alexander Douglas, Sheriff-

* Balquhain Charters, No. 623

CHAP. I. — *William, Fourth Baron of Balquhain.*

depute of Aberdeen, which gave a decreet in favour of James Skene of Skene, against Joneta de Keith, and her uncle Sir William Keith, Great Marischal of Scotland, regarding the lands of Ledoch of Skene, the Kirktown of Skene, and various other lands, at Aberdeen, 21st February
1457 1457.

1457 Sir William Leslie, 5th March 1457, resigned the barony of Pitcaple into the hands of the king, James II., in favour of David Leslie, his son by his third wife, Euphemia Lindsay.*

Sir William Leslie had a seat in parliament, and was one of the committee of parliament for the reduction of the earldom of Mar from the Lord Erskine, at the instance of the Crown, before the Lord Lindsay, Justice-General. The committee of parliament consisted of Alexander, Earl of Huntly; William, Earl of Errol; William, Dominus Keith, Martial Scocie, George Dominus Leslie de Rothes; William Leslie de Balquhane, and others. The decreet of reduction is dated
1457. 5th November 1457.

Sir William Leslie got a charter, 27th March
1460. 1460, from Alexander Leslie, first Baron of that
See App. No. II. Ilk, of the lands of Bracach, the Quyltis, the Milton of Knockenlewis, and the Drummis, in the barony of Leslie, in the regality of the Garioch,

---

* *Collections for Shires of Aberdeen and Banff*, p. 530, note; Spalding Club.

William, Fourth Baron of Balquhain.

which charter was confirmed by King James II., 4th April 1460.

Sir William Leslie married, first, the Honourable Elizabeth Fraser, daughter of Hugh, first Lord Lovat, and by her had—

I. ALEXANDER, his successor.
II. WILLIAM, first Baron of Kincraigie, of whom hereafter.
III. GUILDA, married to Barclay, Baron of Gartly.

Sir William married, secondly, Agnes Irvine of Drum, by whom he had—

I. ALEXANDER, first Baron of Wardis, of whom hereafter.
II. GEORGE, first Laird of New Leslie, of whom hereafter.
III. THOMAS, in holy orders, parson of Kingussie.
IV. ELIZABETH, married to Norman Leith of Barnes.
V. A Daughter, married, first, to Stewart of Laithers, and, secondly, to the Laird of Balquhollie.
VI. A Daughter, married to Cullen in Aberdeen.
VII. A Daughter, married to Cheyne of Straloch.
VIII. A Daughter, married to the Laird of Auchteralter.

Sir William Leslie married, thirdly, Euphemia Lindsay, only child and heiress of William Lindsay of Cairney, second son of David, first Earl of Crawford, by Janet, daughter of King Robert II. With Euphemia Lindsay, Sir William Leslie got the lands of Cairney, and by her had issue—

I. DAVID, first Baron of Pitcaple, of whom hereafter.
II. JAMES, who succeeded his brother David, as second Baron of Pitcaple, of whom hereafter.
III. A Daughter, married to Alexander Menzies, provost of Aberdeen 1475-1486. 1475-86.
IV. MARGARET, married to George Forbes of Auchintoul.

CHAP. I.

William, Fourth Baron of Balquhain.

V. A Daughter, married to Duncan Davidson of Auchenhampers.

VI. A Daughter, married to Alexander Marr.

VII. MAGDALEN BESSIE, married to John Forbes of Terpree.

VIII. A Daughter, married to Thomas Guthrie of Kinblaithmond.

Sir William had also a natural son, Patrick, by Marjory, or Mary, daughter of Sir Thomas Meldrum of Fyvie. From this Patrick are descended the Leslies of Iden, the Leslies of Baccarn, and the Leslies of Crichie.

1467. Sir William Leslie, fourth Baron of Balquhain, died 18th April 1467, and was succeeded by his eldest son, Alexander Leslie, fifth Baron.

Alexander, Fifth Baron of Balquhain.

ALEXANDER LESLIE,

FIFTH BARON OF BALQUHAIN.

ALEXANDER LESLIE, eldest son of Sir William Leslie by his wife the Honourable Elizabeth Fraser of Lovat, succeeded his father as fifth

1467. Baron of Balquhain, 18th April 1467.

He sold Findlater in Tough to Duncan Forbes of Druminnor.

Alexander Leslie married, first, Janet Gordon, daughter of the Laird of Cairnbarrow, whose successors became Barons of Rothiemay. By her he had issue—

I. PATRICK, his successor.

II. ROBERT, who died while at school in France.

III. A Daughter, married to David Ross of Tillesnaught.

IV. A Daughter, married to John Ogilvie of Tillesmachie.

CHAP. I.

He married, secondly, a daughter of Cuming of Coulter, by whom he had three daughters, married respectively to Sir John Rutherford in Aberdeen, David Anderson in Aberdeen, and John Stewart in Strathdon.

Alexander, Fifth Baron of Balquhain.

Alexander Leslie, fifth Baron of Balquhain, died 10th April 1472, and was succeeded by his son Patrick Leslie, sixth Baron. 1472.

PATRICK LESLIE,

SIXTH BARON OF BALQUHAIN.

Patrick, Sixth Baron of Balquhain.

Patrick Leslie, son of Alexander Leslie, fifth Baron of Balquhain, by his wife Janet Gordon of Cairnbarrow, succeeded his father as sixth Baron, 10th April 1472. 1472.

He married Murial Grant, daughter of Sir Donald Grant of Fruchie, a Highland chieftain. By her he had a son—

I. William, his successor.

Patrick Leslie, sixth Baron of Balquhain, died 16th April 1496, and was succeeded by his son William Leslie, seventh Baron. 1496.

WILLIAM LESLIE,

SEVENTH BARON OF BALQUHAIN.

William, Seventh Baron of Balquhain.

William Leslie, son of Patrick Leslie, sixth Baron of Balquhain, by his wife Murial Grant,

CHAP. I.

William, Seventh Baron of Balquhain.

succeeded his father as seventh baron, 16th April 1496.

William Leslie was a proud and boisterous baron, though he lived very honourably according to the fashion of his time. Kennedy, in his *Annals of Aberdeen*, narrates that on Sunday 1st

1525. October 1525, William Leslie, Baron of Balquhain, Alexander Seton of Meldrum, and John Leslie of Wardis, three potent barons in the Garioch, in revenge of an injury supposed to have been done to them, entered the City of Aberdeen at night, with their confederates and retainers, numbering eighty men, armed with spears and other weapons. They attacked the inhabitants with great fury. These instantly flew to arms, and gave battle to the invaders. After a bloody conflict, in which eighty citizens, including several magistrates, were killed or wounded, the invaders were repulsed and driven out of the town. On a complaint made by the citizens to King James V., the affair was investigated, and was finally terminated by the arbitration of certain bishops and nobles.

1527. At Aberdeen, 12th February 1527, before the Lords-Justices and Componitors, William Leslie of Balquhain and John Leslie of Wardis entered

See App. No. III. into an obligation for themselves, their kin, friends, tenents, servants, adherents, and partakers, that they would not molest, vex, inquiet, or trouble, the provost, bailies, council, community and inhabitants of the burgh of Aberdeen, or any one

William, Seventh, Baron of Balquhain.

of them, in any manner of way, in time coming, in their persons, lands, or goods, otherwise than the law will, under a penalty of £2000.

After this affair, great precautions were taken by the Magistrates of Aberdeen to prevent the recurrence of such an assault. The ports or gates of the burgh were ordered to be repaired; the vennels, back-dykes, and waste places, to be built up; a watch to be kept by sixteen persons every night, and two sentinels in every steeple by day, to give the alarm on the appearance of any horsemen; all able men to be supplied with culverins, cross-bows, hand-bows, and shooting-pieces; ten additional gunners to be engaged for the artillery, and wappenshaws to be held weekly.

At this time also, as John Leslie, Bishop of Ross, informs us in his History of Scotland, great feuds existed among the barons of Aberdeenshire, and particularly between the powerful families of Leslie and Forbes. A sharp war was carried on between these two families, in which many barons, gentlemen of great consideration, and others of inferior rank, fell, and many murders were committed. Almost the whole of Aberdeenshire came to be engaged in the quarrel, most families siding with one party or the other, so that the county was divided into two factions. During these feuds in 1526, the Forbeses attacked and burned 1526.
the castle of Balquhain, the stronghold of the Leslies. At length, in 1527, peace was restored 1527.

CHAP. I.

William, Seventh Baron of Balquhain.

by the intervention of Archibald, Earl of Angus, Lord High Chancellor of the kingdom, the lords of the Council, and other noblemen, friends of both parties, who interested themselves, and made these powerful families come to an agreement. But unfortunately, not long afterwards, the Master of Forbes, son of Lord Forbes and the heir of the family, with the Laird of Lentusk, laid wait in ambush for Alexander Seton, the Baron of Meldrum, a great friend and ally of the Leslies, and basely murdered him. The quarrel between the Leslies and the Forbeses broke out again more violently than before, and much injury was inflicted on both sides. The nobility again interfered, and by their intervention peace was restored. The murderers were banished, and took refuge in France. To prevent the recurrence of the feud, John, Lord Forbes, infefted William Leslie of

See App. No. IV.

Balquhain in the lands of Cultercullane and Pettemwk, and in twenty-four shillings of annual rent furth of the alehouse of Fudess, in fulfilment of the decreet-arbitral given at Aberdeen, 11th

1527.

February 1527, and for security and keeping kindness, and eschewing of troubles and inconveniences.

Although this peace continued to be maintained between the Leslies and the Forbeses, yet there always remained animosities between the families, because the house of Balquhain and its numerous branches always adhered to the Earls of Huntly

William, Seventh Baron of Balquhain.

in their quarrels with the Forbeses, and William Leslie of Balquhain was one of those who signed the general band of noblemen and barons of the North, whereby they bound themselves to George, Earl of Huntly, to obey him in his office of Lieutenant of the North, and to search, seek, and apprehend malefactors, and to punish them, or to deliver them to the Judge-ordinary of the said Lord-lieutenant—dated at Elgin 8th December 1544.*

In 1530, William Leslie repaired, or rather rebuilt the castle of Balquhain, which had been burned by the Forbeses, and he erected the noble square tower or keep, so as to make the castle a place of some strength, and capable of offering resistance to any further assault. He also added to the family estates the lands of Whitecross, Inveramsay, Pitbee, and Newlands, which he acquired by purchase. 1530.

William Leslie of Balquhain was one of the jury in the service and retour of Abercromby of Birkenbog, at Banff, 31st October 1506, and he was chancellor of a jury consisting of fifteen persons, at the Burgh Court of Aberdeen, held 12th December 1544 for the trial of defaulters. 1506. 1544.

William Leslie of Balquhain sold to the Rev. Alexander Galloway two acres of the barony of Balquhain, which this excellent man, by a charter

* Gordon Papers, *Spalding Club Miscellany*, vol. iv. p. 213.

CHAP. I.

William, Seventh Baron of Balquhain.

dated at Aberdeen, 21st November 1505, and confirmed by James IV. at Edinburgh, 24th January 1506, annexed to the parish of Bourtie, and granted the said two acres for building a house for the chaplain of Collyhill, who was bound to pray for the souls of Bishop Elphinston of Aberdeen, William Leslie, seventh Baron of Balquhain, Elizabeth Ogilvie his wife, and Sir Walter Ogilvie of Boyne, her father, besides several others.

William Leslie got a precept of Chancery, 23d July 1511, for infefting him in the lands of Balquhain; the Nethertown and Oldtown of Knockinlews; four bovates of the lands of Harlaw; the lands of Selbie, Lochtilloch, Whitecross, and Knockallochy, with the mill; two bovates of the lands of Ressavate; two parts of the lands of Wardis Flemyng, and of Wraes; the lands of Syde, with the mill and alehouse; the lands of Seggyden and Erlesfield, in the regality of the Garioch; and on the 29th July 1511, he obtained from King James IV. a royal charter of the above-mentioned lands united into one free barony, the barony of Balquhain.

1511.

See App. No. V.

1514.

On the 7th April 1514, William Leslie of Balquhain, and Elizabeth Ogilvie his wife, got a charter from King James V. of the lands of Syd, with the mill, Erlisfeild, Segateden, and the Wrays, in the earldom of Mar and lordship of the Garioch.

See App. No. VI.

William Leslie resigned the lands of Erlisfeild,

William, Seventh Baron of Balquhain.

Segydene, and the Wrayis, with the Mill of the Syde, in favour of himself and Marjory Keith his spouse, 24th January 1522, and they received from King James V. a royal charter of the said lands, dated 13th February 1522. *See* App. No. VII.

Sasine followed thereon, 7th April 1522. 1522.

William Leslie resigned the lands of Auldtown of Knockinlews in favour of himself and Marjory Keith his wife, and received a royal charter of the same, dated 15th October 1524.* 1524.

He also resigned the lands of Selbie, in favour of himself and Marjory Keith his wife, 14th November 1536, and they received a royal charter 1536. of the said lands from King James V. on the same day.†

He also resigned the lands of Lochtilloch, in favour of himself and Marjory Keith his wife, 6th January 1538, and on the 18th day of the 1538. same month and year they received a royal charter of the said lands.‡

On the 25th June 1526, George, Earl of Rothes, 1526. entered into an obligation with William Leslie, Baron of Balquhain, mentioning that he had given to the said William Leslie in feu-farm the lands of Rothes, as contained in a charter made

---

* *Registrum Magni Sigilli*, lib. xx. No. 125.

† Balquhain Charters, No. 843 ; and *Registrum Magni Sigilli*, lib. xxv. No. 363.

‡ Balquhain Charters, No. 841 ; and *Registrum Magni Sigilli*, lib. xxvii. No. 28.

CHAP. I.

William, Seventh Baron of Balquhain.

thereupon, and obliging himself, in case the same should prove insufficient, to grant a new right by the advice of lawyers.

Patrick Leith of Harthill, and Janet his wife, granted a letter of reversion of the mid-third of the lands of Knockallochy, in favour of William
1527. Leslie of Balquhain, dated 10th May 1527.*

John Leslie, eldest son of William Leslie, seventh Baron of Balquhain, styled heir-apparent of Balquhain, and who succeeded as eighth baron, had a son also called John Leslie, styled younger or fiar of Balquhain, to whom his grandfather made over his rights to the family estates. But this John the younger died before his father and grandfather, leaving two daughters, Marjory and Janet, to whom their grandfather, John Leslie, the heir-apparent, styled of Syde, was appointed tutor.

William Leslie, seventh Baron of Balquhain, Marjory Keith, his spouse, John Leslie, his son and apparent heir, and John Leslie, younger, son to the said John, are parties to a contract of marriage between the said John Leslie, younger of Balquhain, and Agnes Wood of Bonnington, dated
1539. February 1539.†

William Leslie, Baron of Balquhain, resigned the barony of Balquhain in favour of his grandson, John Leslie, younger of Balquhain, styled "Domino feudo Baronie de Balquhain," and Agnes Wood his wife, and they received a royal

* Balquhain Charters, No. 634. † *Ibid.* No. 845.

William, Seventh Baron of Balquhain.

charter of the same from King James V., dated 19th July 1540.*

John Leslie, younger, fiar of Balquhain, granted a letter of reversion in favour of William Leslie, seventh baron, his grandfather, dated 17th November 1543, submitting that the said William had, out of love, infefted the said John in the fee of all the barony of Balquhain; notwithstanding the said John obliges himself to renounce his rights to the said barony, in favour of the said William, upon payment of a rose noble of gold, at any time when required.† 1543.

John Leslie, younger, fiar of Balquhain, being dead, William Leslie, seventh Baron of Balquhain, in terms of the above letter of reversion, executed an instrument of premonition, under the hand of Thomas Annand, notary-public, dated 15th January 1544, against his son John Leslie of Syde, tutor to his granddaughters Marjory and Janet, daughters of the deceased John Leslie, younger, fiar of Balquhain, for the redemption of the barony of Balquhain.‡ 1544.

William Leslie, seventh Baron of Balquhain, and John Leslie his son, as factor or tutor to his granddaughters Marjory and Janet Leslie, with their consent, executed a contract, whereby, for causes therein mentioned, the said John Leslie

* Balquhain Charters, No. 846; and *Registrum Magni Sigilli*, lib. xxix. No. 117.

† Balquhain Charters, No. 2. ‡ *Ibid.* No. 3.

CHAP. I.

William, Seventh Baron of Balquhain.

obliges himself, in the name of his pupils, to renounce all right which they or their father, the deceased John Leslie, fiar of Balquhain, had to the barony of Balquhain, dated 16th January 1544; whereupon, by an instrument dated 14th February 1544, the said William Leslie consigned into the hands of Andrew Menzies, bailie of Aberdeen, a rose noble for the redemption of the said barony of Balquhain from the said John Leslie of Syde, tutor, and the instrument of redemption was executed under the hand of John Nicholson, notary-public, on the same day.*

1544. Letters of regress under the Privy Seal were granted in favour of William Leslie, Baron of Balquhain, 6th June 1544, on the redemption of the barony of Balquhain. A precept of Chancery, for infefting the said William Leslie in the lands of Balquhain, was issued 20th April 1545, and sasine followed thereon 3d May 1545.†

1545. William Leslie, seventh Baron of Balquhain, resigned the barony of Balquhain into the hands of the king, 19th May 1545, in favour of his son, John Leslie of Syde, heir-apparent of the said barony; whereupon the said John Leslie received a charter under the Great Seal, 19th June 1545, of the said barony, proceeding on the above resignation, and sasine thereon followed 20th July 1545.

1545.

* Balquhain Charters, Nos. 6, 7, 8.

† *Ibid.* Nos. 10, 12, 13.

William, Seventh Baron of Balquhain.

William Leslie married, first, Elizabeth, daughter of Sir Walter Ogilvie, second Baron of Boyne. King James V. granted a charter of the lands of Syd, with the mill, Erlisfeild, Segateden, and the Wrays, in the earldom of Mar and lordship of the Garioch, in favour of William Leslie of Balquhain, and Elizabeth Ogilvie his spouse, dated 7th April 1514. By this marriage William Leslie had issue— *See* App. No. VI.

I. JOHN, his successor.

II. PATRICK.

III. JAMES, who died young.

IV. ISABEL, married first to John Panton or Paton of Pittendreich, and secondly to Alexander Seton of Meldrum.

V. JEAN, married to Patrick Leith, younger of Edengarioch, Barns, and Likelyhead.

VI. MARGARET, married to James Forbes, Auchintoul.

VII. AGNES, married, 1528, to John Strachan. 1528.

VIII. ELIZABETH, married to James Dunbar.

Elizabeth Ogilvie died in September 1518, and William Leslie married, secondly, Marjory Keith, a most virtuous lady, daughter of Alexander Keith of Inverugie and Pittendrum, a son of William, third Earl, and thirteenth Grand Marischal of Scotland. King James V. granted a charter of the lands of Erlisfeild, Segyden, and the Wrais, in favour of William Leslie of Balquhain, and Marjory Keith his spouse, dated 13th February 1522. There is no record of any issue by this marriage. 1518. *See* App. No. VII.

CHAP. I.

William, Seventh Baron of Balquhain.

William Leslie, seventh Baron of Balquhain, died in 1545, and was succeeded by his eldest son, John Leslie, eighth baron.

John, Eighth Baron of Balquhain

JOHN LESLIE,

EIGHTH BARON OF BALQUHAIN.

JOHN LESLIE, eldest son of William Leslie, seventh Baron of Balquhain, by his first wife, Elizabeth Ogilvie, succeeded as eighth baron, on the death
1545. of his father, in 1545.

John Leslie of Balquhain was chancellor of a jury at a Burgh Court, held in Aberdeen, 22d
1546. January 1546, for the trial of William Anderson, a publican, accused of purchasing wine from foreigners, and selling it before the price was fixed by the bailies and council. He was Deputy-
1548. sheriff of Aberdeen in 1548.

On 16th January of that year we find him presiding at the court held in Aberdeen, for taxing all the lands within the sheriffdom of Aberdeen, by command of the Queen and Council, that money might be raised for resisting the threatened invasion of the realm by our old enemies of England. Among the lords and barons forming the assize, we find Alexander Leslie of Wardis, and Alexander Leslie of that Ilk; and among the landowners who were taxed, we find the Laird of Balquhain, for his lands of

John, Eighth Baron of Balquhain.

the same, xx. lib.; the Laird of Leslie, for his lands of the same, x. lib.; the Laird of Pitcaple, for his lands of the same, v. lib.; the Laird of Iden, for his lands of the same, iiij. lib.; the Laird of Coclarachy Leslie, xxx. sh.; Gordoune Leslie, portioneris of Warthill, ilk ane of thaim, xxx. sh.; Alexander Leslie of Wardess, for his lands Gareauche and Kyntour, of old extent, feftie libs.; the Laird of Auchinhuwff, for his lands of the same, ix. libs.*

Soon after this, John Leslie was raised to the office of Sheriff-principal of Aberdeen, and we find that George Leith of Edingarioch was served heir to his uncle, George Leith of Barnes, before John Leslie of Balquhain, Vicecomes de Aberdene, 13th January 1550. 1550.

John Leslie of Balquhain was a staunch adherent of George, Earl of Huntly, and we find him frequently as a witness to the bands of manrent entered into between that nobleman and the barons and gentlemen of the northern counties. John Leslie, styled of Syde, during the lifetime of his father, William, seventh Baron, is witness to the band between James Garioch of Kynstair, and George, Earl of Huntly, 10th June 1536;† to the band of Alexander Gordon of Strathoune, 5th 1536.

* *Collections on the Shires of Aberdeen and Banff*, pp. 113-119; Spalding Club.

† Gordon Papers; *Spalding Club Miscellany*, vol. iv. p. 199.

CHAP. I.

John, Eighth Baron of Balquhain.

See App. No. VIII.

1546.

November 1539;* and, 31st July 1541, he entered into a similar band himself; and after he succeeded as Baron of Balquhain, we find him a witness to the band of James Grant of Freuchie, and John Grant, his eldest son, with the same nobleman, 8th May 1546.† We also find Georgio Comite de Huntlye, and Johanne Lesley de Syde, among the witnesses to a charter of the Bishop of Moray, confirming a letter of sale from Alan Keyr M'Kyntosy de Rothamurcous, granted to George Gordoun, Constabularius de Ruthven de Badyenoch, dated at Inverness, 26th November 1539.‡

As has been related, Alexander Seton of Meldrum, an ally of the Leslies, had been basely murdered by the Master of Forbes and his followers, one of whom was Alexander Forbes, commonly called Spangare. John Leslie, son and apparent-heir of William Leslie of Balquhain, Alexander Leslie of Kincraigie, and an adherent called John Keith, appear to have attacked and slain this Alexander Forbes, or Spangare, on a Sunday, for which they obtained a remission under the Privy Seal, from King James V., 9th February 1527.

See App. No. IX.

1527.

There seems to have been a feud between William, Lord Forbes, and John Leslie, Baron of

* Gordon Papers; *Spalding Club Miscellany*, vol. iv. p. 204.

† *Ibid.* vol. iv. p. 215.

‡ *Registrum Moraviense*, p. 419, No. 449.

CHAP. I.

John, Eighth Baron of Balquhain.

Balquhain, on the one part, and Thomas Menzies of Pitfoddles on the other, for the "slauchteris happenit betwixt Maister Thomas Dauedson, Maister Walter Leslie, and others, ther complices and pairttakkeris." William, Lord Forbes, and John Leslie of Balquhain, on the one part, and James Gordon of Methlic, in the name and behalf of Thomas Menzies of Pitfoddles, on the other part, appeared before George, Earl of Huntly, Lieutenant of the North, at Grantullie, 27th February 1551, and entered into a contract for the settlement of their feuds. *See* App. No. X.

John Leslie of Balquhain, and William Leslie, his son, are witnesses to an inventory of the silver and gold work, sacred utensils, and church-furniture, of the Cathedral of Aberdeen, which were delivered to the keeping of the canons of the said cathedral, by William Gordon, Bishop of Aberdeen, 7th July 1559. Among the items enumerated in the inventory is the following:— "To Mr. John Leslie, parson of Oyne, the image of the Virgin Mary, 114 ounces." The witnesses are John Leslie of Balquhain, William Leslie his son, Alexander Leslie of Pitcaple, William Seton of Meldrum, Duncan Forbes of Monymusk, and others.* 1559.

John Leslie of Balquhain got a lease of the church-lands, called Kirktown of Rayne, from Thomas Myrtoun, Archdeacon of Aberdeen, dated *See* App. No. XI.

* Keith's *Catalogue*, p. 129.

CHAP. I.

John, Eighth Baron of Balquhain.

See App. No. XII.

7th June 1543; a lease of half of the town of Leddintusche, from William Gordon, Bishop of Aberdeen, 7th February 1549; a lease of the barony and shire of Fetternear, from the same, 22d October 1550; a letter of reversion from James Leslie, burgess of Aberdeen, and his spouse, upon the sunny third of the town and lands of Inveramsay, in January 1551;* a charter from Alexander Leslie, fourth Baron of that Ilk, of the sunny half of Aquhorties—namely, the sunny halves of Overtoun, Netherbeggery, Woodhill, and Blairdaff, and half of the mill thereof; sasine

See App. No. XIII.

1554. thereon, 26th February 1554. Christian Menzies, spouse of John Leslie of Balquhain, renounced the lands of Talzeaucht in favour of the said John Leslie, and William Leslie, his son and heir, 9th

1560. September 1560. John Leslie of Balquhain alienated the barony of Balquhain in favour of his son, William Leslie of Kirkhill, 10th September 1560; and granted precept of sasine for infefting the said William in the said lands, and the instrument of sasine was executed under the hand of Andrew Leslie, notary-public, 11th October 1560.† John Leslie, fifth Baron of that Ilk, made a gift of ward, relief, and non-entry, of half of the lands of Aquhorsk, in favour of John Leslie of Balquhain, and William Leslie, his son, 26th

1561. April 1561. John Leslie of Balquhain granted

* Balquhain Charters, No. 683. † *Ibid.* Nos. 18, 19, 20.

John, Eighth Baron of Balquhain.

by deed to his brother-in-law, Patrick Leith of Likelyhead and Edingarioch, the lands of Kirktoun of Rayne, 13th August 1561; and Patrick Leith got a charter of the same in favour of himself and his son, John, from the Archdeacon of Aberdeen.*

John Leslie married, first, Elizabeth Leslie, daughter of Patrick Leslie of Ardoyne, Provost of Aberdeen, and by her had issue—

I. JOHN, who married Margaret Wood of Bonnington in 1539, and by her had issue— 1539.

I. MARJORY, married to Alexander Bisset.

II. JANET, married to Patrick Leslie of Kincraigie.

John Leslie died before his father and grandfather, in consequence of a fall from the battlements of the Tolbooth of Aberdeen. He had been infefted in the estates of Balquhain by his grandfather, William, seventh baron. At his death his grandfather redeemed the estates by the payment of a rose noble, according to the agreement, and John Leslie, his father, received from Queen Mary, 6th June 1544, the gift of 1544. ward and non-entry of all and haile the lands and barony of Balquhain, the mill, multures, fishings, advowson, donation of kirk, chaplainry, benefices, etc., which were in the queen's hands, by reason of ward and non-entry, through the decease of umquhile John Leslie younger; and the said John Leslie of Syde, apparent heir of Balquhain, was appointed and served as tutor to his granddaughters Marjory and Janet Leslie, 23d January 1545.†

II. WILLIAM, who succeeded as ninth baron.

* *Chartulary of Aberdeen;* and Douglas's *Baronage*, p. 226.

† Balquhain Charters, No. 875.

CHAP. I.

John, Eighth Baron of Balquhain.

III. Janet, married to William Duguid of Auchinhove.

IV. Agnes, married to James Harvey of Boyndis.

V. Margaret, married to Dunbar of Bonnyfield.

VI. Barbara, married to William Cumming of Auchray.

VII. Isabella, who died 4th February 1576, as appears from the following entry in the Chronicle of Aberdeen, *Spalding Club Miscellany*, vol. ii. p. 42 :—

"Isabell Lesly, doithair to John Lesly of Balquhain,
1576. departtit the fowrtt day of Februar 1576 yeris."

John Leslie is said to have had another son, James Leslie, who entered the church, and died
1561. at Aberdeen 1st February 1561.

John Leslie married, secondly, Christian Menzies, but does not seem to have had any children by her.

John Leslie, eighth Baron of Balquhain, was much afflicted in his declining years by bodily infirmities. He went to France in the hope of
1561. finding relief, and died there in 1561, and was succeeded by his son, William Leslie, ninth baron.

William, Ninth Baron of Balquhain.

WILLIAM LESLIE,

NINTH BARON OF BALQUHAIN.

William Leslie, son of John Leslie, eighth Baron of Balquhain, by his wife Elizabeth Leslie of Ardoyne, succeeded as ninth Baron of Balquhain,
1561. on the death of his father, in 1561.

William Leslie was a man of great abilities, and acquired so much influence that he was held in great esteem by all the great nobility. Indeed,

CHAP. I.

William, Ninth Baron of Balquhain.

by his means the Earls of Huntly and Atholl, between whom serious feuds existed, were brought to a reconciliation. Hollinshed, in his *Scottish Chronicles*, vol. ii. p. 306, writes, "Great troubles were in divers parts of the realm, and openly betwixt the Earl of Huntly and the Earl of Atholl. There was taking of prisoners and overthrowing of houses on either part, and great preparations made and arms in readiness to invade either other's countries. But this business was pacified by the good mediation of Mr. Alexander Gordon, Postulat of Galloway; Mr. John Leslie, Official of Aberdeen; and William Leslie, the young Laird of Balquhain, who agreed them in all matters of controversie, and caused them to go to either other's houses."

William Leslie had the honour of receiving and entertaining Queen Mary in his castle of Balquhain. The queen being at Aberdeen on her progress to the north, William Leslie invited her to visit him at his castle of Balquhain, which is situated about eighteen miles north-west of Aberdeen, near the great north road to Huntly and Strathbogie. Queen Mary accepted the invitation, and passed the night at Balquhain Castle, 9th September 1562. During her stay there she attended Mass in the chapel of the Blessed Virgin of the Garioch. 1562.

It was on this occasion, and in the castle of Balquhain, that it is said the Earl of Huntly

CHAP. I.

William, Ninth Baron of Balquhain.

designed to sacrifice his rival, the newly-created Earl of Moray, Lord James Stewart, the queen's natural brother, who was one of the guests. But William Leslie would not on any account consent to become accessory to such a deed, and by his influence he dissuaded the Earl of Huntly from the design. The different writers of the period give different versions of the story, each relating it according to his difference of party and religious feelings. The facts seem to be as follows:—

George, fourth Earl of Huntly, who succeeded
1524. to the earldom in 1524, was made Lord Chancellor of Scotland on the death of Cardinal Beaton,
1546. and got the Great Seal in 1546. He also got a grant of the earldom of Moray from Queen Mary,
1548. 13th February 1548, and was appointed the queen's Lieutenant in the North. During the queen's absence in France, Huntly had been deprived of the chancellorship, which the queen, on her return, restored to him, but at the same time took from him the earldom of Moray, which she gave to her natural brother, Lord James Stewart, Prior of St. Andrews, who had recently been created Earl of Mar. This gave rise to implacable enmity between the two earls, of which the enemies of Moray, and of his friend the Earl of Morton, took advantage to plot his ruin. Huntly being at the head of the Catholic party, the queen's maternal relations of the house

CHAP. I.

William, Ninth Baron of Balquhain.

of Guise had great expectations that he would restore that religion, and they held out hopes to him that the queen would marry his second son, Sir John Gordon of Findlater. It is possible that Huntly entertained this project proposed to him, although he never intended to seize the queen, or to force her to it against her will, as his enemies gave out. If this had been his design, he might easily have executed it, as the queen was frequently in his power, had he been disposed to use force.

In a History of the Douglas and Angus family, we are told that Huntly gathered a force under pretence of receiving the queen in her journey north, but really with a view of cutting off Moray and Morton; and that the queen went from Aberdeen to Bowhane in August 1562, the house 1562. of one Master Leslie, a gentleman, twelve miles off, and that this was thought by Huntly and his friends to be a fit place to execute their designs on Moray and Morton; but Leslie, although he was Huntly's friend, would upon no terms give way to have it done in his house.

David Scott, in his *History of Scotland*, book vi. p. 394, says that Queen Mary, in her progress to the north, arrived at Aberdeen about the 15th of August 1562, and on proceeding on her journey 1562. towards Inverness, she lodged the first night with John (William) Leslie of Balquhain at his castle; the next night at Rothiemay; and the third day

CHAP. I.

William, Ninth Baron of Balquhain.

was invited by the Earl of Huntly to his castle at Strathbogie. But the queen denied this, or any favour to him, until his son, John Gordon, had given obedience to her command. So she kept on her journey, and the next day she arrived at Inverness.

1562.

Another account states that the queen being at Aberdeen in August 1562, she was there met by the Countess of Huntly, who interceded in behalf of her second son, Sir John Gordon, who had been taken prisoner for having wounded Lord Ogilvie in a fray, and, having made his escape, had been declared an outlaw. The countess begged that the queen would grant his pardon, and allow him to come into her presence and kiss her hand. The queen replied that she could not admit him into her presence until such time as he should surrender himself to justice; whereupon the countess promised that he would surrender, and Lord Glammis was appointed to conduct Sir John to Stirling Castle. On his way, however, Sir John altered his resolution, and made his escape, and retired to the north, and collected a large body of followers, which much incensed the queen. In the meantime, the queen had proceeded on her journey northward, intending to go to Huntly's house in Strathbogie, where great preparations had been made to receive her. The Earl of Huntly met her on the way, at Balquhain Castle, and he there besought

William, Ninth Baron of Balquhain.

her to pardon his son, Sir John, but she remained inexorable; and the earl having pressed her more solicitously than was proper to go to his castle, she determined not to go. Others say that Mary came to this resolution at the instigation of the Earl of Moray. Be it as it may, the queen proceeded to Inverness without visiting Huntly, and on her arrival there she found, to her surprise, that the Earl of Huntly's deputy-governor refused to admit her into the castle without the orders of Lord Gordon. The queen, having raised the forces of the country, prepared to carry the place by assault, which was rendered unnecessary by the surrender of the governor, who was hanged, and the queen returned to Aberdeen.

Whether Huntly's ambition, which had spurred him on, now necessarily drove him forward as he had gone too far to retrace his steps, and he resolved either to procure a full pardon, or to seize the queen; or whether he dreaded Moray's influence with the queen to effect his ruin; he determined to collect troops to protect or to avenge himself. With his followers he moved towards Aberdeen, threatening to attack Moray, who was there with the queen. It is said that he received secret intelligence from his friends, the Earl of Sutherland, the Laird of Balquhain, Black Arthur Forbes, and others, then within the city, who informed him of all that took place there, and assured him that the town's people, being

CHAP. I.

William, Ninth Baron of Balquhain.

his kindred or allied to him, neither would nor dared oppose him. But the letters of the Earl of Sutherland and of the Laird of Balquhain were intercepted, and the designs of Huntly upon the town were discovered and defeated.

Moray and Morton resolved to attack and disperse the force which Huntly had collected. They had only one hundred men with them, but, armed with the queen's authority, they issued a proclamation calling upon all who could bear arms to attend the queen. About 2000 men answered the summons, and amongst these were a considerable number of Leslies, under their chief, the Laird of Balquhain; Moray trusting that, though they were inclined to favour Huntly, yet their duty and allegiance to their queen would not suffer them to betray her. On the
1562. 28th October 1562, Moray marched with these forces from Aberdeen to attack Huntly, who was lying at the Loch of Skene, about ten miles distant, with a force which had melted away to about 500 men. The principal leaders of Moray's army were the Earl of Errol, Lord Forbes, the Laird of Balquhain, in the vanguard; and John, Prior of Coldingham, with some horsemen: the main body being commanded by the Earls of Moray, Morton, and Atholl. The vanguard drove Huntly from the Loch of Skene to Corrichie, a place on the Hill of Fair, about six miles distant, where they skirmished with him, and sent word

CHAP. I.

William, Ninth Baron of Balquhain.

to the Earl of Moray to come up with the southern men. When Moray came up the vanguard prepared to engage, and began to attack. But, as the chronicler says, " incontinent thereafter thae fled back upon the gentlemen of Louthian; and, as some say, purposing to have causet them to flee also, and to be overrun to the effect that the Earl of Huntly might have obtinet the victory. But the gentlemen of Louthian stand firmle still, and the said Erles company coming upon the Louthian men, was put upon their bakkes with speiris and thereafter fled, quhan followit great slauchter."

The truth seems to be that these unwilling enemies of Huntly marched boldly up as if to attack him, and then turned and fled, calling out, Treason! Huntly, thinking to drive Moray before him during the confusion caused by the retreat of the vanguard, too hastily left his strong ground and advantageous position, and was attacked on the low ground by Moray, Morton, and Atholl, with the horse, and suffered a complete defeat. The Earl of Huntly himself was slain, and his son, Sir John Gordon, was taken prisoner, and was immediately executed. The immense estates of the family were seized by the crown, and the title was forfeited.

David Scott, in his *History of Scotland*, book vi. pp. 394, 395, gives the following account of the defeat of the Earl of Huntly :—

"After the castle of Inverness was taken, the

CHAP. I.

William, Ninth Baron of Balquhain.

queen remained in it a few days, and then set out for Aberdeen, where she arrived in four days. The Countess of Huntly came with offers of submission from her husband, but was denied access. Huntly, finding matters turn out contrary to his expectations, assembled his friends and approached the town of Aberdeen, he having great hopes to attain the queen's pardon for his being in arms, by the intercession of the Earl of Sutherland and the Baron of Balquhain, who were with the queen and kept close correspondence with the Earl of Huntly. But their letters being intercepted, the Earl of Sutherland made his escape, and Leslie of Balquhain being brought before the Council and examined, confessed what he knew, whereupon he was pardoned, and continued in the queen's service. Huntly upon this would have dismissed his forces, and returned home; but hearing that the Earl of Moray was approaching with a party of the queen's forces raised in Lothian, Fife, Angus, Strathern, etc., he resolved to give them battle. The Earl of Moray, with the Earl of Morton and Lord Lindsay, advanced. Finding Huntly resolved to fight, Moray seemed to retire by bringing his men to some ground of greater advantage, which retreat being mistaken for a flight by Huntly's party, they advanced precipitately, and coming disorderly to an engagement, were soon worsted with great slaughter."

CHAP. I.

William, Ninth Baron of Balquhain.

William Leslie was Sheriff of Aberdeen under the queen's Lieutenant of the North, the Earl of Huntly. In this capacity he afforded the utmost assistance in protecting the cathedral of Aberdeen from the ravages of the Reformers, and he preserved that ancient edifice from being demolished by the furious zealots in 1560. As a magistrate he defended from the attacks of the Reformers the Bishop of Aberdeen, William Gordon, brother of the Earl of Huntly, and supported him in his diocese by force of arms when all the other bishops of Scotland were persecuted. The bishop, as a mark of his gratitude for the kindness and services shown to him in those trying times, bestowed on William Leslie the barony of Fetternear, with the palace, which was the bishop's summer-residence, the tower and fortalice of the same, with the salmon-fishing in the river Don, and all other pendicles; the lands of Talzeaucht, lying in the shire of Fetternear; the lands of Bonyngton, with the mill, multures, and crofts of the same; the lands of Lowesk, and the third part of the town and lands of Ledintusche; the lands of Custestoun, in the shire of Rayne; the lands of Auchlyne, with the mill of the same; the croft of Blairdinny, in the shire of Clatt, with all their pendicles, lying within the county of Aberdeen. The bishop granted to William Leslie a charter of all these lands, dated 8th June 1566, which charter was confirmed by a Royal charter,

See App. No. XIV.

1560.

See App. No. XV.

See App. No. XVI.

CHAP. I.

William, Ninth Baron of Balquhain.

dated 10th May 1602, and by a Papal charter granted by Pope Clement X., dated 20th September 1670.

William Leslie got from his father, John Leslie, eighth Baron of Balquhain, a charter, dated 17th
1550. January 1550, of the fourth part of the east half of the west town of Syde, in the regality of the Garioch, in favour of himself, and Janet Forbes his wife, which charter was confirmed by a royal
See App. No. XVII. charter under the Great Seal, dated 29th June 1554.
1554. William Gordon, Bishop of Aberdeen, granted a charter of the lands of Auchlyn, in favour of William Leslie of Kirkhill, and Janet Forbes
1556. his wife, 28th May 1556; sasine thereon followed,
1558. 26th March 1558.* William Leslie of Kirkhill is a witness to a bond of manrent between Duncan Forbes of Monymusk, and George, Earl of Huntly, who had leased to the said Duncan Forbes for nineteen years the town and lands of
1559. Delab and Kemboig; 2d February 1559.† John Leslie, fifth Baron of that Ilk, and superior of the lands of Aquhorties, Aquhorsk, and Blairdaff, granted a precept for infefting William Leslie, younger of Balquhain, in the sunny halves of the lands of Aquhorties, Overtoun, Netherbeggery,
1560. Woodhill, and Blairdaff; 4th October 1560.‡ William Leslie, fiar of Balquhain, entered into a

* Balquhain Charters, No. 668.

† *Gordon Papers;* Spalding Club Miscellany, vol. iv. p. 224.

‡ Balquhain Charters, No. 258.

William, Ninth Baron of Balquhain.

contract with Thomas Gordon, son of James Gordon of Lesmore, and his curators, whereby he obliged himself to infeft the said Thomas Gordon in two parts of the lands of Wraes, and the said Thomas Gordon obliged himself to renounce in favour of the said William Leslie the wadsett rights which he had on the lands of Erlesfield and Seggyden; 6th September 1561. William 1561.
Leslie entered into a bond of manrent with George, Earl of Huntly, 20th August 1562. 1562.
George Mortimer of Aquhorties, and Janet Leslie his wife, granted a letter of reversion of the sunny half of the lands of Aquhorties, in favour of William Leslie of Balquhain, 22d February 1563.* Queen Mary issued a precept, directed to 1563.
John, Archbishop of St. Andrews, to receive and admit William Leslie of Balquhain and his heirs-male as hereditary tenants and feuars of the lands of Seveedlie, lying in the barony of Keig and Monymusk, and regality of St. Andrews, as the same were formerly held by George, Earl of Huntly, attainted; dated 22d June 1563. John 1563.
Leslie, dwelling in Meikle Durno, granted a letter of reversion of the town and lands of Newlands, in favour of William Leslie of Balquhain, 16th August 1563. Duncan Forbes of Monymusk 1563.
granted a letter of reversion of the lands of Abersuethok and Mill of Ramstone, in favour of William Leslie of Balquhain, in 1563. William

* Balquhain Charters, No. 259.

CHAP. I.

William, Ninth Baron of Balquhain.

Leslie of Balquhain and Duncan Forbes of Monymusk entered into a contract, whereby Duncan Forbes obliged himself to renounce the lands of Talzeaucht, lying in the parish of Clatt, which had been wadsett to him by John Leslie, eighth
1564. Baron of Balquhain; dated 1st January 1564.* William Leslie of Balquhain and Thomas Ker of Coclarachy entered into a contract of excambion, whereby William Leslie got rights to the ploughland of the Hauch of Bogie or Blairdinny, 8th
1564. December 1564; and William Gordon, Bishop of Aberdeen, granted a charter of the same in favour of William Leslie, 9th December 1564: sasine
1564. thereupon 18th December 1564.† Thomas Ker of Coclarachy granted a letter of reversion of the sixth part of the lands of Begeshill and others, in favour of William Leslie of Balquhain, 9th Decem-
1564. ber 1564.‡ William Leslie of Balquhain entered into a contract with Alexander Leslie of Pitcaple, whereby, in respect of the said Alexander having become cautioner for the said William Leslie to James Dempster of Auchterless for 600 merks, the said William Leslie obliged himself to infeft the said Alexander Leslie in the lands of Pitbee
1565. for his security; 18th September 1565. William Leslie of Balquhain redeemed the lands of Craigtown and Craigmill from George Gordon of
1566. Lesmore, 26th May 1566. Patrick Leith of

* Balquhain Charters, No. 609.

† *Ibid.* Nos. 596, 597.

‡ *Ibid.* No. 599.

Harthill, and William Leith, his son, granted a letter of reversion of the lands of Newlands, Craigtown, and Craigmill, in favour of William Leslie of Balquhain, 11th June 1566. George Leslie of Tocher granted a charter of the shadow half of the town and lands of Drumdurno in favour of William Leslie of Balquhain, 20th June 1566; sasine followed thereupon 11th July 1566.* 1566.
Thomas Ker of Coclarachy granted a letter of reversion of the lands of Begeshill, containing the sum of 300 merks, in favour of William Leslie of Balquhain, in November 1566.† John Leslie, 1566.
Bishop of Ross, received a gift under the Privy Seal, of the escheat of Barbara Leslie, wife of Mr. William Con, which the bishop assigned to William Leslie of Balquhain; 20th July 1567. 1567.
John Leslie, Bishop of Ross, with consent of the dean and chapter, granted a feu-charter of the lands of Learney, the mill of Avach, the lands of Craighead, and other lands, lying within the bishopric of Ross, in favour of William Leslie of Balquhain, 16th October 1567; sasine followed 1567.
thereupon 18th October 1567:‡ also a charter of the lands of Tulliquiddon, Farnes, and others, within the bishopric of Ross and shire of Inverness, 16th October 1567;§ which two charters 1567.
were confirmed by a charter granted under the

* Balquhain Charters, No. 616.
† *Ibid.* No. 600. ‡ *Ibid.* No. 670.
§ *Ibid.* No. 672.

CHAP. I.

William, Ninth Baron of Balquhain.

Great Seal, 29th November 1567.* William Leslie of Balquhain wadsett to James Arbuthnot, burgess of Aberdeen, three quarters of the town and lands of Logydurno, redeemable for 1000
1568. merks, 6th September 1568; and received a letter of reversion of the same, 25th October 1568. William Leslie of Balquhain gave to Stephen
1570. Leslie, the second Laird of Warthill, about 1570, the other half of Warthill in wadsett, and for nineteen years after its redemption, for the payment of 20 merks yearly. William Leslie redeemed the two parts of the lands of Wraes from
1571. Thomas Gordon of Lesmore, 8th October 1571; and the said Thomas Gordon renounced the said lands, in favour of the said William Leslie, on the same day.

William Leslie, ninth Baron of Balquhain, married, first, Janet Forbes, daughter of John, sixth Lord Forbes, and widow of John, Earl of Atholl, and by her had issue—

I. JOHN, his successor.

II. WILLIAM, who was a courtier in the service of King
1592. James VI. He was a Privy Councillor in 1592, and died in London without issue.

III. ARTHUR, who fell from his horse while crossing the Don near Fetternear, and was drowned.

IV. JEAN, married to Thomas Dempster, Baron of Muiresk,
1588. 1588, as appears by a charter, dated 6th January
1592. 1592, giving to their second son, Robert, the barony of Auchterless. They had a third son, the learned and renowned Thomas Dempster. Their eldest son, James,

* Balquhain Charters, No. 673.

William, Ninth Baron of Balquhain.

succeeded his father as Baron of Muiresk. The line is now extinct.

V. Margaret, married to Alexander Abercrombie of Birkenbog. It is said that she got as her dowry the barony of Fetternear, about 1593, subject to its being redeemed. But whether this was the case, or William Leslie, ninth Baron of Balquhain, wadsett it to Abercrombie on these conditions, it is certain that the second son by this marriage succeeded to Fetternear.

VI. Isabella, married to James Arbuthnot of Lentusk.

William Leslie married, secondly, Margaret Leslie, daughter of the Baron of Bonnymoon, or Balnamoon, by whom he had—

I. Andrew, who died abroad.

II. Gilbert, who was killed in a quarrel by young Dempster at Muiresk.

III. Christian.

IV. Elizabeth.

It is stated in the genealogy of the house of Drummond, that Margaret Drummond, daughter of Andrew Drummond, second Laird of Belliclene in Perthshire, and Janet Dickson his wife, daughter of John Dickson, Laird of Ballachaster, married, about 1550, Leslie, Laird of Bouchain in Aberdeenshire. If this is correct, it would appear that William Leslie was thrice married. 1550.

William Leslie, second son of William Leslie, ninth Baron of Balquhain, got a charter of the lands of Balquhain, from his brother, John, tenth Baron, and declared the same redeemable by the said John, on payment of a rose noble of gold; 1st December 1573. He also got a charter of certain 1573.

CHAP. I.

William, Ninth Baron of Balquhain.

lands which formerly belonged to the order of Friars-preachers, and to the White Friars, dated 14th March, James VI., anno regni 19;* also a charter of the barony of Fetternear, 4th March
1597. 1597.†

William Leslie, ninth Baron of Balquhain, died
1571. in 1571, and was succeeded by his eldest son, John Leslie, tenth baron.

John, Tenth Baron of Balquhain.

JOHN LESLIE,

TENTH BARON OF BALQUHAIN.

JOHN LESLIE, eldest son of William Leslie, ninth Baron of Balquhain, by Janet Forbes his wife, daughter of John, sixth Lord Forbes, and widow of John, Earl of Atholl, succeeded as tenth Baron
1571. on the death of his father in 1571.

John Leslie of Balquhain was Sheriff-principal of Aberdeen for many years. Patrick Leith of Likelyhead was served heir to his father, George Leith of Barns and Edingarioch, before John Leslie of Balquhain, Sheriff of Aberdeen, 4th
1580. October 1580. Again, in 1584, John Leslie of Balquhain succeeded the Earl of Huntly as Sheriff of Aberdeen; and in the Diet-book of the Sheriff-court of Aberdeen we find him frequently
1597. mentioned, as presiding as Sheriff, up to 1597.

* *Retours*, B. 36, No. 69. † *Ibid.* B. 41, No. 248.

John, Tenth Baron of Balquhain.

Under the date 24th April 1597, we find the following entry :—

"Curia Justiciarii xxiv. Aprilis 1597, per honorabiles viros Joannem Leslie de Balquhane vicecomitem de Aberdeen, Thomam Leslie ejus deputatum Alexandrum Rutherford de Robeslaw praepositum dicti burgi."

John Leslie of Balquhain lived in splendid magnificence, and by his expensive habits he much encumbered his estates. He never rode out without an escort of at least twenty vassals or followers, who attended him on horseback. We find the following account of the Baron of Balquhain and his retinue in the *Book of Bon-accord* :—

"On the 6th February 1587, the Laird of Balquhain came to the Justess-port, Aberdeen, with certain horsemen to the number of fiftie to be in the toune contrar to the will of the hail magistrates, and commands, quha was repulsit and gat na entrance, the hail toune beand in armour, withstann the said Laird. On the morne he cam to the crabstane wi his horsemen to see gyff the toune would come out, quha cam outt to the crofties on the north syd of the toune, and thair-after cam to the Womanhill all in ordour and foynd nane o theyme thair."* 1587.

In 1570, a great dispute arose between the 1570.

* *Book of Bonaccord*, p. 225.

CHAP. I.

John, Tenth Baron of Balquhain.

Munroes and the Clan Cheinzie, two families of great power and influence in the county of Ross, owing to the following circumstance:—John Leslie, Bishop of Ross, made over his right and title to the castle of the Channonrie of Ross, with the castle-lands, to his consanguineus, or cousin, John Leslie, then fiar, afterwards tenth Baron of Balquhain. But it happened that the Regent Moray,
1569. some time in 1569, the year before his death, had given the custody of this castle to Andrew Munroe of Miltown, to which he got the Baron of Balquhain to agree, on condition that he was to get a portion of the lands of Tintries, in Buchan, in lieu of the said castle and its lands. But the
1570. untimely death of the regent, 23d January 1570, interrupted this agreement, and Andrew Munroe was disappointed in his hope of retaining peaceable possession of the castle. However, the Earl of Lennox and the Earl of Mar, successive regents of the kingdom, kept Munroe in possession of the castle, whereupon the Clan Cheinzie purchased from John Leslie of Balquhain his right and title to the castle and the castle-lands, and then besieged the castle, which the Munroes defended for three years. Great loss was sustained on both sides, and the castle was finally given up to the Clan Cheinzie by an act of pacification.

1594. In 1594, the three Catholic lords, Huntly, Errol, and Angus, were excommunicated by the Scotch Kirk, and were also attainted by a summary pro-

John, Tenth Baron of Balquhain.

ceeding of the Scottish Parliament, under the pretence that they had conspired against the Kirk and the State. James VI., urged by Queen Elizabeth and his own ministers, much against his will, consented to the forfeiture of these nobles, and the Earl of Argyle was appointed the king's lieutenant-general to reduce them. Argyle, accompanied by the Earl of Tullibardine, Sir Lauchlan Maclean, the Laird of Grant, Macintosh, the whole Clan Campbell, Clan Gregor, and many others, whom hatred of the Gordons or the hope of gain had induced to join him, mustering in all about 12,000 men, marched through the mountains to the Highlands. On the 27th September 1594, 1594.
Argyle attacked the castle of Ruthven in Badenoch, but he was obliged to raise the siege, the castle being gallantly defended by the Clan Macpherson. He then returned to the Lowlands, and, in the king's name he summoned and called on Lord Forbes, Leslie of Balquhain, the Irvines, the Ogilvies, and others, and on Lord Lovat, the Frasers, the Clan Cheinzie, the Munroes, and others in the Highlands, to join him. In the meantime, he had marched from Badenoch towards Strathdown, and on the 2d October 1594 he 1594.
encamped near Drimmin, upon the river Avon.

Huntly and Errol, on learning the great preparations which had been made against them, displayed great courage and resolution: Errol went to Strathbogie, with 100 mounted gentlemen and

CHAP. I.

John, Tenth Baron of Balquhain.

some artillery, to join Huntly. They advanced to Auchindown with 1500 resolute horsemen, all determined to die in the field rather than submit to the mercy of their enemies. Huntly, having got intelligence of the designs of Argyle, and of the route by which he was to descend from the mountains, moved forward on the 3d October from Auchindown, and sent in advance Captain Thomas Ker, with a party of horse, to reconnoitre the country, and to ascertain the movements of the enemy. This patrol, meeting a party of Argyle's men sent out for the same purpose, attacked and killed them. This incident so much encouraged Huntly, that he determined to fight Argyle before Lord Forbes and the other forces could arrive. So he continued his advance towards the enemy, who had passed Glenlivat, and was at Alachanlochan in Strathdown.

Argyle was astonished to find that Huntly, with such a disparity of force, should venture to meet him. He immediately prepared for battle. He arranged his forces upon a steep, rough, heather hill, between Glenlivat and Glenrinnis, the lower slope of which, as well as the foreground, was mossy and full of peat-holes or pits. His advanced corps, consisting of 4000 men, of whom 2000 were hagbuteers and musketeers, was under the command of Sir Lauchlan Maclean and Macintosh; while Argyle himself, and the Earl of Tullibardine, were with the main body.

CHAP. I.

John, Tenth Baron of Balquhain.

Huntly's advanced guard consisted of 300 mounted gentlemen, under the Earl of Errol, Sir Patrick Gordon of Auchindown, Gordon of Gight, and Captain Thomas Ker. Huntly himself followed with the rest of his force, which consisted entirely of cavalry, having the Laird of Cluny-Gordon on his right, and Gordon of Abergeldie on his left flank. Owing to them being all horsemen, the nature of the ground was much against them, because, in order to reach the enemy, they were obliged to pass the mossy ground, and to ride up the rough hill through high heather.

Huntly began the attack by ordering a battery of three field-guns, under Captain Andrew Gray, to open upon the enemy, which was done with much effect, causing great confusion among them, and killing Macneil, the third son of the Laird of Barra, one of their bravest officers, and Campbell of Lochnell, who carried the standard. The advance-guard, perceiving the disorder of the enemy's ranks, instantly charged. Sir Patrick Gordon, with his own men, galloped right up the hill against Sir Lauchlan Maclean, while Errol made a detour to attack the right flank. Maclean received the charge with great firmness, and a furious fight was continued for some time, and Sir Patrick Gordon was slain; Maclean's force being vastly superior, he nearly surrounded his assailants, and the Earl of Errol was in danger of being cut off. Huntly, however, speedily ad-

CHAP. I.

John, Tenth Baron of Balquhain.

vanced to his support, and in doing so, he had a horse shot under him. The battle was renewed, and continued for two hours, when Argyle's main body began to give way, and fled towards the burn of Alachanlochan, leaving Maclean still fighting manfully. At length Maclean retired in good order, and Huntly pursued the enemy beyond the burn of Alachanlochan, when the steepness of the mountains prevented his further progress.

Argyle lost 700 men, and his standard was found on the field of battle, and was taken in triumph to Strathbogie, where it was placed on the top of the Great Tower. On Huntly's side, Sir Patrick Gordon of Auchindown and twenty other gentlemen were slain, and forty or fifty were wounded. Argyle had assured himself of victory, and among his personal baggage, which fell into Huntly's hands, there was found a document in which the lands of Huntly, of Errol, and of their supporters, were promised to the Earl of Argyle and his army.

In the meantime, Lord Forbes, John Leslie of Balquhain, and Irvine of Drum, had, in consequence of Argyle's summons in the king's name, assembled all their followers, in order to join him against Huntly. But on learning Argyle's defeat, some of them, Lord Forbes and others, resolved to join the Highlanders who were coming from Moray and Ross to Argyle's assist-

CHAP. I.

John, Tenth Baron of Balquhain.

ance, and to attack Huntly as he returned from Glenlivat, thinking that it would be no difficult matter to overcome him, and thus revenge old quarrels. With this design, all the Forbeses, with some of the Leslies and Irvines, met at Druminnor, Lord Forbes's place, under cover of a dark night, and commenced their march. During the march, a gentleman of the name of Irvine was killed by a pistol-shot, close by the side of Lord Forbes. The pistols of the whole party were immediately examined, and were all found loaded, so that it was never ascertained who fired the shot. It was conjectured that it was done by some adherent of the Gordons, who might have got close to them in the darkness of the night. The untoward incident created much confusion, and cast such doubts on the minds of the Forbeses and Irvines, every man suspecting his neighbour, that they parted company, and all returned to their homes. The northern clans were prevented from joining Argyle by the persuasion of John Dunbar of Monyness, whose mother had married Sir Patrick Gordon of Auchindown as her second husband.

The king, James VI., on hearing of Argyle's defeat, advanced from Dundee to Strathbogie, and, though much against his own inclination, he permitted the houses of Huntly, Errol, Gordon of Newton, and of other adherents of Huntly, to be burned or destroyed, under the pretext that

CHAP. I.

John, Tenth Baron of Balquhain.

priests were harboured in them. Huntly had retired into Sutherlandshire while the king was marching towards Strathbogie. When the king went south again, he left Lennox as his Lieutenant in the North. Huntly and Errol went to Lennox in Aberdeen, where he resided, and they consented to leave the kingdom during the king's pleasure.
1595. Huntly embarked at Aberdeen in March 1595, and went to Flanders and Germany, where he travelled for some time, till he was recalled by the king, and, together with Errol and Angus, was restored to his honours and estates at a
1596. parliament held at Edinburgh in November 1596.
1599. He was created Marquis of Huntly in 1599, and the Forbeses, Leslies, Irvines, and the northern clans, willingly reconciled themselves with him.

It is certain that the king was not sorry for Argyle's defeat, and that he made jests about it. Lennox, whom he made his Lieutenant in the North, was Huntly's brother-in-law. Gordon of Straloch states that he found among the papers of his father, Sir John Gordon of Pitlurg, letters in the king's own hand to Huntly, giving him advice how to behave in the several conjunctures that might happen, and that his father did service to Huntly by conveying his messages to the king; and that this correspondence continued while the king was at Aberdeen, by means of Pitlurg, who, four nights after the king's departure, gave Lennox a treat (a supper) in his own house in

CHAP. I.

John, Tenth Baron of Balquhain.

that city, at which Straloch himself, then a young man, was present; and that he saw there the Earl of Huntly and John Leslie of Balquhain, a man of prime note in these parts; and that this could not be done without the king's knowledge.* The king's political exigencies compelled him to act against Huntly and Errol, but he never looked on them as his enemies, and his feelings were shared by many who answered Argyle's summons to join him against them, especially by the Leslies and the Irvines. That the Leslies were not Huntly's enemies is plainly shown by the presence of John Leslie of Balquhain at the interview between him and Lennox in Pitlurg's house, and by their subsequent friendship, and by the bond of manrent, executed 21st March 1603, between George, Marquis of Huntly, and his special friend and servant, John Leslie of Balquhain. That the Leslies of Balquhain and the Irvines of Drum were not enemies of the Earl of Errol, is shown by the letter of John Crychtoun, younger of Frendraught, to John Leslie of Balquhain, and by that of Alexander Irvine of Drum and John Crychtoun to John Leslie, purporting that they three—John Leslie of Balquhain, Alexander Irvine of Drum, and John Crychtoun of Frendraught—had been chosen as impartial arbiters in a dispute between the Earl of Errol and the Earl Marischal.

1603.

See App. No. XVIII.

See App. No. XIX. and No. XX.

* *Chronicles of Aberdeen*, p. iii.

CHAP. I.

John, Tenth Baron of Balquhain.

John Cheyne, burgess of Aberdeen, granted a letter of reversion to John Leslie, son and heir of William Leslie of Balquhain, upon a house in the Netherkirkgate of Aberdeen, dated 27th January
1564. 1564.*

John Leslie of Kirkhill, son and heir of William Leslie of Balquhain, got a gift of nonentry of the lands of Balquhain, under the Privy Seal, 6th June
1569. 1569; and also a gift of ward, nonentry, and relief, of the same lands, 6th August 1569.†

John Leslie, son and heir of William Leslie of Balquhain, made a contract with Marjory Leslie, one of the two, and elder daughter of the late John Leslie, brother of the said William Leslie of Balquhain, and Alexander Bisset, her husband, whereby the said Marjory ratified the redemption of the lands of Balquhain. In consideration whereof, John Leslie bound himself to pay to Marjory £5000 Scots. The contract is dated 1st
1569. October 1569, and is registered in the Commissary books of Aberdeen on the same day.‡

Patrick Leslie of Kincraigie, and his spouse Jean Leslie, granted a letter of reversion of the sunny halves of Auldtown and Netherbeggery of Aquhorties, in favour of John Leslie of Kirkhill,
1569. 23d December 1569.§

John Leslie of Balquhain made a contract with John Leslie in Ardlaw, whereby he assigned to

* Balquhain Charters, No. 702.

† *Ibid.* No. 889. ‡ *Ibid.* No. 22. § *Ibid.* No. 984.

CHAP. I.

John, Tenth Baron of Balquhain.

him the reversion of the sunny half of the lands of Aquhorties, formerly granted by George Mortimer, and Janet Leslie his spouse, to William Leslie, ninth Baron of Balquhain, 20th March 1573.* 1573.

John Leslie of Kirkhill was retoured heir to his father William Leslie in the barony of Balquhain, 17th October 1573.† 1573.

John Leslie of Balquhain made a contract, 7th November 1573, with James Leslie, burgess in 1573. Aberdeen, and his spouse, whereby John Leslie was allowed to possess certain wadsett lands of Inveramsay on payment of forty bolls of victual annually.‡

William Leslie, brother of John Leslie of Balquhain, granted a letter of reversion in favour of his said brother John, bearing that the said John had disponed his lands of Balquhain and others to the said William and his heirs-male, and declaring the said lands to be redeemable upon payment of a rose noble of gold; 1st December 1573.§ 1573.

John Leslie of Balquhain assigned, 5th April 1574, to James Harvey of Boyndes a letter of 1574. provision, dated 27th May 1563, granted by 1563. Alexander Strachan, advocate in Aberdeen, to the said John Leslie, upon the lands of Bonnytown, with the brewhouse and croft thereof.‖

* Balquhain Charters, No. 261. † *Ibid.* No. 23.
‡ *Ibid.* No. 684. § *Ibid.* No. 24. ‖ *Ibid.* No. 602.

CHAP. I.

John, Tenth Baron of Balquhain.

John Leslie of Balquhain wadsett to Alexander Letster, burgess in Aberdeen, the lands of Syde, extending to four ploughs, and the teinds thereof, redeemable for 1400 merks; 8th September
1574. 1574.*

John Leslie of Balquhain, and John Erskine of Balhagarty, settled the amount of toll to be uplifted at the Chapel of Garioch, by a submission
1574. and decreet-arbitral, 30th September 1574.†

William, Bishop of Aberdeen, 25th October
1574. 1574, confirmed a charter of the lands of Bonnytown and others, granted by John Leslie of Balquhain to James Harvey of Boyndes, 24th October 1574; and sasine thereon followed, 28th October 1574.‡

John Leslie of Balquhain wadsett to William Leslie of Wardis, and Janet Innis his spouse, and James Leslie their son, the lands of Knockallochy, redeemable for 600 merks, and gave in warrandice
1576. the Mains of Balquhain, 2d February 1576.§

John Leslie of Balquhain made a contract with John Spens, burgess of Edinburgh, whereby he bound himself to infeft the said John Spens in the lands of Nethertown and Blairbowie, 11th
1576. March 1576; and registered in books of Council
1577. 25th November 1577;|| and in terms of the contract John Spens granted a letter of reversion of the

* Balquhain Charters, No. 660.
† *Ibid.* No. 986. ‡ *Ibid.* No. 603. § *Ibid.* No. 636.
|| *Ibid.* No. 661.

said lands, in favour of John Leslie of Balquhain, 15th March 1576.* CHAP. I. *John, Tenth Baron of Balquhain.*

James, Earl of Morton, Regent of Scotland, and John Leslie of Balquhain, executed a contract, whereby, for the sum of 5000 merks, John Leslie obliged himself to make up titles to the lands of Learny, Mill of Awach, Craighead, and others, and also to the lands of Tulliqueden, Farnes, and others, in the bishopric of Ross, which his father, William Leslie, ninth Baron of Balquhain, had acquired in 1567, and to denude himself of the 1567.
whole thereof in favour of the said earl; dated 28th May 1576, and registered in books of Council 1576.
7th June 1576.†

Alexander, Bishop of Ross, granted a letter for giving sasine to John Leslie of Balquhain, as heir to William Leslie, his father, in the hail lands mentioned in the contract of sale between James, Earl of Morton, and the said John Leslie, 15th November 1576;‡ and James, Earl of Morton, 1576.
granted a discharge for 1000 merks, stipulated to be paid as specified in the foresaid contract, 8th April 1577.§ 1577.

James Leslie granted a letter of reversion of the lands of Newmills in favour of John Leslie of Balquhain, 9th November 1576.|| 1576.

Mary Maitland granted a letter of reversion of

* Balquhain Charters, No. 663.
† *Ibid.* No. 674. ‡ *Ibid.* No. 675. § *Ibid.* No. 676.
|| *Ibid.* No. 702.

CHAP. I.

John, Tenth Baron of Balquhain.

the lands of Bonnytown, in favour of John Leslie of Balquhain, 6th February 1578.*

John Leslie of Balquhain wadsett to George Leslie in New Rayne, and Janet Leslie his spouse, two ploughs of the lands of Bonnytown, redeem-
1579. able for 1000 merks, 31st May 1579.†

Marjory Galloway, relict of George Leslie of Lentusk, renounced her liferent of part of the lands of Lowns, in favour of John Leslie of Bal-
1579. quhain, 23d September 1579.‡

John Leslie of Balquhain granted a charter of the sunny third ploughlands of Pitbee, in favour of Walter Gordon of Westhall, 8th December
1580. 1580.§

John, Earl of Argyle, ratified a bond granted by Dame Anna Keith, his spouse, to John Leslie of Balquhain, concerning certain securities and infeftments in her favour upon the Mains of
1581. Balquhain, dated in August 1581.||

John Leslie of Balquhain redeemed the half of the lands of Blairdaff from Marjory Innes, spouse of John Innes of Edengeycht, 10th November
1586. 1586.¶

James Leslie of Newmills, upon his forfeiture, granted a letter of repossession to John Leslie of
1587. Balquhain, dated 21st June 1587.**

Sir Patrick Gordon of Auchindown, and James

* Balquhain Charters, No. 605. † *Ibid.* No. 606.
‡ *Ibid.* No. 707. § *Ibid.* No. 623. || *Ibid.* No. 25.
¶ *Ibid.* No. 268. ** *Ibid.* No. 703.

Leslie of Newmills, executed a renunciation and grant of redemption of the lands of Newmills, in favour of John Leslie of Balquhain, 21st June 1587.*

Norman Leslie, burgess of Aberdeen, and Elspet Spens his spouse, granted a letter of reversion of the lands of Nethertown of Knockinlewes, containing the sum of £1000 Scots, in favour of John Leslie of Balquhain, 1st September 1587. 1587.

Thomas Dempster of Auchterless granted a commission to John Leslie of Balquhain, empowering him to sell the lands of Killesmount to Sir Walter Ogilvie of Findlater, 18th January 1588.† 1588.

Thomas Gordon of Cluny, and John Erskine, fiar of Balhagarty, on one part, and John Leslie of Balquhain, and Patrick Leslie of Kincraigie, as his cautioner, for themselves and as taking burden for William Leslie of Sevedlie, on the other part, executed a contract, whereby, *inter alia,* John Erskine, fiar of Balhagarty, bound himself to grant a letter of reversion of the lands of Drumdurno in favour of John Leslie of Balquhain, 12th May 1588.‡ 1588.

John Leslie of Balquhain wadsett the sunny half of Overtown of Aquhorties, with the mill, and the sunny half of the lands of Bograxie, to

* Balquhain Charters, No. 704.

† *Ibid.* No. 648. ‡ *Ibid.* No. 616.

CHAP. I.

John, Tenth Baron of Balquhain.

Patrick Leslie of Kincraigie, 25th May 1588; and Patrick Leslie granted a letter of reversion of the same to John Leslie of Balquhain, 1st October
1590. 1590.*

John Leslie of Balquhain got a charter, under the Great Seal, of the lands of Drumdennan and
1591. Inveramsay, 1st October 1591.†

1592. John Leslie of Balquhain, in 1592, bought the lands of Ardlaw from the Magistrates and Council of Aberdeen for 400 merks. These lands, which lie in the parish of Clatt, were granted by Alexander Stewart, Earl of Mar, to the Cathedral and Bishop of Aberdeen, by a charter, 10th Feb-
1407. ruary 1407. In 1507, William Elphinston, Bishop of Aberdeen, began to build the romantic
1527. bridge of Don, which was finished in 1527 by Bishop Gavin Dunbar, who gave over the bridge to the Magistrates, Council, and Community of Aberdeen, and gave them the lands of Ardlaw as a fund to support, repair, or rebuild it, if necessary, at any future period.

Marjory Gordon, relict of Captain John Gordon, brother of William Gordon of Gight, granted a letter of reversion of the lands of Kirkhill, containing the sum of 3000 merks, in favour of John
1593. Leslie of Balquhain, 7th June 1593.‡

Andrew Meldrum of Fyvie obliged himself to

* Balquhain Charters, No. 273.

† *Registrum Magni Sigilli*, lib. xxxviii. No. 317.

‡ Balquhain Charters, No. 659.

CHAP. I.

John, Tenth Baron of Balquhain.

infeft John Leslie of Balquhain in a third part of the Mains of Hatton, 3d October 1593;* and John Leslie of Balquhain got a charter of the said lands, 11th October 1593. Sasine followed thereon, 22d October 1593.† 1593.

James Mortimer, fiar of Craigievar, assignee of John Leslie of Balquhain, made premonition for the redemption of the sunny half of Overtown of Aquhorties, with the mill, and the sunny half of the lands of Bograxie, from Patrick Leslie of Kincraigie, in terms of contract, 8th March 1594.‡ 1594.

John Leslie of Balquhain redeemed the middle third plough of the lands of Pitbee from Alexander Davidson in Kintore, and Janet Leslie, his spouse, 20th May 1594.§ 1594.

John Leslie of Balquhain redeemed the middle third plough and the sunny plough of the lands of Knockallochy, from John Leith, Apparent of Harthill, 22d May 1594.|| 1594.

At the instance of John Leslie of Balquhain, son and heir of William Leslie, ninth Baron of Balquhain, the Sheriff of Aberdeen granted a precept against John Erskine of Balhagarty, and John Erskine, his eldest son, for having a contract of marches of the lands of Knockallochy and Pitbee, made in June 1565, transferred active in 1565.

* Balquhain Charters, No. 649.
† *Ibid.* No. 651. ‡ *Ibid.* No. 272. § *Ibid.* No. 625.
|| *Ibid.* No. 636.

CHAP. I.

John, Tenth Baron of Balquhain.

the person of the said John Leslie, 17th August 1594.*

John Leslie of Balquhain granted a procuratory for resigning the sunny half of the lands of Aquhorties, with the mill, in favour of James Mortimer, fiar of Craigievar, and Margaret Gordon
1594. his spouse, 6th December 1594.†

John Leslie of Balquhain obliged himself to infeft John Gordon of Braco, and Agnes Strachan his spouse, in the lands of Whitecorse, and the mill and teind-sheaves of the same, redeemable for 3200 merks; and also in the lands of Nethertown of Knockinlewes, and the teind-sheaves of the same, redeemable for 2200 merks, 8th March
1595. 1595.‡

John Leslie of Balquhain, for himself, and taking burden on him for Lady Elizabeth Hay, his spouse, made a contract with Andrew Lawson, burgess of Aberdeen, and Christina Hay his spouse, whereby, for 3000 merks paid to Andrew Lawson and his spouse, they disposed their lodgings in the Castlegate of Aberdeen to the said
1595. John Leslie, 8th March 1595.§

John Leslie of Balquhain granted a charter of sale of the lands and mill of Syid, with the Peil, and the customs of St. Rule's Fair, the ailhous croft of Syde, Arnbrig, Erllisfeild, Seggydene, Kirkhill, and Mostoun, in the parish of Kineth-

See App. No. XXI.

* Balquhain Charters, No. 706.

† *Ibid.* No. 274. ‡ *Ibid.* No. 160. § *Ibid.* No. 652.

mount, 19th June 1595, in favour of Sir Thomas Gordon of Cluny, which charter was confirmed by King James VI., 24th July 1597.

George Innes, younger of Newbeggery, renounced eight bovates of the lands of Logydurno, and the mill of Auchendellon, in favour of John Leslie of Balquhain, in September 1595.* 1595.

John Leslie of Balquhain executed a contract in 1595, whereby he obliged himself to infeft 1595. John Leith, Apparent of Harthill, in the lands and baronies of Fetternear and Balquhain.†

Patrick, Lord Lindores, granted a discharge to John Leslie of Balquhain, discharging him of the yearly teind-silver of his lands of Balquhain, and obliged himself to grant a new site of the teinds and teind-sheaves for nineteen years, when he should be required to do so by the said John Leslie, 30th September 1596.‡ 1596.

John Leslie of Balquhain executed a contract, 27th September 1596, whereby he disponed his 1596. estate of Wardis to William Leslie, fourth Baron of Wardis. The contract was registered in the Commissary-books of Aberdeen, 13th December 1596.§ 1596.

John Leslie of Balquhain, with the consent of Lady Elizabeth Hay his spouse, wadsett the town and lands of Tullos, and Mistown croft in Whitecorse, including a tack of the teind-sheaves, to

* Balquhain Charters, No. 699.

† *Ibid.* No. 987. ‡ *Ibid.* No. 87. § *Ibid.* No. 647.

CHAP. I.

John, Tenth Baron of Balquhain.

John Gordon of Braco, redeemable for 600 merks, 31st December 1596;* and granted a charter of the said lands to John Gordon on the same day.
1597. Sasine thereon followed, 1st January 1597.†

John Leslie of Balquhain, with the advice and consent of Francis, Earl of Errol, disponed his lands of Balquhain to his eldest lawful son, John Leslie, fiar of Balquhain, under certain conditions, and redeemable upon payment of eight pounds
1597. Scots, 23d September 1597;‡ and granted a charter of the said lands to his said son on the same day: sasine followed thereupon, 26th September 1597.§ This charter was confirmed by a charter under the Great Seal, 9th November
1660. 1600.‖

John Leslie of Balquhain, and his son John Leslie, younger thereof, wadsett the lands of Craigsmill to John Leith of Harthill, redeemable
1598. for 400 merks, 12th March 1598.¶

John Leith of Harthill granted a back-bond to John Leslie of Balquhain, obliging himself to give up all right and claim to the lands of Newmills
1598. on payment of 600 merks, 12th March 1598.**

William Leslie of Seveedlie disponed the lands of Fetternear in favour of John Leslie of Bal-
1598. quhain, 13th November 1598,—the said William having right to the said lands by disposition from

* Balquhain Charters, No. 181. † *Ibid.* No. 185.
‡ *Ibid.* No. 26. § *Ibid.* No. 27. ‖ *Ibid.* No. 30.
¶ *Ibid.* No. 691. ** *Ibid.* No. 692.

John, Tenth Baron of Balquhain.

the king, in virtue of the Act of Annexation of Church Lands.*

John Leslie of Balquhain, and Patrick Leslie of Kincraigie, executed a contract, August 1598, whereby, *inter alia*, Patrick Leslie granted to James Leslie of Middleton the crofts of Pitbee, which were redeemable by John Leslie of Balquhain.† 1598.

John Leslie of Balquhain, for himself, and as taking burden for Jean Erskine, now his spouse, executed a contract with Patrick Coupland, who assigned and disponed the town and lands of Fingask in favour of John Leslie of Balquhain and spouse, 30th September 1598.‡ 1598.

Patrick Leslie of Kincraigie resigned the croft-land called Pitbee Haugh, in favour of John Leslie of Balquhain, and John Leslie, younger thereof, 10th December 1599.§ 1599.

John Leslie of Balquhain wadsett a plough of the lands of the Nethertown of Fetternear to William Leslie of Seveedlie, redeemable for 500 merks, 26th June 1601.|| 1601.

King James VI. granted a charter to John Leslie of Balquhain, and Jean Erskine his wife, of the barony of Fetternear, the office of Constable of the palace and chief messuage of the bishopric of Aberdeen, and an annual rent of £120 from the lands of Auchlyne, Talzeaucht, Blairdinny, Bonynton, Casteltoun, and Louesk, in the parishes *See* App. No. XXII.

* Balquhain Charters, No. 460. † *Ibid.* No. 626.
‡ *Ibid.* No. 644. § *Ibid.* No. 617. || *Ibid.* No. 612.

CHAP. I.

John, Tenth Baron of Balquhain.

of Clatt and Rayne, for the support of the office of Constable, 10th May 1602; sasine followed thereon, 15th April 1603; registered at Aberdeen, 4th
1603. May 1603.

John Leslie of Balquhain disponed the lands of Balquhain, under certain conditions, in favour of
1603. his son, John Leslie, fiar of Balquhain in 1603;* and granted a procuratory of resignation of the said lands in favour of his said son and the other heirs of tailzie therein mentioned.†

John Leslie of Balquhain, and John Leslie, younger thereof, renounced all right of reversion of the lands of Newmills, in favour of John Leith of Harthill, who had paid the sum of 700 merks for the said lands, which were declared irredeem-
1605. able, 12th July 1605. This renunciation was
1606. ratified 11th November 1606.‡

Elspet Spens, and Christian Leslie her daughter, made a judicial renunciation of the lands of Newtown of Knockenlewes, in favour of John
1605. Leslie of Balquhain, 13th July 1605.§

Norman Leslie, burgess of Aberdeen, renounced in favour of John Leslie of Balquhain the sunny third of the plough-lands of Pitbee, which had been wadsett to the said Norman by Walter Gordon of Westhall, and Agnes Leslie his spouse, and assigned to John Urquhart in Aberdeen; 14th
1608. May 1608.||

* Balquhain Charters, No. 31. † *Ibid.* No. 32.
‡ *Ibid.* Nos. 693, 694. § *Ibid.* No. 128. || *Ibid.* No. 624.

CHAP. I.

John, Tenth Baron of Balquhain.

John Leslie, fiar of Balquhain, ratified the alienation of the lands of Syde, with the mill, the Peil, and the customs of St. Rule's fair, the alehouse croft of Syde, Arnbrig, Erllisfeild, Seggydene, Kirkhill, and Mostown, made by John Leslie, tenth Baron of Balquhain, his father, in favour of Sir Thomas Gordon of Cluny; and John Leslie, elder, and John Leslie, younger, of Balquhain, obliged themselves to warrant the said alienation, 15th May 1608; registered in books of 1608.
Council, 13th December 1613.* 1613.

Archibald, Earl of Argyle, for himself, and for the executors of his father, Colin, Earl of Argyle, and for Dame Anna Keith, his mother, with the consent of John Leslie of Balquhain, renounced all right to the lands of Balquhain, and particularly a charter of infeftment granted by the said John Leslie of Balquhain to the said Dame Anna Keith, for security of 2000 merks, in favour of John Leslie, fiar of Balquhain; and the Earl Archibald, and John Leslie of Balquhain, ratified and approved the infeftment of John Leslie, younger, in the lands of Balquhain, 23d June 1609; registered in books of Council, 28th June
1609.† 1609.

John Leslie of Balquhain granted a procuratory of resignation of the sunny half of the town and lands of Aquhorties, Overtown, and Nethertown

* Balquhain Charters, No. 360. † *Ibid.* No. 34.

CHAP. I.

John, Tenth Baron of Balquhain.

thereof, with the half of the mill and the mill-lands thereof, the half of the lands of Blairdaff, and the half of the lands of Woodhill, in favour of his eldest son, John Leslie, fiar of Balquhain, 31st
1610. January 1610 ; and resigned the said lands in the hands of George Leslie, Baron of that Ilk, as superior thereof, 21st March 1610.*

John Leslie of Balquhain resigned all right which he had in the lands and barony of Balquhain, in favour of John Leslie, his eldest son,
1611. 1st April 1611.†

John Leslie of Balquhain, and John Leslie, younger thereof, wadsett the lands of Craigstown, redeemable for 1700 merks, to James Glennie, *alias* Forbes, and Annabella Cruickshanks his
1614. spouse, 9th June 1614.‡

Alexander Gordon of Cluny made an inhibition against John Leslie, elder, and John Lesly, younger, of Balquhain, proceeding upon the
1608. contract and warrandice of 15th May 1608, dated
1616. at Aberdeen, 16th September 1616.§

James Mortimer of Craigievar assigned the gift of ward and nonentry duties of Aquhorties, to John Leslie of Balquhain, 16th September
1616. 1616.||

John Leslie of Balquhain, and John Leslie, fiar thereof, granted a procuratory for resigning the

* Balquhain Charters, Nos. 278, 279.

† *Ibid.* No. 686. ‡ *Ibid.* No. 695. § *Ibid.* No. 363.

|| *Ibid.* No. 880.

lands and barony of Balquhain into the king's hands, for new infeftment to be given to the said John Leslie, fiar of Balquhain, and the other heirs of tailzie therein mentioned, 6th June 1619.* 1619.

John Leslie, tenth Baron of Balquhain, granted a procuratory for resigning the lands and barony of Fetternear into the hands of Patrick, Bishop of Aberdeen, for new infeftment to be given to John Leslie, his eldest son, 3d July 1621. He also 1621. resigned the office of Constable of the Bishop's palace, Aberdeen, in favour of Patrick, Bishop of Aberdeen.†

John Leslie, tenth Baron of Balquhain, married, first, in 1564, Elizabeth Grant, daughter of the 1564. Baron of Grant. The marriage-contract is dated 15th February 1564, and by it William Leslie, ninth Baron of Balquhain, obliged himself to infeft his eldest son and apparent heir, John Leslie, and his future spouse, Elizabeth Grant, in the lands of Kirkhill.‡ By Elizabeth Grant John Leslie had issue—

I. JOHN, who succeeded as eleventh Baron of Balquhain.

II. WILLIAM, who succeeded his nephew John as thirteenth Baron of Balquhain.

John Leslie is said to have divorced his first wife, Elizabeth Grant.

John Leslie married, secondly, Lady Elizabeth Hay, daughter of George, sixth Earl of Errol, by

* Balquhain Charters, No. 44.

† *Ibid.* No. 989. ‡ *Ibid.* No. 847.

CHAP. I. his second wife, Helen, co-heiress of Walter Bruce

John, Tenth Baron of Balquhain. of Pitcullen. John Leslie of Balquhain granted a charter, 20th February 1595, to George, Earl Marischal, of the lands of Pitbee and Inveramsay, during the lifetime of Lady Elizabeth Hay, spouse to the said John Leslie.* By Lady Elizabeth Hay John Leslie had issue a daughter—

ISABELLA, married to Alexander Hay of Dalgety.

Lady Elizabeth Hay obtained a decreet of divorcement against her husband, John Leslie of Balquhain, before the Commissaries of Edinburgh,
1597. 9th March 1597;† and John Leslie, reader at the kirk of Fetternear, granted a certificate that he had read the said decreet of divorcement in the kirk of Fetternear, and proclaimed the said John Leslie his banns to marry when, where, and whom
1598. he pleased, 23d April 1598.‡ John Leslie, fiar of Balquhain, confirmed the provision made by John Leslie of Balquhain in favour of Lady
1597. Elizabeth Hay, 23d September 1597;§ and Lady Elizabeth Hay, Lady Pitcullen, renounced all right which she had in the barony of Balquhain, in favour of John Leslie of Balquhain, her former
1609. husband, 7th April 1609.‖

1598. John Leslie married, thirdly, in 1598, Jean Erskine, daughter of Sir Alexander Erskine, Baron of Gogar, and sister of Thomas, first Earl of

* Balquhain Charters, No. 629.
† *Ibid.* No. 848. ‡ *Ibid.* No. 850. § *Ibid.* No. 630.
‖ *Ibid.* No. 33.

Kellie. The marriage-contract is blank in the date, and is without witnesses.* Mr. John Lindsay, minister of Lethnal, granted a certificate that he had celebrated the marriage of John Leslie of Balquhain and Jean Erskine, 6th July 1598;† and David Wilson, notary-public, executed an instrument of the solemnisation of the said marriage on the same day.‡ Jean Erskine obtained a decreet of adherence, before the Commissaries of Edinburgh, in the same year.§ The presbytery of Brechin accused John Leslie of Balquhain of adultery and unlawful marriage with Jean Erskine; and John Leslie and Jean Erskine defended themselves successfully against the accusation.‖ 1598.

It is said that all the three wives of John Leslie of Balquhain were alive at the same time, and that on one occasion they were all in the same kirk of Chapel of Garioch.

By Jean Erskine John Leslie had issue—

I. Alexander, who succeeded as fourteenth Baron of Balquhain.

II. Walter, born about 1606, who became the first Count Leslie in Germany, of whom hereafter. 1606.

III. Jean, married to Sir Patrick Leslie of Iden, Provost of Aberdeen.

IV. Elizabeth, married, first, to Gilbert Hay, brother of the Baron of Dalgety, and, secondly, to William Grant of Conglass, by whom she had a son, William Grant of Crichie, a celebrated man, who filled many honourable offices.

* Balquhain Charters, No. 849. † *Ibid.* No. 851.
‡ *Ibid.* No. 852. § *Ibid.* No. 854. ‖ *Ibid.* Nos. 855-857.

CHAP. I.

John, Tenth Baron of Balquhain.

It would appear that John Leslie had another son, probably a natural one, who had two sons, one a lawyer in Edinburgh in 1652, named Alexander, and the other, William, who was a bailie in Edinburgh. These two, in letters written by William, thirteenth Baron of Balquhain, and his successor, Alexander, fourteenth baron, are called the nephews of the said barons.

John Leslie, tenth Baron of Balquhain, died in
1622. June 1622, and was succeeded by his eldest son, John Leslie, eleventh Baron of Balquhain.

John, Eleventh Baron of Balquhain.

JOHN LESLIE,

ELEVENTH BARON OF BALQUHAIN.

JOHN LESLIE, eldest son of John Leslie, tenth Baron of Balquhain, by his first wife, Elizabeth Grant of Grant, succeeded, as eleventh Baron of Balquhain, on the death of his father in June
1622. 1622.

In the *Chronicles of Aberdeen* we find the following record of John Leslie :—

"John Leslie, aperand of Balquhane, coyme to Aithakaynt in Buchane thane partinand to Alexander Cullen, with Androw Lesly, Gilbert Lesly, his fader, breder, and oderis, to the nwmer of xx personis, and thair moist cruelly enwaditt the saidis Alexander Cullen bygyne in strikin wp his yeittis, dwiris, kistis, and away takin of clayise

John, Eleventh Baron of Balquhain.

and birnyne of writtins, and slew and mwrdrest onder nycht Dauid Carill, serwand to the said Alexander, the laist day of Marche 1587 yeris, God to revenge."*

For this murder of David Carill, John Leslie, fiar of Balquhain, got a letter of slains, 22d March 1609, from the nearest of kin to the said David; 1609.
and he got a remission for the same under the Privy Seal, 9th March 1620.† 1620.

We find by the Records of the Sheriff-Court of Aberdeen that, 1st October 1616, John Leslie, 1616.
fiar of Balquhain, and John Cheyne of Arnage, at a meeting of freeholders held at the Michaelmas Court in Aberdeen, were elected Commissioners conjunctly to attend Parliament. This appears to be the earliest election of which mention is made. In those times the Members of Parliament for shires were usually elected annually, and they required a qualification of forty shillings land in superiority, holding of the king, of old extent, or when this extent did not appear, then of lands worth £400 Scots rent, holding of the king.

John Leslie, like his father, lived very expensively, and by his extravagant habits he involved the family estates still more. He wadsett or mortgaged great part of his property, particularly the lands and barony of Fetternear,

* Chronicles of Aberdeen; *Spalding Club Miscellany*, vol. ii. p. 58.

† Balquhain Charters, Nos. 889, 890.

CHAP. I.

John, Eleventh Baron of Balquhain.

which he wadsett to his brother-in-law, Sir Alexander Hay of Dalgety, and William Hay, his son, for the sum of 11,000 merks, and gave in warrandice six ploughs of the lands of Balquhain,
1625. 15th June 1625.* He granted a charter of the lands and barony of Fetternear to the said William Hay on the same day; sasine followed
1626. thereupon, 12th January 1626; registered at Edinburgh, 7th February 1626. He also granted a charter *de me* to the same effect, 16th November
1627 1627.† Sir Alexander Hay of Dalgety, for himself, and taking burden for his son William, granted a letter of consent to John Leslie of Balquhain, to sell and dispone his lands of Balquhain and Fetternear, subject to his wadsett
1627. rights, 16th October 1627.‡

Sir Alexander Hay of Dalgety, and William Hay, his son, as wadsettees, with the consent of John Leslie of Balquhain, and Janet Innes, his spouse, as superiors, alienated the lands and barony of Fetternear in favour of Hector Abercromby of Westhall, second son of Alexander Abercromby of Birkenbog, by his wife, Margaret Leslie, daughter of William Leslie, ninth Baron
1627. of Balquhain, 16th November 1627.§ Sir Alexander Hay, William Hay, his son, John Leslie of Balquhain, and Janet Innes, his spouse, granted a

* Balquhain Charters, No. 469.

† *Ibid.* Nos. 472, 473.

‡ *Ibid.* No. 474.

§ *Ibid.* No. 475.

charter of the lands and barony of Fetternear to Hector Abercrombie, on the same day: sasine followed thereon, 26th November 1627; registered at Aberdeen, 1st December 1627. Patrick Forbes, Bishop of Aberdeen, with the consent of the Dean and Chapter, granted a charter containing a *novo damus* of the said lands in favour of Hector Abercromby, 2d February 1628; registered at Aberdeen, 9th February 1628. This charter was ratified by Adam Bellenden, Bishop of Aberdeen, 24th January 1636. The Lords of Session pronounced a decreet of reduction at the instance of Patrick Forbes, Bishop of Aberdeen, for behoof of Hector Abercrombie, against John Leslie of Balquhain, Janet Innes, his spouse, Sir Alexander Hay of Dalgety, and William Hay, his son, 8th July 1629. Hector Abercrombie obtained a charter, under the Great Seal, of the lands and barony of Fetternear, 29th January 1631.*

1628. 1636. 1629. 1631.

Alexander Abercromby, eldest son of Hector Abercromby, obtained a confirmation of the above charters from Pope Clement X., 20th September 1670; and the barony of Fetternear remained in the possession of the Abercrombys until it was redeemed by Patrick, Count Leslie, fifteenth Baron of Balquhain, in 1690.

See App. No. XVI. 1670. 1690.

John Leslie, fiar of Balquhain, with the consent of his father, John Leslie, tenth Baron of Balquhain,

* Balquhain Charters, Nos. 476-485.

CHAP. I.

John, Eleventh Baron of Balquhain.

ratified, in favour of Gilbert Farquhar, the wadsett of the lands of Whitecorse, with a new reversion of 1000 merks, 9th June 1606.*

James Gordon, eldest son of John Gordon of Braco, and John Gordon, now of Braco, heir-male procreate between the said John Gordon and Agnes Strachan, his spouse, made a renunciation in favour of John Leslie, fiar of Balquhain, discharging a precept of *clare constat* granted by the said John Leslie to the said John Gordon, now of Braco, upon the lands of Whitecorse, under a certain victual feu-farm, 10th February
1609. 1609, in respect of an after-precept containing a money feu-farm, granted to him by the said John
1610. Leslie, 7th June 1610. The renunciation and discharge are dated 8th June 1610.†

John Leslie, fiar of Balquhain, resigned the lands of Inveramsay in favour of himself, 10th
1610. June 1610,‡ and he received a charter under the Great Seal, containing a *novo damus* of the lands and barony of Balquhain, Inveramsay, and others,
1610. united into one barony, 30th August 1610, proceeding upon the resignation of his father, John Leslie, tenth Baron of Balquhain, and of Archibald, Earl of Argyle.§ A precept of Chancery for infefting John Leslie, fiar of Balquhain, in the said lands, was issued on the same

* Balquhain Charters, No. 192.

† *Ibid.* No. 163.

‡ *Ibid.* No. 685.

§ *Registrum Magni Sigilli,* lib. xlvi., No. 165.

CHAP. I. *John, Eleventh Baron of Balquhain.*

day, and sasine followed thereupon, 3d November 1610.

John Leslie, fiar of Balquhain, with the consent of his father, John Leslie, tenth Baron of Balquhain, Sir James Balfour of Pitcullen, Patrick Leslie of Badifora, and George Leslie of Kincraigie, wadsett to William Blackhall of that Ilk the lands of Auldtown of Knockinlewes, and the teinds of the same, redeemable for 6000 merks—31st May 1610.* John Leslie granted a charter in conformity with the wadsett, and a procuratory for resigning the said lands into the king's hands for new infeftment to be given to William Blackhall, both dated on the same day, 31st May 1610.† 1610.

George Leslie, seventh Baron of that Ilk, as superior, granted a charter of the sunny half of the farm and lands of Aquhorties, Overtown and Nethertown thereof, with the half of the mill and mill-lands thereof, half of the lands of Blairdaff, and half of the lands of Woodhill, in favour of John Leslie, fiar of Balquhain, 21st March 1610; sasine followed thereupon, 24th March 1610.‡ 1610.

John Leslie, fiar of Balquhain, having received 300 merks from Thomas Smith in Blairdaff, ratified the wadsett over the half of the lands of Blairdaff, made by James Mortimer in favour of

* Balquhain Charters, No. 101.
† *Ibid.* Nos. 102, 103. ‡ *Ibid.* No. 280.

CHAP. I.

John, Eleventh Baron of Balquhain.

the said Thomas Smith; and John Leslie declared the said lands redeemable for 1356 merks—25th September 1610.*

John Leslie, fiar of Balquhain, granted a charter of Nethertown of Knockenlewes, in favour of John Leslie of Keathney, and Janet Wood his
1612. spouse, 4th November 1612.†

Patrick, Lord Lindores, granted a tack of the teinds of the lands of Balquhain to John Leslie, fiar of Balquhain, for the lifetime of the said Lord Lindores, and nineteen years thereafter, for
1604. £72 Scots per annum, 17th October 1604; and of the teind-sheaves of Aquhorties, for nine years from the term of Lambas 1613, for 24 bolls of
1613. victual per annum, 17th September 1613; and of the teind-sheaves of the lands of Balquhain for the lifetime of the longest liver of them two, and for twenty-nine years thereafter; and of the teind-sheaves of the lands of Aquhorties for thirty-six
1615. years from the date of the grant, August 1615; and Lord Lindores obliged himself to dispone heritably to John Leslie the teind-sheaves of Aquhorties as soon as he was able.‡

John Leslie, fiar of Balquhain, granted a moss-licence in the Moss of Fetternear to James Mortimer of Aquhorties; and James Mortimer granted to John Leslie a moss-gate or road through the lands of Aquhorties to Balquhain,

* Balquhain Charters, No. 292.

† *Ibid.* No. 129. ‡ *Ibid.* Nos. 88, 89, 90.

24th August 1614; registered in the books of Council 12th June 1616.*

James Mortimer disponed half of the town and Mains of Aquhorties, the mill and mill-lands thereof, half of Netherbeggery, and half of Blairdaff, the hail town and lands of Bograxy, multures of Aquhorsk, and the superiority of half of the lands of Woodhill, in favour of John Leslie, fiar of Balquhain, to whom he granted a charter of the said lands, 6th September 1616; sasine followed thereupon 10th Septmber 1616.† 1616.

James Mortimer executed an instrument of resignation *ad remanentiam* of the sunny half of the lands of Aquhorties, called the Mains, of the half of the mill and mill-lands thereof, and of the sunny half of the lands of Bograxy and Netherbeggery, in favour of John Leslie, fiar of Balquhain, 10th September 1616.‡ 1616.

John Leslie, fiar of Balquhain, made a requisition against Francis Leslie, eldest son of John Leslie of Keathnie, deceased, for the redemption of the lands of Nethertown of Knockenlewes, 14th April 1618.§ 1618.

William Blackhall of that Ilk, having paid to James Gordon the sum of 3200 merks, the sum for which the lands of Whitecorse had been wadsett to him, James Gordon transferred all his rights in the lands of Whitecorse to William

* Balquhain Charters, No. 285.

† *Ibid.* No. 290. ‡ *Ibid.* No 291. § *Ibid.* No. 130.

CHAP. I.

John, Eleventh Baron of Balquhain.

Blackhall, 9th June 1610; and John Leslie, fiar of Balquhain, having redeemed these lands for the same sum of 3200 merks, William Blackhall renounced all right which he had to them, 27th
1619. January 1619.*

James Harvey in Elrick, apparent heir to James Harvey of Boyndes, his grandfather, obliged himself to John Leslie, fiar of Balquhain, to have himself served heir to his said grandfather in the lands of Bonnytown, which had been
1574. assigned to him in 1574, and thereafter to dispone the said lands to John Leslie—10th May
1619. 1619.†

John Leslie, fiar of Balquhain, wadsett the lands of Nethertown of Knockenlews to John Leslie of Badifora, and Marjory Strachan his spouse, redeemable for 3000 merks, and failing payment thereof in the manner mentioned, redeemable for 4000 merks; and granted a charter of the said lands, and a tack of the teinds, to the said
1619. John Leslie of Badifora, 2d June 1619. Sasine
1620. followed thereupon 6th April 1620, registered at Aberdeen 8th April 1620.‡

Patrick, Bishop of Aberdeen, with the consent of the Dean and Chapter, granted a charter containing a *novo damus* of the lands and barony of Fetternear, in favour of John Leslie, fiar of Balquhain, proceeding on the resignation of John

* Balquhain Charters, Nos. 164, 165.

† *Ibid.* No. 608.

‡ *Ibid.* Nos. 131-134.

Leslie, tenth Baron of Balquhain, 13th November 1621.* Sasine followed thereupon 21st May 1622, registered at Aberdeen 2d July 1622.

CHAP. I.

John, Eleventh Baron of Balquhain.

John Leslie, fiar of Balquhain, with the consent of Janet Innes his spouse, wadsett the lands of Whitecorse, the mill and teinds thereof, excepting Merstown's Croft (which was wadsett to Gilbert Farquhar), to Patrick Leslie, burgess of Aberdeen, Patrick Leslie his son, and Jean Leslie his spouse, redeemable the lands of Whitecorse for 3000 merks, and the mill, mill-lands, and multures for 1000 merks, 18th June 1622; and granted a charter to this effect, 19th June 1622: sasine thereon 8th July, and registered at Aberdeen 20th July 1622.† 1622.

John Leslie, eleventh Baron of Balquhain, with the consent of William, Alexander, and Walter Leslie, his brothers, granted a procuratory for resigning the lands and barony of Balquhain, in favour of himself and the heirs of tailzie therein mentioned, 19th January 1623; registered in the books of Session 5th June 1623.‡ 1623.

James VI. granted a charter, under the Great Seal, of the lands and barony of Balquhain, in favour of John Leslie of Balquhain, proceeding on the resignation of the said John and his brothers, 25th March 1623.§ A precept of Chancery was 1623.

* Balquhain Charters, No. 467.

† *Ibid.* Nos. 166, 169. ‡ *Ibid.* No. 45

§ *Registrum Magni Sigilli*, lib. l. No. 140.

CHAP. I.

John, Eleventh Baron of Balquhain.

issued for infefting the said John Leslie in the said lands and barony on the same day. Instrument of sasine thereon, 16th September 1623, and again 24th July 1624; registered at Aberdeen
1624. 6th August 1624.*

John Leslie of Balquhain granted a moss-licence in the moss of Fetternear, in favour of Janet Innes
1624. his spouse, in May 1624.†

John Leslie of Balquhain bound himself to John Leslie, sixth Baron of Pitcaple, to obtain the consent of Sir Alexander Hay of Dalgety to a contract whereby John Leslie of Balquhain sold to John Leslie of Pitcaple the lands of Aquhorties, the town and lands of Knockallochy, with the mill thereof, and the lands of Pitbee; and John Leslie of Balquhain, and Janet Innes his spouse, obliged themselves to ratify the contract, 27th
1625. August 1625;‡ and on the same day, John Leslie of Balquhain executed a contract whereby he sold and disponed to John Leslie of Pitcaple, and Marjory Cheyne his spouse, irredeemably, for the sum of £8000 Scots, all the foresaid lands.§ Sasine followed thereon 24th December 1625, registered at Aberdeen 1st January
1626. ary 1626.

Robert Gilbert and Jean Irvine obtained letters of horning, execution of charge and denunciation, against John Leslie of Balquhain and his

* Balquhain Charters, No. 50.

† *Ibid.* No. 858. ‡ *Ibid.* No. 299. § *Ibid.* No. 300.

CHAP. I.

John, Eleventh Baron of Balquhain.

cautioners, proceeding on a bond granted by them to Alexander Irvine, 5th August 1626.*

George Leslie, seventh baron of that Ilk, obtained a decreet of resignation of the sunny half of Aquhorties, against John Leslie of Balquhain, John Leslie of Pitcaple, and others, 7th May 1827;† and he assigned the said decreet to James Leslie, second son of John Leslie of Pitcaple, 10th July 1627.‡ 1627.

James Mortimer, John Leslie of Balquhain, John Leslie of Pitcaple, and Marjory Cheyne his spouse, resigned the shadow half of the lands of Aquhorties, in favour of James Leslie, second son of John Leslie of Pitcaple, 5th October 1627.§ 1627.

John Leslie of Badifora, designed of Artannis, made a requisition to John Leslie of Balquhain to redeem the lands of Nethertown of Knockenlewes, in terms of the contract of wadsett, 14th February 1627; and entered a protest against the said John Leslie of Balquhain, 12th May 1627,‖ and ob- 1627.
tained an inhibition against him, 18th June 1628.¶ 1628.

John Leslie of Balquhain wadsett the lands of Logydurno to Hector Abercrombie of Westhall, redeemable for £1000 Scots, 16th November 1627.**

* Balquhain Charters, No. 881. † *Ibid.* No. 307.
‡ *Ibid.* No. 308. § *Ibid.* No. 313. ‖ *Ibid.* Nos. 136, 138.
¶ *Ibid.* No. 139. ** *Ibid.* No. 700.

CHAP. I.

John, Eleventh Baron of Balquhain.

John Leslie of Balquhain made a contract with Thomas Erskine of Balhagarty, whereby, in extinction of certain debts due to the said Thomas Erskine, for which an apprising had been led against the lands of Inveramsay, he corroborated the said apprising, and declared the lands of
1628. Inveramsay irredeemable, 10th June 1628.*

John Leslie of Balquhain wadsett the land in Whitecorse, called Merstown's Croft, to Alexander Watt in Logydurno, redeemable for 300 merks, 4th May 1628; and granted a charter of the same, 9th May. Sasine followed thereupon 20th May,
1628. registered at Aberdeen 18th June 1628.†

Alexander Paterson, minister of Chapel of Garioch, made a declaration that he had no right to cast and lead fuel from the lands of Bogangus, but by the permission and tolerance of John Leslie
1628. of Balquhain, 17th July 1628.‡

The Lords of Session issued a decreet, at the instance of John Leslie of Badifora, and Marjory Strachan his spouse, against John Leslie of Balquhain, declaring the Nethertown of Knockenlewes to be redeemable only by payment of 4000 merks, because John Leslie of Balquhain had failed to make payment of the 3000 merks in the terms of the contract of wadsett, 5th February
1629. 1629.§

John Leslie of Badifora, and Marjory Strachan

* Balquhain Charters, No. 687.
† *Ibid.* No. 199. ‡ *Ibid.* No. 907. § *Ibid.* No. 140.

his spouse, obtained letters of horning against John Leslie of Balquhain, proceeding on a bond granted to them by him, 2d June 1619, obliging himself to relieve them of all feu-duties, taxes, and teinds of the town and lands of Knockenlewes during the time the same should remain unredeemed, 8th June 1629.* 1629.

John Leslie of Balquhain assigned a tack of teind-sheaves of Balquhain, as far as related to the teind-lands of Drymmies, to John Gordon of Cluny, 23d October 1629.† 1629.

John Leslie of Balquhain made an indenture of marches for the lands of Balquhain, with John Gordon of Cluny, for the lands of Drymmies, with a note of marches, 23d October 1629.‡ 1629.

John Leslie of Pitcaple executed a back-bond in favour of John Leslie of Balquhain, obliging himself not to use any diligence against John Leslie of Balquhain, his person or estate, for £8000 Scots, due to him by bond, 1st February 1630.§ 1630.

The Lords of Council issued a decreet, at the instance of John Leslie of Badifora, against John Leslie of Balquhain, ordaining him to warrant, acquit, and defend the lands of Nethertown of Knockenlewes, and the teinds of the same, to the said John Leslie of Badifora, and Marjory Strachan his spouse, safe and free from the action of reduc-

* Balquhain Charters, No. 141.

† *Ibid.* No. 92. ‡ *Ibid.* Nos. 84, 85. § *Ibid.* No. 701.

CHAP. I.

John, Eleventh Baron of Balquhain.

tion at the instance of the Earl of Mar, and also from the payment of £8 Scots yearly, for certain years, of which John Leslie of Badifora had been charged to make payment to Mr. James Milne, minister of Inverurie, for the teinds of the said lands; or otherwise to infeft the said John Leslie of Badifora and his spouse in other lands of the
1630. same value and yearly rent—20th February 1630; execution for charges and denunciation registered
1636. 28th June 1636.* John Leslie of Badifora obtained letters of horning against John Leslie of Balquhain, proceeding on the said decreet, 25th
1630-36. February 1630; caption thereon, 26th July 1636,† and he also obtained letters from the Privy Council against John Leslie of Balquhain, proceeding on the said denunciation, 26th July 1636, with execution thereon, 15th October 1636,‡ and
1636. letters of arrestment, 2d November 1636; with execution thereof on a paper apart, used in the hands of tenants of Balquhain, 3d January
1637. 1637.§

John Leslie in Meikle Durno, and Walter Farquhar, made a declaration that they had no right, but leave and tolerance from John Leslie of Balquhain, and John Leslie, younger thereof, to their desks placed in the east gable of the kirk of Chapel of Garioch. The date is blank.||

---

* Balquhain Charters, No. 143.

† *Ibid.* No. 144. ‡ *Ibid.* No. 146. § *Ibid.* No. 147.

|| *Ibid.* No. 909.

John, Eleventh Baron of Balquhain.

Alexander Strachan, minister of Chapel of Garioch, obtained a decreet of augmentation of stipend, 13th July 1636.*

John, Earl of Mar, disponed the lands of Balquhain to Alexander Leslie of Tullos, during the lifetime of his brother, John Leslie, eleventh Baron of Balquhain, after the lifetime of the said John, to devolve on his widow, Janet Innes, in liferent, and then to John Leslie, younger of Balquhain, in fee—1st December 1636.† 1636.

John Leslie of Balquhain resigned the lands and barony of Balquhain in favour of his brother Alexander Leslie of Tullos, who obtained a charter under the Great Seal of the same, 13th February 1637. A precept under the Great Seal was issued 1637. for infefting the said Alexander in the said lands on the same day; and sasine followed thereupon 11th August 1637, registered at Aberdeen, 12th August 1637.‡

John Leslie of Balquhain disponed the third part of the lands of Drumdurno in favour of his brother, Alexander Leslie of Tullos, 3d December 1636; and the said Alexander assigned the 1636. said disposition to his nephew, John Leslie, younger of Balquhain, 6th December 1636.§ John Leslie of Balquhain executed an instrument of resignation of the said lands in favour

* Balquhain Charters, No. 912.

† *Ibid.* No. 51. ‡ *Ibid.* Nos. 53-55.

§ *Ibid.* Nos. 619, 619

CHAP. I.

John, Eleventh Baron of Balquhain.

of Alexander Leslie of Tullos, and John Leslie, younger of Balquhain, 13th February 1637.*

John Leslie of Balquhain granted a tack of the teind-sheaves of the lands of Balquhain to Janet
1638. Innes, his spouse, 9th February 1638.†

John Leslie, eleventh Baron of Balquhain, married, first, Marjory Gordon, widow of Robert Duguid, fifth Baron of Auchinhove, but he does not appear to have had any issue by this marriage. He married, secondly, Janet Innes, daughter of the Laird of Auchintoul, by whom he had—

I. JOHN, who succeeded as twelfth Baron of Balquhain.

II. ALEXANDER, concerning whom there is the following entry in the old parish records of Inverurie :—

"Jhon Leslie of Balquhyn and Janet Innes ane sone baptisit callit Alex^{r}. witness Alex^{r}. Lesly of Tullos,
1635. W^{m}. Lesly of Carthnie, 7th March 1635, in respect y^{r} was no minister at the chappell after the death of M^{r}. Andro Straq^{n}."

This Alexander Leslie must have died young.

III. JEAN LESLIE, married to James Elphinston of Glack.
1641. The marriage-contract is dated 13th May 1641.‡

John Leslie had also a natural son, Andrew, who adopted the military profession in Germany, where he attained the rank of captain.

John Leslie, eleventh Baron of Balquhain, died
1638. in 1638, and was succeeded by his son, John Leslie, twelfth baron.

---

* Balquhain Charters, No. 620.
† *Ibid.* No. 859. ‡ *Ibid.* No. 860.

CHAP. I.

JOHN LESLIE,

TWELFTH BARON OF BALQUHAIN.

John, Twelfth Baron of Balquhain.

JOHN LESLIE, eldest son of John Leslie, eleventh Baron of Balquhain, by Janet Innes his wife, succeeded as twelfth Baron of Balquhain, on the death of his father, in 1638. 1638.

Owing to the expensive habits and mismanagement of his father and grandfather, the tenth and eleventh barons, John Leslie found the family estates much reduced, and deeply in debt, so that little remained to him but the castle and Mains of Balquhain. He therefore left his estates to nurse, and being a gallant young gentleman, he served in the civil wars from 1639 till 1647, as 1639-47. captain in the troop of Guards of Alexander Leslie, Earl of Leven, General of the Scotch army. After this he left his native country, and went first to Germany, and from thence to Russia, where he entered the Muscovite service, in which he attained the rank of colonel of cavalry.

In the time of John Leslie, twelfth Baron of Balquhain, Alexander Gordon of Kincraigie had the lands of Syde, with the mill, the Peil, the customs of St. Rule's fair, the alehouse-croft of Syde, Arnbrig, Erllisfeild, Seggydene, Kirkhill, and Mostown, adjudged to him from the heirs of Balquhain on the following grounds:—

By a contract, dated 15th May 1608, John 1608.

CHAP. I.

John, Twelfth Baron of Balquhain.

See App. No. XXI.

Leslie, fiar, afterwards eleventh Baron of Balquhain, ratified an alienation of the said lands made by his father, John Leslie, tenth Baron, to Sir Thomas Gordon of Cluny, which contract was registered in the books of Council 13th December
1613. 1613. Sir Alexander Gordon of Cluny got an inhibition against John Leslie, tenth Baron, and his son, John Leslie, fiar of Balquhain, proceeding on the foresaid contract, and execution was
1616. registered at Aberdeen 16th September 1616. He assigned to John Leith of Bucharn all the claims, rights, and titles, competent to him by the
1638. said inhibition, 11th February 1638; and John Leith of Bucharn afterwards transferred all his rights to the said lands to Alexander Gordon of Kincraigie, who had them adjudged to him 24th
1649. December 1649, so that these lands were lost to the Balquhain family.*

John Leslie, fiar of Balquhain, as principal, and Robert Smith in Blairdaff, as cautioner, granted a heritable bond for 600 merks, to John Watt at New Mill of Knockallochy, registered in the books of Council and Session 7th October
1626. 1626.†

John Leslie, eleventh Baron of Balquhain, in
1638. May 1638 assigned to his son, John Leslie, fiar of Balquhain, a contract containing a tack of the teind-sheaves of the lands of Balquhain and

* Balquhain Charters, Nos. 360-364.

† *Ibid.* No. 990.

John, Twelfth Baron of Balquhain.

Aquhorties, granted to him by Patrick, Lord Lindores, in August 1615.*

Alexander Strachan, minister of Chapel of Garioch, obtained a decreet of locality against the heritors of the parish, 20th February 1643, and a correspondence ensued concerning the decreet between John Leslie of Balquhain and the Laird of Pittodrie.† 1643.

John Leslie of Balquhain married Miss Crawford, daughter of Colonel Crawford in Muscovy, and by her had two daughters, who, with their mother, died of the pestilence.

John Leslie, twelfth Baron of Balquhain, was killed at the storming of Igolwitz, 30th August 1655, when the Russians invaded Poland. He was succeeded by his uncle, William Leslie, thirteenth Baron. 1655.

WILLIAM LESLIE,

THIRTEENTH BARON OF BALQUHAIN.

William, Thirteenth Baron of Balquhain.

William Leslie, second son of John Leslie, tenth Baron of Balquhain, by his wife Elizabeth Grant of Grant, succeeded as thirteenth Baron of Balquhain on the death of his nephew John, twelfth baron, without issue, 30th August 1655. 1655.

William Leslie was a man of considerable abilities, and he entered into public life. He

* Balquhain Charters, No. 93. † *Ibid.* Nos. 913-917.

CHAP. I.

William, Thirteenth Baron of Balquhain.

was a Privy Councillor, and a true and faithful servant of King Charles I. both in court and camp. He received several wounds in the king's service. After the execution of the king, he retired to Holland, where he settled with his family, and acquired some property. In his absence, his brother, Alexander Leslie of Tullos, managed his Scotch property.

Besides the family estates of Balquhain, William Leslie acquired considerable property about Stirling, called Cambusbarron, which had formerly belonged to the prior and convent of Stirling, and of which Alexander Erskine, brother of John, Lord Erskine of Kelly, got a charter,
1560. 10th May 1560.* Thomas, Earl of Kelly, disponed these lands to William Leslie, who got a charter of them, under the Great Seal, 12th July
1640. 1640.† William Leslie, designed servitor to the King, Charles I., wadset tthese lands to his brother Alexander Leslie of Tullos, redeemable for 11,000
1642. merks, 3d August 1642,‡ and granted to him a charter of the same. Sasine followed thereupon 12th August 1642, and registered at Stirling on the same day.§ William Leslie obtained letters of horning against the superior of the lands of Cambusbarron, to infeft him therein, proceeding on a
1642. decreet of adjudication, 20th July 1642.‖ Execu-

* Balquhain Charters, No. 794.
† *Ibid.* No. 795. ‡ *Ibid.* No. 796. § *Ibid.* No. 797.
‖ *Ibid.* No. 799.

CHAP. I.

William, Thirteenth Baron of Balquhain.

tion of charge followed thereupon against the magistrates of Stirling, the Earl of Kellie, and Lord Erskine, 11th August 1642;* and another execution of charge against the said Earl and Lord Erskine, 16th November 1647.† William Leslie authorised his brother, Alexander Leslie of Tullos, to sell the lands of Cambusbarron, and to dispose of the house at Stirling, 3d March 1651.‡ An inventory was made of the books which were in the cabinet left by William Leslie at Stirling, and the inventory was signed by Alexander Leslie of Tullos, 13th July 1652.§ An opinion anent the sale of the lands of Cambusbarron was obtained from John Gilmour and other lawyers, 19th August 1652.|| Alexander Leslie of Tullos disponed the lands of Cambusbarron to the town of Stirling, and the disposition was ratified by William Leslie of Balquhain 31st January 1653, and registered in books of Session 29th June 1653.¶ William Leslie granted a discharge to Alexander Leslie of Tullos for his intromissions with the rents of the lands of Cambusbarron for the crop and year 1655, and for 16,000 merks, the price of the said lands received from the town of Stirling, 25th February 1659.** Alexander Leslie obtained an inhibition against William Leslie, proceeding upon the ratification of the sale of the

1647. 1651. 1652. 1653. 1659.

* Balquhain Charters, No. 800. † *Ibid.* No. 801.
‡ *Ibid.* No. 805. § *Ibid.* No. 809. || *Ibid.* No. 810.
¶ *Ibid.* No. 818. ** *Ibid.* No. 822.

CHAP. I.

William, Thirteenth Baron of Balquhain.

lands of Cambusbarron to the burgh of Stirling, and the obligement of relief therein contained, 10th June 1665.*

William Leslie, on succeeding to the estates of Balquhain, found that they were reduced to a low ebb, being much encumbered and involved by the extravagance of the tenth and eleventh barons, and having no son surviving to succeed him, he renounced his rights in the estates to his brother Walter, Count Leslie. But Walter, Count Leslie, having acquired large properties and high rank in Germany, also renounced his right in favour of his elder brother, Alexander Leslie, called the Goodman of Tullos, with whom William made an arrangement, on receiving an annuity, to give up
1659. the succession in his favour, about 1659. Alexander Leslie bound himself to pay an annuity of 700 merks out of the lands of Tullos to Walter, Count Leslie, during the lifetime of William Leslie, 24th June 1659; and by a letter, dated
1660. 17th February 1660, Walter, Count Leslie, desired Alexander Leslie to pay the said annuity to William Leslie.†

William Leslie went to Holland, and left a memorandum with his brother Alexander Leslie, whom he appointed to manage his estates, 18th
1651. March 1651.‡ There is an account of several sums paid by Alexander Leslie to and for William

* Balquhain Charters, No. 830.
† *Ibid.* Nos. 826, 827.
‡ *Ibid.* No. 807.

CHAP. I.

William, Thirteenth Baron of Balquhain.

Leslie from 1642 to 1652.* William Leslie wrote from the Hague to his brother Alexander, 5th September 1652,† and to his nephew Alexander, third son of Alexander Leslie of Tullos, 12th September 1652.‡ William Leslie gave a receipt to Norman Leslie, merchant in Aberdeen, for fifty dollars, on account of Alexander Leslie of Tullos, dated at Rotterdam, 26th April 1655.§ He also granted a discharge to Alexander Leslie for the rents of the lands of Balquhain for the crops of 1655, 1656, 1657, and 1658, dated 31st March 1659, and registered in the Commissary Court books, 16th April 1659.|| William Leslie disponed the lands and barony of Balquhain in favour of Mr. James Leslie, doctor of medicine in Aberdeen, 31st March 1659.¶ William Leslie, designed of Cumbusbarron, was served heir-male of John Leslie, twelfth Baron of Balquhain, the son of his brother, in the dominical lands of Balquhain, with the manor-place of Balquhain, and common pasture in the forest of Benachie in the parish of Logiedurno, and in the third part of the town and lands of Drumdurno, with common pasture in the same forest, all united into the barony of Balquhain, 5th July 1661.** A precept of Chancery

1652. 1655. 1655-58. 1659. 1661.

* Balquhain Charters, No. 808.

† *Ibid.* No. 811. ‡ *Ibid.* No. 814. § *Ibid.* No. 821.

|| *Ibid.* No. 825. ¶ *Ibid.* No. 56.

** *Inquisitiones Speciales Vicecomitatus Aberdonensis*, No. 352; and General Service, Edinburgh, No. 4462.

CHAP. I. — *William, Thirteenth Baron of Balquhain.*

for infefting him in the said lands was issued 12th August 1661; sasine followed thereon 27th August, and was registered at Aberdeen 28th August 1661.*

William Leslie resigned the lands and barony of Balquhain in favour of his brother, Alexander Leslie of Tullos, proceeding upon the disposition of the said lands and barony made by him in favour of Dr. James Leslie in Aberdeen, 31st
1659. March 1659; which disposition Dr. James Leslie had assigned to Alexander Leslie of Tullos 6th
1661. December 1661.†

William Leslie resigned the lands of Auldtown and Nethertown of Knockenlewes, Whitecorse, and Tullos, in favour of Alexander Leslie of
1662. Tullos, 21st February 1662.‡

Thomas Forbes, wadsetter of Aquhorties, obtained a summons of warrandice against William Leslie of Balquhain, for warranting the lands of Aquhorties from a process of reduction at the instance of Alexander Gordon of Kincraigie, 11th
1663. August 1663.§

Alexander Gordon of Kincraigie obtained letters of general charge against William Leslie of Balquhain to enter heir as brother and apparent heir-male of the deceased John Leslie, fiar of Balquhain (eleventh baron), son and apparent heir of the deceased John Leslie elder, tenth

* Balquhain Charters, Nos. 59, 60.

† *Ibid.* No. 61. ‡ *Ibid.* No. 62. § *Ibid.* No. 357.

CHAP. I.

William, Thirteenth Baron of Balquhain.

Baron of Balquhain; and against Janet Leslie, daughter and apparent heir of line of the said deceased John Leslie, fiar of Balquhain, and James Elphinstone, younger of Glack, her husband, 1st August 1665.* 1665.

Alexander Gordon of Kincraigie, and Patrick Gordon, his eldest son, transferred the warrandice of the lands of Syde and others to Alexander Leslie of Tullos, 18th August 1665.† 1665.

The Lords of Session pronounced a decreet *cognitionis causa*, at the instance of Alexander Gordon of Kincraigie, against William Leslie of Balquhain, Janet Leslie, and James Elphinstone her spouse, finding the rents of the lands of Syde and others, which had been evicted by the Earl of Mar, by a decreet dated 26th March 1635, 1635. and the price of the said lands to extend to £46,445 : 12 : 2 Scots,—31st July 1667.‡ And 1667. Alexander Gordon of Kincraigie obtained a decreet, 30th June 1668, against William Leslie 1668. of Balquhain, Janet Leslie, and James Elphinstone her spouse, adjudging all and haill the lands of Aquhorties, with the mill and multures thereof, and the lands of Bograxie, to the said Alexander Gordon, in payment of the foresaid £46,445 : 12 : 2.§ Alexander Gordon obtained letters of horning on the above decreet, 20th August 1668.‖

Janet Leslie, daughter of John Leslie, eleventh

* Balquhain Charters, No. 365. † *Ibid.* No. 366.
‡ *Ibid.* No. 368. § *Ibid.* No. 369. ‖ *Ibid.* No. 370.

CHAP. I.

William, Thirteenth Baron of Balquhain.

Baron of Balquhain, and James Elphinstone of Glack, her husband, granted a discharge to William Leslie of Balquhain of the provision contained in their contract of marriage, 20th July
1670. 1670; registered in Sheriff-Court books, Aberdeen, 1st August 1670.*

William Leslie of Balquhain married Marjory Bernard, an English lady, by whom he had five sons and five daughters, who all died in their minority, except one daughter, Mary, who married Sir Elias Lechton, knight, who was colonel of a regiment.

The *Laurus Leslæana* observes that it is remarkable that of all the Barons of Balquhain none of them hitherto had failed to have a male heir of their own bodies to succeed them, except this William, the thirteenth baron, and his predecessor, John, the twelfth baron, who were the only two of the family who had become Protestants, and the *Laurus* says the same has happened in other Scotch families. It may also be remarked that James, Count Leslie, the seventeenth baron, Ernest, Count Leslie, the eighteenth baron, and Peter Leslie Grant, the nineteenth baron, who were Protestants, also died childless.

William Leslie, thirteenth Baron of Balquhain,
1671. died in Holland at an advanced age in 1671, and was succeeded by his half-brother, Alexander Leslie of Tullos.

* Balquhain Charters, No. 862.

Alexander, Count Leslie, Fourteenth Baron of Balquhain.

COUNT ALEXANDER LESLIE,

FOURTEENTH BARON OF BALQUHAIN.

ALEXANDER LESLIE of Tullos, third son of John Leslie, tenth Baron of Balquhain, by his third wife, Jean Erskine, sister of Thomas, first Earl of Kellie, succeeded as fourteenth Baron of Balquhain on the death of his brother, William Leslie, thirteenth baron, in 1671. He had held the estates of Balquhain since 1659, when William Leslie resigned them in his favour, but he did not assume the title of Baron of Balquhain during his brother's lifetime, but was styled Alexander Leslie of Tullos. 1671. 1659.

Alexander Leslie lived long very frugally upon the small property of Tullos, and his brother Walter, Count Leslie, frequently remitted to him considerable sums of money from Germany, which, with his own prudence, enabled him wonderfully to retrieve the family fortune, and, in some measure, to restore it to its ancient splendour. He was created a count of the Holy Roman Empire by the Emperor Leopold I., by patent dated at Vienna, 31st May 1662; the Emperor bestowing this honour on him to show his appreciation of the services rendered to the empire by his brother Count Walter Leslie. The *Laurus Leslæana* states that "in gratiam comitis Walteri fratris sui ab augustissimo Romanorum Imperatore S. R. I. Comes de Leslie cum tota sua posteritate creatus." 1662.

CHAP. I.

Alexander, Count Leslie, Fourteenth Baron of Balquhain.

Gilbert Farquhar, having acquired the lands of Tullos, with the teind-sheaves of the same, from Gordon of Braco, who held them by wadsett from John Leslie, eleventh Baron of Balquhain, alienated the said lands and teind-sheaves in favour of Alexander Leslie, and Jean Elphinstone his spouse, 20th May 1630, and granted a charter of the same on the same day; sasine followed thereon 31st July 1630, and was registered at Aberdeen 6th August 1630.*

1630.

An inventory of the houses of Tullos was made at the entry of Alexander Leslie, and was signed by him, and by John Leslie, eleventh Baron of Balquhain, 10th June 1630.†

John, Earl of Mar, and John Leslie, eleventh Baron of Balquhain, renounced the lands of Tullos in favour of Alexander Leslie, 25th July 1630.‡

John Leslie, eleventh Baron of Balquhain, confirmed the former securities of the lands of Tullos in the person of his brother, the said Alexander Leslie, with a warrandice, containing a new reversion of 1300 merks, 27th October 1630.§

1630.

Alexander Leslie of Tullos wrote a letter to Patrick Leslie of Whitehall, burgess of Aberdeen, and wadsetter of the lands of Whitecorse, requesting him to allow Alexander Robertson, minister of Chapel of Garioch, some feal which he had cast by mistake, on the lands of Whitecorse, 26th

* Balquhain Charters, Nos. 193-195.

† *Ibid.* No. 197. ‡ *Ibid.* 198. § *Ibid.* No. 196.

August 1630 and the day following; Alexander Robertson also wrote to the said Patrick Leslie, offering to pay for the feal, and declaring that he cast it thinking that the bounds on the west side of the burn had been commonty to Balquhain, as he had been informed—27th August 1630.* 1630.

John Leslie, eleventh Baron of Balquhain, disponed to his brother, Alexander Leslie of Tullos, the right of reversion of the lands of Whitecorse, wadsett to Patrick Leslie of Whitehall, burgess in Aberdeen, 10th October 1636.† 1636.

Patrick Leslie, younger of Whitehall, burgess, late Provost of Aberdeen, disponed the lands of Whitecorse in favour of Alexander Leslie of Tullos, 19th June 1637; and granted a charter to him of the said lands, to be holden of John Leslie, eleventh Baron of Balquhain, as superior of the same, 19th June 1637:‡ sasine followed thereon 31st July 1637.§ John Leslie of Balquhain granted a discharge of the feu-duty of the lands of Whitecorse, bygone and in time coming, to Alexander Leslie of Tullos. 1637.

Alexander Leslie of Tullos, and John Leslie, eleventh Baron of Balquhain, got a charter under the Great Seal of the lands of Balquhain united in one barony, 13th February 1637.‖

Alexander Watt, wadsetter of Merstown's croft

* Balquhain Charters, Nos. 170, 171.

† *Ibid.* No. 172. ‡ *Ibid.* Nos. 175, 177. § *Ibid.* No. 178.

‖ *Registrum Magni Sigilli*, lib. lv. No. 306.

CHAP. I.

Alexander, Count Leslie, Fourteenth Baron of Balquhain.

in the lands of Whitecorse, disponed his right and title to the said croft in favour of Alexander Leslie of Tullos, and Jean Elphinstone his spouse, 16th August 1638.*

John Leslie, twelfth Baron of Balquhain, renounced and discharged all former reversions granted to him by Patrick Leslie of Whitehall, for the redemption of the lands of Whitecorse, and all reversions granted to him or his father by Alexander Leslie of Tullos, or by Gilbert Farquhar, or any of their predecessors, in favour of Alexander Leslie of Tullos, and Jean Elphin-
1640. stone his spouse, 13th May 1640.†

Robert Farquhar, bailie of Aberdeen, with the consent of John Blackhall of that Ilk, and of his mother and three sisters, alienated all right which he had to the two ploughs of the lands of Auldtown of Knockenlewes in favour of Alexander
1649. Leslie of Tullos, 30th November 1649.‡

John Blackhall of that Ilk, with the consent of his mother, alienated the haill lands of Auldtown of Knockenlewes in favour of Alexander Leslie of Tullos, and granted the lands of Blackhall as
1649. warrandice, 3d December 1649.§

John, Lord Erskine, as taking burden on himself for John, Earl of Mar, his father, and Sir Francis Erskine, his brother, made a minute of sale, whereby he agreed to dispone the lands of

* Balquhain Charters, No. 203.

† *Ibid.* No. 204. ‡ *Ibid.* No. 118. § *Ibid.* No. 122.

Alexander, Count Leslie, Fourteenth Baron of Balquhain.

Auldtown and Nethertown of Knockenlewes in favour of Alexander Leslie of Tullos, 11th April 1650.* The disposition was effected 27th June 1650, and John, Earl of Mar, and his sons, granted a charter of the said lands to Alexander Leslie of Tullos, to be holden "*de me*," 27th June; sasine followed thereon 10th July, and was registered at Aberdeen 26th July 1650.† 1650.

John Leslie of Badifora and Artannis, designed also of Nethertown of Knockenlewes, disponed in favour of Alexander Leslie of Tullos all right which he had to the lands of Nethertown of Knockenlewes, 6th May 1650; and granted a charter of the said lands in his favour on the same day; sasine followed thereupon 9th May 1650, and was registered at Edinburgh 24th June 1650.‡ 1650.

Sir Patrick Leslie of Whitehall and Thomas Ronald, on behalf of John Galloway junior, burgess of Aberdeen, sold to Alexander Leslie of Tullos the rood and other lands disponed by George Leslie, bailie of Inverurie, to Sir Patrick Leslie, 20th November 1652; and Sir Patrick Leslie granted a bond of warrandice to Alexander Leslie of Tullos for relieving him of the warrandice contained in the contract of sale, 27th May 1653.§ 1652.

Alexander Abercrombie of Fetternear granted a bond to Alexander Leslie of Tullos, obliging himself to discharge any right that he or his son

* Balquhain Charters, No. 206.
† *Ibid.* Nos. 207-211.
‡ *Ibid.* Nos. 148-150.
§ *Ibid.* No. 792.

CHAP. I.

Alexander, Count Leslie, Fourteenth Baron of Balquhain.

Francis should acquire in the lands of Auldtown of Knockenlewes flowing from John or William Blackhall, and that in respect that the said Alexander Leslie had renounced in favour of Francis Abercrombie his right of warrandice of the lands of Blackhall, granted to him by John Blackhall,
1657. 24th January 1657.*

Gilbert, Earl of Erroll, set and disponed to Alexander Leslie of Tullos the teind-sheaves of half of the
1657. town and lands of Whiterashes, 17th April 1657.†

John, Earl of Loudon, as having right, disponed in favour of Alexander Leslie of Tullos all the annuities of teinds which were due to the king,
1633. Charles I., by the Act of Parliament of June 1633, furth of the teinds of the lands of Auldtown and Nethertown of Knockenlewes, and also of the lands of Balquhain, for all the years bygone and
1659. in time coming, 4th February 1659.‡

Mr. Alexander Strachan, minister of Chapel of Garioch, made a declaration to Alexander Leslie of Tullos concerning the lands of Whitecorse,
1661. 25th July 1661.§

Alexander Leslie of Tullos got a charter under the Great Seal of the lands of Balquhain united into one barony, proceeding on the resignation of William Leslie, thirteenth Baron of Balquhain, 21st February 1662.|| A precept for infefting

* Balquhain Charters, No. 125.

† *Ibid.* No. 95. ‡ *Ibid.* No. 96. § *Ibid.* No. 919.

|| *Registrum Magni Sigilli*, lib. lviii. No. 81.

him in the said barony was issued on the same day; sasine followed thereon 21st April 1662, and was registered at Aberdeen 31st May 1662.*

Alexander Leslie of Tullos got a charter under the Great Seal of the lands of Whitecorse, 29th July 1664;† and of the lands of Scotstown Hill, 19th August 1664.‡ 1664.

Alexander Leslie of Tullos resigned the lands of Auldtown and Nethertown of Knockenlewes in favour of Patrick Leslie, his second surviving son, and Elizabeth Douglas his spouse, and the heirs-male to be procreated of their bodies, and the other heirs of tailzie; and also the lands and barony of Balquhain, in favour of the said Patrick, and his heirs-male and of tailzie, proceeding on the procuratory of resignation contained in the contract of marriage between the said Patrick Leslie and Elizabeth Douglas, 29th July 1664. 1664.

Alexander Leslie of Tullos got a charter of the plough-lands of Listhoghill, 23d November 1666.§ 1666.

A precept was issued furth of the Chancery for infefting Alexander Leslie of Tullos in the lands of Pitbee, as assignee of Alexander Gordon of Kincraigie, 10th November 1668; sasine followed thereon 5th April 1669, and was registered at Aberdeen 15th May 1669.‖ 1669.

---

* Balquhain Charters, Nos. 63-65.

† *Registrum Magni Sigilli*, lib. lviii. No. 207.

‡ *Ibid.* No. 362.

§ *Ibid.* lib. lxi. No. 189.

‖ Balquhain Charters, Nos. 632, 633.

CHAP. I.

Alexander, Count Leslie, Fourteenth Baron of Balquhain.

1671. Alexander Leslie of Tullos assigned to Alexander Strachan of Kinaldie a bond for 2000 merks of principal and annual rent, contained in a bond granted to him by Thomas Forbes of Aquhorties, 4th January 1671.*

1673. Alexander Forbes of Ardo disponed the lands of Largie, Meikle Wardis, and the teinds of the same, in favour of Alexander Leslie of Balquhain, and Patrick Leslie, his son, and the other heirs of tailzie, 10th September 1673.†

1673. Alexander, Lord Pitsligo, with the consent of Alexander Forbes of Ardo, resigned the lands of Largie and Meikle Wardis into the hands of the king for new infeftment to be given to Alexander Leslie of Balquhain, 19th December 1673.‡

1674. Alexander Farquharson of Wardis renounced all right which he had in the lands of Brankstone in favour of Alexander Leslie of Balquhain, 16th January 1674.§

1674. Alexander Leslie of Balquhain got a charter of the lands of Largie, Meikle Wardis, and the teind-sheaves of the same, under the Great Seal, 20th January 1674;‖ sasine followed thereon 23d January 1674, registered at Aberdeen 3d April 1674.¶

Alexander and Thomas Smith, sons of the

---

* Balquhain Charters, No. 993. † *Ibid.* No. 544.
‡ *Ibid.* No. 547. § *Ibid.* No. 548.
‖ *Registrum Magni Sigilli,* lib. lxiv. No. 60.
¶ Balquhain Charters, No. 550.

CHAP. I. — *Alexander, Count Leslie, Fourteenth Baron of Balquhain.*

deceased William Smith in Blairdaff, disponed the lands of Middleton, which had been wadsett to them in 1638, in favour of Alexander Leslie of Balquhain in liferent, and Patrick Leslie, his son, in fee, 9th December 1673;* which disposition was ratified by John Gordon of Braco, 28th January 1674.† 1674.

Alexander, Count Leslie, fourteenth Baron of Balquhain, married, about 1634, Jean Elphinstone, 1634.
daughter of James Elphinstone of Glack, descended from a brother of the celebrated Bishop Elphinstone of Aberdeen, who was of Lord Elphinstone's family. By her he had—

I. JOHN, who died young at Dundee in returning from France, 1659. 1659.

II. JAMES, who went to Germany, and succeeded his uncle Walter, Count Leslie, as second Count Leslie, of whom hereafter.

III. PATRICK, who succeeded his father as fifteenth Baron of Balquhain, of whom hereafter.

IV. WILLIAM ALOYSIUS, who went abroad, and having studied for the church, received holy orders, and was made a canon of the cathedral church of Wratislaw. He afterwards resigned his benefice and entered the society of Jesus, and was successively Professor of Philosophy at Perugia, Rector of the Scotch College at Douai, Superior of the Missions in Scotland, and Rector of the Scotch College at Rome. He was the author of the *Laurus Leslœana*, published at Gratz in 1692, and entitled "Laurus Leslæana explicata, sive clarior enumeratio personarum utriusque sexus cognominis Leslie, unacum affinibus, titulis, officiis, dominiis, gestisque celebrioribus breviter indicatis, quibus a sex-

* Balquhain Charters, Nos. 233 and 243. † *Ibid.* No. 244.

CHAP. I.

Alexander, Count Leslie, Fourteenth Baron of Balquhain.

centis et amplius annis prosapia illa floret, ex variis authoribus, manuscriptis et testimoniis fide dignis in unum collecta. Graecii, Apud Heredes Widmanstadij, Anno 1692. The Honourable John Gordon, aged 80, second son of John, third Earl of Aboyne, stated in his evidence, given in 1760, in the law-process between Anthony, Count Leslie, and Peter Leslie Grant, that he had been educated at the Scotch college at Douai, where he became acquainted with the Rev. William Leslie, who was residing in the Scotch college there, and was remarkable for having a hare-lip ; and he afterwards saw the Rev. William Leslie in Scotland, where he was superior of the Catholic missions ; and that he knew that some time afterwards he went to be rector of the Scotch college at Rome. During the
1693. time that he was at Douai, in 1693, the Rev. William Leslie informed him that he was the chief compiler of the *Laurus Leslæana*—a work containing the genealogy and the history of the family of Leslie, published
1692. in 1692, and also presented him with a copy of the work. He recollected seeing in the college at Douai a picture in oil, said to be the portrait of one of the German branch of the family of Balquhain—a copper-plate copy of which picture is at the beginning of the *Laurus Leslæana*, which is dedicated to James, second Count Leslie. There is a great eulogium of the Rev. William Leslie in Sir Andrew Balfour's "Advice for Travelling." Besides the *Laurus Leslæana*, the Rev. William Leslie also wrote in Italian *La Vita di Santa Margarita, Regina di Scozia*, published at Rome in
1691. 1691. In the *Laurus Leslæana*, under Alexander, fourteenth Baron of Balquhain, he makes the following mention of himself :—"Tertiogenitus Guilielmus Aloysius relicto canonicatu Wratislaviensi Romae Societatem Jesu ingressus, ibidem postea fuit Colegii Scotorum Rector." In his enumeration he calls himself the third son of Alexander, fourteenth baron, not counting the first-born son John, who died young.

V. ALEXANDER, a Count of the Holy Roman Empire, who went over to Germany to his brother James, second

Alexander, Count Leslie, Fourteenth Baron of Balquhain.

Count Leslie, by whom he was educated. Being a man of genius, he first applied himself to letters, and made great progress in learning. But on receiving the rank of lieutenant-colonel in Mansfeld's regiment from the Emperor, he quitted the closet and signalised himself as much in the field of Mars as he had done in the school of Minerva. He was also appointed chamberlain to the Emperor. During the famous siege of Vienna by the Turks in 1683, Alexander, 1683. Count Leslie, commanded his regiment with great gallantry. Being ordered by Count Staremberg, the governor, to make a sortie on the besiegers, while commanding and leading on his men, he was mortally wounded, and died with pious resignation 8th August 1683, and was buried in the Leslie Chapel at the Scotch Benedictine Abbey in Vienna. He married Cressentia Christina, Countess Heberstein, only daughter and heiress of George Guntherens, Count Heberstein, and by her had a son, Francis James, Count Leslie, who died without issue in 1700. 1700.

Besides these five sons, Alexander, Count Leslie, fourteenth Baron of Balquhain, had three daughters, who all died young.

Alexander, Count Leslie, fourteenth Baron of Balquhain, died 3d March 1677, in the eightieth 1677. year of his age, and was succeeded by his second surviving son, Patrick, Count Leslie, fifteenth Baron of Balquhain.

PATRICK, COUNT LESLIE,

FIFTEENTH BARON OF BALQUHAIN.

Patrick, Count Leslie, Fifteenth Baron of Balquhain.

Patrick, Count Leslie, second surviving son of Alexander, Count Leslie, fourteenth Baron of Balquhain, by his wife Jean Elphinstone of Glack,

CHAP. I.

Patrick, Count Leslie, Fifteenth Baron of Balquhain.

1667. succeeded as fifteenth Baron of Balquhain, on the death of his father, 3d March 1677, in consequence of his elder brother, James, having succeeded his uncle, Walter, Count Leslie, in Germany, in 1667.

1640. Patrick, Count Leslie, was born in 1640. He was made a Privy Councillor by King James VII. in 1686. The *Laurus Leslæana* says of him "Est hic Patritius a serenissimo nostro rege et clementissimo Domino Jacobo VII., in intimum Scotiæ consilium adlectus, vir prudens justus et fidei avitæ tenax." Patrick, Count Leslie of Balquhain, is on the roll of freeholders, 8th October 1690, who were obliged to give suit, service, and presence, at the three head-courts held yearly by the Sheriff of Aberdeen.

1686.

1690.

Patrick, Count Leslie, was a frugal and virtuous gentleman. With the aid of money which he received from his brother, James, Count Leslie, in Germany, he redeemed much of the property which had formerly belonged to the family, but which had been alienated or mortgaged by his predecessors, particularly the barony of Fetternear, which, as has been related, was alienated by John Leslie, eleventh Baron of Balquhain, in 1625, to his brother-in-law Sir Alexander Hay of Dalgety, who transferred his wadsett rights to Hector Abercromby of Westhall, second son of Alexander Abercromby of Birkenbog, in 1627. By documents in the charter-room at Fetternear, and by

1625.

1627.

Patrick, Count Leslie, Fifteenth Baron of Balquhain.

others in the possession of the Birkenbog family, it appears that Count Patrick Leslie purchased or redeemed the barony of Fetternear, 20th August 1690, from Francis Abercromby, Lord Glassford, who married Lady Sempill. Alexander Abercromby of Aquhorsk, a member of the Birkenbog family, who rented the mansion-house of Fetternear, renounced his possession in favour of Patrick, Count Leslie, 23d August 1690. Patrick, 1690.
Count Leslie, after his succession to the Leslie estates in Germany, on the death of his brother Count James in 1694, also made additions to the 1694.
Balquhain property, purchasing the lands of the barony of Insch, Boddam, Greenhall, Muiryheadless, Knockenbaird, Scotstown, and Aquhorties.

We gather much information regarding Patrick, Count Leslie, from the evidence given by witnesses in the law proceedings which took place during the disputed succession after the death of his grandson, Ernest, Count Leslie, eighteenth Baron of Balquhain, who died without issue in 1739. William Watt in Nethertown of Fetter- 1739.
near stated in his evidence that he was upwards of 75 years of age; that he knew Count Patrick Leslie, and was aware that he received remittances of money from his brother, Count James Leslie in Germany, with which he redeemed the lands of Fetternear, which had been alienated to the Abercrombys.

After recovering possession of Fetternear, Count

CHAP I.

Patrick, Count Leslie, Fifteenth Baron of Balquhain.

Patrick Leslie occasionally resided there. In the law proceedings above alluded to, Jean Erskine, widow of James Moir of Stoneywood, deponed that she often visited Count Patrick Leslie both at Balquhain Castle and at Fetternear. John Steel, Mill of Fintray, aged 85, deponed that his father was gardener at Fetternear, and that when very young he used to go with his father and carry fruit from Fetternear over to Balquhain, and that he afterwards lived with Count Patrick Leslie both at Balquhain and at Fetternear.

Count Patrick Leslie afterwards abandoned Balquhain Castle as his principal residence, and took up his abode at Fetternear House per-
1692. manently about 1692. Fetternear House then possessed many advantages, being built on a fine site near the banks of the Don, commanding a splendid view of the surrounding country. The domain was richly wooded, having extensive avenues of magnificent trees. The pleasure-grounds were curiously laid out, and there were excellent gardens, which were renowned as being peculiarly productive. The mansion-house was extremely spacious and commodious, and formed three sides of a square. It was handsomely furnished, and was adorned with a fine collection of paintings, including many family portraits, amongst others those of James Ernest, Count Leslie in Germany, of his lady the Princess Berne de Lichtenstein, and of their son Count Joseph Patrick

Patrick, Count Leslie, Fifteenth Baron of Balquhain.

Sigismund Leslie, and of their daughter Maria Antonia Leslie.

Count Patrick Leslie had also a town-house in Aberdeen. It is recorded in the Journal of the Presbytery of Aberdeen that there were four priests residing in Aberdeen in 1698, and that 1698.
mass was publicly celebrated in the dwelling-house of Count Patrick Leslie of Balquhain in Aberdeen, by his brother the Rev. William Leslie. In the list of Catholics sent by the Presbytery of Aberdeen to the General Assembly in 1700, 1700.
eighty were named, and amongst them were Count Patrick Leslie, Lady Wartle, and the Laird of Hilton.

Count Patrick Leslie, seeing that his elder brother, Count James Leslie in Germany, had no children, and that he himself was the next heir to the family estates in Germany, thus having the prospect of uniting the Scotch and German estates in his own person, was desirous of establishing two families. Therefore, in 1692, he executed 1692.
a primary deed of entail, settling the estates of Balquhain on his second son, George Leslie, with clauses regulating the succession of heirs-male to the Scotch and German properties. On the death of his brother, James, second Count Leslie, in 1694, without issue, Count Patrick succeeded 1694.
as he expected to the German estates, and henceforth was known by the style and title of Count Patrick Leslie. John Lumsden, law-agent in

CHAP. I.

Patrick, Count Leslie, Fifteenth Baron of Balquhain.

Edinburgh, deponed, in the law-process already mentioned, that he knew Patrick Leslie of Balquhain, who was styled count after, but not before, the death of his brother, Count James Leslie in Germany in 1694, although he had a right to the title previously through his father, Count Alexander Leslie, fourteenth Baron of Balquhain.

Count Patrick Leslie now proposed to put his son, Count James Ernest, in immediate possession of the German estates, on condition that he should renounce all claim to the Scotch estates in favour of his younger brother, George Leslie, Count Patrick's son by his second marriage. To this proposition James Ernest acceded, as is testified by a letter written by him to his father, 9th
1695. December 1695, in which he says that if he were put in possession of the German estates he would have enough, and that it would be a prouder thing for the family to be represented by him in Germany, and by his half-brother George in Scotland, than if both fortunes were held by the same person. In this letter James Ernest refused to bear the title of count during his father's lifetime.

In consequence of this agreement, Count Patrick Leslie executed another deed of entail in
1700. 1700, in which he revoked some clauses of the
1692. former entail of 1692, and altered others, at the same time confirming the settlement of the

CHAP. I.

Patrick, Count Leslie, Fifteenth Baron of Balquhain.

Scotch estates on his second son, George Leslie; and he added new clauses in case of failure of direct heirs-male, regulating the succession of the male issue of his daughters, Ladies Marjory, Ann Francisca, Teresa, Mary, Margaret, and Jean, with regard both to the Scotch and German estates. These entails were written by William Grant of Crichie, from Count Patrick Leslie's directions.

Patrick Leslie, and Elizabeth Douglas his spouse, got a charter under the Great Seal of the lands of Auldtown and Nethertown of Knockenlewes, and also of the lands and barony of Balquhain, to them and the heirs-male of tailzie, proceeding on the resignation of Count Alexander Leslie, fourteenth Baron of Balquhain, 29th July 1664;* sasine following thereupon 2d December 1664, and was registered at Aberdeen 3d January 1665.† 1664. 1665.

Patrick Leslie executed a bond of tailzie of the lands and barony of Balquhain in favour of himself and the other heirs of tailzie therein mentioned, 22d November 1666.‡ 1666.

Patrick Leslie got a charter of the barony of Balquhain under the Great Seal from King Charles II., anno regni 18, 23d November 1666.§ 1666.

Patrick Leslie got a gift under the Privy Seal,

* Balquhain Charters, Nos. 66, 67.

† *Ibid.* No. 68. ‡ *Ibid.* No. 70.

§ *Registrum Magni Sigilli*, lib. lxi. No. 188; and lib. iii. folio 69.

CHAP. I.

Patrick, Count Leslie, Fifteenth Baron of Balquhain.

of the escheat of John Leslie, twelfth Baron of Balquhain, 22d July 1666.*

The Lords of Session pronounced a decreet of general declarator, at the instance of Patrick Leslie, against Count Walter Leslie in Germany, and William Leslie, thirteenth Baron of Balquhain, then residing in Holland, upon the above gift of
1666. escheat, 8th December 1666.†

Patrick Leslie got a gift under the Privy Seal of the escheat of William Leslie, thirteenth Baron
1667. of Balquhain, 8th February 1667.‡

Patrick Leslie of Balquhain got a charter under the Great Seal of the lands of Over and Nether Boddam, from King Charles II., 7th
1667. May, anno regni 19, A.D. 1667.§

Patrick Leslie of Balquhain got a charter under the Great Seal of the barony of Balquhain, in favour of himself and the heirs of tailzie therein mentioned, proceeding on his own resignation,
1670. 4th February 1670;|| sasine following thereon 31st March 1670, registered at Aberdeen 2d May 1670.¶ This charter was ratified by act of parliament 22d August 1670.**

William Forbes, minister of Inverurie, obliged

* Balquhain Charters, No. 882.

† *Ibid.* No. 883. ‡ *Ibid.* No. 886.

§ *Registrum Magni Sigilli*, lib. lxi. No. 256; and lib. iii. folio 94.

|| Balquhain Charters, No. 76.

¶ *Registrum Magni Sigilli*, lib. lxii. No. 185; and Balquhain Charters, No. 79.

** Balquhain Charters, No. 80.

himself to Patrick Leslie of Balquhain to accept a certain sum of money and a quota of victual, as stipend, out of the lands of Knockenlewes, 11th May 1677.* He also made a disposition of the haill houses upon the manse-lands in favour of the heritors, 8th March 1678.† 1678.

CHAP. I.

Patrick, Count Leslie, Fifteenth Baron of Balquhain.

Mary Irvine, spouse of Patrick Leslie of Balquhain, renounced in favour of the said Patrick Leslie 12 chalders of victual, part of the 30 chalders provided for her by her contract of marriage, 17th November 1680; registered in General Register, Edinburgh, 2d December 1680. 1680. She made another renunciation to the same effect before one of the bailies of Inverurie.‡

Patrick Leith, second son of George Leith of Freefield, disponed his wadsett rights in the town and lands of Greenhall in favour of Patrick Leslie of Balquhain, 18th June 1683.§ And 1683. Charles, Earl of Mar, and John Keirie of Gogar, disponed the said town and lands, and the lands of Muiryheadless, in favour of Patrick Leslie of Balquhain, and the heirs-male of his body, to be holden in feu of the said earl, for the yearly payment of £3 Scots, 24th March 1683, and granted a charter to this effect on the same day; sasine followed thereon 4th July, and 1683. was registered at Aberdeen 12th July 1683.||

Patrick Anderson, wadsetter of the lands of

---

* Balquhain Charters, No. 983. † *Ibid.* No. 895.
‡ *Ibid.* No. 864. § *Ibid.* No. 568. || *Ibid.* Nos. 570-572.

CHAP. I.

Patrick, Count Leslie, Fifteenth Baron of Balquhain.

1680. Knockenbaird, with the mill and mill-lands thereof, renounced the said lands in favour of Charles, Earl of Mar, the superior thereof, and John Keirie of Gogar, of whom he held the same in wadsett, 30th November 1680; and the said earl, with the consent of John Keirie and Dame Jane Mackenzie, Countess Dowager of Mar, granted a charter of the said lands and mill to Patrick Leslie of Balquhain, and his heirs therein mentioned, to be held of the said earl in feu for 16 merks yearly, 23d December 1680; sasine followed 21st May 1681, and was registered at Aberdeen 8th June 1681.*

1680.

1681.

Patrick Leslie of Balquhain got a charter under the Great Seal, confirming the charters granted to him by Charles, Earl of Mar, and John Keirie of Gogar, of the lands of Knockenbaird, Scotstown, Greenhall, and Muiryheadless, 4th April 1683.†

1683.

Alexander Johnston, burgess of Inverurie, made a disposition of a desk in the parish church of Inverurie in favour of Patrick Leslie of Balquhain, 30th June 1683.‡

1683.

Patrick Leslie of Balquhain made a contract of marches with James Gordon, younger of Lesmore, with the consent of Sir William Gordon of Lesmore, settling the marches of the hill of Foundland between the lands of Meikle Wardis

* Balquhain Charters, Nos. 577-579.

† *Ibid.* No. 584. ‡ *Ibid.* No. 898.

Patrick, Count Leslie, Fifteenth Baron of Balquhain.

and Largie, and the lands of Johnsleys, 2d August 1683.*

Adam Urquhart of Meldrum assigned to Francis Abercromby of Fetternear an obligement granted by Arthur Forbes of Brux, concerning a decreet of adjudication of the lands of Aquhorties, and a charter of the same, 5th December 1683; 1683.
and Francis Abercromby translated the said assignation to Patrick Leslie of Balquhain, 22d June 1685; and on the same day, Francis Aber- 1685.
cromby, and Dame Anne Sempill his spouse, executed a disposition in favour of Patrick Leslie of Balquhain, and the heirs-male of his body, whereby, for the sum of 16,000 merks paid by the said Patrick Leslie to Dame Anne Sempill in payment *pro tanto* of her liferent right over the lands of Sempill, the said Francis Abercromby, and Dame Anne Sempill his spouse, dispone to the said Patrick Leslie all and haill the lands and manor-place of Aquhorties as therein contained.†

Francis Abercromby resigned the lands of Aquhorties into the hands of the king, for new infeftment to be given to Patrick Leslie of Balquhain, 3d August 1688.‡ 1688.

The Commission for repairing Highways and Bridges granted a warrant in favour of the Laird of Balquhain, 22d May 1688.§ 1688.

* Balquhain Charters, No. 553.

† *Ibid.* Nos. 441-443. ‡ *Ibid.* No. 446. § *Ibid.* No. 899.

CHAP. I.

Patrick, Count Leslie, Fifteenth Baron of Balquhain.

Mr. George Clerk, minister of Chapel of Garioch, granted a discharge to Patrick Leslie of Balquhain for crop 1690, dated 31st August 1690; also one for crop 1693, dated 22d February 1695; and another for teind-money 2d September 1698.*

1698.

Francis, Lord Glassford, and Anne, Lady Sempill, his spouse, disponed the barony of Fetternear in favour of Patrick Leslie of Balquhain, and Mary Irvine his spouse, and granted a charter of the same to them in liferent, and to their son, George Leslie, and the other heirs of tailzie therein mentioned, in fee, 20th August 1690; sasine followed thereon 30th December 1690, registered at Aberdeen 16th January 1691.† Alexander Abercromby of Aquhorsk renounced his possession of the fortalice and manor-place of Fetternear, in favour of Patrick Leslie of Balquhain, 23d August 1690.‡ Anne, Lady Sempill, ratified the disposition of the barony of Fetternear in favour of Patrick Leslie, before one of the bailies of the burgh of Inverurie, 29th August 1690.§

1690. 1691. 1690. 1690.

Patrick Leslie of New Rayne granted a bond for 27,000 merks of principal, and 9000 merks of penalty, in favour of Patrick Leslie of Balquhain, bearing annual rent from the date thereof, and payable at Martinmas then next, dated 27th

* Balquhain Charters, No. 928.

† *Ibid.* Nos. 498, 499. ‡ *Ibid.* No. 503. § *Ibid.* No. 504.

CHAP. I.

Patrick, Count Leslie, Fifteenth Baron of Balquhain.

October 1691, registered in books of Session 16th December 1691.* Count Patrick Leslie of Balquhain obtained letters of charge against Patrick Leslie of New Rayne to enter as heir to his great-grandfather, John Leslie of Wardis, 19th December 1695.† The Lords of Session pronounced a decreet, at the instance of Count Patrick Leslie of Balquhain, against Patrick Leslie of New Rayne, for himself and as lawfully charged to enter heir in special, as said is, adjudging all and haill the lands of Scotstown, Knockenbaird, Greenhall, and Muiryheadless, to Count Patrick Leslie, in payment and satisfaction to him of £29,220 Scots, 11th November 1696.‡ 1695. 1696.

Count Patrick Leslie assigned the foresaid decreet in so far as relates to the lands of Meikle Durno, to Mr. James Elphinstone of Logie, 28th May 1697.§ 1697.

James Elphinstone, writer to the signet, transferred all right which he had to the lands of Middletown of Knockenlewes, by virtue of the gift of ward, nonentry, and marriage, in favour of Count Patrick Leslie of Balquhain, 24th December 1691.‖ 1691.

Count Patrick Leslie disponed the haill lands and barony of Balquhain in favour of George Leslie, his eldest son by Mary Irvine, his second

* Balquhain Charters, No. 587.
† *Ibid.* No. 589. ‡ *Ibid.* No. 590. § *Ibid.* No. 592.
‖ *Ibid.* No. 253.

CHAP. I.

Patrick, Count Leslie, Fifteenth Baron of Balquhain.

wife, and the other heirs of tailzie, reserving his own liferent, 15th June 1694.*

Count Patrick Leslie of Balquhain, and George Leslie his son, got a charter under the Great Seal of the lands and barony of Insch, and also of the
1699. lands of Boddam, 21st July 1699, William and Mary, anno regni 11.†

Robert Forbes of Learney granted a tack of the teind-sheaves of the lands of Balquhain, as advocate titular and hereditary proprietor of the same, to Count Patrick Leslie, for nineteen years from and after the expiry of any other rights the
1701. said Count Patrick had thereto, 10th May 1701.‡ He also granted a discharge to the said Count Patrick of all the annual teind tack-duty stipulated by the said tack for all the years of the tack, 10th
1701. May 1701.§

William Leslie, minister of Chapel of Garioch, gave a receipt to the Laird of Balquhain for part
1707. payment of the vicarage dues for the years 1707 and 1708, dated 15th January 1709.‖

John Pirie, collector of money for repairing the manse of Chapel of Garioch, gave a receipt to Count Patrick Leslie of Balquhain for £6 Scots, as his proportion for the said repairs, 1st July
1709. 1709.¶

* Balquhain Charters, No. 585.

† *Registrum Magni Sigilli*, lib. lxxv. Nos. 123, 124.

‡ Balquhain Charters, No. 99.

§ *Ibid.* No. 100. ‖ *Ibid.* No. 932. ¶ *Ibid.* No. 934.

CHAP. I.

Patrick, Count Leslie, Fifteenth Baron of Balquhain.

Patrick, Count Leslie, married first, 24th November 1661, Elizabeth Douglas, daughter of Gavin Douglas of Bridgford, son of William, Earl of Angus. In the legal proceedings already alluded to we find that Walter Leith, merchant in Aberdeen, aged 30 years, produced a Latin copy of the Bible in folio, printed at Paris in 1537, which he had bought from David Angus, 1537. bookseller in Aberdeen, in 1744, and on which 1744. there were written on two leaves, then produced, the following entries:—

"Anno Domini 1661, die 24 Novembris, nempe Dominica 1661. P. G. L. Conjunxit in Matrimonium Patritium Leslie et Elizabetham Douglas—quo die praedictae dominae Pater Robertus Douglas a Pseudoministris excommunicatus fuit."

"1669. 20 June, Sunday, was born James Leslie, Baptized 1669. the same day."

"1678. 21 November, died Elizabeth Douglas, mother of 1678. the above, in childbed of a daughter Elizabeth."

"The 3rd August 1679, was married Patrick Leslie of Bal- 1679. quhain, and Mary Irvine, daughter of the Laird of Drum."

"1682. August 26th, Saturday, George Leslie was born and 1682. baptized this day."

By Elizabeth Douglas Count Patrick Leslie had issue—

I. James Ernest, born 20th June 1669. He succeeded 1669. his uncle James, second Count Leslie in Germany. See hereafter.

II. Alexander, born 1670. He died young in Germany. 1670.

III. Marjory, born 1663; married, about 1693, Alexander 1663. Leslie of Pitcaple. Their son, Sir James Leslie, claimed the Balquhain estates in 1740, against Charles Cajetan, 1740. Count Leslie. See hereafter.

CHAP. I.

Patrick, Count Leslie, Fifteenth Baron of Balquhain.

IV. ANNE FRANCISCA, born about 1664. She was a pensioner for six years in a convent at Mons, under Madam Leslie, the lady abbess. She returned to Scotland in 1680, and was married in November 1689 to John Grant of Ballindalloch. John Watson, aged 85, deponed that he got money from George Leslie of Balquhain when he was playing as a piper on the occasion of the marriage of Anne Francisca Leslie, Count Patrick's daughter, with John Grant of Ballindalloch. Their grandson, Peter Leslie Grant, claimed and recovered the estate of Balquhain from Anthony,
1762. Count Leslie, in 1762, and became twentieth Baron of Balquhain. See hereafter.

1672. V. TERESA LESLIE, born about 1672; married in 1699 to Robert Duguid of Auchinhove. Their son, Patrick Leslie Duguid, eventually succeeded to Peter Leslie Grant as next heir of entail, and became twenty-first Baron of Balquhain. See hereafter.

1678. VI. ELIZABETH LESLIE, born in November 1678. She became a nun, and was lady abbess of the Ursuline convent at Lisle. She was usually styled Lady Betty
1767. Leslie. She died in 1767, having lived to a great age, much esteemed by all who knew her. There is a painting of her in the dining-room at Fetternear House.

Elizabeth Douglas died in childbed of her
1678. daughter Elizabeth, 21st November 1678; and Count Patrick Leslie married, secondly, 3d
1679. August 1679, Mary Irvine, eldest daughter of Alexander Irvine of Drum by Lady Mary Gordon, daughter of John, Marquis of Huntly. By
1679. the marriage-contract, dated 23d July 1679,* Count Patrick Leslie bound himself to secure the estates of Balquhain to the eldest son of this

* Balquhain Charters, No. 863.

marriage, and to provide 30,000 merks for the younger children of the same. The issue by this marriage was— CHAP. I. *Patrick, Count Leslie, Fifteenth Baron of Balquhain.*

I. GEORGE, born 26th August 1682, and was baptized on the same day. He succeeded his father as sixteenth Baron of Balquhain.

II. MARGARET, born in 1683, married to George Leslie of Iden. Their marriage-contract is dated 8th January 1709.* Margaret Leslie is sometimes styled Lady Kinnaires. She died 17th June 1744. 1683. 1709. 1744.

III. JEAN, born 1685, married 3d November 1713 to Patrick Gordon of Aberlour, as appears from a deed in which George Leslie of Iden and Robert Duguid of Auchinhove are trustees for her portion. 1685-1713.

IV. HENRIETTA, who died young.

V. MARY, who also died young.

Patrick, Count Leslie, fifteenth Baron of Balquhain, died in 1710, and was succeeded by his eldest son of his second marriage with Mary Irvine of Drum, George, sixteenth Baron of Balquhain; James Ernest, Count Leslie, his eldest son of his first marriage with Elizabeth Douglas, having succeeded to the German estates in 1694. 1710. 1694.

GEORGE, COUNT LESLIE,

SIXTEENTH BARON OF BALQUHAIN.

George, Count Leslie, Sixteenth Baron of Balquhain.

COUNT GEORGE LESLIE, born 26th August 1682, eldest son of Patrick, Count Leslie, fifteenth Baron of Balquhain, by his second wife, Mary 1682.

* Balquhain Charters, No. 874.

CHAP. I.

George, Count Leslie, Sixteenth Baron of Balquhain.

Irvine of Drum, succeeded as sixteenth Baron of Balquhain, on the death of his father in 1710, in accordance with the agreement made with his elder brother, Count James Ernest Leslie, and in conformity with the deed of entail executed by

1700. Count Patrick Leslie in 1700.

From the evidence given in the law process regarding the succession to the Balquhain estates, we learn the following circumstances:—John Steel, Mill of Fintray, deponed that when he was a servant to Count Patrick Leslie at Fetternear, he heard the Count tell his company or visitors that George, his second son, had gone abroad to meet his elder brother, James Ernest, and to get from him a right to the Balquhain estates. William Watt in Nethertown of Fetternear, another witness, stated that George Leslie

1695. went abroad in 1695 to arrange with his brother the family affairs, on which occasion George Leslie had wished to go to his brother's place of residence, but James Ernest sent him word that if he could not appear with a retinue of horse and men amounting to the value of 30,000 merks, he behoved not to come to the place of his residence in Germany; but that he, James Ernest, would meet him at Cologne, where George Leslie accordingly went, and met his brother, James Ernest, who there, by an agreement, made over to him his right of succession to the Balquhain estates. Patrick Gordon of Aberlour, another

CHAP. I.

George, Count Leslie, Sixteenth Baron of Balquhain.

witness, who had married Count Patrick Leslie's youngest surviving daughter, Jean, stated that George Leslie went abroad to meet his elder brother, Count James Ernest, which he did at Cologne. They there arranged and made a final settlement with regard to the succession of the Balquhain estates, which Count James Ernest resigned in favour of his brother George, who, on his part, gave up all claim to the annual remittance which had been promised to him out of the German estates.

When Count Patrick Leslie went to reside at Fetternear, George Leslie continued to occupy the old castle of Balquhain. We find by the Poll-books of the Shire of Aberdeen for 1696, 1696.
vol. i. p. 292, that George, Count Leslie, son of Patrick, Count Leslie, was residing at Balquhain with his family and servants. After his father's death he removed to Fetternear.

George Leslie got a charter under the Great Seal of the lands and barony of Balquhain, proceeding on the resignation of his father, Count Patrick Leslie, fifteenth Baron of Balquhain, 9th March 1694.* 1694.

George Leslie got a charter of the lands of Largie, proceeding on the resignation of his father, Count Patrick Leslie, 13th June 1694; sasine followed 9th July 1694.† 1694.

* *Registrum Magni Sigilli*, lib. lxxiii. No. 76.
† Balquhain Charters, No. 554.

CHAP. I.

George, Count Leslie, Sixteenth Baron of Balquhain.

John Leslie, schoolmaster of Chapel of Garioch, gave a receipt for £16 : 3 : 4 Scots to George Leslie of Balquhain, 2d August 1707.*

1709. John Pirie, collector of money for repairing the manse of Chapel of Garioch, gave a receipt to George Leslie of Balquhain for £33 Scots, as his proportion for the said repairs, 4th June 1709.† The Honourable Margaret Elphinstone, spouse of George Leslie of Balquhain, got a charter of the lands of Tullos and of an annuity of 2000 merks out of the lands of Balquhain, proceeding upon an obligation made to her by Count Patrick Leslie, father of the said George Leslie, 9th June 1711.‡ (1711.)

Mr. William Leslie, minister of Chapel of Garioch, gave a discharge to George Leslie of Balquhain for £23 : 2s. Scots, being his proportion for repairing the kirk of Chapel of Garioch, 21st June 1710 (1710.);§ also for £10 : 10s. for repairs, 21st November 1712 (1712.);|| also for £20 : 11s. for repairing the kirkyard dykes, and building a new school-house, 21st November 1712;¶ also for the money and victual stipend for crop 1711, dated 23d January 1713 (1713.); and another for crop 1712, dated 6th February 1713.**

1706. Count George Leslie married, 1706, the Honourable Margaret Elphinstone, second daughter of

* Balquhain Charters, No. 931. † *Ibid.* No. 933.
‡ *Ibid.* No. 873. § *Ibid.* No. 936. || *Ibid.* No. 1712.
¶ *Ibid.* No. 942. ** *Ibid.* Nos. 943, 944.

George, Count Leslie, Sixteenth Baron of Balquhain.

John, eighth Lord Elphinstone, and by her had issue—

I. James, born 25th May 1711, who succeeded as seventeenth Baron of Balquhain.

II. Ernest, born in 1714, who succeeded his brother as eighteenth Baron of Balquhain.

III. A Son, who died soon after his birth.

Count George Leslie died 17th June 1715 at Fetternear, aged 34 years, in the vigour of manhood, as appears by an inscription on a stone above the gateway of the old family burying-place at the chapel at Fetternear. He was succeeded by his eldest son Count James Leslie, seventeenth Baron of Balquhain, then a child four years old. From this time the ancient splendour of the house of Balquhain began to wane, and the bitterness of anti-Catholic prejudice brought ruinous consequences on the family, which firmly adhered to the religion of its forefathers. 1715.

JAMES, COUNT LESLIE,

SEVENTEENTH BARON OF BALQUHAIN.

James, Count Leslie, Seventeenth Baron of Balquhain.

James, Count Leslie, born 25th May 1711, 1711.
eldest son of George, Count Leslie, sixteenth Baron of Balquhain, by the Honourable Margaret Elphinstone his spouse, succeeded on the death of his father, 17th June 1715, as seventeenth Baron 1715.
of Balquhain, being then a child in his fourth year.

CHAP. I.

James, Count Leslie, Seventeenth Baron of Balquhain.

His mother, having been left the tutor of her children, resolved to bring them up Protestants, as is shown in the following evidence. The Honourable Mary Elphinstone, wife of Thomas Buchan of Cairnbulg, advocate, stated that her sister, the Honourable Margaret Elphinstone,
1706. married George Leslie of Balquhain in 1706; that George Leslie and his sisters were all bigoted papists; that she knew there was a popish chapel in their house, and a popish priest always kept at Fetternear; that when her brother-in-law,
1715. Count George Leslie, died in 1715, his widow, her sister, sent for the popish priest, and desired him to pack up the popish trinkets, vestments, baubles, and many popish books, and to carry them away, which he accordingly did; and that she was resolved to bring up her children, James and Ernest, and to educate them, as Protestants, which she did. The Honourable Mrs. Buchan added that the family of Balquhain had then several trinkets and vestments which, she was informed, had been sent from Germany by James, Count Leslie, for the use of the chapel and priest. These church vestments and plate, which were thus· sent away were of the richest brocaded stuffs, gold and silver cloth, and precious metals and jewels, being made out of articles taken from the Turks in various battles in which Field-Marshal James, Count Leslie, had defeated them. Besides these, many other valuable articles were

carried away from Fetternear, amongst the rest many family portraits, much silver plate and rich furniture.

CHAP. I.

James, Count Leslie, Seventeenth Baron of Balquhain.

Not content with this, the Honourable Margaret Elphinstone also induced her son, Ernest, Count Leslie, eighteenth Baron of Balquhain, to dismember the family estates. She had a locality, that is the revenue of certain lands for her jointure on the lands of Insch and Boddam, belonging to the Balquhain estates. After her husband's death, about 1720, she married Sir James 1720.
Gordon of Park, by whom she had a son, James Gordon, styled of Cobairdy, and she prevailed on her son Ernest, when he succeeded to the Balquhain estates, to dispone part of the lands of Insch, and the lands of Boddam, to the said James Gordon, his uterine brother, which was in defraud of the deed of entail made by Count Patrick Leslie, fifteenth Baron, in 1700. Count Anthony 1700.
Leslie, nineteenth Baron of Balquhain, sought to reduce this iniquitous disposition, but he did not succeed, as will be shown hereafter.

While still a minor, Count James Leslie went abroad to travel, and on his way home again he died at Paris, 29th January 1731, in the twentieth 1731.
year of his age, unmarried. Some time afterwards his body was brought over to Scotland, and interred in the old chapel at Fetternear. In digging the grave for Violet Dalzel, widow of John Leslie, twenty-second Baron of Balquhain, in

CHAP. I.

James, Count Leslie, Seventeenth Baron of Balquhain.

September 1836, his leaden coffin was dug up, and was again replaced above the coffin of Mrs. Leslie in the same grave. There was found lying on the lid of the coffin a long piece of metal rounded at one end and pointed at the other, on which were engraved the family crest, a griffin's head, and the motto, "Grip fast," with the following inscription :—

"Jacobus Leslie de Balquhain
Natus 25 Maij. 1711.
Obiit Parisiis. 29 Januarii 1731."

The following inscription is engraved on a metal plate preserved at Fetternear House :—

S. D. G.
In memoriam *Iuvenis* ingentis speciei,
Dum vixit
Majoris spei si fata sivissent
Honorandi Domini D. Jacobi Leslie
de Balquhain.
Cujus si prosapiam spectes
Quid antiquius ?
In Martis et Minervae scholis
Quid illustrius ?
Si Rem familiarem, amplam satis
Honesti partam.
Industria et bonis artibus auctam
Et adhuc augendam.
Reperies.
Si corporis dignitatem
Statura erecta et procera.
Vultu erecto, gravi, verecundo.
Hilari tamen.
Et amabili.

CHAP. I.

James, Count Leslie, Seventeenth Baron of Balquhain.

Pietatem, si spectes, Dei, Principis
Et Patriae
Cultorem Invenies.
Sanctissimum simul
Ac fidissimum
Si probitatem, sobrius erat et equanimus
Omnibus aequus, omnibus gratis.
Facile omnes ferebat
Et patiebatur.
Nunquam se praeponens alijs.
Ita laudem inveniebat et amicos,
Parabat.
Verbis inerat fides, Comitas, et humanitas.
Factis aequitas et charitas.
Parenti optimae, praeceptoribus paedagogis
Et Tutoribus
Semper morigerus.
Nec prodigus nec parcus,
Qui dum in exteras Regiones
Ad Ingenium Excolendum
Et Majorem
Cognitionis & Experientiae suppellectilem struendam
Tendebat.
Parisiis. A.D. MDCCXXXI. Jarij 29
Fatis concessit
Et quod mortale fuit
Hic posuit.
Hunc tantum terris ostendunt fata nec ultra
Esse sinunt.
Qualem amisit patria civem
Uno avulso, non deficit alter
Aureus.

The following invitation, addressed to John Leslie seventh Laird of Warthill, by Count Ernest Leslie, eighteenth Baron of Balquhain, to attend the funeral of his brother, Count James Leslie,

CHAP. I.

James, Count Leslie, Seventeenth Baron of Balquhain.

seventeenth baron, is preserved among the family papers at Fetternear :—

Sir,—The Corpse of James Lesley of Balquhain, my brother, Lyeing in Saint Paules Chappell of Aberdeen are to be transported from thence, and Interred in his Chappell at Fetterneir, upon the twenty-third day of Aprile current. Your presence here at eight of the clock before noon To witness the same, Is earnestly Intreated by Sir, your most humble servant,

ERNEST LESLIE.

Aberdeen, Pitfodles Lodgeing,
1731. *16th Aprile* 1731.

Count James Leslie, seventeenth Baron of Bal-
1731. quhain, dying unmarried 29th January 1731, was succeeded by his brother, Count Ernest Leslie, eighteenth baron.

Ernest, Count Leslie, Eighteenth Baron of Balquhain.

ERNEST, COUNT LESLIE,

EIGHTEENTH BARON OF BALQUHAIN.

COUNT ERNEST LESLIE, second son of Count George Leslie, sixteenth Baron of Balquhain, by his wife the Honourable Margaret Elphinstone, succeeded his brother James, Count Leslie, seventeenth baron, as eighteenth Baron of Balquhain,
1731. 29th January 1731—he being still a minor.

We have seen that immediately after the death of his father, his mother, the Honourable Margaret Elphinstone, expressed her determination to bring up her two infant sons as Protestants, which she did accordingly, as is stated in a letter from Count

Ernest, Count Leslie, Eighteenth Baron of Balquhain.

Charles Cajetan Leslie to Sir James Leslie of Pitcaple, 7th July 1740, in which he says:— "The possession of the lands of Balquhain has always been in the hands of Catholics except the last, the late Ernest Leslie, who was educated, contrary to the inclination of his father George Leslie, in the Protestant religion."

Count Ernest Leslie was served heir to his brother, Count James, in the lands of Balquhain, 17th July 1739, and established in his own person the proper titles both to the estates of Balquhain and to the lands of Insch and Boddam; but in the retour of his service to the lands of Insch and Boddam he neglected to insert the prohibitive, irritant, and resolutive clauses of the entails of 1692 and 1700, against alienation of the property. On the 26th July 1739 he resigned the whole of the lands of Balquhain mentioned in the entail, excepting the lands of Greenhall and Knockenbaird, in favour of himself and the heirs-male of his body; and on the same day he got a charter, under the Great Seal, of the lands and barony of Balquhain; sasine followed thereon 16th October 1739, and was registered at Aberdeen 20th October 1739.* Thereafter he granted a procuratory for resigning the lands of Insch and Boddam in favour of himself and the heirs-male of his body, with remainder to James Gordon of

1739. 1692-1700. 1739. 1739.

* General Retours, lib. xcvi. No. 164; and Balquhain Charters, No. 83.

CHAP. I.

Ernest, Count Leslie, Eighteenth Baron of Balquhain.

Cobairdy, his half-brother, the son of his mother by her second husband Sir James Gordon of Park, and the heirs-male of his body, with remainder to the sister of the said James Gordon of Cobairdy and the other heirs therein mentioned. This breach of the entail was made by Count Ernest Leslie at the instigation of his mother, the Honourable Margaret Elphinstone, and the consequence was that, on the death of Count Ernest

1739. without issue in 1739, James Gordon of Cobairdy took possession of the lands of Insch and Boddam, which were thus lost to the true heirs of the Balquhain estates.

Count Ernest Leslie is said to have been a thoughtless youth, who, having an opulent fortune unexpectedly thrown upon him by his brother's death, led a wild life, and made too free with his constitution, and thereby undermined his health. He went abroad to travel, and when in Germany it seems he had proposed to visit his relations there; but the German branch of the family were so disobliged at their Scotch relatives, because Count Patrick had prevailed on his elder son, James Ernest, Count Leslie, to renounce his birthright to the Balquhain estates, that Count Charles Cajetan Leslie, the son of Count James Ernest, would not receive a visit from his cousin Ernest Leslie of Balquhain. Count Ernest Leslie therefore returned to Scotland, and after remaining a short time there he went abroad again. His in-

CHAP. I.

Ernest, Count Leslie, Eighteenth Baron of Balquhain.

temperate habits brought on disease, and he was obliged to return home again. He died at Edinburgh 20th November 1739, aged 25 years. His remains were buried in Lord Balmerino's burial-place in the chapel of Holyrood.

Count Ernest Leslie was the last male heir of the house of Balquhain in Scotland. The succession to the estates was disputed by Count Charles Cajetan Leslie, and his two sons, Count Joseph Leopold and Count Anthony, and Sir James Leslie of Pitcaple, and was decided in favour of Count Anthony Leslie, nineteenth Baron of Balquhain, by a judgment of the House of Peers, 29th April 1742. 1742.

ANTHONY, COUNT LESLIE,

NINETEENTH BARON OF BALQUHAIN.

Anthony, Count Leslie, Nineteenth Baron of Balquhain.

By a decision in his favour, pronounced by the House of Peers 29th April 1742, Count Anthony Leslie, second son of Count Charles Cajetan Leslie, the son of James Ernest, Count Leslie, the elder son of Count Patrick Leslie, fifteenth Baron of Balquhain, succeeded his cousin Count Ernest Leslie as nineteenth Baron of Balquhain. 1742.

By the death of Count Ernest Leslie, eighteenth Baron of Balquhain, without issue, 20th November 1739, the succession to the lands and barony of Balquhain opened to Charles Cajetan, Count 1739.

CHAP. I.

Anthony, Count Leslie, Nineteenth Baron of Balquhain.

Leslie, second son of James Ernest, Count Leslie, as heir of provision under the deeds of entail. But Count Charles Cajetan having succeeded to the family estates in Germany by the death of his elder brother, Count Joseph Leopold, and of his
1738. father, Count James Ernest, in 1738, he could not also hold the Balquhain estates in Scotland, as by the deeds of entail the Scotch and German estates could not be united in the same person. He was therefore bound to convey the Balquhain estates to that person who by the entail stood next in the order of succession thereby established. Such being the case, the next heirs of entail in the order of succession preferred their claims, and three processes were brought against Count Charles Cajetan Leslie: one at the instance of Count Joseph Leopold, his eldest son; another at the instance of his second son, Count Anthony; and a third at the instance of Sir James Leslie of Pitcaple, as the son and heir-male of his mother, Lady Marjory Leslie, eldest daughter of Count Patrick Leslie, the entailer. The scope of these three actions was to have it declared that Count Charles Cajetan Leslie could not hold both the Scotch and German estates, and that he was bound to denude himself of the Balquhain estates in favour of one or other of the pursuers. Sir James Leslie of Pitcaple took steps immediately to prosecute his claims to the succession, and wrote the following letter to Mr. James Cattanach,

advocate in Aberdeen, whom he appointed his agent:—

Paris, January the 16th, 1740, *N. S.*

Sir—I am told by late Count Leslie's entail, and my cosen, the late Balquahn's death, the entailed estate of Balquhan devolves to me. I therefore empower you, as my procator, to procure warrants from the Lords of Session, or Commissars of Aberdeen, for inspecting the papers of that estate, and consult Lawiers by the advice of Sir Alexander Reid of Barra, Mr. Erskine of Pittoderie, Mr. Horn of Horn Castel, Mr. Elphinston of Glack, and Captain Urquhart, or any two of them, and to doe everything as my procator and Lawier, and to expedd my service if necessar, for which this is your power, authority, and warrant, and will obleage Your humble servant, JA. LESLIE.

This missive letter was registered in the Commissary Court books of Aberdeen 26th January 1740 1740.

Count Charles Cajetan Leslie, with the view of dissuading Sir James Leslie of Pitcaple from disputing his succession to the Balquhain estates, wrote to him two letters, in which he states the grounds of his claim, and endeavours to persuade Pitcaple from entering into litigation, and offers him the management of the estates in the most liberal terms. The following is a copy of these two letters, translated from the originals written in French:—

Gratz in Styria, 30th April 1740. 1740.

My dear Cousin—Being informed by my aunt, the holy sister Mary Elizabeth, Abbess of the Ursulines at Lisle, of the favourable inclinations you entertain to favour my

Anthony, Count Leslie, Nineteenth Baron of Balquhain.

interests in the succession to my deceased cousin, Mr.
Ernest Leslie, Baron of Balquhain, which falls to me in
consequence of an agreement made at Paris in 1700
between my father and grandfather, by which it is evidently
stipulated that if one branch should fail through want of
issue, the succession to the failing branch should fall to the
second son of the other; consequently, my late uncle, Count
George, son of the late Count Patrick, leaving none but the
deceased Mr. Ernest Leslie, who was never married, the
succession belongs to me as the second son of my father,
Count James Ernest, my elder brother Joseph having
1732. died in 1732, leaving only one daughter, who died of the
1738. small-pox in 1738. This is only consistent with justice,
since, *vice versa*, if my branch had come to fail of issue,
their estates would have belonged directly to those who
had survived of the descendants of Count George. However,
should my succeeding be disputed, the succession at least
belongs lawfully to the second of my sons, in order that
the foresaid agreement be faithfully executed according to
the intentions of the contractors. I have three sons: the
1728. eldest, Joseph Leopold, born 1728, aged 12 years; the
1733. second, Anthony, born 1733, aged 7; the third, Charles,
1730. aged 4 months; and three daughters, the eldest born 1730,
1732. aged 10; the second born 1732, aged 8; and the third
1737. born 1737, aged 3.

They may perhaps occasion me some difficulties with regard to my religion before they grant me free administration of succession in Scotland; but I hope these will be easily removed when they consider that the said contract was agreed upon solely by two persons who were Catholics, and that the government of Scotland has permitted it, and caused it to be registered in the public records. They may also require that either I or my son should come to Scotland to take personal possession, which would not be practicable at present on account of the tender age of my son, and the risk he would run of changing his religion; and with regard to myself, the places and employments which I hold under his Imperial and Catholic majesty, and other circumstances would likewise prevent my doing so. I have therefore determined to empower some person to take up the said possession, either in my name, or in that of my son. I entreat you, my dear cousin, to inform me without delay what would be the best method for me to manage this affair. It will be easy for you to do so, as you are acquainted with the laws and customs of Scotland. I would wish to be indebted to your friendship for these hints on account of the blood whereby we are so closely connected. As for me, I should avail myself of every opportunity of rendering you every service in my power; and if you consider that anything that I can do would be useful to you, pray address yourself freely to me, who beg to assure you with the utmost sincerity of the tender affection with which I am, and ever will be, with all respect, my most honoured cousin, your obedient and humble servant,

CHARLES CAJETAN, Count Leslie,
Baron of Balquhain, Privy Councillor
of His Imperial and Catholic Majesty.

P.S.—Pray do me the honour to let me hear from you, if only to show that you have received this.

To this letter Sir James Leslie of Pitcaple replied, 28th May 1740, asserting his own claims, and stating the opinion of lawyers whom he had consulted; and Count Charles Cajetan Leslie answered as follows:— 1740.

Gratz, 7th July 1740. 1740.

My dear Cousin—Your sincere and affectionate expressions of esteem, contained in your letter of the 28th May, have afforded me great pleasure; in consequence of which I frankly confess I should have no regret to see you in quiet possession of the barony of Balquhain in Scotland, if that only regarded myself, being well aware that from my possessing the lands, and fidei commiss, and feoffment in trust in Germany, I cannot, by the entail, at the same

CHAP. I.

Anthony, Count Leslie, Nineteenth Baron of Balquhain.

time, hold or enjoy those in Scotland. But in consequence of the substitution made in favour of our family, it is clearly stipulated that in the event of the branch of Balquhain in Scotland happening to fail, the succession ought to belong to the second son of the same family in Germany, before the succession can fall to the line of Pitcaple. Therefore, as I informed you in my last letter that I have three sons, it is not in my power to allow others to enjoy what belongs to my second son; but, on the contrary, it is my duty, as an affectionate father, to do everything I possibly can to obtain for him the possession of an estate which justly belongs to him by the laws of God and man. The opinion of the lawyers you mention is certainly so far correct that the succession cannot belong to me, because, at the death of our cousin, Ernest Leslie, I was not the second son. But surely these lawyers could not have been informed that I have several sons, the second of whom cannot be excluded from enjoying the said succession; but who, according to the family agreement, ought to be called to it, because, if the Scotch line should happen to fail, the inhibition is not at all limited, but will fall to my family, and as long as the survivor shall have sons, the second ought to possess the Scotch succession; nor can I comprehend how it can be considered an obstacle that I and my second son were both born in this country, as the condition is not at all mentioned; particularly as the Scotch government made no objection of the kind when they caused it to be registered in the Public Records, while they knew very well that I and my deceased cousin Francis James, Count de Leslie, who were expressly named in the said inhibition, were not born in Scotland. Hence it is natural to conclude that they cannot at present legally propose such a difficulty with regard to my second son, since such objection could only refer to me myself by the literal terms of the said inhibition, and which constitutes the justice of his claims. For the same reason, the obstacles which they might raise on account of our religion cannot avail, seeing that the possession of the lands of

CHAP. I.

Anthony, Count Leslie, Nineteenth Baron of Balquhain.

Balquhain has always been in the hands of Catholics except the last, the late Ernest Leslie, who was educated, contrary to the inclination of his father George Leslie, in the Protestant religion; and who, although consequently being of different religious opinions to those of his ancestors, yet was not able to change the nature of the property, which the said inhibition guaranteed to the German branch in the event of the Scotch failing in issue. You see, my dear cousin, all that I can write to you concerning this affair, I put all my confidence in you, trusting to your conscience and the regard you have for my interest, entreating you to interest yourself not only for our house, but also for our religion, in order that we may not lose these lands, and that those to whom they lawfully belong may possess them according to the disposal and intentions of our ancestors. And as I am too far from Scotland, where I have no acquaintance, I make no doubt, my dear cousin, but that, considering justice and the sense of friendship, and the blood whereby we are related, you will take up the cause of me and my family, and I hope that you will look upon my second son as a second father. Should such prove the case, I assure you that if you are inclined to take possession of these lands in the name of my second son, I will make over to you the management of them during my life, only reserving to myself the right to advise with you, in a manner which I feel certain will prove most satisfactory to you, with respect to the rents, so that both you and my second son shall reap advantage from it. Although you write to me that these lands are of little consequence, yet I must tell you that Ernest Leslie alienated a great deal of those which were included in the entail, as the lands of Telernes and Tolos, and others, whereof he had no liberty to dispone, and which ought to be restored to the true possessor of Balquhain, agreeable to the destination of my grandfather Count Patrick. I hope, my dearest cousin, that on an occasion so interesting to our family, you will apply yourself very effectually, and do all that lies in your power that our family may not lose their property; and I

CHAP. I.

Anthony, Count Leslie, Nineteenth Baron of Balquhain.

promise you that I will make such a contract with you, in the name of my second son, as will be quite to your own satisfaction; and I assure you that I reckon myself extremely happy to have found an occasion to make myself acquainted with you, nor shall I neglect to avail myself of every opportunity of testifying to you the inward consolation it affords me. All my family beg to assure you of their affectionate friendship, as well as myself, who am with the sincerest attachment, dearest cousin, your obedient servant,

CHARLES CAJETAN, Count Leslie.

Sir James Leslie of Pitcaple did not accept these offers of Charles Cajetan, Count Leslie, but resolved to assert his own rights to the succession, relying on the following clause contained in the deed of entail executed by Count Patrick Leslie,
1700. in 1700:—"In case it should happen that any heirs-male of the said Count Patrick Leslie's body should succeed to both the said estates, the estate of Balquhain in Scotland and the estate in Germany, in that case the foresaid estate of Balquhain, and others above specified, should fall and belong to the next heir-male to have been procreate of the said Patrick's body of his then present or any other marriage; which failing, to the subsequent heirs of tailzie aforesaid, in the order of succession above mentioned, to whom, and in whose favours, the said heir-male, and the heirs of his body, who should succeed to the said lands and estate of the said Count Leslie in Germany, should be holden and obliged, by their acceptation of the said deed of tailzie, to dispone

CHAP. I.

Anthony, Count Leslie, Nineteenth Baron of Balquhain.

and resign the said lands and estate of Balquhain; and the same should from thenceforth be redeemable by the other and next heirs-male, and the other heirs of tailzie foresaid, from the said heirs-male, who should succeed to both the said estates, and his heirs-male foresaid, by payment of the sum of ten merks Scots."

This case had now happened, and Sir James Leslie of Pitcaple claimed to be the next heir of tailzie, to whom Count Charles Cajetan Leslie was bound to dispone the estate of Balquhain in terms of the deed of tailzie; and he brought an action of declarator in the Court of Session for ascertaining the devolution of the succession in his favour.

Count Charles Cajetan Leslie, having no acquaintance in Great Britain, placed himself entirely in the hands of Abbé Bernard Baillie, Abbot of the Scotch Benedictine Abbey of St. James's in Ratisbon, who took a great interest in his cause, and who recommended his cousin, Thomas Dundas of Fingask, a lawyer in Scotland, as a suitable person to conduct the Count's law affairs in Scotland. Under Thomas Dundas's direction, Count Charles Cajetan Leslie defended himself against the action of Sir James Leslie of Pitcaple, on the ground that he claimed the estate of Balquhain in virtue of the following clause contained in the deed of entail executed by his grandfather, Count Patrick Leslie, regulating the

CHAP. I.

Anthony, Count Leslie, Nineteenth Baron of Balquhain.

succession to the said estate :—"which failing" (viz. the heirs of Count George, sixteenth Baron of Balquhain), "to the said Charles Cajetan, Count Leslie, second son lawfully procreate betwixt the said James Ernest, Count Leslie, and Berne, Princess of Lichtenstein, his spouse, and the heirs-male lawfully to have been procreate of his body." Therefore Count Charles Cajetan claimed the estate in virtue of this express limitation to him by name; and though he was already in possession of the estate in Germany, yet he was entitled to hold both estates, and was not bound to resign or denude the estate of Balquhain, either to his own sons or to Sir James Leslie of Pitcaple, because he was not called to the succession to the estate of Balquhain as the heir-male of Count Patrick Leslie's body, or of his son, Count James Ernest Leslie, his own father, but by being specially named.

For greater security it was deemed advisable to bring two other actions at the instance of Count Joseph Leopold and Count Anthony Leslie, the two eldest sons of Count Charles Cajetan Leslie.

Count Joseph Leopold raised his action on the ground that if his father, Count Charles Cajetan, was obliged to resign the estate of Balquhain, it must be in favour of him, Count Joseph Leopold, as next heir of tailzie, and who was not entitled to the estate in Germany during his father's lifetime, and whose right to the estate of Balquhain

CHAP. I.

Anthony, Count Leslie, Nineteenth Baron of Balquhain.

ought not to terminate till he got possession of the German estate, which may not happen during his lifetime.

Count Anthony Leslie raised his action on the ground that his father, Count Charles Cajetan, having succeeded to both estates, he was bound in terms of the entail to resign the estate of Balquhain in favour of him, Count Anthony, his second son, who could not, in any sense, during his brother's lifetime, be considered either heir-presumptive or heir-apparent to the estate in Germany; and Count Charles Cajetan, and his eldest son and heir, Count Joseph Leopold, being to be considered one person, are both bound to denude in favour of the next substitute, and he, Count Anthony, was that next substitute.

Upon the report of the Lord Ordinary, Arniston, the Court of Session, 11th February 1741, pronounced judgment, finding "That Charles Cajetan, Count Leslie, being an heir-male of Patrick Leslie of Balquhain's body, and having succeeded to both estates, he and the heirs-male of his body were obliged to denude of the estate of Balquhain in favour of the next heir of tailzie, and that the said Charles Cajetan, Count Leslie, and the heirs-male of his body, being thus excluded from the estate of Balquhain, in the event that had happened of his succeeding to both estates, James Leslie of Pitcaple was the next heir of tailzie, on whom the estate of Balquhain 1741.

CHAP. I.

Anthony, Count Leslie, Nineteenth Baron of Balquhain.

then devolved; and that Charles Cajetan, Count Leslie, was obliged to denude in his favour; and that Count Joseph Leopold and Count Anthony Leslie being by the substitution in the entail called to the succession in their order, only as heirs-male of the body of the said Count Charles Cajetan, they were, in like manner, as heirs-male of his body, excluded from the succession to the estate of Balquhain, in the event that had happened of their father succeeding to both estates; and that therefore Count Charles Cajetan, their father, could not denude in their favour, but ought to denude in favour of James Leslie of Pitcaple."

In consequence of this decision, Sir James Leslie took possession of the estate of Balquhain, and lifted the rents from Martinmas 1739 to
1742. Whitsunday 1742. But Count Charles Cajetan Leslie, and his sons, Count Joseph Leopold and Count Anthony, carried the case by appeal to the
1742. House of Lords, who, 29th April 1742, reversed the decision of the Court of Session, and pronounced "That the said appeals of Charles Cajetan, Count Leslie, and Leopold, Count Leslie, be dismissed; and that Anthony, Count Leslie, second son to Charles Cajetan, Count Leslie, was the next heir of tailzie, to whom the estate of Balquhain, in the event which had happened, devolved, according to the true intent and meaning of the deeds of entail mentioned in the said

Anthony, Count Leslie, Nineteenth Baron of Balquhain.

appeals ;" and it was thereby ordered that the said Charles Cajetan, Count Leslie, should denude himself of the estate of Balquhain in favour of the said Anthony, Count Leslie, and that the same should be redeemable by the said Anthony from the said Charles Cajetan, Count Leslie, and his eldest son, or his heirs-male, by payment of the sum of ten merks Scots, in terms of the said entail; and that the Lords of Session give the necessary directions for carrying that judgment into execution.

In obedience to this order, the Lords of Session, by interlocutor, dated 29th June 1742, "Found and declared that the said Anthony, Count Leslie, second son of the said Charles Cajetan, Count Leslie, was the next heir of entail to whom the estate of Balquhain, in the event which had happened, devolved, according to the true intent and meaning of the deeds of entail in the said judgment and decree mentioned; and decerned and ordained the said Charles Cajetan, Count Leslie, to denude himself of the said estate of Balquhain in favour of the said Anthony, Count Leslie; and found and declared that the said estate was redeemable by the said Anthony, Count Leslie, from the said Charles Cajetan, Count Leslie, and the said Leopold, Count Leslie, his eldest son and heir-male, for payment of the sum of ten merks Scots money." 1742.

During all the pleadings of this lawsuit no

CHAP. I.

Anthony, Count Leslie, Nineteenth Baron of Balquhain.

objection was ever made to Count Charles Cajetan Leslie and his sons on the ground of being aliens. Sir James Leslie had the assistance of several of the most eminent counsel then at the bar; particularly Robert Craigie, afterwards Lord President of the Court of Session; James Graham, afterwards Lord Easdale; and James Ferguson of Pitfour, afterwards Dean of Faculty. As it was then generally supposed or believed that Count Charles Cajetan himself, as well as his two sons, Leopold and Anthony, though descended from the family of Balquhain, were born in foreign parts, it could not escape so many eminent and acute lawyers to consider with suitable attention what influence that circumstance might have on the question then depending, touching the right of succession to the Balquhain estate; whether, supposing Count Charles Cajetan and his two sons to be born in foreign parts, outwith the allegiance of the sovereign of this country, they were thereby to be considered as aliens, and consequently incapable of succeeding to or holding any land-estate in Scotland, whether as heirs by descent or as heirs of tailzie. That this point was specially under the consideration of these eminent lawyers is a certain fact, as appears from the testimony of Arthur Gordon of Wardhouse, a witness adduced by Peter Leslie Grant in his action of reduction, brought a few years afterwards against Count Anthony Leslie. But it appeared to them that

CHAP. I.

Anthony, Count Leslie, Nineteenth Baron of Balquhain.

this exclusion or disability, under the circumstances of the case, had no foundation or authority either in the principles or practice of the law of Scotland, and it was resolved that no such plea should be made. Arthur Gordon of Wardhouse stated, in his evidence above alluded to, that, in a conversation with Mr. Graham, afterwards Lord Easdale, who was one of the lawyers engaged by James Gordon of Cobairdy in defending the action brought against him by Count Anthony Leslie for the reduction of the deed whereby the lands of Insch and Boddam were settled on him, in which defence it was pleaded successfully that Count Anthony was an alien, and had no right to pursue or raise the action, he asked Mr. Graham why the same plea had not been made in behalf of Sir James Leslie of Pitcaple against Count Charles Cajetan Leslie, and Mr. Graham answered that he was for doing it, but an eminent lawyer, who was also one of Pitcaple's counsel, did not think it proper at the time; and that he afterwards asked the said lawyer why he did not think it proper, and he answered that he did not think the Court of Session would have paid any attention to that plea. Hence it would seem that Sir James Leslie of Pitcaple lost his lawsuit and the estate of Balquhain through this erroneous opinion of his counsel.

The decision of the House of Lords in favour of Count Anthony Leslie is thus noticed in

CHAP. I.

Anthony, Count Leslie, Nineteenth Baron of Balquhain.

the *Scots Magazine*, April 1742, vol. iv. p. 193:—

"The Lords, April 28 and 29, were upon the appeal, Cajetan Leslie, a Count of the Roman Empire, against James Leslie of Pitcaple, Esq., in Aberdeenshire, and reversed the decree of the Court of Session, so that the count gets the estate of Balquhain."

Count Charles Cajetan Leslie, as tutor and administrator to his son, Count Anthony, appointed Thomas Dundas of Fingask to be commissioner and manager of the Balquhain estates for behoof of Count Anthony, who was served heir of entail to Count Ernest Leslie, last of Balquhain, 2d
1742. August 1742.

During the dependence of the process with Sir James Leslie of Pitcaple, discovery had been made of the deed of settlement executed by Count Ernest Leslie, eighteenth Baron of Balquhain, whereby he had granted procuratory for resigning the lands of Insch and Boddam in favour of himself and the heirs of his body; with remainder to James Gordon of Cobairdy, his uterine brother, and the heirs of his body; whom failing, to the other heirs therein mentioned, in prejudice of Anthony Count Leslie's rights to
1692. these lands under the deeds of entail of 1692 and
1700. 1700; whereby not only the estate of Balquhain and the other lands therein mentioned, but also all the lands which Count Patrick Leslie, the

CHAP. I.

Anthony, Count Leslie, Nineteenth Baron of Balquhain.

entailer, then had, or should thereafter acquire, were limited and devised to a series of heirs, under the usual prohibitive, irritant, and resolutive clauses *de non alienando.* Count Charles Cajetan Leslie therefore, in the name of his son Count Anthony, still a minor, brought an action against James Gordon of Cobairdy, who had assumed the possession of the lands of Insch and Boddam under the settlement, to have the said settlement reduced, and to have it found and declared that those lands did of right belong to Count Anthony under the two deeds of settlement above mentioned; and consequently that Count Ernest Leslie, eighteenth Baron of Balquhain, had not power gratuitously to give away these lands to James Gordon of Cobairdy, his uterine brother.

No compearance was made for Cobairdy himself, but his sister Elizabeth, Lady Forbes, and the other substitutes under the settlement, having appeared for their interest, it was objected *in limine,* that as Count Anthony, in whose name the action was brought, was in foreign parts, process could not be maintained at his instance without a proper mandate, or power of attorney authorising the same; that the commission or power of attorney granted by Count Charles Cajetan, as administrator-in-law to his infant son, to Thomas Dundas of Fingask, produced and referred to for obviating the said objection, did allenarly respect the estate of Balquhain, and

CHAP. I.

Anthony, Count Leslie, Nineteenth Baron of Balquhain.

therefore could not be sustained as a proper mandate for carrying on the suit respecting the lands of Insch and Boddam; besides, that as Count Charles Cajetan professed the popish religion, he was, by the laws of Scotland disabled to act as guardian or administrator in-law to his son.

1747. The Lord Ordinary, by interlocutor dated 24th July 1747, sustained the factory produced as sufficient to begin the process, the pursuer's procurator producing a more explicit one before extract. This interlocutor was acquiesced in by both parties; and though the factory produced was thereby sustained to the effect only to begin the process, matters were so slovenly conducted, that the cause was carried on to the final conclusion thereof by an interlocutory sentence of the Court of Session, without any other factory or mandate having been produced.

In the further proceedings in this cause, the defenders averred that Count Anthony Leslie was born in foreign parts, outwith the allegiance of the sovereign of this country, and consequently that he was an alien; and this fact being supposed or admitted by the counsel for Count Anthony, they proceeded, upon that supposition, to argue the abstract point, whether, by the laws of Scotland, one born in foreign parts, and in that respect most erroneously supposed to be an alien, was capable of succeeding to, or of holding and enjoying, any land-estate in this country. It was

CHAP. I.

Anthony, Count Leslie, Nineteenth Baron of Balquhain.

doing great injustice to Count Anthony's interest in this cause to confine the question to this abstract point of law. For, though no man can be an alien to that country in which he is born, it does not follow, by necessary consequence, that every person born out of the country is an alien. Indeed, the consequences would be dreadful were the child of every British subject casually born in foreign parts to be deemed an alien, and, as such, incapable of succession to his inheritance in this country. Various other circumstances, unknown or not adverted to by those who conducted this process in Count Anthony's name, and which were essential and necessary to be taken into consideration in the decision of the cause, were totally overlooked.

Upon this imperfect state of the case, the Court of Session, by an interlocutor dated 9th June 1749, found that by the common law of Scotland an alien not naturalised cannot succeed to any heritage in this country; and that the pursuer, Count Anthony Leslie, is an alien, and therefore has no right to carry on this action for the recovery of a land-estate. This interlocutor declared Count Anthony to be an alien upon no other evidence or foundation but its being supposed or admitted by the counsel employed for him that he was born in foreign parts, upon which the erroneous consequence was grafted that therefore he was an alien.

1749.

CHAP. I.

Anthony, Count Leslie, Nineteenth Baron of Balquhain.

Thus James Gordon of Cobairdy succeeded in keeping possession of the lands of Insch and Boddam, which actually belonged to the estate of Balquhain, and which the true heirs have lost for ever.

1754. Count Anthony Leslie, on attaining his majority in 1754, came over to Scotland to take personal possession of the estate of Balquhain.

The extraordinary judgment pronounced by the Court of Session respecting the lands of Insch and Boddam had the effect of instigating Peter Grant, son of Captain John Grant, late of Ballindalloch, whose mother was Anne Francisca, second daughter of Count Patrick Leslie, a remote substitute under the entail of the Balquhain estates, to abjure the Catholic religion, in which he had been born and educated, and had professed, and which his own father continued to profess; and, under the pretence of being the next Protestant heir, he brought an action to evict the estate of Balquhain from the true and nearest heirs, including his own father.

1689. Lady Anne Francisca Leslie, second daughter of Count Patrick Leslie, married John Roy Grant of Ballindalloch in November 1689. By him she had a son, John Grant, who was a captain in the Dutch service, and who professed the Catholic religion. He married the daughter of an Episcopal clergyman in Fife, and she became a convert to the Catholic faith. They had a son,

Peter Grant, born in 1741, who was baptized by a Catholic priest. But one of his mother's relations, David Orme, a lawyer in Edinburgh, aware of the penal laws existing against Catholics, brought him over to Scotland from Holland when he was fifteen years of age, and induced him to take the formula prescribed by law, by which he renounced the Catholic faith and professed himself to be a Protestant. Thereafter, in September 1756, David Orme, as *curator ad litem* for Peter Grant, brought an action of reduction in the Court of Session against Charles Cajetan, Count Leslie, and his son Count Anthony Leslie, then in possession of the Balquhain estates, and the other sons of Count Charles Cajetan Leslie, and Sir James Leslie of Pitcaple, and his own father Captain John Grant, the next heirs of tailzie to the said estates, and sought to have it declared that he, Peter Grant, was the true heir to these estates on the following grounds:— 1756.

I. That the defenders were either aliens, and consequently, by the laws of Scotland, incapable to succeed, or to hold any land-estate in Scotland; or,

II. That the whole defenders were either professed Papists, or born of parents professing the Popish religion, and educated therein; and, as such, by the statute of 1700, entitled "Act for preventing the growth of Popery," rendered incapable to succeed to or to take and enjoy any land-estate in Scotland until they should renounce that religion in the form and manner, 1700.

CHAP. I.

Anthony, Count Leslie, Nineteenth Baron of Balquhain.

1700.

and within the time limited and appointed by the act, by taking and subscribing the formula.

III. That the pursuer was the nearest Protestant heir called to the succession of the estate of Balquhain under the deed of settlement executed in 1700.

Therefore he concluded against Charles Cajetan, Count Leslie, that, in terms of the devolving clause contained in the settlements of the said estate, he should be decerned and ordained to grant, subscribe, and deliver, a valid and sufficient disposition, containing procuratory of resignation, and all other necessary clauses, of the said lands and estate of Balquhain, to and in favour of the said Peter Grant.

See App. No. XXIII.

David Orme produced in Court a letter addressed to him, 1st October 1755, from Captain John Grant, informing him that his eldest son, Peter Grant, was born 5th April 1741, and this proved that Peter Grant was fifteen years of age at the date of the action. He also produced a certificate under the hands of the moderator and clerk of the Presbytery of Edinburgh, dated 2d March 1755, testifying that Peter Grant had taken the formula by which he had abjured Popery. The Lord Ordinary, 30th June 1757, found it proved that the pursuer, Peter Grant, was the eldest son of Captain John Grant, late of Ballindalloch, in the service of the States-General of Holland, who was the son of John Roy Grant of Ballindalloch, and Anne Francisca Leslie, and

1755. 1741. 1755. 1757.

CHAP. I.

Anthony, Count Leslie, Nineteenth Baron of Balquhain.

that the pursuer was entitled to bring and maintain the said action.

In order to prove that the defenders were Catholics and aliens, David Orme, as *curator ad litem* for Peter Grant, collected evidence at home and abroad, and exposed to public view all the transactions, both public and private, of Charles Cajetan, Count Leslie, and of Count Anthony Leslie, and their family.

By proofs taken at Venice in November 1759, before a notary, in order to prove that Count Charles Cajetan Leslie and his sons were papists, it was shown that Count Charles Cajetan had a chapel with three altars in his palace at Pernegg in Upper Styria, and that mass was said there daily; and that, as far as could be judged, the count and his sons were devout persons, and on meagre days ate no flesh meat; and a witness deponed that he had seen the count receive the sacrament at the Romish church at Marioncelli, where he had a large estate, and that if the Counts Leslie had not been Roman Catholics, they could not have held public offices about the Imperial Court, and could not have been admitted to the posts and dignities which they enjoyed in the empire; Count Charles Cajetan being a Councillor of State, Actual Privy Councillor to the Empress Queen, and President of the Revisary Court of Justice of Lower Austria, *in causis privatorum;* Count Joseph Leopold being actual

1759.

CHAP. I.

Anthony, Count Leslie, Nineteenth Baron of Balquhain.

Imperial and Royal Councillor of Lower Austria; and Count Anthony Leslie being a gentleman of the bed-chamber of the Archduke Joseph, for which reason he always resided in Vienna.

1759. In a letter from Jerome Reccunct, a merchant in Venice, dated 11th September 1759, to Thomas Gordon, merchant in Aberdeen, it was stated that, "With regard to the papers you sent relating to Count Leslie's affair, I shall send them over to my friend in Germany, but am apprehensive it will be almost impossible to succeed according to your wishes. The family of Count Leslie resides in Styria, and is held in great consideration, not only in that part of the country but likewise at the Court of Vienna."

1754. Lord Newark stated that about the year 1754 he visited Count Charles Cajetan Leslie at Gratz, in Styria, as he had learned from Mr. Thomas Dundas of Fingask that the count had desired that he would wait upon him; and that Count Leslie told him that one of his sons had gone over to Scotland with the Austrian ambassador, and also spoke of a lawsuit which he had regarding the estate of Balquhain. He also stated that the count talked in French, and none in English.

John Frederick Ordos, a Hanoverian, stated that he was house-porter to the Imperial ambassador in London, Count Coloredo, who had a private Romish chapel in his house, and that he

Anthony, Count Leslie, Nineteenth Baron of Balquhain.

had often seen Count Anthony Leslie, when in London, in 1753 and afterwards, go with the ambassador into the chapel, and that Count Anthony Leslie, when disengaged, generally dined with Count Coloredo.

Jacob Frey, a German tailor, stated that in August 1753 he saw Count Anthony Leslie at Count Coloredo's, the Austrian ambassador's in London, for whom he used to work; that he was engaged by Count Anthony to make clothes for him and his servants; that he had seen Count Anthony at mass in the chapel of Count Coloredo's country house at Brentford; that Count Anthony lodged, on his first coming to England, at Mr. Rosenberg's in Bury Street, St. James's, and afterwards at a milliner's in Great Grosvenor Street; and, on his return from Scotland, he lodged again with Mr. Rosenberg; that he had often observed a crucifix at the head of Count Anthony's bed, and that he had found in the pockets of one of the count's coats sent to be mended by him, a handkerchief, gloves, and a set of beads; and that, happening to be in the count's room when he was undressing, he saw the pictures of two saints on his breast and back next the skin. 1753.

Archibald Campbell, vintner in Aberdeen, stated that about five years before, in 1754, a gentleman who had come from Edinburgh, and who was called Count Leslie, lodged in his house, and was on his way to his own house of Fetternear; and 1754.

CHAP. I.

Anthony, Count Leslie, Nineteenth Baron of Balquhain.

that, from his dialect, he took him to be a foreigner, although he spoke English pretty well.

The Rev. Patrick Simpson, minister at Inverurie, stated that he was often with Count Anthony Leslie during the time he was at Fetternear in
1754. July 1754; that there was a painting of Count Charles Cajetan's house at Gratz in the dining-room of Fetternear, and Count Anthony recognised it as his father's house on first entering the room; and that Count Anthony, from his language, appeared to be from Germany, and the witness did not imagine that Count Anthony was a native of Great Britain.

The Rev. Alexander Simpson, minister at Monymusk, stated that when Count Anthony Leslie
1754. was at Fetternear about 1754, he met him at the house of his son, Patrick Simpson, then minister at Kemnay, and that Count Anthony spoke with a foreign accent.

John Clerk senior, advocate in Aberdeen, stated that he was several days with Count
1754. Anthony Leslie in July 1754, at Fetternear and other places in Scotland; and that he was also in company with him for several days in the south
1758. country in July 1758, during the count's second visit to Scotland.

Count Anthony Leslie, in a letter dated 18th
1780. November 1780, addressed to the Rev. Charles Leslie, S. J., son of Patrick Leslie Duguid, twenty-
1758. first Baron of Balquhain, says, "The year 1758 I

was myself in Scotland during the war, when everybody said and believed it to be the highest injustice if I ever lost the inheritance which had been for so many years in the family of Leslie; even the former king (George II.) spoke to me concerning it."

The Rev. Robert Farquhar, minister at Chapel of Garioch, aged sixty, stated in his evidence that he had been twenty years a minister of the parish, in which a great part of the estate of Balquhain lay; that in 1754 Count Anthony Leslie came 1754.
and stayed some days at the house of Fetternear, and came one Sunday and heard divine service performed by him at the kirk of Chapel; and that he conversed that day and the next day with Count Anthony at Fetternear, and could perceive from his dialect that he was not a native of this country.

Mrs. Isobel Leslie, sister of Sir James Leslie of Pitcaple, stated that about five years before, in 1754, when Count Anthony Leslie was at Fetter- 1754.
near, she saw the Rev. James Hamilton, a religious, abbot of Augsburg, who told her that he was at the Scotch College at Ratisbon, along with Count Anthony Leslie and his brother, when they were studying there, and that he had received a letter from Count Charles Cajetan Leslie, desiring him to take care of Count Anthony while in Britain, particularly in matters of religion, meaning that he should not deviate from the Catholic religion,

CHAP. I.

Anthony, Count Leslie, Nineteenth Baron of Balquhain.

and that he intended to have come to Scotland with Count Anthony, but the Count gave him the slip, and went off to Scotland before him. The witness stated that Mr. Hamilton mentioned these facts to her after she had told him that Count Anthony Leslie had been hearing divine service at the kirk of Chapel of Garioch.

Mrs. Teresa Leslie, sister of Mrs. Isobel Leslie, stated that the Rev. James Hamilton told her that, when travelling down to this part of the country, he met Count Anthony Leslie returning south again, and that the Count told him he had been at mass the preceding Sunday; and that, when Mr. Hamilton came to Pitcaple, the witness informed him that the mass which the Count had been at was that he had been that Sunday at the kirk of Chapel of Garioch.

Christian Rosenberg, oculist to her Royal Highness the Princess of Wales, stated that Count Anthony Leslie lodged in his house in Bury Street, St. James', both before and after his
1754. journey to Scotland in 1754, and that the Count's servant had told him laughing, that the Count had been at a church of the established religion, and had given five guineas in charity on that occasion, and that the Count had done it out of frolic.

1758. Another witness stated that, in 1758, Count Anthony Leslie passed through Rotterdam on his way to London, and it was also stated that he was at Fetternear in July 1758.

Anthony, Count Leslie, Nineteenth Baron of Balquhain.

In order to obviate one objection to his title to retain the estate of Balquhain, Count Anthony Leslie took the legal formula purging himself of popery; and his counsel produced a certificate to that effect, signed by the moderator and clerk of the presbytery of Stirling, dated the 15th July 1758. 1758.

At a meeting of the freeholders of the county of Aberdeen at the Michaelmas head-court, held 3d October 1758, John Clerk senior, advocate 1758. in Aberdeen, produced a petition from Count Anthony Leslie, praying to be enrolled among the freeholders of the county, in virtue of a charter under the Great Seal, dated 26th July 1743, of 1743. the lands and estate of Balquhain. Against this it was objected by Sir Archibald Grant of Monymusk, that Count Anthony Leslie was an alien, and therefore could not hold any heritable subject in Great Britain, and he craved that the meeting would delay enrolment as there was a lawsuit depending before the Court of Session upon the point. Mr. Clerk admitted that there was a lawsuit depending at the instance of Peter Grant, who claimed the estate as next Protestant heir, but that the objection to Count Anthony's title had been removed, he having qualified himself in terms of the law, and had taken the necessary formula; and that, though the Court of Session had found Count Anthony presumed to be a foreigner or alien, yet the House of Peers had reversed the

CHAP. I.

Anthony, Count Leslie, Nineteenth Baron of Balquhain.

interlocutor of the Court of Session ; and, as Count Anthony had been in possession of the estate of Balquhain since 1743, he ought to be enrolled among the freeholders of the county. On a vote of the meeting to enrol or to delay enrolment, the latter was carried by a majority, and it was determined to delay enrolment till the action then pending was decided.

While the law process was lingering on, Sir James Leslie of Pitcaple, one of the nearer heirs
1757. of entail, died, 12th March 1757; and a short time afterwards Captain John Grant, father of Peter Grant, also died, so that then Peter Grant fairly stood the direct and nearest heir of the female line of Count Patrick Leslie's daughters.

On the death of Count Charles Cajetan Leslie
1760. in 1760, his eldest son, Count Joseph Leopold,
1750. having died in 1750, Count Anthony Leslie succeeded to the family estates in Germany, and, in terms of the deeds of settlement, was bound to denude himself of the estate of Balquhain to the next heir of entail; and having no surviving brother and no son, that next heir of entail was Peter Grant, who had now a better ground for claiming the estate than his former invidious grounds of action. However, the case continued to be argued on the former grounds, and was finally decided against Count Anthony Leslie in favour of Peter Grant, by an interlocutor of the
1761. Court of Session, 4th December 1761, finding it

Anthony, Count Leslie, Nineteenth Baron of Balquhain.

proved that Captain John Grant, the pursuer's father, was a professed papist; that Charles Cajetan, Count Leslie, and his sons Leopold and Anthony were born abroad, out of the king's allegiance, whereby they, being aliens, cannot succeed to any heritage in Scotland; and therefore they found the retour of Count Anthony Leslie, as heir of tailzie to Ernest Leslie, last of Balquhain, 2d August 1742, with the instrument 1742.
of sasine following thereon, to be null and void; and by another interlocutor, dated 5th February 1762, by which the Court found and declared 1762.
Peter Grant to be the nearest Protestant heir entitled to succeed to the estate of Balquhain; and found the Counts Leslie obliged to denude of the said estates in favour of Peter Grant, and repelled all the other defences. This decision having been confirmed by the House of Peers, Peter Grant became twentieth Baron of Balquhain. For the life of Anthony, Count Leslie, see the Records of the Counts Leslie in Germany. *See* App. No. XXIV.

PETER LESLIE GRANT,

TWENTIETH BARON OF BALQUHAIN.

Peter Leslie Grant, Twentieth Baron of Balquhain.

By a decision of the Court of Session, 5th February 1762, Peter Leslie Grant, son of Captain John Grant, son of John Roy Grant of Ballindalloch, and Lady Anne Francisca, second daugh- 1762.

CHAP. I.

Peter Leslie Grant, Twentieth Baron of Balquhain.

ter of Count Patrick Leslie, fifteenth Baron of Balquhain, was declared nearest Protestant heir of tailzie to the estate of Balquhain; all the other nearer heirs being declared incapable to succeed because they were either aliens born out of the allegiance of the crown of Great Britain, or were persons professing the popish religion. Therefore Count Anthony Leslie, who had succeeded to the estate of Balquhain as nineteenth baron, in virtue of a decision of the House of Lords in his
1742. favour, 29th April 1742, was obliged to denude himself of the estate of Balquhain in favour of Peter Leslie Grant, who became twentieth Baron of Balquhain.

Lady Anne Francisca Leslie, second daughter of Count Patrick Leslie, married John Roy Grant
1689. of Ballindalloch in November 1689. Her husband, John Roy Grant, being a man of no prudence, and being of irregular habits, very unhappy differences arose between them, and he not only ruined his own estate, but also involved several of his friends and neighbours. He mortgaged his estate of Ballindalloch, and lost it by adjudication, when it was sold to Ludovic Grant of Grant in
1710. 1710. They had one son, John Grant, who was educated in the Catholic religion. Having little or nothing of his paternal inheritance to depend on, John Grant determined to try his fortune abroad. He went to Holland and entered the Dutch service, in which he attained the rank of

Peter Leslie Grant, Twentieth Baron of Balquhain.

captain, as appears from the evidence of witnesses in the law proceedings between his son Peter Grant and the Counts Leslie. We find Colonel William Murray of the Dutch service stating in his evidence that he had known Captain John Grant since 1708, when Captain Grant first entered the Dutch service; that he was a very good officer, but his being a Roman Catholic prevented his promotion; that they served together in General Colzier's regiment; and that he had received letters from Captain Grant within seven or eight years, informing him that his children had been baptized by Catholic priests. 1708.

Edward Manhard, a merchant, stated in his evidence that he had known Captain John Grant since 1727, when he went over to Holland along with him as a volunteer; that he was in the Captain's house when his son Peter Grant was born; and that he, as well as the captain's other children, was baptized by a Romish priest; and that Captain Grant was a Roman Catholic, and converted his wife, who was the daughter of an Episcopal clergyman in Fife. 1727.

Captain Robert Johnston stated in his evidence that he had served with Captain John Grant in Colzier's regiment from 1739 to 1742; and that in the nomination for promotion returned by General Colzier to the States of Holland, Captain Grant was always returned as a Papist, which 1739-42.

CHAP. I.

Peter Leslie Grant, Twentieth Baron of Balquhain.

was the reason given for his being so often disappointed in preferment.

Captain John Grant married, about 1740, the daughter of an Episcopal clergyman in Fife, and she afterwards became a Catholic. By her he had—

I. PETER, who became twentieth Baron of Balquhain.

II. ELIZA, who, late in life, married Patrick Leslie Duguid of Auchinhove.

Although Peter Grant was born of Catholic parents, and was baptized and educated as a Catholic, yet, on attaining the age of fifteen years, by the persuasion of a relation of his mother, David Orme, a lawyer in Edinburgh, he renounced the Catholic faith, and then claimed the estate of Balquhain as the nearest Protestant heir of tailzie, and brought an action of reduction against all the nearer heirs, including his own father, Sir James Leslie of Pitcaple, and the Counts Leslie in Germany, as being either persons professing the popish religion, or aliens born out of the king's allegiance, and consequently incapable of inheriting any land-estate in Scotland. As has been shown, after a litigation of six years, during which time the Court of Session pronounced several interlocutors, and several appeals were carried to the House of Lords, Peter Grant was declared nearest and true and lawful heir professing the Protestant religion to the estate of
1762. Balquhain, 5th February 1762, and was served

CHAP. I.

Peter Leslie Grant, Twentieth Baron of Balquhain.

heir to the deceased Ernest Leslie, eighteenth Baron of Balquhain, 11th March 1763, and obtained a precept of chancery for infeftment in the lands and barony of Balquhain, 25th April 1763.* He then assumed the name and arms of Leslie.

Peter Leslie Grant entered the Dutch service, and during the period of his service he used occasionally to come over to Scotland and reside at Fetternear. But having lived rather freely, he fell into delicate health, and was obliged to retire, when he took up his permanent abode at Fetternear. He was a most gentlemanlike man in his manners, and had a very amiable disposition. He used frequently to have to stay with him Patrick Leslie Duguid of Auchinhove, the next heir to the estate of Balquhain.

Peter Leslie Grant was deeply in debt to his law-agent, David Orme, who had rendered him much assistance in obtaining possession of the estate of Balquhain, and had advanced sums of money at various times. In payment of this debt, Peter Leslie Grant in 1769 granted to David 1769.
Orme a lease of the whole estate of Balquhain for five times nineteen years, for a yearly rent of £733 : 13 : 4, payable to him and the next heirs of entail, during the currency of the lease, in which were included the manor-house and domain

* Balquhain Charters, Nos. 1000-1001.

CHAP. I.

Peter Leslie Grant, Twentieth Baron of Balquhain.

of Fetternear. This lease was radically unjust and illegal, seeing that the whole estate was most strictly entailed, and could in no manner be disponed, and the manor-house and domain of Fetternear could in no case, by law, be let beyond the lifetime of the heir of entail in possession.
1774. This lease, which was registered 7th July 1774, proved of ruinous consequence to the family, as will be shown.

Peter Leslie Grant was never married. He
1775. died at Fetternear in 1775, and was succeeded by Patrick Leslie Duguid of Auchinhove, son of Teresa Leslie, third daughter of Count Patrick Leslie, fifteenth Baron of Balquhain.

Patrick Leslie Duguid, Twenty-first Baron of Balquhain.

PATRICK LESLIE DUGUID,

TWENTY-FIRST BARON OF BALQUHAIN.

Patrick Leslie Duguid, tenth Baron of Auchinhove, eldest son of Robert Duguid, ninth Baron of Auchinhove, by his wife, Teresa Leslie, third daughter of Patrick, Count Leslie, fifteenth Baron of Balquhain, succeeded his cousin, Peter Leslie Grant, as twenty-first Baron of Balquhain in
1775. 1775. Patrick Leslie Duguid was born in 1700, and succeeded his father in the estate of Auchin-
1731. hove in 1731.

We find by the evidence given by Patrick Leslie Duguid in the law-process between Peter

CHAP. I.

Patrick Leslie Duguid, Twenty-first Baron of Balquhain.

Leslie Grant and the Counts Leslie regarding the succession to the estate of Balquhain, that he was educated abroad. He stated that his cousins, Counts Joseph and Charles Cajetan Leslie, the sons of his uncle Count James Ernest Leslie, his mother's brother, while making a tour with their tutor, paid a visit to their and his aunt, Lady Betty Leslie, abbess of the Ursuline convent at Lisle; and on her informing them that he, Patrick, their cousin, was at Douai, they came over to see him. He also stated that for several years he used to go from Douai to Lisle and stay there for eight or ten days at a time with his aunt Lady Betty Leslie, and that, since his return to Scotland he had frequently corresponded with her. He also stated that when his half-uncle, George Leslie, second son of Count Patrick Leslie by his second wife, Mary Irvine of Drum, went over to Paris to meet his elder brother, Count James Ernest Leslie, it was arranged that George should succeed their father, Count Patrick Leslie, in the estate of Balquhain, and James Ernest in the German estates; also that Count James Ernest wrote to his sister, Teresa, Patrick Leslie Duguid's mother, that as he never intended to return to Britain, he had sent her by his brother George his picture and a ring set round with diamonds.

Patrick Leslie Duguid returned from Douai before 1715. On the breaking out of the rebellion 1715.

CHAP. I.

Patrick Leslie Duguid, Twenty-first Baron of Balquhain.

in that year, he espoused the cause of the Stuarts with the utmost zeal, so that, though he was only a lad of fifteen years old, he was "out," as the Jacobite expression was. Again, when Prince Charles Edward landed in Scotland in 1745, Patrick Leslie Duguid joined his standard, with a considerable body of men which he had raised on his own estate, and in other parts of Aberdeenshire, and which he maintained at his own expense, for which purpose he borrowed large sums of money on the security of his estate of Auchinhove. He was present and was wounded in the engagement which took place at Inverurie,
1745. 23d December 1745. He joined the force under Lord Lewis Gordon at Aberdeen, 27th November 1745, with about fifty men. Lord Lewis Gordon was appointed by the Prince Lord-Lieutenant of the counties of Aberdeen and Banff, where from his family connection he had considerable interest. He commenced immediately to raise men: every proprietor was obliged to furnish a man or £5 sterling for every hundred pounds Scots of his valued rent. By this means two battalions were raised, one of which was placed under the orders of James Moir of Stoneywood, and the other under Gordon of Abbachy. He also raised a considerable sum of money, notwithstanding that his views were much thwarted by his brother, Cosmo, Duke of Gordon, who kept up a fair appearance with the government.

Patrick Leslie Duguid, Twenty-first Baron of Balquhain.

To put an end to Lord Lewis Gordon's recruiting and exactions, Lord Loudon, the king's Commander-in-chief in the North, despatched the Laird of Macleod, 10th December 1745, from Inverness with 500 of his clansmen, followed by 200 men under Major Munro of Culcairn, and 500 men under the Laird of Grant. Lord Lewis Gordon ordered his forces to fall back on Aberdeen, where he assembled a number of men raised in Forfarshire and Kincardineshire, and some of Lord John Drummond's French troops, lately landed at Montrose, and 300 Farquharsons and others under the Laird of Monaltrie, and the Aboyne battalion, and the Aberdeen battalion under James Moir of Stoneywood.

The Laird of Grant, fearing for his own country, returned homeward; Munro took post at Old Meldrum, and Macleod advanced and occupied Inverurie, 16 miles north of Aberdeen. Lord Lewis Gordon, on learning this incautious movement, determined to attack his opponents with all despatch. He moved from Aberdeen on the morning of the 23d December with about 1100 men and five small pieces of cannon, which had been taken from a vessel in the harbour. With the main body of his army he crossed the bridge of Don, and took the route by Fintray up the left bank of the river, while he sent a detachment of 300 men, French and others, by the Tyrebagger road, the usual road to Inverurie, so as to deceive

CHAP. I.

Patrick Leslie Duguid, Twenty-first Baron of Balquhain.

the enemy with regard to the true point of attack.

About four o'clock in the afternoon, when it was getting dark, the French party, who had marched by the right bank of the Don, dashed into and waded across the river, and attacked the enemy on the south-west side of Inverurie. Lord Lewis Gordon, who had reached the Urie on the east side of the town, hearing the din of battle, immediately crossed that river near the church, and attacked the town on that side. He came on the enemy so unexpectedly, that they were completely surprised. The Macleods opened a fire from the ditches and from behind walls, but being vigorously pressed, they gave way and fled in all directions. Their chief was placed in great peril, particularly as his men were not over zealous in the cause against the Stuarts. He got his followers together as well as he could, and retreated for some time fighting by moonlight. Many of his men were killed or wounded, and about fifty were taken prisoners, among whom were Gordon, younger of Ardoch, Forbes of Echt, and John Chalmers, formerly Principal and Professor of King's College, Aberdeen. The Macleods continued to retreat till they crossed the Spey and reached Elgin. There they told their chief that he had deceived them by making them believe that he had raised them and brought them out of their country to serve the Prince, and had

Patrick Leslie Duguid, Twenty-first Baron of Balquhain.

afterwards told them so at Inverness. They promised to follow him still if he would return to his duty, and be faithful to Prince Charles Edward, but otherwise they would return to their country, which latter they did.

Patrick Leslie Duguid was also engaged in the battle of Culloden, fought 16th April 1746. He was excepted from the general pardon granted by the government of King George to those engaged in the rebellion, on account of the bold and active part which he had taken in the unfortunate cause of him whom he considered his rightful sovereign. 1746.

After the suppression of the rebellion, Patrick Leslie Duguid could not return to his own house at Auchinhove, because a party of the king's troops, under Captain Hardy, was quartered on the estate and occupied the castle. He was therefore obliged to skulk about the country. Being a most resolute man, he determined to sell his life as dearly as possible, particularly as Captain Hardy had sworn and declared in the most brutal boasting manner, that if Auchinhove was out of hell, he would take him dead or alive. Patrick Leslie Duguid got a guard for his safety and protection, a band of six faithful old followers and companions in arms, who were well armed, and remained constantly with him in the various places to which he resorted for security, in the fastnesses of Coul, and the neighbouring hills and mountains, where he concealed himself and dex-

CHAP. I.

Patrick Leslie Duguid, Twenty-first Baron of Balquhain.

terously evaded every attempt of the king's troops to surprise or take him. He frequently observed the soldiers searching the neighbourhood for him.

During this unhappy period, his wife, Lady Auchinhove as she was usually called, remained with her three infant children at the castle of Auchinhove, and was kept in a state of continued alarm and anxiety not only with regard to her husband's safety, but also for her own, and on account of the continual intrusion of the soldiers into her privacy under the pretence of searching for her husband. One day Captain Hardy abruptly entered her room, and hearing some noise in an adjoining closet in which her son James, then a child only five years old, usually slept, he thought that it was perhaps the laird who might have got secretly into the castle, and was concealed there. He rushed in great haste to examine the closet, when, to his great mortification, he found only the little fellow. Captain Hardy was not a little abashed, but, to conceal his chagrin, he flourished his gay cocked hat and feathers, and told the child that he would give it to him if he would cry Hurrah for King George! To his surprise the boy smartly answered, "Na, na; I'm a Prince's man."

Some time afterwards, Captain Hardy, finding that he had little chance of succeeding in apprehending the Laird of Auchinhove, and becoming enraged at being baffled in all his attempts,

Patrick Leslie Duguid, Twenty-first Baron of Balquhain.

cruelly ordered the castle to be burned, without giving notice or warning of any kind to the unfortunate lady or her family. At the hour of midnight, he barbarously gave the order to set fire to the castle. After it was in a blaze, Lady Auchinhove made her escape with her children by a window, and retired to the top of a neighbouring hill, where she sat shivering in the cold, mournfully looking on until the castle and all its valuables were reduced to ashes. She took refuge afterwards in the gardener's house.

Lady Auchinhove, on afterwards seeing Captain Hardy, made no reproach to him, but simply remarked that her uncle General Irvine, the Commander of the Forces in the North, would not thank him for what he had done. The captain was thunderstruck, and tried to excuse himself, saying that if he had known she was a relation of General Irvine he would not have done it. She replied, "That shows your evil disposition, as you had no orders to do it." His employers were equally culpable, however, as no merited punishment followed the crime, and no redress was ever obtained. The laird witnessed the heartrending sight of his ancient castle in flames from a spot on the hill of Coul, which is still pointed out by the country people. A gable-end and the foundations of the castle of Auchinhove still exist, and the traces of the fire may still be seen in the

CHAP. I.

Patrick Leslie Duguid, Twenty-first Baron of Balquhain.

blackened walls of a house which formed part of the barn-yards or office-houses.

In addition to his other misfortunes, Patrick Leslie Duguid had incurred large debts in consequence of borrowing money to raise and to maintain his men during the rebellion, so that his barony of Auchinhove was deeply mortgaged. Trustees, one of whom was his brother-in-law, James Irvine of Kingcaussey, were appointed over his estates to manage them and to pay his debts; but, with every endeavour to save the estates, they were obliged to sell them to pay the encumbrances. The estate of Auchinhove passed into the possession of the Farquharsons of Finzean.

1763. About 1763, Patrick Leslie Duguid got from his cousin, Peter Leslie Grant, twentieth Baron of Balquhain, the house of Tullos, on the estate of Balquhain, to live in, and a small piece of ground, about a boll and a half sowing. There, with his children, he was supported by an allowance of twelve bolls of meal out of a public mortification called Dr. Anderson's, which was managed by several gentlemen, among whom was James Irvine of Kingcaussey, his brother-in-law, and other twelve bolls of meal which he got for some time from the granary of Balquhain. His miserable situation at this period appears from letters which he wrote to Mr. Orme, writer in Edinburgh, who produced them in the law-process which afterwards took place regarding the lease of the estate of Balquhain. He was reduced to the necessity of selling some of the meal allowed to him for the sustenance of his family, in order to get money to pay the wages of the maid-servant. CHAP. I. *Patrick Leslie Duguid, twenty-first Baron of Balquhain.*

On the death of Peter Leslie Grant, twentieth Baron of Balquhain, without issue, in 1775, 1775. Patrick Leslie Duguid of Auchinhove, the next heir of entail, succeeded as twenty-first Baron of Balquhain. Patrick Leslie Duguid, eldest son and heir of Teresa Leslie, third daughter of Count Patrick Leslie of Balquhain, was served heir of tailzie to the late Peter Leslie Grant, of Balquhain, in the lands and barony of Balquhain, 17th April 1775. 1775. A precept was issued furth of the Chancery for his infeftment as aforesaid, 25th April 1775. Sasine followed thereon 11th May 1775, registered at Aberdeen 22d May 1775.*

On succeeding to the estate of Balquhain, Patrick Leslie Duguid found that he had new difficulties to contend with. The last possessor, Peter Leslie Grant, being of careless habits, by these, and by the expenses incurred in disputing the succession with the Counts Leslie, had involved himself deeply in debt, particularly to David Orme, a lawyer in Edinburgh. To relieve himself from his difficulties, and having no family to provide for, as has been related he granted to this David Orme, in 1769, a lease of the whole 1769.

* Balquhain Charters, Nos. 1003, 1004, 1005.

CHAP. I.

Patrick Leslie Duguid, Twenty-first Baron of Balquhain.

estate of Balquhain for five times nineteen years, or ninety-five years, for the small consideration of a yearly rent of £733 : 13 : 4, payable to himself and his heirs of entail during the currency of this long lease, in which were included the manor-house and domain of Fetternear. This lease was manifestly unjust, and contrary to all established law, seeing that the whole estate was strictly entailed, and could not in any manner be alienated; and further, the manor-house and domain of Fetternear could in no case by law be let to any tenant beyond the lifetime of the heir of entail in possession.

By this iniquitous settlement, Patrick Leslie Duguid found himself not only deprived of the revenue from the estate of Balquhain which he had a right to enjoy, but he was also excluded from his own family mansion-house of Fetternear, David Orme having taken possession of the house, and acting as lord and master of the whole estate. Being unwilling to submit to such in-
1776. justice, Patrick Leslie Duguid, 2d July 1776, raised an action of reduction against David Orme, for reducing the lease.* In the meantime he was obliged to continue to occupy the house of Tullos, which had formerly been a hunting-seat of the Barons of Balquhain, and was situated in a small open plain at the foot of Bennachie, which rises majestically behind it.

* Balquhain Papers, No. 1006.

CHAP. I.

Patrick Leslie Duguid, Twenty-first Baron of Balquhain.

Besides his difficulties with David Orme, Patrick Leslie Duguid found himself exposed to new vexations on his accession to the estate of Balquhain. His brother, James Duguid, had an illegitimate son, Joseph Duguid, and this Joseph took advantage of an act of the sixth Parliament of King James VI., entitled "Act anent the youth and others beyond sea suspected to have declined from the true religion," to declare himself a Protestant, and as a Protestant to be the nearest and rightful heir of entail in the estate of Balquhain to Peter Leslie Grant, twentieth Baron of Balquhain. He brought an action against Patrick Leslie Duguid; James Duguid, his eldest son; Charles Duguid, his second son; John Duguid, his third son; Patrick Duguid, his fourth son; Alexander Duguid, his brother-german; and Ernest Leopold Patrick, son of John, third son of Patrick Leslie Duguid; who, he contended, should all be passed over and excluded from the possession of the estate of Balquhain, because they all professed the Popish religion. The summons is dated 30th May 1775.

See App. No. XXV

Patrick Leslie Duguid, finding his age and infirmities increase, and being unable to undergo all the anxieties and trouble attending the management of the legal proceedings and the affairs of his estate, and being desirous of securing his property to his own family, formally renounced his liferent right and title to the lands and

CHAP. I.

Patrick Leslie Duguid, Twenty-first Baron of Balquhain.

barony of Balquhain in favour of his third surviving son, John Leslie, his two elder sons being in holy orders, and being thereby excluded from the succession by the terms of the entail.

Patrick Duguid granted a bond of corroboration in favour of Count Ernest Leslie, then eighteenth Baron of Balquhain, as heir served and retoured to the deceased Count James Leslie, seventeenth Baron of Balquhain, his brother, for six thousand
1734. pounds, dated 14th December 1734. He disponed a piece of moss, part of the Mains of Auchinhove, in favour of Francis Farquharson of
1737. Finzean, 11th July 1737. He sold to Francis Farquharson of Finzean the lands of Meikle and
1738. Little Tillylair, 17th June 1738; and granted him a disposition of the same, dated 5th July and 13th November 1738. He also granted to him a disposition of heritable tolerance of a road to the Lochs in 1738. Ernest, Count Leslie, eighteenth Baron of Balquhain, disponed and translated the several bonds granted to him by Patrick Duguid, with the letters of inhibition and decreet of adjudication therein contained, in favour of Francis
1738. Farquharson of Finzean, 6th December 1738, who obtained letters of inhibition on the said disposition against Patrick Duguid, 19th February
1740-50. 1740. In 1750, Patrick Duguid paid Elspet
1745. M'Combie for a horse taken from her in 1745.

Patrick Leslie Duguid married, first, Isabella Dickson. Their marriage-contract is dated 27th

Patrick Leslie Duguid, Twenty-first Baron of Balquhain.

and 28th August 1731. By it Robert Duguid of Auchinhove, and Teresa Leslie his spouse, disponed the lands of Tillylair and others, under the burden of a bond for £6000, due to James, Count Leslie, seventeenth Baron of Balquhain, in favour of Patrick Leslie, their eldest son, and Isabella Dickson, his spouse, in liferent, and the heirs-male of their marriage. This marriage-contract was registered in the Sheriff-Court books of Aberdeen, 29th December 1735. Patrick 1735. Leslie Duguid had three sons and one daughter by his first wife, Isabella Dickson, but they all died young. He married, secondly, 16th July 1740, Amelia Irvine, daughter of James Irvine of 1740. Kingcaussey, by his wife, Lady Mary Forbes, daughter of the Earl of Granard. By her he had—

I. JAMES, born 21st October 1741. He was sent 1741. abroad at an early age for his education. He received holy orders, and entered the Society of Jesus, and then returned to England. Being in holy orders, he was excluded from the succession to the Balquhain estates. He came to Scotland when his father died, in 1777, but, being disgusted with the 1777. prejudices then prevailing against Catholics, and with Lord George Gordon's riots in Edinburgh in 1780, he returned to England, and served the 1780. Grafton Mission for nine years. He was afterwards chaplain to Anthony, Earl of Newburgh, at Slindon Hall, in Sussex. He then succeeded his brother, the Rev. Charles Leslie, in the Oxford mission in 1806. He left Oxford in 1812, and became 1806-12. chaplain to Peter Middleton, Esquire, at Stockhill Park, in Yorkshire. He received the honour of the Croix de la Fleur de Lys from Louis XVIII., King

CHAP. I.

Patrick Leslie Duguid, Twenty-first Baron of Balquhain.

of France, 16th September 1814. He died, 25th August 1816, aged 75 years, and was buried at Spofforth.

II. CHARLES, born 8th January 1748. He was sent to France for his education at an early age. He also entered the Society of Jesus, and was a fellow-novice with the learned Père le Pointe. He returned to England, and served in several missions; first at Woodstock, then at Tusmore, and lastly, at
1793. Oxford, where, in 1793, he built a handsome Catholic church. By his amiable manners and classical taste he commanded the respect and acquired the esteem of many learned members of the University. He was carried off by a paralytic
1806. stroke, 28th December 1806, and was buried in the sanctuary of his church. The following epitaph is inscribed on his tomb :—

Here lies the body of
The Reverend Charles Leslie,
Who built this Chapel
1793. In the year 1793.
1806. He died the 28th of December 1806,
Aged 59.
Requiescat in Pace.

1749. III. HENRY, born 6th May 1749. He died unmarried at
1762. Lumphanan in 1762.

1751. IV. JOHN, born 13th January 1751. He succeeded his father as twenty-second Baron of Balquhain.

1753. V. PATRICK, born 24th August 1753. He studied Medicine, and resided at Durham. Falling into delicate health, he went to Lisbon to try a change of
1783. climate, and died there in 1783.

1743. VI. MARGARET, born 12th March 1743. Died at Aber-
1762. deen in 1762.

1744. VII. AMELIA, born 8th July 1744. Died at Aberdeen in
1762. 1762.

1754. VIII. MARY, born 1754. Married to Mr. Reid, Aberdeen.

Patrick Leslie Duguid, Twenty-first Baron of Balquhain.

IX. MARYANNE, born 26th May 1756. Died at Aberdeen in 1762.

X. ELIZABETH, born 8th November 1757. Married to Captain Macdonell of Leich, by whom she had issue—

I. WOLFE, who entered the army, and attained the rank of Lieutenant-Colonel. He died without issue in London in 1830. 1830.

II. GEORGE, a colonel in the army and C.B. He married the Honourable Laura Arundel, daughter of Lord Arundel of Wardour, by whom he has a son, Ignatius, born 24th March 1825, Lieutenant-Colonel 71st Regiment. 1825.

III. JACOBINA, married to Sir Joseph Radcliff, Baronet, and had issue. She died at Rudding Park 10th May 1868. 1868.

IV. ELIZA, married to Arthur Clifford.

XI. JACOBINA, married to Edward Clavering Esquire, of Berrington. She was born 21st October 1760, and 1760.
died at Edinburgh 3d February 1840, and was 1840.
buried in Greyfriars churchyard.

Patrick Leslie Duguid's second wife, Amelia Irvine, died of an infectious fever, along with three of her daughters, Margaret, Amelia, and Maryanne, in 1762, at Aberdeen. Among the 1762.
family papers there is a voucher for the expenses of Lady Auchinhove's funeral, amounting to £9 : 10 : 7, dated June 1762. 1762.

Patrick Leslie Duguid married, thirdly, in 1773, his second cousin, Eliza Grant, sister of 1773.
Peter Leslie Grant, twentieth Baron of Balquhain, but by her he had no issue.

In a letter dated at Tullos, 28th May 1776, 1776.
written by John Leslie, to his wife, Violet Dalzell,

CHAP. I.

Patrick Leslie Duguid, Twenty-first Baron of Balquhain.

then at Terregles with her infant son, Ernest, John Leslie mentions that his father, Patrick Leslie Duguid, was at Tullos, and was not very well. Patrick Leslie Duguid wrote a letter to his daughter-in-law, Violet Leslie, dated at Edinburgh, 15th January 1777. By a letter, written
1777 11th April 1777, by John Leslie to his wife Violet, addressed to her at Kingswells, it appears that Patrick Leslie Duguid was then dead. He was succeeded by his third surviving son, John Leslie, twenty-second Baron of Balquhain. His third wife, Elizabeth Grant, died in the following year.

John, Twenty-second Baron of Balquhain.

JOHN LESLIE,

TWENTY-SECOND BARON OF BALQUHAIN.

1751. JOHN LESLIE, born 13th January 1751, third surviving son of Patrick Leslie Duguid, twenty-first Baron of Balquhain, by Amelia Irvine of Kingcaussey, his second wife, succeeded as twenty-second Baron of Balquhain on the death of
1777. his father in April 1777; his two elder brothers, James and Charles, being excluded from the succession by a clause in the deeds of entail excluding heirs who were in holy orders.

Scotland being at the time in a very unsettled
1745. state, in consequence of the troubles of 1745, and there being then no schools for the education of young people professing the Catholic religion,

John, Twenty-second Baron of Balquhain.

John Leslie was sent abroad at an early age, about 1761, to be educated at the Scotch college at Ratisbon, where the Counts Leslie in Germany had made a foundation for the education of members of the family. John Leslie prosecuted his studies with great success, and became an elegant classical scholar and an excellent linguist, speaking most of the modern languages with fluency.

During the time John Leslie was at Ratisbon, Peter Leslie Grant, then in possession of the estate of Balquhain, fell into delicate health, and there appeared to be no probability that he would marry Patrick Leslie Duguid and his family, therefore, became anxious that John Leslie should return to Scotland, which he was induced to do at their urgent request, as appears by a letter from his eldest brother, the Rev. James Leslie, written 17th March 1770. John Leslie returned 1770.
home with some reluctance, because he had made up his mind to enter the Austrian service. It was desirable that he should relinquish this plan, as, in the event of the death of Peter Leslie Grant without issue, he became immediate heir-apparent of entail to the estate of Balquhain, his elder brothers being excluded from the succession, being in holy orders.

On his return home, in order to improve himself and to obtain a knowledge of the laws of the country, and so to qualify himself to understand

CHAP. I.

John, Twenty-second Baron of Balquhain.

the duties of a country gentleman, John Leslie studied civil and canon law at the University of Edinburgh, and attended various other classes there. By these studies, combined with the accomplishments acquired in foreign lands, he became a most finished gentleman, and, being of a lively disposition, a most agreeable companion. During this period he used frequently to pay visits to his cousin, Peter Leslie Grant, at Fetternear.

Peter Leslie Grant, twentieth Baron of Bal-
1775. quhain, died in 1775, and was succeeded by Patrick Leslie Duguid of Auchinhove as twenty-first Baron of Balquhain. Finding himself unable from his years to manage the estates and the lawsuits in which he found himself involved, as has been narrated, he resigned his estates in
1776. favour of his son John, in 1776. Patrick Leslie Duguid did not long survive his resignation: he
1777. died in the following April, 1777.

As has been narrated, Peter Leslie Grant, having been in difficulties with regard to money, granted a lease of the whole estate of Balquhain to David Orme, writer in Edinburgh, for a period of five times nineteen years, from Whitsunday
1769-1864. 1769 to Whitsunday 1864, being a duration of ninety-five years, at the rent of £733 : 13 : 4 a-year. On the death of Peter Leslie Grant in
1775. 1775, his successor, Patrick Leslie Duguid, brought an action of reduction against David Orme, to

John, Twenty-second Baron of Balquhain.

reduce this long lease; but during his lifetime little progress was made in the action. When John Leslie succeeded his father in the estates, he continued the process for the reduction of the lease. In the meantime, he was put to the greatest inconvenience, as David Orme had taken possession of the mansion-house of Fetternear, as appears by a letter written by John Leslie to his wife, dated 28th April 1776. In consequence of 1776.
this, John Leslie was obliged to remain at Terregles with his father-in-law for upwards of a year, and his first child, Ernest, was born there. After that he took up his residence at Kingswells in 1777, 1777.
a place belonging to his law-agent Mr. Durno, several miles from Fetternear, on the Skene road to Aberdeen. Afterwards he went to live at Tullos, a small and inconvenient house on the estate of Balquhain. During this period he was subjected to every sort of annoyance and persecution on account of his religion. Few of the country people would afford his family even the smallest assistance or service for any money; they would hardly sell them an egg or a chicken. There were some honourable exceptions—people who were attached to the cause of the Stuarts, and who had been out with Mr. Leslie's father in 1745. These worthy people and their descendants 1745.
continued faithful adherents to Mr. Leslie through life, on account of the difficulties to which the family was subjected. But they were the excep-

CHAP. I.

John, Twenty-second Baron of Balquhain.

tion. When Mr. Leslie's brothers, the Rev. James and the Rev. Charles Leslie, visited him, and said mass privately in his house, the women of the neighbourhood, getting to hear of it, threatened to break the windows. Being obliged to go to
1780. Edinburgh in 1780, on law business, accompanied by his brother the Rev. James Leslie, and his sister-in-law Miss Margaret Dalzell, they happened to arrive during the anti-Catholic riots raised by Lord George Gordon, and no person would take them into a house, and they were obliged to take a small boat and cross the Frith of Forth on a dark and stormy night, and seek shelter on the opposite coast.

To add to these difficulties, David Orme, fearful of losing the power which he had acquired over the estate of Balquhain, carried his ill-will and prejudice so far, that he used every endeavour to produce a Protestant claimant to the estate; and he attempted to set up as such one Joseph Duguid, an illegitimate son of James Duguid, a brother of Patrick Leslie Duguid, twenty-first Baron of Balquhain.

James Duguid was the third son of Robert Duguid, ninth Baron of Auchinhove, by his wife, Teresa Leslie. Being of a very unsettled disposition, he fell into difficulties and enlisted in the 42d Highland Regiment, in which he became a sergeant. He married a woman of the name of Brodie, who went with him when he accompanied

CHAP. I.

John, Twenty-second Baron of Balquhain.

his regiment to America. When he returned home again, his wife remained in America, and was kept by a lieutenant in the regiment, and afterwards became a common prostitute. James Duguid then took up with another woman in this country, and cohabited with her while his own wife was still living. This woman had a son called Joseph, and James Duguid was supposed to be his father. But James Duguid, on his death-bed, solemnly declared that he never was married to Joseph's mother. The said Joseph was at best an adulterous bastard. But this did not prevent Mr. Orme from bringing him forward as a Protestant heir to the estate of Balquhain.

Mr. Orme founded Joseph Duguid's claim to the estate of Balquhain on the seventy-first act of the sixth parliament of King James VI., entitled "An Act anent the youth and others beyond sea suspected to have declined from the true religion," and the third act of the 8th and 9th sessions of the first parliament of William III., dated 3d November 1700, entitled "An Act for preventing the growth of popery;" by which acts persons professing the popish religion, and neglecting to purge themselves of popery by taking the formula prescribed by law, or who sent their children, or had themselves been sent abroad to be educated in popish religious houses, were excluded from any right which they might have to succeed to any real estate in Scotland, and the nearest Protestant

1700.

CHAP. I.

John, Twenty-second Baron of Balquhain.

heir was entitled to succeed to such estate, in the same manner as if the nearer Catholic heirs were dead.

Joseph Duguid founded his claim on these acts of parliament, and brought an action of reduction against Patrick Leslie Duguid, late of Auchinhove, now designed of Balquhain; James Duguid, his eldest son; Charles Duguid, his second son; John Duguid, his third son; Patrick Duguid, his fourth son, and Alexander Duguid, his brother-german; and sought to have it found and declared that all these were persons professing the popish religion, or had been educated in popish religious houses abroad, and as such incapable to succeed to, or to take, hold, enjoy, or possess, the lands and estate of Balquhain, but were obliged to resign the same in favour of him, Joseph Duguid, the next Protestant heir of entail.

See App. No. XXV.

Foreseeing that the legitimacy of Joseph Duguid would be disputed, David Orme brought an action of declarator of his legitimacy before the Commissary of Edinburgh. Appearance was made for John Leslie of Balquhain, who offered to prove that the said Joseph Duguid was an adulterous bastard, the reputed son of James Duguid, born to him during the lifetime of his wife, from whom he was separated. This offer put an end to this process. David Orme then bethought him of the device of serving Joseph Duguid as heir-in-general to James Duguid, his supposed father, before the

CHAP. I.

John, Twenty-second Baron of Balquhain.

bailies of the Canongate, without attempting to serve him as Protestant heir-in-special to Peter Leslie Grant; finding it impossible to accomplish the latter on account of Joseph's bastardy and the existence of nearer heirs of entail.

On the part of Joseph Duguid, David Orme further raised objections to the service and retour of John Leslie of Balquhain, on the ground that John Leslie had two elder brothers, who, although in holy orders, were not excluded from the succession by the clause of the deed of entail, because the clause did not exclude such heirs as were in holy orders at the time the succession opened to them, but only such as should receive holy orders after the succession opened to them; also on the ground that John Leslie was a papist, and as such his service to the estate of Balquhain ought not to proceed.

On the report of Lord Kames, one of the assessors in the competition of breves between John Leslie and Joseph Duguid, the Lords of Session found that the service of John Leslie could not proceed, and that the service of Joseph Duguid might proceed; and they remitted to the macers to proceed in the service of Joseph Duguid accordingly.

By this judgment matters were brought to an extremity; and there being no appeal against the unjust law of which David Orme had taken advantage, John Leslie thought it prudent to

CHAP. I.

John, Twenty-second Baron of Balquhain.

get a Protestant friend of the family to take charge of his infant son and heir, Ernest, who was born while the process was pending, and who would be considered by law as a nearer Protestant heir to the estates while under the guardianship of a Protestant, than Joseph Duguid. Accordingly, James Irvine of Kingcaussey, John Leslie's maternal uncle, applied by petition to the Court of Session that it might be ordained that Ernest Patrick Leslie, the son of John Leslie of Balquhain, now an infant, should remain under the keeping of James Irvine of Kingcaussey, to the end that he might be educated suitably to his station, and especially that he might be instructed in the principles of the Protestant religion by law established, and that he might remain under his charge till further orders of the court, and that such a sum might be appointed in name of aliment, to be paid to James Irvine out of the means of John Leslie, the father, to defray the expense of the education and maintenance of the said Ernest Patrick Leslie; and this in virtue of an act of
1661. parliament passed in 1661, entitled "An Act against popish priests and Jesuits," which, after discharging them from saying mass within the kingdom, commands all sheriffs and magistrates to send to parliament or to the Privy Council lists of such persons as are known or suspected to be papists, that course might be taken with them conform to the laws, enacts as follows :—" Like-

CHAP. I.

John, Twenty-second Baron of Balquhain.

wise his Majesty, considering how dangerous it is that children be educated by persons popishly affected, do therefore, in conformity to former acts of parliament, appoint that children under popish parents or curators, shall be taken from them and committed to the education of some well-affected and religious Protestant friend, by order of his Majesty's Privy Council." The Court of Session granted to James Irvine the prayer of his petition, and he got possession of the infant, Ernest Leslie. The child was seized with an alarming illness, of which he nearly died, and his parents got permission to visit him. Mrs. Leslie risked her life in visiting her sick child. It was in November, and the snow fell so fast and heavily that the carriage could not proceed, and Mrs. Leslie with her infant daughter, whom she was then nursing, had to get out and wade through the snow. It was only when John Leslie, compelled by the necessity of the case, submitted to a degrading form of law, that his infant son was restored to him.

John Leslie, having the prospect before him of being deprived of his estate, and seeing his son taken from him to be educated in a religion different from that which he and his ancestors had professed for so many centuries, had been frequently urged by his legal advisers and Protestant friends to take the formula, by which means, nominally renouncing his religion, he

CHAP. I.

John, Twenty-second Baron of Balquhain.

might have his son restored to him, and his estate secured. John Leslie was very reluctant to do this, and for a long time he refused. His uncle, James Irvine of Kingcaussey, wrote to him the following well-meant letters, urging him to comply with the requirements of the law.

1777. *Edinburgh*, 25*th November* 1777.

Dear Nephew—We got safe here Friday last, but too late to meet with the Lord Advocate. Yesterday I had a long conversation with Mr. Colquhoun Grant upon your affairs. It seems there is a necessity for taking the formula within the Presbytery of Garioch. Here it cannot be done, and all your lawyers are of opinion if that is not done little Pat must be served heir, and the widow also for her terce. This you must know will be destruction and beggery, and the child taken away from you for ever. I have at a distance talked with two of our judges, and I assure you they said just what Mr. Grant will tell you by this post. You have an army of the best lawyers against you, and it really gives me great concern to think of the consequences if you do not do what you should do. I need say no more, but compliments to Mrs. Lesly and Miss Dalzell, and that I am always, dear nephew, yours, &c.

JAMES IRVINE.

To John Leslie, Esq., of Balquhain,
At Mr. Durno's, Aberdeen.

1777. *Edinburgh*, 6*th December* 1777.

Dear Nephew—Altho' I have had no answer to my last, yet as your affairs are now in that situation that a few days more must, if you still persist in not doing what you ought, you and all your family ever live in beggery and want, and I am sure with good reason heartily curse you, and lament you ever were born. If you had not married, I should not have felt what I now do, and from henceforward shall not trouble you upon this subject. Do not flatter yourself with idle nonsense of a division of the House of Peers. That will not do, and Mr. Grant is determined to serve your son heir, and Mrs. Leslie in her terce, and by this post Mr. Durno will have orders for doing so, and indeed you have not a friend that can condemn him. How soon this service is over, little Pat shall be sent for, and neither his mother, nor you, nor any of his Roman Catholic friends, must have anything more to say to him. Mr. Grant will write to you this day, and altho' I expect no answer to this, yet I can answer to myself that I have done everything in my power to save you and your family from utter ruin; and with compliments to Mrs. Lesly and Miss Dalzell, I am, your aff. uncle and humble servt., JAMES IRVINE.

John Leslie was deeply moved by the opinion which his Protestant friends expressed with regard to his conscientious scruples against taking the formula, and at last, after much reluctance, and with great repugnance, he took it before the Presbytery of Aberdeen. But David Orme persisted in his plan of opposition, and brought an action in the Court of Session to reduce the proceedings of the Presbytery of Aberdeen, alleging that John Leslie did not then live within the bounds of that presbytery, and that he had only signed the formula without repeating the words. To put an end to these objections, John Leslie was obliged to take the formula again before the Presbytery of the Garioch.

He was then required to prove that his two elder brothers, James and Charles, were in holy orders, and thereby excluded from succession to

CHAP. I.

John, Twenty-second Baron of Balquhain.

1778. the estate by an express clause in the deeds of entail. This he proved, and the Court of Session pronounced a declarator against the said James and Charles Leslie as papists and priests of the Romish Church, 21st January 1778. John Leslie was then served and retoured heir to his father, Patrick Leslie Duguid, in the lands and barony of Balquhain, 26th January 1778; and a precept of Chancery for infefting him in the said barony was issued to the sheriff and bailies of Aberdeen,
1778. 31st January 1778.*

Thus were the claims of Joseph Duguid disposed of. It was not possible that it could long be the law of the land that such a claimant could bring an action to eject lawful proprietors from their estates on account of their religion. In the
1779. very following year, 1779, an act of parliament was passed allowing Roman Catholics in Great Britain and Ireland to educate their own children without incurring the punishment of perpetual imprisonment; and Catholics were declared capable of acquiring landed property by purchase or inheritance, and of transmitting it to others. England and Ireland acquiesced in this small measure of favour granted to fellow-Christians. But in Scotland the intolerant spirit of presbytery stopped the current of brotherly love, and stirred up a spirit of hatred which terminated in the

* Balquhain Charters, Nos. 1009, 1010.

CHAP. I. *John, Twenty-second Baron of Balquhain.*

riots of 1780, when Lord Mansfield's house in London was sacked and burned by a mob led by the fanatic Scotchman Lord George Gordon; and the Catholic church and Bishop Hay's house in Edinburgh were destroyed, and the house of Principal Robertson was attacked by a furious populace, who were restrained only by military force from sacrificing the Principal's life to their vengeance, because he had said in the General Assembly that these slender concessions ought to be made to Catholics.*

Years had now passed, and the law-plea which was to decide the validity of the lease granted by Peter Leslie Grant to David Orme was still pending. The deeds on which David Orme defended his claim were the following:—

I. A Lease of the whole estate of Balquhain, granted to him by Peter Leslie Grant in 1765 for nineteen years. 1765.

II. A Lease of the whole estate of Balquhain, granted to him by Peter Leslie Grant for four times nineteen years, from Whitsunday 1769, for a rent of £733 : 13 : 4. 1769.

III. An Assignation, dated 29th March 1769, to him by Peter Leslie Grant of the said rent of £733 : 13 : 4, with the exception of a sum of £300 a-year to be paid to Peter Leslie Grant—the balance of rent being assigned to pay his debts. 1769.

* See *Stewart's Life*, p. 177; and *Presbyterian Empire: its Origin, Decline, and Fall*, by John Macfarlane of Ballindereck.

CHAP. I.

John, Twenty-second Baron of Balquhain.

IV. A Ratification of the above three deeds, dated 14th September 1769, by Patrick Leslie Duguid, the next heir of entail.

1773. V. A Lease, dated 7th September 1773, to him by Peter Leslie Grant of the Manor and House of Fetternear, for four times nineteen years from Whitsunday 1773.

1773. VI. A Lease, dated 11th September 1773, to him by Peter Leslie Grant of the whole estate and premises contained in the former leases, for nineteen years, to commence at the termination of

1845. the second lease, viz. at Whitsunday 1845.

David Orme's views at first seem to have extended no further than to get every possible security for the repayment of the money due to him by Peter Leslie Grant. But afterwards he came to entertain ideas of a very different kind. He availed himself of Peter Leslie Grant's necessities, and of the confidence which he reposed in him, and aimed at getting possession of the estate of Balquhain under the form of a lease for a number of years amounting nearly to a perpetuity, coupled with such other deeds as would render his possession absolute. Indeed, Peter Leslie Grant, in spite of his inexperience and want of reflection, and the unlimited confidence which he placed in David Orme, became sensible of the unfair advantage which had been taken of him, as appears by

1773. a letter written, 8th February 1773, to John Leslie, declaiming in the most bitter terms against the whole transactions as a piece of gross imposition put on him under the mask of friendship.

But his turn for dissipation was continually leading him into fresh extravagance, and his debts went on accumulating so as to render any redress impossible.

In the law proceedings it came out that the lease for four times nineteen years, from Whitsunday 1769, was sent to Peter Leslie Grant, then in Edinburgh, on the 28th March 1769, 1769. with a note in David Orme's handwriting, informing him that he might keep the lease till next day, but must bring it with him to dinner at a tavern named. On Peter Leslie Grant's part no friend or lawyer had been consulted, and being permitted only one day for reflection, he had not time to give sufficient consideration to so important a matter. He went to the tavern next day, 29th March 1769, and there signed the lease 1769. without further inquiry. In order to secure this lease, David Orme applied to Patrick Leslie Duguid, the next heir of entail, to get a ratification of it, so that it might not be reduced on his succession. David Orme invited Patrick Leslie Duguid to dine at Fetternear, and after dinner he produced a ratification of the lease, and by artifice he induced him to sign it, 14th September 1769. 1769.

David Orme, in his defence, stated that the execution of the lease and deed of assignation and restriction was witnessed by one of the judges of the Court of Session; that the whole transaction

CHAP. I.

John, Twenty-second Baron of Balquhain.

was known to Patrick Leslie Duguid, the then next heir of entail, who resided on the estate, and who, 14th September 1769, executed a deed mentioning the obligations which all the heirs of entail lay under to him, David Orme; that the lease for four times nineteen years which Peter Leslie Grant had given him, and the deed of assignation and restriction, were just and equitable; that it was reasonable that he and Peter Leslie Grant's other creditors should have every security which it was in the power of the heir of entail in possession to grant; that having taken opinion of counsel how far Peter Leslie Grant, then an infant, the nearest Protestant heir called to succeed to the estate of Balquhain, and who was a native of Great Britain, could exclude the other heirs named before him in the entail, in respect of their being papists and aliens, and having been advised that his claims were well founded, he, David Orme, who was Peter Leslie Grant's first cousin, brought him over from Holland, where he resided with his father; that he maintained and
1756. educated him, and, in 1756, when he was fifteen years of age, he raised an action in his name for the recovery of the estate of Balquhain from the Counts Leslie; that he had involved himself in great expense to prove that the Counts Leslie were Roman Catholics and aliens; that a great part of the evidence to prove these points being taken by commission in foreign parts, particularly

at Vienna, whither it was necessary to bring witnesses from Gratz in Styria, where the Counts Leslie resided; that he had himself to go abroad several times in the cause; that he gave up his whole time and business to it, and staked all that he had, and all the credit that he could command, on it; that the action against the Counts Leslie commenced in 1756, and they, being people of great opulence and power, contested every point; that no less than thirty-six interlocutors were pronounced in the cause by the Court of Session, and five appeals carried to the House of Lords; that the cause was continued for more than six years, when it was decided in favour of Peter Leslie Grant; that the expenses of the process were very great, and the whole were defrayed by him, David Orme—Peter Leslie Grant having neither money nor credit of his own, except £343 lent to him by Sir Ludowic Grant, and £150 lent to him by his relations, which he, David Orme, paid; that Peter Leslie Grant, sensible of the service which he had rendered to him, settled an account on his coming of age, 15th April 1762, for the money expended by him in the lawsuit since 1756, with an allowance for his trouble and advances, and granted a bond for £3080, with interest from 16th April 1762; and that he settled a second account, 26th April 1763, for further expenses incurred, and gave him a bond for the balance of £155 : 3 : 3; that on the 25th

1756. 1762. 1756. 1762. 1763.

CHAP. I.

John, Twenty-second Baron of Balquhain.

1765.

April 1765, with a view to pay him and others what he owed them, Peter Leslie Grant executed a deed whereby he leased the whole estate of Balquhain to him for nineteen years from Whitsunday 1765, for the rent of £300 a-year, to be paid to him, his heirs, and assigns—the surplus rent to be applied to the payment of Peter Leslie Grant's debts, after deducting necessary charges, provided Peter Leslie Grant did not apply such surplus rent to other necessary purposes; that for four years after the date of this lease, Peter Leslie Grant found it necessary to apply the surplus rent to other purposes, and, in consequence, his debts increased; that Peter Leslie Grant, being sensible that some other plan must be adopted for the payment of his debts, took the opinion of counsel, with respect to his power under the entail to grant a long lease of the estate as a security to his creditors; that what followed was in conformity with the opinion of counsel; that John Lumsden, a tenant on the estate, and his brother, were appointed to make out a statement of the rents and of the fines or grassums which the tenants paid for their leases, and to give their opinion what grassum each farm would likely yield, supposing the lease to be out; that their report was laid before Mr. Farquharson, accountant in Edinburgh, with a memorial that Peter Leslie Grant had resolved to grant a total lease of the estate of Balquhain for four times

nineteen years, at the present rent, in favour of him, David Orme; and desiring him to make a calculation as to what the various farms might yield by way of grassum in present money, supposing the farms to be worth the appraised money at the commencement of each term of nineteen years, and at what rate the victual or meal rent should be taken on an average of the fiars for the preceding twenty years; that Mr. Farquharson stated in his report that, supposing the current leases to be as stated, the grassums for four times nineteen years would amount to £992 : 15 : 6 sterling; and that, in respect of the endurance of the tack, and that the last seven years had been years of scarcity all over Britain, he was of opinion that the price of bere should not exceed £7 Scots, or 11s. 8d. sterling, per boll, and the whole meal should not exceed £5 : 14s. Scots per boll, and that at these prices he had drawn up an abstract of the whole rental, amounting to £9062 : 8 : 3 Scots; that, in consequence of this report, the lease for nineteen years granted to him in 1765 was annulled, and, on the 29th 1765.
March 1769, Peter Leslie Grant gave him a new 1769.
lease, whereby, for the sum of £992 : 15 : 6 sterling premium or grassum, he let or devised to him, his heirs and assigns, the whole lands and barony of Balquhain for the term of four times nineteen years; and he, David Orme, became bound to pay to Peter Leslie Grant, his heirs and

CHAP. I.

John, Twenty-second Baron of Balquhain.

assigns, the yearly rent of £9062 : 8 : 3 Scots, or £733 : 13 : 4 sterling, the amount of the rental as valued by Mr. Farquharson—always deducting the minister's stipend and other public burdens; that the lease contained a clause to the effect that if Peter Leslie Grant, his heirs or assigns, chose to possess the house, gardens, and Mains of Fetternear, he, David Orme, should be obliged to yield them up upon twelve months' warning, being
1769. allowed a discount from the rent; that in 1769 Peter Leslie Grant's debts were as follows, viz.—due to him, David Orme, after deducting £992 : 15 : 6 paid as a grassum for the lease, £2398 : 11 : 5½; repaid by David Orme to Sir Ludowick Grant, principal and interest, £411, 14s. 9d.; fees of counsel, for which David Orme had given bond in trust for him, £851 : 13 : 10. Balance due to London solicitors for last appeal, £560 : 3s.; due to physicians, during a long illness, and to the surgeon in whose house Peter Leslie Grant had lived in London, £867 : 4 : 8; due to sundry persons, for which David Orme became security, £558 : 15 : 11 :—in all £5648, 3s. 7½d.; that to make a sinking-fund for the payment of these debts, and to provide an allowance for Peter Leslie Grant himself, and to put his affairs on a clear footing for the time to come, another deed was executed on the same day as the lease, whereby, after reciting the lease and the debts due as above, Peter Leslie Grant as-

signed to him, David Orme, his heirs and assigns, for himself, and in trust for the other creditors, the sum of £4770 : 1 : 9 Scots, being the yearly rent or tack-duty due for the lease, being the balance, after deducting the sum of £3600 Scots, reserved to himself and his heirs, and £692 : 1 : 9 Scots, being minister's stipend and other public burdens; which annual sum of £4770 : 1 : 9, he, David Orme, was bound to apply—first, in payment of an annuity of £60 to Elizabeth Grant, only sister of Peter Leslie Grant, in case she should survive him, and the remainder for the extinction of the principal and interest of the debts due by Peter Leslie Grant; and to the end that the said sum should be punctually applied to the said purposes, Peter Leslie Grant discharged him, David Orme, and his heirs and assigns, as lessees, of that portion of the rent until all the said debts were extinguished; and he provided that, in the event of the heir of entail who should succeed to him refusing to ratify these deeds, by virtue of the power vested in him to set tacks for any yearly rent he might think proper, being satisfied that all the sums due to him, David Orme, and the other creditors, except the debts lately contracted, were spent *in rem versam* of all the heirs of entail, he restricted the rent of £9062 : 8 : 3 Scots, payable by the lessee, to the sum of £300 sterling, payable to himself and the heir of entail in possession

CHAP. I.

John, Twenty-second Baron of Balquhain.

CHAP. I.

John, Twenty-second Baron of Balquhain.

for the time being, till the whole debt should be paid off; that under this lease, he, David Orme, entered into possession of the estate of Balquhain, and went and resided with his family on it, but found that it would be necessary either to build a dwelling-house or to repair the house of Fetternear, which was in ruins; that from the latter course he was deterred by the power reserved to Peter Leslie Grant, his heirs and assigns, to resume possession of the mansion-house of Fetternear; but that, to obviate this difficulty, Peter Leslie Grant executed another deed, dated 4th
1769. August 1769, restricting this right to himself and his heirs, exclusive of assigns, and permitting him, David Orme, to cut barren timber for building or repairing the tenants' houses, and for restoring Fetternear House, and fencing such fields as he should take into his own possession, and obliged himself to give an allowance for such repairs as should be made in the house of Fetternear, and in the office-houses; also that he should take down such parts as could not be repaired, and use the materials for other building, and that no additional rent was to be charged for the privilege of cutting timber; and, in the event of limestone being found on the estate, he, David Orme, was to pay at the rate of a penny a boll for what he should dispose of after serving his own tenants; that, having been at considerable expense in repairing Fetternear House, he thought it would be

a hardship if the succeeding heirs were to turn him out of possession of it and the surrounding enclosures; therefore he prevailed on Peter Leslie Grant to restrict the power of recovering possession of it to himself and the heirs-male of his body; and, in consideration of the extensive repairs done at Fetternear House, and for a grassum of £55, to grant to him, his heirs and assigns, a lease of the manor and house of Fetternear, with the avenues, gardens, enclosures, office-houses, and Mains, for four times nineteen years from Whitsunday 1773; and further, another lease for nineteen years, to commence on the expiry of the former lease for four times nineteen years, for a grassum of £25 sterling; that Peter Leslie Grant died in 1775, and was succeeded by Patrick Leslie Duguid, who was not in a position to assail the above leases and deeds, on account of his ratification of the same, 14th September 1769.

1775.

1769.

After a lengthened process, the Lord Ordinary, having advised the process of reduction at the instance of John Leslie of Balquhain against David Orme, and the counter-process of the said David Orme; the two deeds of entail made by Count Patrick Leslie in 1692 and 1700; the tacks and other deeds under challenge; the memorials for both parties, and the answers thereto, pronounced an interlocutor, 18th July 1788, to the following effect, viz.—

1692-1700.

1788.

CHAP. I.

John, Twenty-second Baron of Balquhain.

I. With respect to the first deed—viz. a lease of the whole estate of Balquhain granted in 1765 by Peter Leslie Grant in favour of David Orme, for nineteen years—as it was renounced, the Lord Ordinary assoilzies the defender David Orme.

II. With respect to the second lease of the whole estate of Balquhain for four times nineteen years
1769. from Whitsunday 1769, granted by Peter Leslie Grant in favour of David Orme, the Lord Ordinary finds that by a clause in the deeds of entail, Count Patrick Leslie permitted heirs of tailzie to grant tacks of any part of the estate, and that under the then rental if such heirs should think fit; and therefore that the tack in dispute is not liable to be challenged by the pursuer John Leslie.

III. With respect to the deed of assignation, dated 29th
1769. March 1769, whereby Peter Leslie Grant reserved to himself the sum of £300 out of the rental, and assigned the balance for the payment of his debts, the Lord Ordinary finds that such assignation cannot be effectual beyond the lifetime of Peter Leslie Grant and such of the other heirs of tailzie as should have ratified the same; and as it was ratified by Patrick Leslie Duguid, the pursuer's father, he therefore assoilzies the defender from the reduction of the said deed for the period during the life of Peter Leslie Grant
1777. and of Patrick Leslie Duguid, till 1777, but reduces the same in so far as regards the assignation of the said rent from and after Patrick Leslie Duguid's death.

IV. With respect to the ratification of the leases abovementioned, and the assignation of the rental payable under the same, made by Patrick Leslie
1769. Duguid, 14th September 1769, the Lord Ordinary sustains the same.

V. With respect to the lease made by Peter Leslie Grant, 7th September 1773, in favour of David Orme, of the manor-place and house of Fetternear for four times nineteen years, and the restriction of resuming possession of the same to the said Peter Leslie Grant, and his heirs-male, excluding heirs of entail, the Lord Ordinary finds that as Peter Leslie Grant was under no limitation for granting tacks of all or any part of the estate, and for such rent as he thought proper, therefore the pursuer cannot challenge the said lease as comprehending the manor-place and mansion-house of Fetternear, or as restricting the privilege of resuming possession of the same to the heirs-male of Peter Leslie Grant; and further finds no evidence that Fetternear is the mansion-house of the family, or has been occupied as such for many years; therefore, as the entail makes no exceptions, he repels also that reason for reducing the said lease.

VI. With respect to the lease, dated 11th September
1773, whereby Peter Leslie Grant not only 1773.
ratified the former lease of the whole estate of
Balquhain in favour of David Orme for four times
nineteen years from Whitsunday 1769, but also 1769.
grants a new lease of the same for another period
of nineteen years, to commence at the expiry of
the former lease, thus giving the lease a duration
of five times nineteen years, or ninety-five years,
from Whitsunday 1769 to Whitsunday 1864, 1769-1864.
the Lord Ordinary sustains the said lease, and
assoilzies the defender, David Orme, from the
reduction of the same.

By this interlocutor all these ruinous leases were sustained, notwithstanding the act of parliament of 1685, which declares that it shall 1685.

CHAP. I.

John, Twenty-second Baron of Balquhain.

not be lawful for heirs of tailzie to sell, alienate, or dispose of, any part of their entailed lands, or to contract debts, or do any other deed whereby the same may be oppressed, adjudged, or evicted from the other heirs of entail. John Leslie made representations against the interlocutor, but they were rejected by the Lord Ordinary. Neither was David Orme satisfied with it, because it reduced the deed whereby the balance of the rent payable under the lease was assigned to him. Therefore both John Leslie and he appealed to the Court of Session.

In the further proceedings, John Leslie endeavoured to show, by investigation of the transactions and deeds, that Peter Leslie Grant had suffered gross lesion, and that, in making the bargains, some of the most essential circumstances had been misrepresented or fraudulently concealed from him, which amounted to a breach of trust.
1781. At length, in 1781, the Court of Session pronounced a decision to the effect that David Orme's lease should stand good for four times nineteen years, and that the mansion-house of Fetternear, with the manor-place, should be restored to John Leslie.

By this decision, only nineteen years were struck off from the duration of the lease, and the unwarrantable dispositions made by Peter Leslie Grant, contrary to the entail, were sustained. The grounds on which the Court of Session

John, Twenty-second Baron of Balquhain.

sustained a lease of such unusual duration, contrary to the terms of entail, appear to have rested on the plea of equity. The court seems to have considered that David Orme was entitled to indemnification for the expenses incurred by him in recovering the estate of Balquhain from the Counts Leslie in Germany, and thus opening the succession to the descendants of the daughters of Count Patrick Leslie. But the decision is contrary to all decisions given by the Court of Session ever since.

When John Leslie recovered possession of the once fine family seat and mansion-house of Fetternear, with its once magnificent domain, he found it in desolation, and reduced almost to a barren waste. The fact was, that David Orme, being aware that John Leslie was a Catholic, and knowing how unfavourable the laws were to Catholics, thought he was quite secure, and would be enabled by law to keep undisturbed possession of everything granted to him by his lease. He carried his insolence so far, that he refused John Leslie, or any member of his family, permission even to enter the house of Fetternear, although they wished to do so only as a matter of curiosity to see it. When, therefore, he found himself likely to be ejected, with great malice he did everything possible to dilapidate and destroy the place. He ordered all the woods to be cut down, even the ornamental timber and the superb old

CHAP. I.

John, Twenty-second Baron of Balquhain.

avenue of trees which led up to the house in triple rows on either hand. Some of the neighbouring gentlemen and friends of the family, with the view of preserving the woods from destruction, and of saving them for the family, purchased them, and left them standing. But David Orme insisted that this was a breach of bargain, as the woods were sold under condition of being cut down. Therefore he repossessed himself of them, and in consequence of this, the finest trees were sold for the smallest trifle. He swept them all away, and destroyed the fine old gardens. Orchards, shrubberies, and walks were allowed to go to ruin; and then he pulled down the two side wings of the house of Fetternear, and used the beams and timbers as firewood. Since the death of Count Ernest Leslie, eighteenth Baron of
1739. Balquhain, in 1739, without issue, and the consequent disputed succession, first between Sir James Leslie of Pitcaple and Count Charles
1740. Cajetan Leslie in 1740, and the continued absence of Count Anthony Leslie in Germany, then the law-process between him and Peter Leslie Grant, and, lastly, the alienation of the property to David Orme, the estate of Balquhain had been for upwards of forty years under the control and management of lawyers and factors, who took no interest in improvements, or in keeping up the condition of the estate.

John Leslie, on obtaining possession of the

John, Twenty-second Baron of Balquhain.

mansion-house of Fetternear in 1781, put it into a state of repair, and set about improving the domain according to the newest and most approved mode of agriculture. He had the merit of introducing one of the finest breeds of cattle ever seen at that period in the north of Scotland. They were originally of the pure Galloway breed, and by crossing with others of an approved description produced a breed which was held in great esteem by the farmers in the country. He lost no time in planting trees about the place. He planted the Cottown and Gallowhill parks, and extensive tracts of barren ground, besides ornamental plantations on the domain.

Soon after the ending of the lawsuit in 1781, 1781.
David Orme became bankrupt, and his lease of the estate of Balquhain devolved to William Keith, as trustee for the creditors. William Keith,
by an assignation dated 17th July 1782, and 1782.
recorded in the Register of Sasines 30th July
1786, transferred the lease to Henry Lumsden, 1786.
advocate in Aberdeen, from Whitsunday 1781, 1781.
and Henry Lumsden made Alexander Lumsden a partner with himself in it from Whitsunday
1789. Articles of agreement were executed 1789.
between Henry and Alexander Lumsden, and assignation was made of the lease by Henry Lumsden, in favour of himself and the said
Alexander Lumsden, 21st December 1790, and 1790.

CHAP. I.

John, Twenty-second Baron of Balquhain.

recorded in the Sheriff-Court books at Aberdeen 24th December 1790.*

Several kind neighbours, knowing the untoward position in which John Leslie was placed, came forward and most handsomely offered their security to him if he could succeed in buying up the lease from the Lumsdens. This, after a lengthened negotiation, he succeeded in doing. Henry and Alexander Lumsden agreed to dispose of their remaining interest in the lease from
1795. Whitsunday 1795, on consideration of receiving the sum of £3727 : 10s. for the lease, and £20 a-year to Henry Lumsden for his lifetime in lieu of his factorship. In consequence of this agreement, Henry and Alexander Lumsden assigned the lease to Charles Bannerman, advocate in Aberdeen, agent for the trustees, 26th April
1796. 1796.† These trustees were Miss Elizabeth Fraser of Castle Fraser, Alexander Burnett, Esq. of Kemnay, and Colonel Horne Dalrymple Elphinstone of Logie, who had become security for John Leslie until the price of the lease should be paid up by yearly instalments.

1813. In 1813, the whole sum, £3727 : 10s., the price of the lease, being paid up, the trustees were released, and John Leslie got the lease into his own possession, so that he became full proprietor, and had the command of his paternal

* Balquhain Charters, No. 68.

† *Ibid.* No. 69.

John, Twenty-second Baron of Balquhain.

inheritance. With a view of providing better for his younger children, instead of renouncing the lease in his own favour and then destroying it, he kept it up as a distinct right in his own person, which could be transmitted to his heirs and assigns whomsoever, as a separate fund from the annual rent of £733 : 13 : 4 payable to the heir of entail in possession under the lease. This arrangement proved a serious misfortune. Having little knowledge of business, and the management of country affairs, and being of an easy temper, and being embarrassed by having borrowed money to pay the price of the lease and to maintain his family, he found himself in difficulties. To relieve himself from these, for inconsiderable grassums he let excellent farms at rents far under their value, and agents lent him money at ruinous interest on the security of the lease. One agent actually got possession of the lease as security for money advanced by him, and thus matters were as bad as if the lease had never been purchased.

John Irvine got a lease of Old Town of Balquhain for four times nineteen years, or seventy-six years, from John Leslie in 1814. Colonel 1814.
Charles Leslie, twenty-sixth Baron of Balquhain, John Leslie's fifth son, in 1859, purchased the 1859.
remainder of this lease, 31 years, from John Irvine's representatives for £2192 : 8 : 11.

At length John Leslie got so involved in his

CHAP. I. — *John, Twenty-second Baron of Balquhain.*

difficulties, that, 23d June 1825, he assigned the lease and the woods of the estate of Balquhain, valued at £6000, to his eldest son, Ernest Leslie, and to Mr. Fraser of Strichen, Mr. Fraser of Lovat, and John Ewing, advocate in Aberdeen, as trustees, reserving to himself an annual sum for his maintenance, and appointing the balance for the payment of his debts and for providing patrimonies for his younger children.

1796. In 1796 the farm of Aquhorties, consisting of nearly 800 acres, was out of lease. It was in a miserable state, only some scattered fields here and there being under cultivation. The other parts were either hills covered with heath, or low marshy lands. It happened that the venerable Bishop Hay, Vicar-Apostolic of the Lowland district of Scotland, at that time was anxious to get a place where he might establish a college for the education of young men destined for the priesthood to serve on the Scotch mission, the French revolution having obliged the Scotch colleges at Paris and Douai to be closed. The good bishop having private property of his own, which he piously devoted to the service of the church and the good of religion, took a lease of the farm of Aquhorties for ninety-nine years. He built a college, and commenced agricultural operations. He was so successful that in the course of a few years the face of the barren country was completely changed. The whole farm was regularly laid out in fields and enclosed and fenced. Every acre capable of cultivation was brought in by trenching and draining, and the remainder was planted so as to be ornamental and useful. Aquhorties remained the only Catholic college in Scotland till 1829, when the college was transferred to Blairs in Kincardineshire. In 1844, the representatives of Bishop Hay renounced the lease of Aquhorties on condition of receiving an annual sum during the currency of the lease.

CHAP. I. — *John, Twenty-second Baron of Balquhain.*

1829.

1844.

John Leslie married, at Terregles Castle in Dumfriesshire, 14th November 1774, Violet Dalzell, daughter of John Dalzell, Esq. of Barncrosh (grandson of Sir Robert Dalzell, Bart. of Glenae, and cousin of Robert, Earl of Carnwath, who was attainted and condemned to be beheaded in 1715, but obtained a reprieve), by his wife, the Honourable Harriet Gordon, only daughter of William, sixth Viscount Kenmure, Lord Lochinvar, who suffered for his zeal in the cause of the Stuarts, being beheaded on Tower Hill 24th February 1716. William, Viscount Kenmure, had married the Honourable Lady Mary Dalzell, sister of Robert, Earl of Carnwath, so that Violet Dalzell's father and mother were cousins. She was a lady possessing great beauty and personal charms, adorned with every virtue, and of graceful and pleasing manners. By her John Leslie had issue—

1774.

1715.

1716.

CHAP. I.

John, Twenty-second Baron of Balquhain.

I. Ernest Leopold Patrick, who succeeded him as twenty-third Baron of Balquhain.

1795. II. John, born at Tullos 1st May 1780. He was sent with his elder brother, Ernest, to the Scotch college at Ratisbon in Bavaria, in 1789, when he was only nine years of age. In 1795 he returned to Scotland, and, as he intended to enter the Austrian service, he prepared himself for the military profession by studying mathematics and the art of fortification.
1797. He left Fetternear 4th October 1797, and sailed from Leith 13th October for the Continent, and proceeded to Vienna. In a letter to his mother, dated 4th December 1797, he stated that he had been kindly received by Major-general Worensdorff, of the Polish Guards, also by Prince Lobkowitz, to whose regiment of Light Dragoons he had been appointed, and that he was about to proceed to Italy, to join his regiment, which was then serving in that country; and that he proposed to call on Count Leslie as he passed through Gratz in Styria, on his way to Italy, because the English ambassador at Vienna had told him that Madame Buchenberg, wife of Count Lilsen, colonel of the regiment in which his brother Ernest was serving, had mentioned to the ambassador that Count Leslie had said that he wished to see some member of the family. By another letter from him,
1798. dated at Padua, 1st February 1798, we learn that he left Vienna 12th January of that year, and had called upon Count Leslie in Gratz, and that he had joined Prince Lobkowitz's Light Cavalry regiment as a cadet. He likewise mentions that his brother Ernest was then with his corps in Bohemia. In
1798. another letter, dated 18th February 1798, he says that his uniform was white with blue facings, and that he was learning his exercises. In a letter written to his father, dated in camp under the Alps at Venola, three miles behind Genoa, 22d December
1798. 1798, he states that he had been wounded in the leg on the 17th October, but that he did not go to the hospital at Lodi, as he had soon got well again, and

had since been in several engagements. The greatest battle, he says, was at Genola, 4th December 1798. He was at the siege of Alexandria, July 1799. By a letter, dated near Tortona, 29th July 1799, he informs his friends that he had been engaged on the 19th, 20th, and 22d June at the battles which took place at the castle of St. Giovanni. He was promoted to the rank of first lieutenant, and attached to the staff of Marshal Suwarroff as an orderly officer. He was present at the battle of Novi, 15th August 1799; at 1799. the siege of Genoa, in April 1800; at the battle of 1800. Marengo, 14th June 1800; at the battle of the Mincio, 25th December 1800. He afterwards returned to Scotland, and attended the funeral of his brother-in-law, Alexander Fraser of Strichen, in 1803. 1803. He took a passage in a foreign vessel then lying at Aberdeen, and about to sail for Dantzig, he having the intention of rejoining his regiment then in Poland. The vessel sailed from Aberdeen 3d December 1803, 1803. and was never afterwards heard of. It was supposed that she foundered at sea, and that all on board perished.

III. JOSEPH EMMANUEL LESLIE, born 5th October 1781, 1781. and died 21st December 1784. 1784.

IV. JAMES MICHAEL, born 25th April 1784. 1784. He succeeded his nephew Count John Leslie as twenty-fifth Baron of Balquhain in 1844. 1844.

V. CHARLES, born 24th April 1785. 1785. He succeeded his brother, James Michael Leslie, as twenty-sixth Baron of Balquhain in 1849. 1849.

VI. ANTHONY, born 30th November 1787. 1787. He entered the British army in 1808, 1808. and served in North America with the 8th Regiment. He got a lieutenancy in the Glengary Rifle Corps, and was present at all the engagements in which that distinguished corps signalised itself during the war in Canada, from 1812 to 1814. 1812-14. He settled in Canada, where he remained for many years, and then returned to England and took up his residence in London, where he still lives. He married, in January 1840, Ann Monagan, but has no issue. 1840.

CHAP. I.

John, Twenty-second Baron of Balquhain.

VII. EDWARD, born 30th September 1792. He was an Ensign in the German Legion. He died of a decline at Fetternear, 20th May 1813.

VIII. LOUIS XAVIER, born 14th October 1793. Twin brother of Francis Robert. He entered the British army, in which he attained the rank of major. He
1813. served in Canada in 1813, during the war; in France, after the battle of Waterloo; at the Cape of Good Hope, during the Caffre war, where he was much engaged with his regiment, the 72d Highlanders. He resides at Tillydrone, Old Aberdeen.

1793. IX. FRANCIS ROBERT, born 14th October 1793. Twin brother of Louis Xavier. He entered the British army, and served in the German Legion. He joined the army in Spain under the Duke of Wellington, and was present at the battle of the Pyrenees, and
1814. during the operations in the south of France in 1814. He was at the siege of Bayonne, the battle of Toulouse, and the battle of Waterloo. He was one of the officers who took possession of the Bariere de
1815. l'Etoile at Paris in 1815. He died at Leslie Lodge,
1831. 17th July 1831.

1777. X. AMELIA, born at Kingswells 24th April 1777;
1801. married in 1801 to Alexander Fraser, Esq. of Strichen, by whom she had a son, Thomas Alexander,
1860. Lord Lovat. She died 27th August 1860.

1778. XI. HARRIET ANN, born at Tullos 24th November 1778.
1805. She died unmarried at Fetternear 6th June 1805, and was buried in the old chapel there.

1783. XII. TERESA FRANCES, born 27th March 1783. She died unmarried at Fetternear, of a decline, 31st May
1801. 1801.

1786. XIII. HELEN, born at Fetternear 17th May 1786. She died unmarried at Edinburgh of a decline, 20th
1811. December 1811, and was buried in the Canongate church.

XIV. VIOLET WINEFRED, born at Fetternear 18th April
1789. 1789. She is unmarried, and resides in Aberdeen.

XV. MARGARET CATHERINE, born 5th June 1790. She died unmarried, of a decline, at Leslie Lodge, 4th September 1830, and was buried in the old chapel at Fetternear.

CHAP. I.

John, Twenty-second Baron of Balquhain.

John Leslie, twenty-second Baron of Balquhain, died 27th February 1828, aged seventy-seven, and was succeeded by his eldest son Ernest, Count Leslie, twenty-third Baron of Balquhain. After the death of her husband, Mrs. Violet Leslie went to live at Leslie Lodge, or Aquhorties, where she died, 23d September 1836, in the eighty-eighth year of her age. This venerable lady was upwards of sixty years resident on the estate of Balquhain, beloved and respected by all classes in the country. She retained all her faculties to the last; and as she possessed a peculiarly retentive memory, her conversation was most interesting and entertaining, especially when she related stories of 1715 and 1745, which she had heard from her relations and friends, many of whom had suffered in the Stuart cause. She used to tell how she and her sisters dressed themselves up in the cloak and gown of the brave Countess of Nithsdale, in which her husband, the Earl, effected his escape from the Tower of London—the relics being preserved in the Castle of Terregles, of which her father had a lease from the Nithsdale family. She used also to tell how, when she was at school at the convent at York, the head of her grandfather, Lord Kenmure, still

See App. No. XXVI.

1836.

1715-45.

CHAP. I.

John, Twenty-second Baron of Balquhain.

remained on the Michaelgate Bar, and when it was taken down by order of the government, all the people congratulated her.

Ernest, Count Leslie, Twenty-third Baron of Balquhain.

ERNEST, COUNT LESLIE,

TWENTY-THIRD BARON OF BALQUHAIN.

Ernest, eldest son of John Leslie, twenty-second Baron of Balquhain, by his wife Violet Dalzell, succeeded as twenty-third Baron of Balquhain,
1828. on the death of his father, 27th February 1828.

Ernest Leslie was born at Terregles Castle 28th
1775-88. November 1775. In 1788 he was sent, with his brother John, to the Scotch college at Ratisbon for his education. Having finished his studies there, he determined to make the army his profession. Being precluded at that period by his religion from entering the British army, he resolved to enter the Austrian service. He did this the more willingly, as several members of the family had risen to great distinction in
1795. that service. In 1795, when he was twenty years of age, he joined La Tour's Dragoons as a cadet. In the following year he served at the siege of Kehle, and was promoted to the rank of
1798. lieutenant. In 1798 he served with his regiment in Bohemia, as appears by a letter written to his mother by his brother John, dated at Padua, 1st
1798-9. February 1798. In April 1799 he returned to Scotland to visit his friends. He left Fetternear,

Ernest, Count Leslie, Twenty-third Baron of Balquhain.

23d September 1799, for Edinburgh, but not finding a vessel there, he returned to Aberdeen, and sailed from thence to Hamburg, 3d October 1799, and reached that city on the 7th after a stormy passage of four days. On the 27th he was at Nuremberg, and in November he was in Augsburg. He was appointed to Hohenloe's Dragoons, and was present at the battle of Hohenlinden, fought 3d December 1800. In 1803 he was at Horodenka, as appears by a letter written to him by his agent at Vienna, 10th February 1803, informing him that he had 335 florins to be forwarded to him. In 1803 he again returned to Scotland. He arrived at Aberdeen in a ship from Dantzig. His brother Charles went aboard to meet him, and next day he went out to Fetternear, where he met his brother John for the first time since they had left the college at Ratisbon. He was present at a dinner given on the occasion of his nephew, Thomas Alexander Fraser of Strichen, now Lord Lovat, being served heir to his father. He returned to Germany, and was employed in partisan service. When General Mack surrendered with the Austrian army at Ulm, Lieutenant Leslie had the good fortune to give timely notice of the disaster to Prince Ferdinand of Austria, who was marching with an army to join General Mack, and thus a portion of the Austrian army was saved. Afterwards Lieutenant Leslie was made a captain in Prince Ferdinand's

1800-3.

1803.

CHAP. I.

Ernest, Count Leslie, Twenty-third Baron of Balquhain.

Hussars. In 1806 he got a troop in Mehrfeldt's Hulans or Lancers. In 1809 he was appointed to a squadron in Prince Ferdinand's Hussars. He was present at the battles of Eckmuhl and Ratisbon in April 1809, and at Aspen, Eslang,
1809-11. and Wagram, in June 1809. In 1811, he was in Upper Hungary.

When the Emperor Napoleon compelled Austria to join him, and to declare against England, and commenced his campaign against Russia, Ernest Leslie, not wishing to serve in the army of a power which was then acting against his country, obtained leave of absence. He returned to Scotland with his wife, the Baroness Fanny Stillfried, whom he had just married. So strictly were Napoleon's decrees of blockade of the ports of Europe against England observed, that he had considerable difficulty in leaving the Continent. He was obliged to travel under an assumed name, and at last he reached Denmark, from whence he
1813. succeeded in embarking for Scotland. In 1813 he again left Scotland, and went to Prague, where he left his wife and joined his regiment. Soon afterwards he was promoted to a majority in Mehrfeldt's Hulans, and was present at the
1813. battle of Dresden, 17th August 1813. He was wounded on the following day, and was taken prisoner and sent to France. In passing through Verdun he received assistance from Captain Pattison of the 29th British regiment. He was

Ernest, Count Leslie, Twenty-third Baron of Balquhain.

released at the peace of Paris in May 1814, when he returned to Prague. In 1816 he again visited Scotland, and on the 31st May 1817 he was again at Prague in Bohemia. Soon afterwards he went to Brussels, where his wife's aunt, the Baroness de Mirwart, lived. At her death she left him her house and plate and some lands in the Ardennes, which, being wooded and wild, he sold far under their value to Mr. Cockerel, who found coal there, and made a large fortune. In 1825 Ernest Leslie again visited Fetternear. In 1825.
1831 he took up his residence there. In 1834 1831-34.
he went to live at Frankfort.

Ernest Leslie assumed the title of Count, which had been so long borne by the German branch of the family, and the title was allowed him by the Austrian government, who addressed him in all official and military documents as Count Ernest Leslie; and as such he appears in the *Almanach de Gotha,* among the Counts of the Holy Roman Empire.

Count Ernest Leslie married, 22d January 1812, 1812.
at Cassorie, in Upper Hungary, the Baroness Fanny Stillfried, daughter of Emmanuel, Baron Stillfried, Chamberlain of the Emperor and Knight of Malta, by his wife Teresa, Baroness Steinbach. She was born at Horn in Austria 20th November 1794—her father, then in the 1794.
army, being stationed there. By her Count Ernest Leslie had issue—

CHAP. I.

Ernest, Count Leslie, Twenty-third Baron of Balquhain.

1839.

I. John Edward, who succeeded him as twenty-fourth Baron of Balquhain.

II. Augusta, born 30th May 1815, at Prague, and died there 2d April 1839.

III. Mary, born 17th January 1817, at Aberdeen. She married, 21st October 1839, Edward, Baron Stillfried, her cousin, then aide-de-camp to General Baron Staner. She has one daughter, Francisca.

Count Ernest Leslie, twenty-third Baron of
1836. Balquhain, died at Frankfort 15th March 1836, and was buried there with military honours. Afterwards his body was brought to Scotland, and was buried in the old chapel at Fetternear,
1837. 19th September 1837. He was succeeded by his son John Edward, Count Leslie, twenty-fourth Baron of Balquhain.

John Edward, Count Leslie, Twenty-fourth Baron of Balquhain.

JOHN EDWARD, COUNT LESLIE,

TWENTY-FOURTH BARON OF BALQUHAIN.

John Edward Leslie, born at Brussels 22d
1820. June 1820, son of Ernest, Count Leslie, twenty-third Baron of Balquhain, by his wife the Baroness Fanny Stillfried, succeeded as twenty-fourth Baron of Balquhain, on the death of his father,
1836. 15th March 1836.

Count John Edward Leslie was sent to the Catholic college of Oscot, near Birmingham, for
1828-34. his education, in 1828. In 1834 he left college, and was sent to Wiesbaden to finish his education

when his parents went to live at Frankfort. After the death of his father in 1836, he entered the Austrian service as a cadet. In the Austrian Army-list for 1843, we find Herr Graff John Edward Leslie, as a lieutenant in the 9th Regiment of Hussars, of which Nicholas, Emperor of Russia, was colonel.

CHAP. I.

John Edward, Count Leslie, Twenty-fourth Baron of Balquhain.

Count John Edward Leslie became of age 22d June 1841. He returned to Scotland in July of that year to take possession of his estates; on which occasion the tenantry, to testify their respect for their landlord, entertained him at dinner at the old castle of Balquhain, when his cousin Lord Lovat and all the neighbouring gentry joined the tenants in welcoming the young Count.
In October 1841 Count Leslie was present at the Inverness meeting. 1841.
In the following winter he went abroad and travelled in Belgium, France, and Italy, and visited Rome. In 1842 he re- 1842.
turned to Scotland, and was present at the Aberdeen steeple-chases, and at the Inverness meeting and races of that year. In the winter he went to live at Manheim, in the Grand Duchy of Baden, where he became acquainted with Mr. Greville, then visiting the Grand-Duchess Stephanie of Baden, and he proposed to marry Mr. Greville's daughter, who was companion to the Princess Mary Amelia of Baden, who married the Duke of Hamilton. But the intended marriage was broken off.

CHAP. I.

John Edward, Count Leslie, Twenty-fourth Baron of Balquhain.

1844. In 1843 Count Leslie returned to Scotland, and was present at the races and ball held at Aberdeen 30th March, and at the steeple-chases and fancy ball held there during the following winter; and also at the Aberdeen races, 24th May 1844.

Count John Edward Leslie went out to shoot grouse on the hill of Bennachie, with his friend

1844. Mr. Gordon of Nethermuir, 12th August 1844. When he was overheated he drank a glass of cold water from one of the springs on the hill. Inflammation ensued, and he died in consequence,

1844. 19th August 1844. He was succeeded by his uncle James Michael Leslie, twenty-fifth Baron of Balquhain.

The following lines by William Thom, the Inverurie poet, were written on the death of John Edward, Count Leslie, and were published in the second edition of Thom's *Poems*, p. 67 :—

LINES OCCASIONED BY THE SUDDEN DEATH OF COUNT JOHN LESLIE OF BALQUHAIN AND FETTERNEAR,

1844. AUGUST 1844.

Beloved by all—cut off in the dawn of manhood—he was borne to the grave by a weeping tenantry.

OH why? but God alone knows why—
Do churls cling aye to earth,
While the brave, and the just, and the generous die—
The hour that owns their worth?
Alas! and woe! so sad, so true,
The blink that's brightest, briefest too.

CHAP. I.

John Edward, Count Leslie, Twenty-fourth Baron of Balquhain.

'Twas a dolefu' dawn yon morning saw
On the turrets of brown Balquhain,
When the Leslie lay on red Harlaw,
Wi' his six good sons a' slain;
But nane less leal the sigh and the tear,
And the waesome hearts round Fetternear.

Don's waters deftly wandered on
Sae wantonly and sae clear,
And dazzling danced beneath the sun
That gleamed o'er Fetternear;
While the lov'd of the land is bounding away,
Like his own bold stream, to the risen day.

O bid him bide, ye birdies that sing,
Or bid him nae fend sae fast;
Haud back your tears, ye witchfu' spring,
Whase waters weird his last: *
But away and away, he bodes a bier,
For the woods look fay round Fetternear.

We lend no lay to living man,
Nor sing for fee or fear;
Our cheek, though pale, yet never faun
The stain of a mimic tear:
In *truth* we mourn the bud that sprung,
Unblossom'd, blighted, fair, and young.

JAMES MICHAEL LESLIE,

TWENTY-FIFTH BARON OF BALQUHAIN.

James Michael Leslie, Twenty-fifth Baron of Balquhain.

1784.

JAMES MICHAEL LESLIE, born at Fetternear 25th April 1784, fourth son of John Leslie, twenty-

* Alluding to the spring, the water of which Count Leslie drank while overheated, and which caused his death.

CHAP. I.

James Michael Leslie, Twenty-fifth Baron of Balquhain.

second Baron of Balquhain, by Violet Dalzell his wife, succeeded his nephew, John Edward, Count Leslie, twenty-fourth Baron of Balquhain, as twenty-fifth Baron, 19th August 1844.

1796. James Michael Leslie went to the grammar-school in Aberdeen for his education in 1796. On finishing his education he was sent to Liverpool, where he entered a West India mercantile house; but, having no turn for mercantile pursuits, he went to Jamaica—then the most flourishing of the British colonies—where he acquired some property. On his accession to the estate of Balquhain, he returned to Scotland to take possession in 1845. (1845.) He roofed the remains of the old chapel at Fetternear, which was used as the family burial-vault, and adjoining to it he built a new chapel.

1849. James Michael Leslie was a magistrate and deputy-lieutenant of Aberdeenshire. He never married. He died at Fetternear 2d January 1849, and was succeeded by his brother Colonel Charles Leslie, K.H., twenty-sixth Baron of Balquhain.

Colonel Charles Leslie, K.H., Twenty-sixth Baron of Balquhain.

COLONEL CHARLES LESLIE, K.H.,

TWENTY-SIXTH BARON OF BALQUHAIN.

COLONEL CHARLES LESLIE, K.H., fifth son of John Leslie, twenty-second Baron of Balquhain, by his wife Violet Dalzell, succeeded his brother James

Michael Leslie as twenty-sixth Baron of Balquhain, 2d January 1849.

Colonel Charles Leslie, K.H., Twenty-sixth Baron of Balquhain.

Charles Leslie was sent to the grammar-school in Aberdeen for his education, and there he was a fellow-student with Lord Byron. He entered the army, and served with the 29th Regiment in the Peninsula, under the Duke of Wellington; and was present at the battles of Roleca, Vimiera, Oporto, Talavera, Albuera, the siege of Badajos, the Lines of Torres Vedras, Redenha, besides various other affairs and skirmishes, for which he received the Peninsular war-medal and four clasps. He was severely wounded at the battle of Talavera, and he has still the musket-ball in his right leg.

Colonel Charles Leslie is a Knight of the Royal Hanoverian Guelphic Order, a Colonel in the army, late of the Grenadier Guards, and a deputy-lieutenant and magistrate in Derbyshire and Aberdeenshire.

Colonel Leslie married, first, 24th November 1826, Mary Holloway, daughter of Major-General Sir Charles Holloway. By her, who died 3d October 1832, he had issue— 1826. 1832.

I. John Charles, born 3d September 1827, at London, and died on the same day. 1827.

II. Charles Stephen, born at Omagh in Ireland 28th April 1832. He married, in 1853, Jane, daughter of John Rounding, Esq., by whom he has issue— 1832-53.

I. Violet Winefred, born 25th August 1856. 1856.

CHAP. I.

Colonel Charles Leslie, K.H., Twenty-sixth Baron of Balquhain.

II. CHARLES RADCLIFF, born 3d November 1857; died 9th March 1858.

III. CHARLES RADCLIFF ALOYSIUS, born 13th May 1859.

IV. ANTHONY IGNATIUS, born 7th February 1861; died 31st December 1861.

1862. V. DOROTHY, born 10th July 1862.

1864. VI. MARY GEORGINA, born 3d December 1864; died
1865. 26th January 1865.

VII. MARY JOSEPH FRANCES, born at Slindon Hall,
1866. Sussex, 15th April 1866.

VIII. MARY TERESA, born at Hassop Hall, Derbyshire,
1867. 7th October 1867.

IX. JOHN CUTHBERT EYRE LESLIE, born at Slindon
1869. Hall, Sussex, 24th April 1869.

Colonel Leslie married, secondly, 21st July
1836. 1836, the Right Honourable Lady Dorothy Eyre, eldest daughter of Francis, sixth Earl of Newburgh, and granddaughter of Charles Radcliff, Earl of Derwentwater. She succeeded as Countess of Newburgh, on the death of her brother Francis,
1852. eighth earl, in October 1852. She died 22d
1853. November 1853, leaving Hassop, Slindon, and all her other estates in the counties of Derby, Sussex, Gloucester, and Northumberland, to her husband Colonel Leslie, whom she appointed her sole executor.

CHAPTER II.

WALTER,

FIRST COUNT LESLIE.

Walter, First Count Leslie.

THE family of the Counts Leslie of the Holy Roman Empire is descended from the ancient family of Leslie of Balquhain in Scotland. Walter, first Count Leslie, was the second son of John Leslie, tenth Baron of Balquhain, by his third wife, Jean Erskine, daughter of Sir Alexander Erskine, Baron of Gogar, and sister of Thomas, first Earl of Kelly. He was born in 1606, and went over to Germany when he was but a youth, and entered the Imperial service, in which he served with great distinction and honour in the war against the Swedes during the reign of the Emperor Ferdinand II. 1606.

After the death of Count Tilly, Wallenstein was reappointed to the command of the Imperial army, and immediately began operations against Gustavus Adolphus, who had intrenched himself at Nürnberg. Wallenstein appeared before Nürnberg 26th June 1632. Finding Gustavus entrenched, when urged to attack him, Wallen- 1632.

CHAP. II. *Walter, First Count Leslie.* stein said that battles enough had been fought already, and that it was time to try another method. He resolved, therefore, to subdue by famine those whom he could not subdue by arms, and with great judgment took up a position about five miles to the south-west of Nürnberg, so as very much to narrow and nearly block up the channels through which Gustavus received his supplies.*

We find in Grant's *Memoirs and Adventures of Sir John Hepburn*, who served in the Swedish army under Gustavus Adolphus, that on the 28th
1632. July 1632, Gustavus Adolphus, having received powerful reinforcements, and provisions becoming scarce in the camp and city, "marched one thousand musketeers and eight hundred horse to Bergtheim, to cover an attack that Colonel M'Dougal (whose *nom de guerre* was Dewbattel) was about to make on an Imperial magazine. These fell suddenly on the forces of Sparre, a sergeant-major *di battaglia,* whom Wallenstein had ordered to drive back M'Dougal. Sparre led his own regiment of musketeers, four troops of Gonzaga's horse, and four of Coloredo's, with twenty squadrons of Croatians, and a thousand Scottish and Irish musketeers, led by Colonel Gordon and Major Lesly, two Scottish officers who served the Emperor.

"Among the rough and rocky ground, three

* Mitchell's *Life of Wallenstein*, p. 254.

miles from Altenburg, a long and desperate but desultory conflict ensued between these forces and those of Gustavus, which were ultimately successful. Each after the other the Imperial regiments were swept away in succession, and the one thousand musketeers of Gordon and Lesly alone stood firm, maintaining their posts behind every tree, rock, and wall, with the most steady gallantry. Gustavus frequently applauded their valour, and declared that if these were Scots and fell into his hands as prisoners, he would release them unransomed: adding that, if all the Imperialists had fought as well, he must have lost the field that day.

"Long and resolutely these brave Scots and Irish fought side by side, and from the cover of a thick wood kept the Swedish troops in check until the mass of their less gallant comrades, the Germans, had effected a safe retreat; but on the flight of Gonzaga (whom, although the nephew of the Empress, Wallenstein tried by a court-martial), being left single-handed, Sparre, Colonel Gordon, and Major Lesly, were taken prisoners, and brought to the Swedish camp. Having on a former occasion violated his parole of honour, the first officer remained a prisoner; but three days after, Gordon and Lesly were released by the Swedish conqueror, who complimented them on their valour and spirit. Hepburn, Munro, and other Scottish officers, would not allow them to

CHAP. II.

Walter, First Count Leslie.

return for five weeks, during which time they had to visit and make merry with them all in succession, and were not permitted to bid adieu to Nürnberg until Gustavus was preparing to attack the Imperialists.

"They returned to the camp of Wallenstein; and these were the two Scottish officers who, on the treachery of that great noble being discovered, so boldly slew him in the now ruined castle of Eger in Bohemia.

"Colonel Gordon was a presbyterian, yet he was created a Marquis of the Empire, Colonel-General of the Imperial Army, and bearer of the gold key as High Chamberlain to the Emperor.

"Major Walter Lesly was the youngest son of Lesly of Balquhain in the Garioch: he was captain of the body-guards and colonel of a regiment. By the Emperor Ferdinand III. he was created Count Lesly, and Lord of Neustadt in Bohemia, an estate worth two hundred thousand florins. He became a Field-Marshal, Governor of Sclavonia, and Knight of the Golden Fleece,—an order which he received from Leopold I. before his departure as ambassador to Constantinople."*

Walter Leslie served with great reputation under Wallenstein during all his splendid exploits.

* *Memoirs and Adventures of Sir John Hepburn, Knight, Governor of Munich, Marshal of France under Louis XIII., and Commander of the Scots Brigade under Gustavus Adolphus,* by James Grant, pp. 188-190.

CHAP. II.

Walter, First Count Leslie.

He was one of the captains of his guards, and was very much in his confidence. But when Wallenstein's ambitious views and his treasonable design of betraying the Emperor and the Imperial army to the enemy, as discovered by his letters to the Swedes, became known, and appeared to be fully confirmed by the movement to Eger, towards the enemy, Walter Leslie found that he was called to choose between treason and duty—between a legitimate sovereign and a fugitive rebel; and although Wallenstein had been his benefactor, yet he felt that his choice could not be doubtful, and that he was bound to lend his aid to frustrate the traitor's designs, and to secure him as a prisoner.

On arriving at Eger in the suite of the Duke, Walter Leslie revealed the designs of Wallenstein to Colonel Gordon, a Scotchman, who was commandant of the town, and to Colonel Butler, who commanded a regiment of dragoons, and who had also come to Eger with the Duke. They resolved on the bold step of taking Wallenstein prisoner, and delivering him up alive to the Emperor. However, when Wallenstein imparted to them his resolution of delivering Eger and the passes of the kingdom into the hands of the enemy, the Palatine of Birkenfield, and told them that he expected the immediate approach of Duke Bernard of Weimar, they altered their plan. The urgency of the case admitted no delay, as Eger

CHAP. II.

Walter, First Count Leslie.

might be in the hands of the enemy at any moment. To prevent such a misfortune, they resolved to put Wallenstein's chief associates to death.

In execution of this design, Colonel Gordon, the commandant, and Colonel Butler, invited Wallenstein and his friends, Counts Illo, Terczka, and Kinsky, and Rittmeister Naumann, to an entertainment to be given in the citadel the next evening. They all came except Wallenstein, who was too agitated to enjoy company, and who seldom joined such convivial parties. The guests were in high spirits at the thought of being beyond the reach of their enemies, meaning the Emperor's faithful generals. But after the dessert was placed, parties of dragoons, who had been placed in rooms at opposite ends of the saloon, rushed in with drawn sabres, shouting, "Viva! viva! la Casa di Austria! Wer ist gut Kaiserlich!" Butler, Gordon, and Leslie immediately sprang up, and called out, "Vivat Ferdinandus!" The unfortunate guests, surprised and thunderstruck, said nothing, and the dragoons immediately attacked them and cut them down.

Walter Leslie hastened to the town below to prevent tumult. He declared to the different guards the whole circumstances of Wallenstein's conspiracy, and the means which were already taken to frustrate it by the fall of the four officers. He exacted from the troops an oath to be faithful to the Emperor, and admitted into the town one

CHAP. II.

Walter, First Count Leslie.

hundred dragoons, to whom he gave orders to patrol and maintain tranquillity. A detachment was sent to surround Wallenstein's residence, to prevent him from escaping or receiving assistance, it still being the intention to secure him alive as a prisoner.

However, after the tragedy in the citadel, a council was held to consider what was to be done. Colonel Gordon raised a feeble voice in the cause of humanity, to save the life of Wallenstein. But his scruples were overruled by Butler, who represented the near approach of the Swedes and Saxons, and urged that the only chance of the final success of the Emperor's cause lay in the immediate death of the Duke. Towards midnight, Colonel Butler, taking with him Captain Devereux and six Hollanders, went to Wallenstein's quarters, as if to call on him. The guards allowed him to enter, and while Butler remained below, Captain Devereux and his party burst into the chambers of the Duke, who, alarmed by the noise, was standing half-dressed at a window. Seeing their design of taking his life, he threw his arms wide open, and received the deadly thrusts in his breast, and fell down dead without a groan, 25th February 1634. 1634.

Walter Leslie was despatched to Vienna to convey to the Emperor the important intelligence of Wallenstein's death and the defeat of his conspiracy. For his fidelity on this occasion the Emperor Ferdinand II. made him captain of

CHAP. II. *Walter First Count Leslie.* 1637. his body-guard, the colonel of a regiment, and governor of a garrison; and also bestowed on him other testimonies of imperial favour. Ferdinand III., who succeeded his father as Emperor in 1637, also held Walter Leslie in great esteem, and presented him with the lordship of Neustadt in Bohemia, valued at 200,000 florins; created him a Count of the Holy Roman Empire, Lord of Neustadt and Pittau, by a patent dated 15th

1637. March 1637; made him Imperial Chamberlain, Privy Councillor, Lieutenant and Governor of Verusden, and Warden of the borders or confines of Sclavonia and Petrinia, and a Field-Marshal of the Imperial army. The Emperor Leopold I. created him a Knight of the Golden Fleece.

Walter Count Leslie's patent of the dignity of Count of the Holy Roman Empire was granted to him and his two brothers, William and Alexander, and their heirs, that, in case he died without issue, they might succeed him in his titles and estates.

Being possessed of great wealth, Count Walter Leslie frequently remitted sums of money to his brother Count Alexander Leslie, fourteenth Baron of Balquhain, and his nephew Count Patrick Leslie, fifteenth Baron, and enabled them to retrieve their estates, then very much embarrassed by the extravagance of former possessors.

After the victory gained by the Imperial General Montecuculi against the Turks at St. Gotthard, on the banks of the Raab, 1st August

CHAP. II.

Walter, First Count Leslie.

1664, Count Walter Leslie was sent as Imperial Ambassador Extraordinary and Plenipotentiary by the Emperor Leopold I. to the Sublime Porte, for the purpose of adjusting the terms of a lasting peace. Count Leslie arranged everything relating to the embassy on the most magnificent scale. His retinue was the most splendid which ever went from Europe to Constantinople, and amongst those who accompanied him was Lord Henry Howard, afterwards fifth Earl of Arundel. They proceeded in great state down the Danube in gay barges to Presburg and Buda, and arrived at Belgrade, from whence they proceeded in state-coaches by easy journeys through Samandria, Nissa, Philippopolis, to Adrianople. Two hundred waggons were employed to convey the baggage. The entrance into Constantinople bore all the characteristics of a triumphal march. Indeed, so superb was his brilliant *cortége*, that the Grand Signor himself, who beheld from a window the entry into the seraglio, where he received them, and granted the Count an audience, was heard to say that in all his life he never saw so splendid a show, as is related in Monsieur Riccati's preface to his book on Turkish fashions, where he speaks of Count Leslie in terms of high commendation.

An account of this embassy was published at Vienna, in 1672, by the Rev. Father Paul Tafferner, a Jesuit, who had been chaplain to Count

CHAP. II.

Walter, First Count Leslie.

Walter Leslie. In this work, dedicated to Count Walter's nephew and successor, James, second Count Leslie, Walter Leslie is styled Count of the Holy Roman Empire, Imperial Legate to the Ottoman Porte, Lord of Pittau and Neustadt on the Moldau, Imperial Privy Councillor, Member of the Aulic Council, Field-Marshal, and General of the Marches of Sclavonia and Petrinia. An account of the embassy was also written by John Burbury, in his "Relation of a Journey of the Right Honourable Lord Henry Howard, and his brother the Honourable Edward Howard, from London to Vienna, and thence to Constantinople, in the suite of his Excellency Count Leslie, Knight of the Golden Fleece, Councillor of State to his Imperial Majesty, Ambassador-Extraordinary from Leopold, Emperor of Germany, to the Grand Signor Sultan Mahomet Hau the Fourth. By
1671. John Burbury. Printed in London, 1671."

1640. Count Walter Leslie married, in 1640, the Princess Anne Francisca de Dietrichstein, daughter of Maximilian, Prince de Dietrichstein, Prime Minister and Grand-Chamberlain to the Emperor; with her he received considerable possessions. Having no issue, he entailed his estates on his nephew, Count James, eldest son of his brother, Count Alexander Leslie, fourteenth Baron of Balquhain, and his heirs-male; whom failing, on Patrick Leslie, younger son of the said Count Alexander Leslie, and his heirs-male; failing whom, on the heirs-male of his father-in-law, Maximilian, Prince Dietrichstein; failing whom, on the heirs-female of the said James and Patrick Leslie, his nephews, when the entail was to be exhausted. CHAP. II. *Walter, First Count Leslie.* *See* App. No. XXVII.

Walter, Count Leslie, died at Vienna 4th March 1667, aged sixty-one years, and was buried with great pomp in the Leslie chapel in the Scotch Benedictine Abbey there. He was succeeded by his nephew James, second Count Leslie. 1667.

JAMES,

James, Second Count Leslie.

SECOND COUNT LESLIE.

James, Count Leslie, eldest son of Alexander, Count Leslie, fourteenth Baron of Balquhain, by his wife Jean Elphinstone of Glack, succeeded as second Count Leslie in Germany on the death of his uncle Walter, Count Leslie, 4th March 1667. 1667.

When but a youth, he was called over to Germany by his uncle Count Walter Leslie, in 1655. Count Walter, having no children, adopted him as his heir, and gave him a finished education, 1655. to complete which he sent him to travel through Germany, Poland, France, Spain, and Italy. When his education was completed, he entered the Austrian service, in which he greatly distinguished himself, and gained the highest honours. He was much esteemed by the Emperor Leopold, who appointed him one of the gentlemen of the Imperial bed-chamber in 1660, and, in the same 1660.

CHAP. II.

James, Second Count Leslie.

year, gave him the gold key as Chamberlain. We find by the Austrian Army-list that Major General Count James Leslie was colonel or proprietor of the Galizisches Infantry Regiment, No.
1665-75. 24, from 1665 to 1675, during which period it was called Leslie's Regiment, after his name. Count James Leslie was afterwards raised to the rank of Field-Marshal, and in the Austrian Army-list it is stated that Field-Marshal Count James
1675. Leslie in 1675 raised the Bohemian Infantry Regiment, No. 36, and remained colonel of it till
1694. his death in 1694, when Prince Philip Erasmus de Lichtenstein got the regiment.

Count James Leslie held a distinguished command under the generalissimo of the Imperial forces, the Duke of Lorraine, during the famous siege of Vienna by the Turks under Kara Mustapha, when the siege was raised and the city delivered by John Sobieski, King of Poland. The Turks began the siege 16th July, and were compelled to raise it 12th September 1683. John Sobieski, King of Poland, passed the Danube,
1683. 8th September 1683, at Kremps, and gained the heights of Calemberg on the right bank of the river above Vienna. On the 11th September he moved down to prepare to attack the enemy, and on arriving in the evening at the plain at the foot of Camaldoli, he ordered Count Leslie to take post with his troops at the opening of a wood which extended to Vienna, and to erect a battery to

secure the pass. Count Leslie's gallantry was most conspicuous on this occasion. The city being in great distress on account of the want of men and provisions, he seized a favourable opportunity and broke through the Turkish army, and threw a large force and supplies into the city, and thus afforded a most seasonable reinforcement and relief, which greatly contributed to the success of the Imperialists. In the battle which took place the following day, 12th September 1683, the Turks were completely defeated and were obliged to raise the siege. The banner of Mohammed was taken and sent to the Pope as a trophy, and Count Leslie received much valuable spoil; amongst others were cloths of gold and silver brocade, which were made into church vestments and sent to Fetternear, where they are still preserved; and also jewelled arms, which were also sent to Fetternear, and remain there. These church vestments and jewelled Turkish arms, and the portraits of Counts Walter and James Leslie, also preserved at Fetternear, were exhibited during the meeting of the British Association held in Aberdeen in 1859, and were especially noticed by the late Prince-Consort.

1683.

1859.

In 1685 Count James Leslie was sent to act on the Drave, having a body of Croats under his command. He stormed and took Verovilaze, and having defeated the Turkish army, he drove the enemy out of Essick, and took possession of the

1685.

CHAP. II. *James, Second Count Leslie.* town. But the castle or citadel holding out, and he being pressed for time, he blew up the Turkish magazines, plundered the town, burned the famous bridge, and recovered great part of Hungary.

Essick is a large and populous city in eastern Sclavonia. It lies very low, and the streets are planked or paved with wood instead of stones. It is a place of great commerce, being the principal thoroughfare between Turkey and Hungary. It is not naturally a strong place, but the Turks bestowed great pains in fortifying it. It is remarkable for its bridges, built of oak, one being 8565 paces long and 17 paces broad. Leading from the city it passes over the Save, through broad marshes, and across the river Tennes, to the fort of Darda in Lower Hungary. Another bridge leads from Essick over the Drave and the marshes on each side of the river, which bridge is five miles long, and so broad that three waggons may go abreast. It had wooden fortified towers every quarter of a mile. These bridges were
1521. erected by Solyman the Magnificent, in 1521, after he had taken Belgrade. By them the Turkish armies were enabled to pass from Constantinople into Hungary. Near this place the unfortunate Louis, King of Hungary, was defeated in attempting to arrest Solyman's passage into his kingdom. The latter bridge was the one burned by Count Leslie, and it was again
1687. destroyed by the Duke of Lorraine in 1687.

James, Second Count Leslie.

Soon after this exploit, Count Leslie, suffering much from gout and ill-health, was obliged to relinquish his command. During his long services he performed many glorious achievements, especially during the last two years of his command against the Turks. Indeed, in twenty pitched battles in which he commanded against the Turks, he always came off victorious. Prince Louis of Baden was bred under his orders. The *Historical Observer and Fun*, published by Sir John Lauder of Fountainhall, from 1680 to 1687, gives the following account of the siege of Vienna, and the war against the Turks which followed:— 1680-87.

"On the 2d September 1683, Vienna had been besieged by a Turkish army, 150,000 strong, for upwards of two months, under Cara Mustapha Bassa, the Grand Vizier. The Turks had at one time gotten possession of the Scotch part (so called from a monastery there founded by Scotsmen, and whereof the foundation required Scotsmen to be abbots), standing near the river Vien, which there falls into the Danube. But Count Starenberg, a Swede, defended it with great courage, until the last extremity of famine, with bloody and diminished numbers. 1683.

"At last, the Christian army commanded by the Duke of Lorraine, John Sobieski King of Poland, the Electors of Bavaria and Saxony, attacked and defeated the Ottoman forces, taking 120 cannon, many standards, all the baggage, rich

CHAP. II.

James, Second Count Leslie.

tents, etc. The Christians sustained but small loss, there not being above 1000 killed, and few of them of note, except our countryman, young Count Leslie, Alexander.

1684. "In June and July 1684, the Imperial forces, under the Duke of Lorraine and Count James Leslie, defeated the Turkish forces, forcing them to abandon Vacerse, Vuvitzie, and Pest. They then besieged the city of Buda, the capital of Hungary, took the lower town, and drove the Turks into the higher town and castle.

1685. "In the summer of 1685 it proved very fatal to the Ottomans, because, besides the defeats they sustained in Greece by Morofine, general of the Republic of Venice, our valiant countryman, James, Count Leslie, of the house of Balquhain, defeated the Turks at the Bridge of Essick, so that the Serasqueer Basha, by a letter closed up in satin to the Duke of Lorraine, humbly asked for peace."*

Count James Leslie was several times employed as ambassador on important missions to different foreign courts. He was a Privy Councillor, and was appointed Governor of Lower Austria, and President of the Council of War of that province. In the *Laurus Leslæana, or History of the Family of Leslie*, written by his brother, the Rev. William Leslie, and dedicated to him, Count James Leslie is styled "Illustrissimus et Excellen-

* *Historical Observer and Fun*, pp. 106, 136, 218.

James, Second Count Leslie.

tissimus Dominus Jacobus, Sancti Romani Imperii Comes de Leslie, Liber Baro de Balquhane, Dominus Neostadii ad Mettoviam, Pettovii, Pernegg, etc. S. C. M. Camerarius et Consiliarius actualis intimus, concilii Aulae bellici int. Aust. praeses, Generalis Campi Mareschallus, Pedestris Regiminis Colonellus, etc.

Count James Leslie married, in 1666-7, the Princess Maria Teresa de Lichtenstein, daughter of Charles Eusebius, Prince de Lichtenstein and Duke of Troppau. Their marriage was celebrated in the most magnificent manner. The Emperor Leopold, the Empress Margaret Teresa, and all the principal nobility of the court, attended the marriage out of respect to him and his uncle, Count Walter. The expenses incurred on the occasion were estimated at 50,000 rix-dollars, which were defrayed by Count Walter Leslie. 1666-7.

But there was no issue by this marriage, and after several years, Count Leslie, finding that it was not likely he would ever have children of his own, called over from Scotland his nephew, James Ernest Leslie, the elder son of his brother, Count Patrick Leslie, fifteenth Baron of Balquhain, and adopted him as his heir. He was also in the habit of remitting sums of money to his brother, Count Patrick, to enable him to redeem the mortgaged portions of the estate of Balquhain, and to add to the property.

Count James Leslie made his will in 1690, and 1690.

CHAP. II.

James, Second Count Leslie.

appointed his nephew, James Ernest, his successor to his titles and principal estates. He bequeathed Pernegg, which he purchased himself, to his nephew, Francis James, Count Leslie, the son of his deceased younger brother, Colonel Alexander, Count Leslie, who was killed at the siege of Vienna 1683. He built a military asylum or hospital for invalided soldiers at Neostad, in Bohemia, and left his estate of Neostad for its support. He also left an annual provision to the Scotch Benedictine Abbey at Ratisbon, for the education of young Scotch gentlemen of small fortune, and particularly for those of the name of Leslie.

1683.

Count James Leslie retired from court to his country seat near Pittau. He suffered much from gout, and at last he was seized with apoplexy, which carried him off in 1694. His widow, the Princess Maria Teresa de Lichtenstein, married John Balthasar, Count Wagenberg, and died 4th February 1715-16.*

1694.

1715-16.

James Ernest, Third Count Leslie.

JAMES ERNEST,

THIRD COUNT LESLIE.

On the death of James, second Count Leslie, in 1694, his brother Patrick, Count Leslie, fifteenth Baron of Balquhain, succeeded to his honours and estates in Germany, in terms of the entail made

1694.

* Anderson's *Genealogical Tables*, No. 319, p. 565.

James Ernest, Third Count Leslie.

by Count Walter Leslie in 1667. But in 1692 and in 1700, Count Patrick Leslie made an entail by which he settled that the family estates in Germany should belong to the eldest son, and those in Scotland to the second son, so that they might always remain distinct and separate. In order to obtain the consent of his eldest son, James Ernest, to this arrangement, Count Patrick resigned the German estates to him immediately on the death of Count James Leslie; and thus James Ernest became third Count Leslie in Germany, and Count George, Count Patrick's second son, succeeded to the family estates in Scotland as sixteenth Baron of Balquhain, at Count Patrick's death in 1710. 1710.

Count James Ernest Leslie was the eldest son of Count Patrick Leslie, fifteenth Baron of Balquhain, by his first wife, Elizabeth Douglas of Bridgeford, and was born 20th June 1669. In 1669.
1686, when he was seventeen years of age, he 1686.
was sent over to Germany to his uncle, Field-Marshal James, second Count Leslie, who took most paternal charge of him, and had him educated with the utmost care. In the law-process regarding the succession to the Balquhain estates on the death of Count Ernest Leslie, eighteenth Baron of Balquhain, Jean Erskine, widow of James Moir of Stoneywood, and upwards of sixty-seven years of age, deponed that when she was four years old she went with her father and

CHAP. II.

James Ernest, Third Count Leslie.

mother, Mr. and Mrs. Erskine of Pittodrie, to the castle of Balquhain, they having been invited there to an entertainment given to the friends of the family on the occasion of James Ernest, Count Patrick Leslie's eldest son, going away to Germany, and she thought him a pretty young boy of about sixteen years of age. She recollected going with him into the garden, where was also Count Patrick's lady, his second wife, who, James Ernest told her, was not his mother. He then brought her into the castle, and showed her his own mother's picture, and Count Patrick afterwards joked her and him for remaining so long together in the garden. Several years after-
1696. wards, about 1696, Count Patrick sent her a message to come and see pictures which his son, James Ernest, her old acquaintance, had sent over from Germany, of his children, a son and a daughter. She thought there were also pictures of Count James Ernest himself and his lady. William Nicol in Blairdaff, aged 100 years, then,
1758. 1758, living on charity, deponed that James Ernest, Count Patrick Leslie's eldest son, went over to Germany previous to Count Patrick's leaving the castle of Balquhain to go to live at
1692. Fetternear, which he did about 1692.

On the death of James, second Count Leslie, as already mentioned, his brother, Count Patrick Leslie, fifteenth Baron of Balquhain, succeeded also to the family estates in Germany, and being

CHAP. II.

James Ernest, Third Count Leslie.

desirous of establishing two families, he proposed to his eldest son, James Ernest, to put him in immediate possession of the German estates, if he would consent to give up his right to the estate of Balquhain in Scotland in favour of his half-brother, George, Count Patrick's son by his second wife, Mary Irvine of Drum. James Ernest consented to this proposal, as is proved by a letter to his father, dated 9th December 1695, in which he 1695. says that if put in possession of the German estates he would have enough, and that it would be a prouder thing for the family to be represented by him in Germany and by his half-brother George in Scotland, than if both fortunes were held by the same person. But he declined to take up the title of Count during his father's lifetime. John Lumsden, writer in Edinburgh, in the law-plea which afterwards took place regarding the succession to the Balquhain estates, stated that his father, John Lumsden, who was agent for Counts Charles Cajetan and Anthony Leslie, had in his possession the disposition and resignation of the estate of Balquhain made by Count James Ernest Leslie in favour of his half-brother, George Leslie, dated 9th December 1695. 1695.

Through the influence of his uncle, Count James, Count James Ernest Leslie made a high matrimonial alliance. He married, in 1692, the 1692. Princess Berne Maria Aloysia de Lichtenstein,

CHAP. II.

James Ernest, Third Count Leslie.

the daughter of Prince Maximilian James Maurice de Lichtenstein, and widow of Francis William, Count of Hohen Ems, who died 27th August 1691. By her he had issue—

1695. I. COUNT JOSEPH PATRICK SIGISMUND, born 1695, who
1719. married, 26th June 1719, Anna Josepha Maria Eleanora, Duchess d'Eggenberg, who was born 20th
1694. April 1694. By her he had an only daughter,
1738. Charlotte, who died of small-pox, unmarried in 1738.
1732. Count Joseph died before his father in 1732.

1696. II. COUNT CHARLES CAJETAN, born 1696, who succeeded his father as fourth Count Leslie.

III. MARIA ANTONIA.*

It appears by a letter written by Lady Betty Leslie, abbess of the Ursuline convent at Lisle, fourth daughter of Count Patrick Leslie of Balquhain, and sister of Count James Ernest Leslie,
1756. dated at Lisle, 15th July 1756, and addressed to Captain John Grant, Pension sur South Holland dans Gertrudenberg, that Count James Ernest Leslie had come with his two sons, Joseph and Charles Cajetan, to Flanders to visit her; and that her half-brother, George Leslie of Balquhain, and James Leslie of Pitcaple, had met them there. She writes, "With regard to my nephews, the two Counts Leslie of Germany (Joseph and Charles Cajetan), with whom you came to see me with your cousin Mr. Leslie (of Pitcaple), both

* See Pedigree in the Case before the House of Lords, 1757-1762; and Anderson's *Genealogical Tables*, No. 319, page 565; and No. 324, page 569.

James Ernest, Third Count Leslie.

returned to their studies; and my eldest brother (Count James Ernest) went off immediately to Paris to see the King of France and the Chevalier de St. George; and my brother Balquhain (George Leslie) returned to Scotland. These two sons of my brother came to see me in 1717, and their father recalled them both to marry them to two princesses, d'Eghemberge or Eggenberg. The elder, Count Joseph, died without children (male issue); and the other, Count Charles Cajetan, has several, one of whom (Count Anthony) has taken possession of our estates in Scotland, but does not wish to reside there on account of the religion." 1717.

Count James Ernest Leslie lived chiefly at Gratz in Styria. There he received a visit from his nephew the Rev. Alexander Leslie, a Jesuit, brother of Sir James Leslie of Pitcaple, who was on his way home from Rome.

James Ernest, third Count Leslie, died in 1738, and was succeeded by his only surviving son, Charles Cajetan, fourth Count Leslie. 1738.

CHARLES CAJETAN,

FOURTH COUNT LESLIE.

Charles Cajetan, Fourth Count Leslie.

CHARLES CAJETAN, only surviving son of James Ernest, third Count Leslie, by his wife, the Princess Berne Maria Aloysia de Lichtenstein, succeeded to the titles and estates as fourth Count Leslie, at the death of his father, in 1738. 1738.

CHAP. II.

Charles Cajetan, Fourth Count Leslie.

Patrick Leslie Duguid, afterwards twenty-first baron of Balquhain, son of Teresa Leslie, third daughter of Count Patrick Leslie, states that Counts Joseph and Charles Cajetan Leslie, sons of Count James Ernest Leslie, his mother's brother, when travelling with their tutor, paid a visit to their aunt, Lady Betty Leslie, abbess of the Ursuline convent at Lisle; and on her informing them that he, their cousin, was at Douai, they came there to visit him, about the year
1717. 1717; and, as has been related, Lady Betty, in a letter to her nephew, Captain John Grant, says—"These two sons of my brother (Joseph and Charles Cajetan) came to see me in 1717, and their father recalled them to marry them to two princesses, d'Eghemberge or Eggenberg."

On the death of Count Ernest Leslie, eighteenth
1739. Baron of Balquhain, without issue, in 1739, the direct line of heirs-male of the Scotch branch of the family failed—all the heirs in Scotland being sons or grandsons of Count Patrick Leslie's daughters. Count Charles Cajetan therefore claimed to succeed to the Balquhain estates as being next in the order of nomination in the deed of entail executed by Count Patrick Leslie. Count Charles Cajetan's claim was opposed by Sir James Leslie of Pitcaple, and by his own sons, Count Joseph Leopold and Count Anthony Leslie. The Court
1741. of Session, 11th February 1741, decided in favour of Sir James Leslie of Pitcaple; but the Counts

CHAP. II.

Charles Cajetan, Fourth Count Leslie.

Leslie carried the case by appeal to the House of Lords, who, 29th April 1742, reversed the decision of the Court of Session, and pronounced in favour of Count Anthony Leslie, Count Charles Cajetan's second son.*

During the law-process many interesting particulars relating to Count Charles Cajetan Leslie and his family were brought forward in the evidence of the various witnesses. One witness stated that in 1753 he visited Count Charles Cajetan Leslie, who was then living at his house at Pernegg in Upper Styria; that he was very good-humoured, and would often make his chaplain drink with him, and would lay wagers which could drink most; and that Count Charles Cajetan had the character of wishing to make everybody who came to his house happy and merry. By proofs taken at Venice in November 1759, before a notary, in order to prove that Count Charles Cajetan Leslie and his sons were papists, it was shown that they had a chapel with three altars in their palace, where mass was said daily; and, as far as could be judged, the Counts were devout persons, and on meagre days ate no flesh meat. One witness deponed that he had seen Count Charles Cajetan receive the sacrament at the Romish church at Marioncelli, where he had

1753.

1759.

* For a full account of the law-process regarding the succession to the Balquhain estates, see "Records of Anthony, Count Leslie, nineteenth Baron of Balquhain."

CHAP. II. *Charles Cajetan, Fourth Count Leslie.*

a large estate; and that if the Counts had not been Roman Catholics they could not have held public offices about the Imperial Court, and could not have been admitted to the posts and dignities which they enjoyed in the empire—Count Charles Cajetan being a Councillor of State, Actual Privy Councillor to the Empress Queen, and President of the Revisary Court of Justice of Lower Austria *in Causis Privatorum;* Count Joseph Leopold being Actual Imperial and Royal Councillor of Lower Austria; and Count Anthony being a gentleman of the Bed-chamber of the Archduke Joseph, for which reason he always resided in Vienna. In a letter from Jerome Reccunct, a
1759. merchant in Venice, dated 11th September 1759, addressed to Thomas Gordon, merchant in Aberdeen, it is stated that, "with regard to the papers you sent relating to Count Leslie's affair, I shall send them over to my friend in Germany, but am apprehensive it will be almost impossible to succeed according to your wishes. The family of Count Leslie resides in Styria, and is held in great consideration, not only in that part of the country, but likewise at the Court of Vienna."

Count Charles Cajetan Leslie married, 26th
1719. June 1719, the Princess Maria Teresa Josepha,
1695. Duchess d'Eggenberg, born 14th October 1695, and daughter of John Anthony Joseph, Prince d'Eggenberg, and sister of the wife of his brother

Joseph Patrick Sigismund, Count Leslie. By her he had issue— CHAP. II.

Charles Cajetan, Fourth Count Leslie.

I. JOSEPH LEOPOLD, born 1728, who married, first, in 1746, the Countess Elizabeth Kinsky, who died without issue; he married, secondly, the Countess Francisca de Walstein. Count Leopold was Kammerherr to the Emperor, and Imperial and Royal Councillor of Lower Austria. He died without issue, before his father, in 1750. 1750.

II. ANTHONY, born 1733, who succeeded his cousin Count Ernest Leslie as nineteenth Baron of Balquhain in Scotland, and his father as fifth Count Leslie in Germany. 1733.

III. CHARLES ALBERT, born 1739, Knight of St. John of Malta. He died without issue. 1739.

IV. ROSALIA, born 1730; married to Antonio, Count Attems. 1730.

V. CAROLINE CAJETANA, born 1732; married to Charles, Count Lamberg. 1732.

VI. ELEONORA, born 1737, who died without issue; and eight other children, who all died young. 1737.

Count Charles Cajetan Leslie died in 1760, and was succeeded by his eldest surviving son, Anthony, fifth Count Leslie. 1760.

ANTHONY,

FIFTH COUNT LESLIE.

Anthony, Fifth Count Leslie.

ANTHONY, eldest surviving son of Count Charles Cajetan Leslie, by his wife the Princess Maria Teresa Josepha, Duchess d'Eggenberg, succeeded as fifth Count Leslie, on the death of his father, in 1760. 1760.

Count Anthony Leslie was born in 1733, and 1733.

CHAP. II.

Anthony, Fifth Count Leslie.

was educated in the Scotch college at Ratisbon. By a judgment pronounced by the House of Lords, 29th April 1742, he was declared next heir of entail to his cousin Ernest, Count Leslie, eighteenth Baron of Balquhain, in the estate of Balquhain in Scotland, and was served heir accordingly.
1747. In 1747 his tutors raised an action of reduction against James Gordon of Cobairdy, for reducing the settlement made by Count Ernest Leslie, eighteenth Baron of Balquhain, whereby he settled the lands of Insch and Boddam, part of the entailed lands of the barony of Balquhain, on his uterine brother, James Gordon of Cobairdy. James Gordon of Cobairdy pleaded that Count Anthony Leslie was an alien, born out of the king's allegiance, and consequently was incapable of bringing an action for recovering a land-estate in Scotland. The Court of Session, 19th June
1749. 1749, sustained this plea, and Cobairdy was allowed to retain the lands of Insch and Boddam, which the true heirs of the Balquhain estates have lost for ever.

1756. Afterwards, in 1756, Peter Leslie Grant, son of Captain John Grant, son of John Roy Grant of Ballindalloch, and Anne Francisca, second daughter of Count Patrick Leslie, claimed the estate of Balquhain as the nearest heir of entail professing the Protestant religion—all the nearer heirs being either aliens, born out of the allegiance of the Crown of Great Britain, or persons pro-

Anthony, Fifth Count Leslie.

fessing the Popish religion, among which latter he included his own father Captain John Grant. After a long litigation, the Court of Session, 5th February 1762, found that the pursuer Peter Leslie Grant was the nearest Protestant heir entitled to succeed to the estate of Balquhain, and this judgment was affirmed by the House of Lords 2d February 1763. Consequently Count Anthony Leslie had to resign the Balquhain estates to Peter Leslie Grant, who became twentieth Baron of Balquhain.* 1762. 1763.

In the *Almanach de Gotha* for the year 1841, p. 226, it is stated that Count Anthony Leslie, Chamberlain and Privy Councillor to the Emperor of Austria, married, 20th February 1785, the Countess Marie Wilhelmine de Wurmbrand, born 3d September 1764, sister of Count Henri Gundaccar de Wurmbrand. But this seems to be a mistake, or perhaps it may be a second marriage. In a letter, written 18th November 1780, to the Rev. Charles Leslie, S.J., son of Patrick Leslie Duguid, twenty-first Baron of Balquhain, Count Anthony says—"I have quitted the Court these three years, since that I married, and established my family here in Styria." 1841. 1785. 1764. 1780.

Count Anthony Leslie died without issue, 22d February 1802, and being the last heir-male of 1802.

* For a full account of the law-process regarding the succession to the Balquhain estates, see "Records of Anthony, Count Leslie, nineteenth Baron of Balquhain."

CHAP. II.

Anthony, Fifth Count Leslie.

the family of Leslie in Germany, the entailed estates or *fidei commis.* in that country went to the heir-male of Charles John, Prince de Dietrichstein, in conformity with the will and entail exe-
1667. cuted by Walter, first Count Leslie, in 1667. These estates remained in the Dietrichstein family till the death of the last heir-male of the line,
1858. Joseph, Prince de Dietrichstein, in July 1858, when the succession opened to the descendants of the heirs-female of Count Patrick Leslie, fifteenth Baron of Balquhain. By Count Walter Leslie's will, the entail was now at an end, and the estates were liable to be divided.

1859. In 1859 the Austrian Government published an edict, calling upon all those who considered themselves heirs to set forth their claims, which edict was several times inserted in the *Times* newspaper. The following are those entitled to claim :—

I. The Descendants of Teresa, third daughter of Count Patrick Leslie—viz. Colonel Charles Leslie, K.H., of Balquhain, his brothers and sister; Colonel Macdonell and his brothers and sisters, children of Elizabeth, daughter of Patrick Leslie Duguid, twenty-first Baron of Balquhain, married to Captain Macdonell of Leich.

II. The Descendants of Jean, youngest daughter of Count Patrick Leslie—viz. the Gordons of Aberlour, Camerons, and others.

III. The Descendants of the daughters of Count Charles Cajetan Leslie—viz. the Counts Attems and Lamberg.

A pedigree extracted from the public and family records, authenticated by the Herald Office, Edinburgh, and all the other documents required, were transmitted to an eminent advocate in Vienna, who opened the case in the Austrian Courts. The Court at Gratz, 18th January 1861, 1861. decided by a decree, No. 14,648, that the Scotch claimants had proved their claim.

The Counts Attems and Lamberg appealed against this decision, which prolonged the legal proceedings until 1867. Then they proposed a 1867. compromise by which they were to receive seven-twelfths of the whole heritage, and the Scotch claimants were to receive the remaining five-twelfths. This compromise was carried into effect by a formal agreement in 1868. The legal 1868. agent at Vienna, in a letter dated 1st February 1869. 1869, stated that the agent at Gratz had informed him that all the parties had agreed to the above terms, and that he hoped to be able very soon to state that the affair was favourably settled. In March 1869, the Gratz agent stated that the re- 1869. venue arising from the accumulation of the rents during the legal proceedings would most likely be divided shortly, but that the sale of the estates to realise the money might yet require a year or two.

The portraits of Count Walter and Count James Leslie, and also of Count James and Count Ernest Leslie, seventeenth and eighteenth Barons

CHAP. II.

Anthony, Fifth Count Leslie.

of Balquhain, are at Fetternear House. The portraits of Count Charles Cajetan, Count Joseph Patrick, and Count Anthony Leslie, were in the possession of the late Colonel Tytler, Edinburgh, who got them from Mr. Dundas of Carron Hall. These had been sent from Germany to Mr. Thomas Dundas of Fingask, the agent for the Counts Leslie in their lawsuit with Peter Leslie Grant. It may also be mentioned that the portraits of Count Patrick Leslie, fifteenth Baron of Balquhain, of Count George Leslie, sixteenth baron, and of Sir James Leslie of Pitcaple, are at Logie Elphinston—being three of the family portraits which were sent away from Fetternear House by the Honourable Margaret Elphinstone, widow of George, Count Leslie, sixteenth Baron of Balquhain.

CHAPTER III.

THE FAMILY OF LESLIE OF WARDIS, *Leslie of Wardis.*

BARONETS.

THE family of Leslie of Wardis, Baronets, is a branch of the family of Leslie, Barons of Balquhain.

Alexander Leslie, first Baron of Wardis, born about 1445, was the eldest son of Sir William Leslie, fourth Baron of Balquhain, by his second wife, Agnes Irvine of Drum. He got from his father the lands of Wardis, Drummies, Middleton, and others * about 1465. Sir William Leslie of Balquhain, styled of Wardis, granted a charter of sale to his kinsman Duncan Forbes, son of Alexander Forbes, of the half of the lands of Corbanchory, in the barony of Cushney, dated at Aberdeen, 20th July 1464; and to this charter, Alexander de Leslie, afterwards first Baron of Wardis, and George de Leslie, afterwards first Laird of New Leslie, sons of the said Sir William Leslie, are witnesses. King James III. granted a charter of the lands of Balcomy in Fife to his

1445.

1464.

See App. No. XXVIII.

* *See* Note, Wardis.

CHAP. III.

Alexander Leslie, First Baron of Wardis.

familiar Esquire, Alexander de Leslie, and Isabella de Lauder, his spouse, which lands belonged in heritage to the said Isabella, and which in her virginity she had resigned into the hands of the king; dated at Stirling, 27th September 1465.

See App. No. XXIX.

Alexander Leslie, Dominus de Balcomie, granted a charter of sale of the lands of Corbanchory to Duncan Forbes of Drummellache, dated at Aberdeen, 30th January 1469, and confirmed by Queen Mary 24th May 1545.

1469.

See App. No. XXX.

James III. granted to his familiar Esquire, Alexander Leslie of Wardis, a charter of the king's lands of the thanage of Kintore, to be held by him and his heirs for an annual payment of four pounds four shillings Scots to the Bishop of Aberdeen, and of three pounds Scots to the Sheriff of Forfar, and his successors, the heirs of the deceased Alexander Ogilvie of Ochterhouse; dated at Edinburgh, 30th September 1473.

See App. No. XXXI.

King James III. granted a charter, mortifying an annual rent of twelve merks from the lands of Balcomie in Fife, which failing, from the lands of Wardis and Quylpat, in the Sheriffdom of Aberdeen, given by Alexander Leslie of Wardis for the support of a chaplain at the chapel of St. Mary of Garioch, for behoof of the souls of the said Alexander Leslie, and Isabella, his spouse, dated 28th November 1474.

See App. No. XXXII.

1479.

King James III. granted a charter, dated 4th February 1479, confirming a charter by John of Ila, Lord of the Isles, to his kinsman, Alexander

Leslie of Wardis, of the lands of the barony of Kynnedward, commonly called the Casteltown, and the lands of Estirtiry, Kynnaroquhy, and Faithly; but reserving to the granter three merks of the lands of Casteltown, with the Castlehill, for the service due to the king from the lands and barony of Kynnedward; dated at Edinburgh, 22d December 1478.

CHAP. III.

Alexander Leslie, First Baron of Wardis.

See App. No. XXXIII.

Alexander Leslie, first Baron of Wardis, was Quæstor or Receiver-General under King James III.; he was also king's shield-bearer. He married Isabella Lauder, heiress of Balcomie in Fife, with whom he got the lands of Balcomie. By her he had issue—

I. John, his successor.

II. Walter, one of the Marischals of the king's household. He got a charter of the lands of Balcomie from James IV. on the resignation of Isabel Lauder, his mother, 1st September 1499. *See* App. No. XXXIV.

III. Elizabeth, married, first, to William Seton, Baron of Meldrum, and secondly, to John Collison, in Aberdeen, and had issue by both. Willelmus Seton de Meldrum, et Elizabeth Leslie, his spouse, got a charter under the Great Seal of the lands of Balcairn, 15th March 1490. They had a son, Alexander, who was 1490. served heir to his grandfather in 1512. 1512.

Alexander Leslie had four other daughters by his wife Isabella Lauder, married respectively to Spence of Boddam, Robert Livingston, provost of Dysart, John Sinclair, and Robert Keith, who was killed at Flodden in 1513. Alexander 1513. Leslie, first Baron of Wardis, died in 1500, and 1500.

CHAP. III.

Alexander Leslie, First Baron of Wardis.

was succeeded by his eldest son, John Leslie, second Baron of Wardis.

John Leslie, Second Baron of Wardis.

JOHN LESLIE,

SECOND BARON OF WARDIS.

1460. JOHN LESLIE, born in 1460, succeeded as second Baron of Wardis on the death of his father in
1500. 1500.

George Lord Gordon, John Leslie of Wardis, and Walter Leslie, his brother, were witnesses in a compromise regarding the marches of the parishes of Croy and Kildrummy, between Andrew, Bishop of Moray, and Hugh Ross of
1492. Kilravock, at Nairn, 13th August 1492.* John Leslie of Wardis was appointed one of the Sheriffs of Aberdeen by King James IV., to give sasine of the barony of Invernochty to Alexander Elphinstone, and Elizabeth Barlay, his wife, 8th
1507. August 1507.†

As has been related, William Leslie, seventh Baron of Balquhain, and John Leslie, second Baron of Wardis, with Alexander Seton of Meldrum and others, in revenge for some injury done to them or their friends, entered the city of Aberdeen
1525. during the night, 1st October 1525, with eighty men armed with spears and other weapons, and

* *Registrum Moraviense*, p. 245, No. 202.

† *Antiquities of Shires of Aberdeen and Banff*, vol. iv. p. 738.

John Leslie, Second Baron of Wardis.

attacked the citizens. A bloody conflict ensued, and by the bravery of the citizens the invaders were expelled, but in the fray eighty citizens were either killed or wounded, including some of the magistrates in the number. It appears that John Collison, a former Provost of Aberdeen, was the instigator of this affair, which was afterwards terminated by the arbitration of Robert Bishop of Moray, James Bishop of Ross, John Earl of Moray, and William Earl of Montrose.

King James IV. granted a charter to John Leslie of Wardis of the lands of Balcomie in Fife, resigned by his brother Walter, dated at Stirling, 14th February 1500. Also, the king granted a charter to John Leslie of Wardis, in recompense of certain sums due by the king's father to the father of the said John Leslie of Wardis, the deceased Alexander Leslie of Wardis, when he was the king's comptroller, of the office of bailie of all the king's lands of the regality of the Garioch—namely, Glanderstoun with the mill, Tulyfoure, Duncanstoun, Donydure with the mill, Rochmuriel, Knokinbard with the mill, Ardoun, Buchanstoun with the mill, Harlaw, Mekle Durno with the mill, Torreys, Rihill, Warthill, and the Davach of Inverurie with the mill—the office of bailie being annexed to the lands of Wardis; dated at Edinburgh, 16th June 1508. King James IV. also granted a charter of feu-ferme to John Leslie of Wardis, of the lands of the thanage

See App. No. XXXV.

See App. No. XXXVI.

CHAP. III.

John Leslie, Second Baron of Wardis.

of Kintore—namely, the Over Davach and Nether Davach of Kintore, with the mills; the lands of Crichie, Tavilty, Mekil Kynnaldy, with the mill; Litill Kynnaldy, Petmeddene, Nether Dyce, with the annual rents, and the fishings on the Water of Don, and the lake and bogs; dated at Edinburgh, 17th June 1508. On the same day King James IV. issued a precept to William, Bishop of Aberdeen, Keeper of the Privy Seal, to infeft the said John Leslie of Wardis in the lands, rents, and fishings of the thanage of Kintore. King James IV. granted a charter of feu-ferme to John Leslie of Wardis, of the king's lands of the Garioch—namely, Duncanstoun, Gillanderstoun with the mill, Donydure with the mill, Rochmurriel, the Davach of Ardune with the mill, Dornoch and the Mylnetoun, the Mill of Dornoche, Harlaw, Inverurie with the davach and mill, Tullifoure, Torreis, Knokinbarde with the mill, and Knokmorgin, in exchange for the lands of Balcomie, with the manor-place and rabbit-warrens, in Fife; dated at Edinburgh, 27th March 1510. King James V. granted a charter to John Leslie of Wardis, and Annabella Chalmer, his wife, of the lands of Tulifour, Tavelte, and the mill and milltoun of Dornoy, in the regality of the Garioch; dated at Edinburgh, 20th January 1525.

See App. No. XXXVII.

See App. No. XXXVIII.

See App. No. XXXIX.

See App. No. XL.

John Leslie of Wardis married, first, Miss Stewart, daughter of Alexander, Bishop of Moray, grandson of James II. She died childless. He

John Leslie, Second Baron of Wardis.

married, secondly, the Honourable Margaret Crichton, daughter of William, Lord Crichton of Frendraught, and had issue—

I. ALEXANDER, his successor.
II. MARGARET, married to the Laird of Cobairdy.

He married, thirdly, Margaret Forbes, daughter of the Laird of Echt, and relict of Walter Stewart of Dryland, and had issue—

I. WILLIAM, first Laird of Warthill, of whom afterwards.
II. WALTER, who died without issue at Frendraught.

He married, fourthly, Agnes Gordon, daughter of Patrick Gordon of Haddo, ancestor of the Earls of Aberdeen, and had issue—

I. ANDREW, progenitor of the Leslies of Bucharn, and of the Leslies of Clisson in France, of whom afterwards.
II. BESSIE, married, first, to Robert Winton, and, secondly, to Andrew Menzies.
III. MARJORY, married to James Keith of Aquhorsk.
IV. Another Daughter, married to John Leith, third son of Patrick Leith of Edingarioch, in 1520. 1520.

He married, fifthly, Annabella Chalmer of Balbithan, before 20th January 1525, when he 1525. and Annabella Chalmer got a charter of the lands of Tulifour and others. By her he had issue—

I. ROBERT, killed at Pinkie, 10th September 1547. 1547.
II. CLARA, married to Patrick Leith of Harthill. Patrick Leith of Harthill, and Clara Leslie, his spouse, got a charter from King James V. of the lands of Auchleven, Ardour, Buchanston, Harlaw, and others, dated 8th December 1531. 1531.
III. ISABELLA, married, first, to William Troup of Colmaleggie, and, secondly, to Andrew Craig of Balmellie.
IV. ANNABELLA, married to Andrew Bremner in Aberdeen.

CHAP. III.

John Leslie, Second Baron of Wardis.

Besides these children, John Leslie of Wardis had several natural children; amongst them Andrew Leslie in Glanderston, John Leslie, employed by the Earl of Sutherland, and Catherine and Jean Leslie. He died 1st April 1546, and was succeeded by his eldest son, Alexander Leslie, third Baron of Wardis.

1546.

Alexander Leslie, Third Baron of Wardis.

ALEXANDER LESLIE,

THIRD BARON OF WARDIS.

ALEXANDER LESLIE, third Baron of Wardis, married, first, Margaret Forbes, daughter of Alexander Forbes of Towie. They got a charter from Queen Mary of the lands of Taviltye, dated at St. Andrews, 13th October 1546. They had issue—

See App. No. XLI.

I. WILLIAM, who succeeded as fourth Baron of Wardis.

II. PATRICK of Duncanston, married Isabella Seton of Meldrum.

III. ALEXANDER, who got a charter of the lands of Dyce, 8th July 1585. He married, first, Isabella Leslie of Pitcaple, and, secondly, Miss Fraser, and had issue—

See App. No. XLII.

- I. ALEXANDER LESLIE of Dyce, who married Miss Harvey, and had issue, who all died young, and he gave the lands of Dyce back to Wardis.
- II. WILLIAM LESLIE, who married Miss Leslie of Tochers.
- III. JAMES LESLIE, who was a captain under Montrose, and married Miss Lindsay.
- IV. ROBERT LESLIE.
- V. ANDREW LESLIE.

CHAP. III.

Alexander Leslie, Third Baron of Wardis.

IV. CATHERINE, married to George Crichton of Conzie.

V. AGNES, married, first, to Hurry of Pitfichie, and, secondly, to Laurence Leith in Kirktown of Rayne, in 1580.

VI. JANE, married to John Innes of Achluncart.

VII. MARY, married to Alexander Burnett of Craigour, Kincardine O'Neil.

VIII. JOHANNA, married, first, to Patrick Gordon, Auchindoir, and, secondly, to the Laird of Foveran. Others say she was married to Barclay of Kincarrachy.

IX. ANNE, married to Alexander Forbes, Goodman of Thainston.

Alexander Leslie married, secondly, Elizabeth Seton, daughter of William Seton, Baron of Meldrum; and, thirdly, when he was in the eightieth year of his age, Isabella Menzies. He had other two sons, Leonard and James, who both died young. He died in 1573, and was succeeded by his eldest son, William Leslie, fourth Baron of Wardis. Alexander Leslie of Wardis departtit in Old Aberdeen, the xxix day of September, the yeir of God 1573 yeiris.* 1573.

WILLIAM LESLIE,

FOURTH BARON OF WARDIS.

William Leslie, Fourth Baron of Wardis.

WILLIAM LESLIE was falconer to King James VI., being a man of great nimbleness and extraordinary agility. It is said that he cut the ground when he leaped, and as none of the nobles

* Chronicles of Aberdeen; *Spalding Club Miscellany*, vol. ii. p. 40.

CHAP. III.

William Leslie, Fourth Baron of Wardis.

could reach the score, the king called him William Cutt.

Queen Mary granted a charter, dated at Newbottle, 24th July 1557, confirming a charter by Alexander Leslie, third Baron of Wardis, to William Leslie, his son and heir-apparent, of the lands of the Garioch underwritten: that is to say, Duncanstoun, Gillanderstoun with the mill, Donnydure with the mill, Rochmureill, the davach of Ardune with the mill, Warthill, Dornocht with the mill, Harlaw, Inverurie with the davach and mill, Tullifour, Torreis, Knokinbarde with the mill, and Knokmorgowne, with the foggage and fogmaill of the Kirktown of Une and Westhall, with the tolbeir of Auchlevin and Bourtie; and of the lands of the thanage of Kintore underwritten: that is to say, the Over Davach and Nether Davach with the mill, the fermes and the tolbeir of Kintore, the lands of Creyche, Taviltie, Mekill Kynnaldie with the mill, Litill Kynnaldie, Petmeddene, Nether Dyce, with the annual rents, the fishings on the Don, and the lochs and bogs; dated at Aberdeen, 21st July 1551. William Leslie of Wardis granted a lease for nineteen years, from Whitsunday 1582, of the Long Croft of Meikle Warthill, with the teindsheaves and teinds of the vicarage of the same, to Stephen Leslie of Little Warthill.*

See App. No. XLIII.

* *Antiquities of Shires of Aberdeen and Banff*, vol. iii. p. 439.

CHAP. III.

William Leslie, Fourth Baron of Wardis.

King James granted a licence to John Erskine of Balhagardie, notwithstanding the proclamation regarding the pest, to pursue William Leslie of Wardis, and John Leslie, his son, for wrongous molestation and troubling of him in his possession of the lands of Bennachie and woods of Ardellochie, 11th March 1589.* *See* App. No. XLIV.

William Leslie of Wardis married Janet Innes, daughter of Robert Innes of Innermarkie, and had issue—

I. John, his successor.

II. George of Crichie, married Marjory, daughter of John Leslie of Kincraigie, in the parish of Tarland, and had issue—

I. The Right Rev. Dr. John Leslie, Bishop of Orkney, Clogher and Raphoe, progenitor of the Leslies of Glasslough in Ireland; of whom afterwards.

III. William, got a charter of lands in the Garioch and of the thanage of Kintore from his father, 12th April 1596.† He married Elizabeth Ogilvie, daughter of 1596. Sir George Ogilvie of Banff, and had a son who died young. William Leslie died in 1606. 1606.

IV. James of Miltown, married Margaret Erskine of Pittodrie, and had issue—

I. John, ancestor of the Leslies of Tarbet in Ireland, of whom afterwards.

II. James, a clergyman of the Established Church in Ireland.

James Leslie of Miltown died in the hospital at Aberdeen.

---

* Pittodrie Papers; *Miscellany of Spalding Club*, vol. ii. p. 205.

† *Registrum Magni Sigilli*, lib. xlviii. No. 326; *Antiquities of Shires of Aberdeen and Banff*, vol. iv. p. 526, note.

CHAP. III.

William Leslie, Fourth Baron of Wardis.

V. FRANCIS, died without issue.

VI. WALTER. William Leslie of Wardis, Janet Innes his spouse, and Walter Leslie his sixth son, got a charter of the lands of Wardis, and of the two parts of the town and lands of Wraes, from King James VI., 3d June 1575.

VII. DUNCAN, married Agnes, daughter of George Knowels, burgess in Aberdeen.

VIII. PETER, died without issue.

IX. GRIZEL, married to James Arbuthnot of Lentusch.

X. BESSIE, married to John Collison, burgess in Aberdeen.

He had also two other daughters, married respectively to Sir George Meldrum of Fyvie and George Chalmers of Balbithan. He died before 1602. 13th April 1602, when his eldest son, John Leslie, fifth Baron of Wardis, was served heir to him.

John Leslie, Fifth Baron of Wardis.

JOHN LESLIE,

FIFTH BARON OF WARDIS.

JOHN LESLIE, fifth Baron of Wardis, was present at the Michaelmas Head Court held at Aberdeen 1616. in 1616, when John Leslie, Fiar of Balquhain, was elected Commissioner to serve in Parliament. He got a charter under the Great Seal of the 1618. lands of Largie, 31st July 1618; also of the lands of Duncanston, and of the patronage of the church of Leslie; also of the lands of Balcomie in Fife, 1619. 30th July 1619. He engaged in a bond of manrent with George, Marquis of Huntly, 13th May 1609.

See App. No. XLV.

CHAP. III.

John Leslie, Fifth Baron of Wardis.

John Leslie of Wardis married Jane Crichton, daughter of Sir James Crichton of Frendraught, and had issue—

I. JOHN, his successor, created a Baronet of Nova Scotia.
II. WILLIAM, who succeeded his nephew, Sir John, as third Baronet.
III. NORMAN, ancestor of the fourth and succeeding Baronets.
IV. ELIZABETH.
V. ANNE, married to John Leith of Edingarioch about 1570. 1570.
VI. MARIOT or MARJORY, married to Gilbert Johnston, Overtown of Dyce, second son of Sir Gilbert Johnston of Caskieben, who died in 1590. 1590.
VII. CHRISTIAN, married to George Leslie of Old Craig.

John Leslie, fifth Baron of Wardis, died in 1620, and was succeeded by his eldest son, Sir John Leslie of Wardis, Baronet. 1620.

SIR JOHN LESLIE OF WARDIS,

FIRST BARONET.

Sir John Leslie of Wardis, First Baronet.

JOHN LESLIE, eldest son of John Leslie, fifth Baron of Wardis, succeeded as sixth Baron of Wardis on the death of his father in 1620. He married Elspet Gordon, daughter of John Gordon of Newton. John Leslie of Wardis, and Elspet Gordon, his wife, were summoned by the presbytery of Aberdeen, 2d January 1601, for having failed to subscribe the covenant and to communicate at the Lord's table. John Leslie promised to comply with the desire of the kirk, and he was required to cause his lady to communicate with

1620.

1601.

CHAP. III.

Sir John Leslie of Wardis, First Baronet.

him; but to this he answered that he had no power to command her in things concerning her soul and conscience, nevertheless, he would do what he could to persuade her. The presbytery does not seem to have been satisfied with this limited promise, and therefore the moderator, in name of the rest, ordained that he and his lady should be present and satisfy the kirk, under pain of excommunication. The presbytery met again,
1601. 6th February 1601, when John Leslie was accused of not having compeired at the kirk of Dyce according to his promise, but sent a letter instead, excusing himself because it was a weighty matter, and he was a young man, and not well resolved in the heads of his faith, and desiring that the kirk should wait till he was better informed, when he would do as he was desired; whereupon the presbytery, according to their idea, finding that he had mocked both God and his kirk, and that he had violated his promise made to them, ordered Mr. William Neilsone to summon him to appear before them on the 20th day of the month, to hear the censures of the kirk pronounced
1601. against him. On the 20th February 1601, Mr. William Neilsone produced before the presbytery the summons duly executed against John Leslie, and Elspet Gordon, his spouse, who, being willfully contumacious, were ordered to lie under the censures of the kirk. On the 27th February the presbytery ordered John Leslie and Elspet Gordon

Sir John Leslie of Wardis, First Baronet.

to be excommunicated after admonitions and prayers, and ordered Mr. William Neilsone to give them the first admonition on the following Sunday. The presbytery met again 13th March 1601, when Mr. William Neilsone excused himself for not having given the admonition, because Elspet Gordon had offered to subscribe the covenant and to communicate within forty days. The presbytery required John Leslie to satisfy their requirements within forty days, under a penalty of two thousand merks. On the 10th April 1601, Mr. 1601. William Neilsone reported that he gave the last admonition to the Laird of Wardis and his lady on the preceding Sunday, the 5th day of the month; and in respect of their obstinacy and the admonitions already past, Mr. William Neilsone was ordered under pain of deprivation to pass to the kirk of Dyce, and there proceed against them with the first prayer for them, and Mr. Robert Mercer to pass there on the Sunday following, and proceed to the second prayer. *See* App. No. XLVI.

John Leslie, sixth Baron of Wardis, was created a Knight Baronet of Nova Scotia, and received a charter of the free barony and regality of Leslie in Nova Scotia, from King Charles I., 1st September 1625. The dignity of Baronet was granted 1625. to him, his heirs-male and assigns whomsoever. *See* App. No. XLVII. He also got a charter of the lands of Balcomie in Fife, 30th July 1629. 1629.

It is said that Sir John Leslie was a very dissi-

CHAP. III.

Sir John Leslie of Wardis, First Baronet.

pated gentleman, and that Sir Alexander Gordon of Cluny being in the habit of staying much with him, became too intimate with his wife, Elspet Gordon. After this, says an old manuscript history of the family, Wardis never prospered, God Almighty most wonderfully overthrowing that once opulent estate, and that by such small and trifling circumstances as visibly made it appear that the finger of God was in their destruction. The first occasion of his getting into trouble was his selling a bargain of oatmeal to Sir Robert Farquhar in Aberdeen, under certain penalties, as is ordinary on such occasions, of so much for each boll not duly delivered at the specified time. Wardis, not fulfilling his bargain with Sir Robert, suffered his estates to be compromised. It so happened just at this time that the Earl of Mar, who held the superiority of much of the lands of Wardis, pursued him for the payment of feu-duties long in arrear. To avoid this inconvenience, Wardis, being infatuated to his own destruction, for the whole debts on the estate were not very large, made over his lands to Cluny, of whom he received back-bonds. But Cluny himself being at the horn or under summons for debt, and an inhibition having been pressed against him three years before, the creditors of Cluny, as well as those of Wardis, seized upon the estates of Wardis. Sir John Leslie, finding himself thus entangled, and being unable to extricate himself, disponed his whole estate in 1634 to the Earl of Rothes, in the expectation of getting some part of it restored to him should the Earl recover it. But neither the Earl of Rothes, to whom it was disponed, nor his son, the Duke of Rothes, ever intermeddled. CHAP. III. *Sir John Leslie of Wardis, First Baronet.*

By his wife Elspet Gordon Sir John Leslie had issue—

I. JOHN, his successor.

II. FRANCIS. } Both went to Germany, and were killed in
III. ALEXANDER. } the wars there, neither leaving any issue.

IV. JANET, married, first, to John Gordon of Avochie, and, secondly, to George Gordon of Newton.

V. ELIZABETH, married, first, to Sir John Gordon of Cluny. They went to England during the civil war. The Earl of Huntly went to the castle of Tillyfour, 24th May 1644, and took possession of certain bonds, and of the rents in their name. Elizabeth Leslie was married, secondly, to Colonel Sir George Currier. 1644.

VI. MARJORY, married, first, to Sir Alexander Bannerman of Elsick, and, secondly, to Sir John Fletcher, King's Advocate.

Sir John Leslie of Wardis, first Baronet, died at Tillyfour 29th November 1640, "and was buried in his own chapel at Tillyfour, where never Laird of Wardis was buried before, and himself being the last Laird of Wardis was first buried there."* His widow, Elspet Gordon, married, 22d June 1641, Sir Alexander Gordon of Cluny, and died at Durham, 2d December 1642, "and wes," says Spalding, "bureit honestlie 1640. 1641. 1642.

* Spalding's *History of the Trubles in Scotland*, vol. i. p. 357.

CHAP. III.

Sir John Leslie of Wardis, First Baronet.

out of hir awin native soyll: a woman of suspect chastetie, and thocht over familiar with Sir Alexander Gordon of Cluny forsaid, thir many yeiris bygone, in hir first husbandis time, and thocht an evill instrument to the dounethrowing of both ther fair and florishing estaites."*

Sir John Leslie of Wardis, Second Baronet.

SIR JOHN LESLIE OF WARDIS,

SECOND BARONET.

SIR JOHN LESLIE succeeded as second baronet on
1640. the death of his father, 29th November 1640. Spalding, in his *History of the Trubles in Scotland* (vol. ii. p. 189), says, in the Chronicles
1642. of 1642—"About this time Sir John Leslie, eldest son of the defunct Laird of Wardis, came home out of Germany, but his father's fair estate was dilapidated, and little or nothing left him whereupon to live, so that he behoved to shift for himself, and went south to Edinburgh." Sir John Leslie did not long survive his accession to the baronetcy. "Upon the third of February,
1645. anno 1645," says Spalding,† "Sir John Leslie of Wardis, Knight-baronet, departed this life in New Aberdeen, a great enemy to the Laird of Cluny, who had mellit with his estate, Cluny wairdit in the Tolbooth of Edinburgh." Sir John Leslie was

* *Trubles*, vol. ii. p. 210.

† *Ibid.* p. 441.

buried at Insch. He, being unmarried, was succeeded in the title by his uncle, Sir William Leslie of Wardis, third baronet; but what little of the family property remained went to Sir John's sisters, Janet, Elizabeth, and Marjory.

Sir John Leslie of Wardis, Second Baronet.

SIR WILLIAM LESLIE OF WARDIS,

THIRD BARONET.

Sir William Leslie of Wardis, Third Baronet.

Sir William Leslie, second son of John Leslie, fifth Baron of Wardis, succeeded as third baronet on the death of his nephew, Sir John, 3d February 1645. Having got none of the Wardis estates, Sir William Leslie allowed the title to lie dormant, and John Gordon of Beldorny acquired the barony of Wardis. Sir William Leslie married Helen, daughter of George Gordon of Newton, and had issue— 1645.

I. John, married Miss Gordon of Milton, and died without issue in Germany.

II. Patrick, killed at the battle of Kilsyth, and left no issue.

III. Alexander, married Mrs. Dunbar, widow of the Laird of Overhall, but had no issue.

IV. William, who survived all his brothers. He usually lived with his cousin, Lady Bannerman of Elsick. He was a poor, simple, indolent man, very unfit to recover a sinking estate. He died unmarried.

Sir William Leslie had also three daughters: one married to Mr. Leith, a second died unmarried, and the third was married to Sir George Johnston of Caskieben.

CHAP. III.

SIR JOHN LESLIE OF WARDIS,

FOURTH BARONET.

Sir John Leslie of Wardis, Fourth Baronet.

On the death of Sir William Leslie and of his sons without issue, the title went to the descendants of Norman Leslie, third son of John Leslie, fifth Baron of Wardis, and brother of Sir John Leslie, first baronet.

Norman Leslie married Marjory, daughter of John Leith of Harthill, and had issue—

I. John, his heir, styled of New Rayne.

II. Alexander of Overtulloch. He married Miss Morison of Bognie, by whom he had a numerous family. He acquired the lands of Tulloch, near Strathbogie. Alexander, his eldest son, succeeded him, and married Jane, daughter of George Gordon of Rothnie, by whom he had two sons, George and Norman, and one daughter, Christina.

Norman Leslie was succeeded by his eldest son, John Leslie of New Rayne, who married Janet Gordon of Newton, and had issue—

I. Patrick, his heir.

II. Alexander, married Miss Jackson, and had several
1741. children. He was living at Little Warthill in 1741, and was maintained in a great measure by the Warthill family.

Patrick Leslie, the eldest son, succeeded on the death of his father, John Leslie, to the lands of New Rayne. He sold the sun-side of the lands of New Rayne, the lands of Barreldicks, and others, to George Ogilvie, portioner of Rayne, in 1700. He married Margaret Gordon of Braco in Aberdeenshire, and had issue—

CHAP. III.

Sir John Leslie of Wardis, Fourth Baronet.

I. William, who lived in Aberdeen. Some say he married, and had a son, also called William, who died without issue.

II. John, who had a son, also called John, who claimed and was allowed the title of Baronet after the death of Sir William Leslie of Wardis, third baronet.

Sir John Leslie, great-great-grandson of Norman Leslie, youngest brother of Sir John Leslie, first baronet, claimed and was allowed the title as fourth Baronet of Wardis. He married, in 1794, Caroline Jemima, only daughter and heiress of Abraham Leslie of Findrassie, by whom he got the estate of Findrassie. He had issue— 1794.

I. Charles Abraham, his successor, born 4th July 1796. 1796.

II. John.

III. Thomas, married Penuel, eldest daughter of John Grant, late of the 78th Regiment, and had two sons.

IV. Caroline Jemima, married to John Murray.

V. Rothes Beatrix, married, 16th July 1831, to Hugh Inglis. 1831.

VI. Cecilia Margaret.

Sir John Leslie of Wardis, fourth baronet, died in 1825, and was succeeded by his eldest son, Charles Abraham, fifth baronet. 1825.

SIR CHARLES ABRAHAM LESLIE OF WARDIS,

FIFTH BARONET.

Sir Charles Abraham Leslie of Wardis, Fifth Baronet.

Sir Charles Abraham Leslie of Wardis, fifth baronet, married Anne, daughter of Adam Walker, and by her, who died 17th March 1845, had issue— 1845.

CHAP. III.

Sir Charles Abraham Leslie of Wardis, Fifth Baronet.

I. NORMAN ROBERT, his successor, born 10th December 1822.

II. JOHN LLOYD, born 24th July 1824.

III. ELIZABETH GEORGIANA GORDON.

IV. ADELA.

Sir Charles Abraham Leslie was succeeded by his eldest son, Sir Norman Robert Leslie, sixth baronet.

Sir Norman Robert Leslie of Wardis, Sixth Baronet.

SIR NORMAN ROBERT LESLIE OF WARDIS,

SIXTH BARONET.

SIR NORMAN ROBERT LESLIE of Wardis, sixth baronet, was killed in India during the Sepoy
1857. mutiny, 12th July 1857, leaving a son, Sir Charles Henry Leslie of Wardis, seventh baronet.
1868. His widow died at Wanstead, 7th October 1868.

Sir Charles Henry Leslie of Wardis, Seventh Baronet.

SIR CHARLES HENRY LESLIE OF WARDIS,

SEVENTH BARONET.

SIR CHARLES HENRY LESLIE of Wardis, seventh
1848. baronet, born in 1848, is an officer in the 107th Regiment.

Arms: Quarterly, 1st and 4th Arg. on a bend az. three buckles or, for Leslie; 2d and 3d or, a lion rampant gu. debruised by a ribbon sa., all within a bordure, chequy vert and of the first for Abernethy.

Crest: A demi-griffin, ppr.

Supporters: Two griffins, per fesse, arg. and gu.

Motto: Grip Fast.

CHAP. III.

THE FAMILY OF LESLIE OF WARTHILL.

Leslie of Warthill.

The family of Leslie of Warthill is descended from the Wardis branch of the family of Leslie, Barons of Balquhain.

William Leslie, first Laird of Warthill, born 1490, was the second son of John Leslie, second 1490. Baron of Wardis, by his third wife, Margaret Forbes of Echt, widow of Walter Stewart of Dryland. He was a prudent and clever man, and was bailie of the courts of his father John, and of his brother Alexander Leslie, Barons of Wardis, who at that period had a great inheritance. He got from his father a lease of the Kemmils of Durno for his lifetime, and to his heirs for nineteen years after his death. He got in wadsett the lands of Ryehill, which being redeemed, he took in tack, and was in possession of them till his death.

Some years before his death, William Leslie of Warthill was struck to the ground by one Tullidaff, possessor or wadsetter of the other half of Warthill, at Laurence fair, at Old Rain, which was so resented by the Baron of Wardis and his sons, who supposed him to be killed, that they followed Tullidaff to the Kirk of Rayne, about two miles off, where they overtook him, and he, being almost surrounded, returned back, and was slain at a place on the Moor of Rayne, where there re-

CHAP. III.

William Leslie, First Laird of Warthill.

mains at this day a small heap of stones, called Tullidaff's Cairn.

William Leslie married, first, a daughter of William Rowan, burgess in Aberdeen, in 1511, and by her he had a son, John, who was slain at the battle of Pinkie along with his uncle, Robert Leslie, son of John Leslie, second Baron of Wardis,
1547. in 1547.

1518. William Leslie married, secondly, in 1518, Janet Cruickshank, heiress of Warthill, only surviving child of John, son of Adam Cruickshank
1482. of Tillymorgan, who in 1482 acquired the lands of Little Warthill and two ploughgates of the lands of Harlaw from Alexander Glaster of Glack. With his wife, Janet Cruickshank, William Leslie got the half of the lands of Little Warthill, and became first Laird of Warthill of the name of Leslie. He had issue twenty-one children, of whom the following were married.

1520. I. STEPHEN, his successor, born 1520.

II. NORMAN, who married, it is said, Isabella Gordon, daughter of William, Bishop of Aberdeen, son of the Earl of Huntly.

III. WILLIAM, who married Elizabeth Gordon, daughter of the Laird of Auchindoir. He was killed by William Gordon of Gight in a quarrel between George Troup of Begshall and William Gordon, but more by accident than design.

IV. ALEXANDER, who married Isabel, daughter of George Leslie of Kincraigie.

V. GEORGE, who married Margaret Dunbar, widow of George Leslie of New Leslie.

William Leslie, First Laird of Warthill.

VI. James, who married Isabella Chalmers, daughter of the Laird of Balbithan.

VII. Patrick.

VIII. Walter, who married, and had issue two sons, William and Patrick, and two daughters, Margaret and Marjory.

IX. Marjory, married to John Lamb of Rothie, commonly called Laird Lamb.

X. Margaret, married, first, to Alexander Leslie in Meikle Durno, and, secondly, to Alexander Anderson of Bonniton.

XI. Janet, married, first, to Alexander Cruickshank, son of the Laird of Tillymorgan, and, secondly, to George Leslie, Overboat of Spey.

XII. Christian, married to John Leslie of Buchanston.

XIII. Clara, married to John Singer or Seinzour of New Rain.

XIV. Isabella, married to James Cruickshank, son of the Laird of Tillymorgan.

XV. Jane, married to David Archibald, commonly called the Laird of Lewis. She was married, secondly, to Robert Abercrombie, son of the Laird of Birkenbog.

XVI. Elizabeth, married to Alexander Lyall of Middlehall, and had three sons and a daughter. At her marriage her father and mother were so strong and vigorous that they danced at a ball given on the occasion in the hall at Warthill. The family party, including the old couple, their children, and their children's wives and husbands, amounted to thirty-four in number.

William Leslie, first Laird of Warthill, died in 1561, upwards of seventy years of age. His widow, Janet Cruickshank, being a spirited lady, though upwards of sixty years old, and having had twenty-one children, took another husband, Michael Leslie, according to some a son of George 1561.

CHAP. III.

William Leslie, First Laird of Warthill.

Leslie, third Laird of New Leslie; according to others, of George Leslie, fourth Baron of Kincraigie.

Stephen Leslie, Second Laird of Warthill.

STEPHEN LESLIE,

SECOND LAIRD OF WARTHILL.

STEPHEN LESLIE, eldest son of William Leslie by his wife Janet Cruickshank, heiress of Warthill, succeeded as second Laird of Warthill on the
1561. death of his father in 1561. He got from his father the lands of Sigehill, and from William Leslie, ninth Baron of Balquhain, the other half of Warthill in wadsett during his life, and for nineteeen years thereafter, for the payment of twenty merks yearly. This half of Warthill had been held in wadsett by Tullidaff from Balquhain, but upon the quarrel in Laurence fair William Leslie of Balquhain paid off Tullidaff's heirs, and wadsett the lands to Stephen Leslie of Warthill, there being now blood between him and the Tullidaffs. Stephen Leslie also got a
1582. lease for nineteen years, from Whitsunday 1582, of the Long Croft of Mekil Warthill with the teind-sheaves and vicarage dues of the same, from William Leslie, fourth Baron of Wardis, who ordered John Murray, his bailie in Old Rain, to give Stephen Leslie sasine in the said lands and pertinents, 1st March 1582.

See App. No. XLVIII.

Stephen Leslie was much given to field sports,

CHAP. III.

Stephen Leslie, Second Laird of Warthill.

as most of the family were. It is related that, being once very ill, there came a bird in at the window of the room where he was lying, and sat and sang at his bedside although several people were in the room, and on going away it dropped a feather, which Stephen kept carefully and wore about him till his dying day.

Stephen Leslie married, first, Marjory Leith, daughter of Patrick Leith of Likelyhead, and had issue—

I. William, his successor, born 1560. 1560.

II. Alexander, married Isabella Runciman, daughter of John Runciman, parson of Oyne.

III. Julia, married to John Anderson, son of William Anderson of Bonniton. Her husband being dangerously ill, she took his sickness so much to heart that she died of grief.

IV. Margaret, married to Andrew Edwards, son of William Edwards of Old Rain, and had a son and two daughters.

Stephen Leslie married, secondly, Bessie Spence, daughter of the Laird of Boddam, and widow of the Laird of Largie. He died in 1610, and was succeeded by his eldest son, William Leslie, third Laird of Warthill. 1610.

William Leslie, Third Laird of Warthill.

WILLIAM LESLIE,

THIRD LAIRD OF WARTHILL.

William Leslie, third Laird of Warthill, bought the lands of Cushieston, Little Folla, and the other half of Little Warthill. He married Mar-

CHAP. III.

William Leslie, Third Laird of Warthill.

garet Gray, daughter of Gilbert Gray of Tullo, and had issue—

I. James, his successor, born 1584.

1799. II. William, who got from his father the lands of Little Folla, which his male descendants enjoyed for six generations, and then, in 1799, succeeded to the patrimonial inheritance of Warthill.

III. Margaret, married to her cousin John Gray of Tullo, who got the lands of Cushieston in wadsett from his father-in-law.

IV. Beatrix, married to Gordon, Laird of Tillichoudie, who sold to his father-in-law the lands of Little Folla.

1640. William Leslie, third Laird of Warthill, died in 1640, and was succeeded by his eldest son James Leslie, fourth Laird of Warthill.

James Leslie, Fourth Laird of Warthill.

JAMES LESLIE,

FOURTH LAIRD OF WARTHILL.

James Leslie, fourth Laird of Warthill, married Beatrix Abercrombie, daughter of Walter Abercrombie, Archdeacon of Aberdeen and minister of Rayne, son of Alexander Abercrombie of Birkenbog. They lived together nearly sixty years, and, it is said, had twenty-one children, of whom the following came of age :—

1623. I. William, who succeeded as fifth Laird of Warthill, born 1623.

1624. 1650. 1651. II. John, born 1624. After serving as a cornet in the troop commanded by Leslie of Pitcaple, at the battle of Dunbar in 1650, and at the battle of Worcester in 1651, he married Janet Innes, daughter of Jerome Innes, minister of Fyvie. He did not enjoy much happiness in this marriage, and died young, without issue. He was a tall, handsome man. CHAP. III.

James Leslie, Fourth Laird of Warthill.

III. JAMES, born 1625, married Isabella Logie, daughter of Andrew Logie, minister of Rayne and Archdeacon of Aberdeen, and had two sons and two daughters, who all died young. He bought the lands of Tochers from Sir Alexander Abercrombie of Gallcross in 1676, and sold them again in 1695 to his nephew, Alexander Leslie, sixth Laird of Warthill. He died in 1695, aged seventy. 1676-95. 1695.

IV. ALEXANDER, who got from his father the lands of Cushieston. He was a gentleman of good repute and was much respected. Being educated for the church, he was settled as minister of Crail in Fife. Being a Nonconformist, he was deprived of his benefice at the Revolution by the act of the Privy Council, 17th September 1689. He died in 1705, leaving by his wife, Helen Seymour, daughter of John Seymour, minister of Macgill, two sons, namely— 1689-1705.

I. JAMES, who was concerned in the troubles of the times, and was out in 1715, in the Stuart cause. He was sheriff-clerk of Fife, and factor to the Earl of Wemyss. He married Catherine Mills, and died in 1730, having had three sons, Alexander, John, and James, who all died unmarried; and three daughters, Jane, Helen, and Anne, the two youngest of whom died unmarried; Jane, the eldest, was married, first, to William Robertson, writer in Edinburgh, and secondly, to the Rev. David Rae. 1715. 1730.

II. DAVID, a merchant in Anstruther. He married, first, Catherine Wood, and had a son Robert, who died unmarried in Jamaica. He married, secondly, Alison Patallo of Balhousie, by whom he had no issue. He married, thirdly, Helen Crawford of Monargan, by whom he had a son, David, and two daughters, Helen and Anne, who all died unmarried.

CHAP. III.

James Leslie, Fourth Laird of Warthill.

V. Patrick, who had the farm of Over Tocher. He married Elspet Keith, daughter of the Laird of Aquhorsk, and by her had—

I. James, who went abroad, and died unmarried.

II. John, who married Margaret Keith, daughter of the parson of Old Deer. He was curator to Alexander Leslie, ninth Laird of Warthill. He left a son, George, who died at an
1785. advanced age in 1785, and a daughter Ann, married to George Seton of Mounie.

III. George, who was one of the ministers of Aberdeen. He married a daughter of Keith of Keithfield, and had an only son, who died young.

IV. Elizabeth.

VI. Elspet, married to John Garden of Brackles.

VII. Marjory, married to Robert Burnet, parson of Oyne.

VIII. Beatrix, died unmarried.

James Leslie, fourth Laird of Warthill, getting advanced in years, resigned his estates to his
1660. eldest son William Leslie, fifth laird, about 1660;
1679. but he survived his son, and died in 1679, aged 96; some say he died aged 105 years old.

William Leslie, Fifth Laird of Warthill.

WILLIAM LESLIE,

FIFTH LAIRD OF WARTHILL.

William Leslie, fifth Laird of Warthill, was a great sportsman, and one of the strongest men of his time. He married Anne Elphinstone, daughter of James Elphinstone of Glack, and grand-niece of Bishop Elphinstone of Aberdeen, and had issue—

William Leslie, Fifth Laird of Warthill.

I. Alexander, his successor, born 1656.

II. William, born 1657. After going through a course of classical studies at the school of Rain, and finishing his academical studies at the University of Aberdeen, he was settled as schoolmaster in the parish of chapel of Garioch, where he remained for some years. In 1684 he left Scotland for foreign parts, and went to study at the University of Padua, where he became a Catholic, and received holy orders. He was so greatly noted for his learning, that Cardinal Barbarigo appointed him Professor of Theology at Padua. It appears that he next went to Germany, and attended Count James Leslie at Pittau, near Gratz, during his illness, and arranged all his affairs. After the death of Count James Leslie in 1692, William Leslie remained in Germany with Count James Ernest Leslie, son of Count Patrick Leslie, fifteenth Baron of Balquhain, assisting him in the management of his family affairs. By his own abilities and merits, and through the influence of his relatives the Counts Leslie, William Leslie was made Bishop of Waitzen in 1716, and in 1718 he was promoted to the bishopric of Laybach in Styria, and was made metropolitan of Carniola, and a Prince of the Holy Roman Empire. He wrote to his brother, Alexander Leslie, sixth Laird of Warthill, the following letter, dated 25th February 1718 :—" Dear Brother—I have endeavoured to purchase here credit and esteem in all stations, and am more and more assured of his Majesty the Emperor's grace and clemency. It has pleased his Majesty to transport me out of Hungary, which is a country not much civilised or cultivated as yet for conversation, nor secure from foreign or intestine wars, and he gave me a much more honourable preferment and seat in the hereditary countries at Laybach, the metropolis of Carniola, to which belong many estates with fine castles, near the castle of Petau, which belongs to Count Leslie. By means of this promotion I am advanced to the dignity of Prince of the Empire, which is a great honour to our name and family, seeing none before was elevated

1684. 1692. 1716-18. 1718.

CHAP. III.

William Leslie, Fifth Laird of Warthill.

to this title. This Emperor, whom God preserve! not by reason or regard of borrowed merit, but without vain-glory for my own comportment, has advanced me within three years to three steps of honour, one higher than the other. I would needs adventure the present to let you know that I live—how long God knows, and his will be done—in a most honourable station. Be pleased to present my duty to all friends and relations. My residence is on the high post-way between Vienna and Venice. In the meantime I
1725. remain, with all fraternal affection," etc. In 1725 he sent home an original portrait of himself, with his diploma from the University of Padua, to his brother, Alexander Leslie, sixth Laird of Warthill, and they are still preserved in the family. In a letter, dated
1725. 1st July 1725, he says, "You may direct to me in this manner—'To the Bishop of Laibach, Metropolitan of Carniola, betwixt Vienna and Venice, Privy Councillor to his Imperial Majesty.' The title of Right Reverend here is due to others who are inferior to Bishops; and albeit I be a Prince of the Empire, which the Emperor himself and all the other Princes in Germany allow me who enjoy their courtesy of their grace, yet I am nowise desirous of those titles in a foreign kingdom, much less in the Land of Cakes. I judge, nevertheless, fitting that the graces and honours which his Majesty has bestowed on me be known to my best friends and nearest relations, as a badge of the esteem of the greatest of monarchs, and as an evidence of my comportment and behaviour, whereby I have not degenerated from my birth and pedigree." In another letter he says, "I represent a greater person in the theatre of this world than I ever could have aspired to, or flattered myself to obtain; far higher than I deserved, for which I wish I may be grateful to God and my master." In these high stations, William Leslie, Prince Bishop of Laybach, continued till his death, and in every scene in life he demeaned him-
1727. self with great dignity. He died in 1727, universally regretted and looked up to as an honour to his country.

CHAP. III.

William Leslie, Fifth Laird of Warthill.

III. James, a merchant in Aberdeen. He married Janet Ragg, but had no issue.

IV. John, a writer to the Signet in Edinburgh. Having joined the army of King James at the Revolution, he was obliged to take refuge in France, and was never heard of again.

William Leslie, fifth Laird of Warthill, died, aged fifty-six, in 1676, three years before his father. He was succeeded by his eldest son, Alexander Leslie, sixth Laird of Warthill. 1676.

ALEXANDER LESLIE,

SIXTH LAIRD OF WARTHILL.

Alexander Leslie, Sixth Laird of Warthill.

Alexander Leslie, sixth Laird of Warthill, according to an old manuscript history of the family, was a man of good natural parts, and learning sufficient for a gentleman. He married, first, Elizabeth Gordon, daughter of the Laird of Badenscoth, and had issue—

I. George, who died a youth at college.

II. John, who succeeded as seventh Laird of Warthill, born 1683. 1683.

III. William, who died unmarried.

Alexander Leslie married, secondly, Janet Gordon, daughter of the Laird of Cocklarachie, but he had no issue by her. He died in 1721, and was succeeded by his eldest surviving son, John Leslie, seventh Laird of Warthill. 1721.

CHAP. III.

John Leslie, Seventh Laird of Warthill.

JOHN LESLIE,

SEVENTH LAIRD OF WARTHILL.

John Leslie, seventh Laird of Warthill, sold the lands of Barnes, not out of necessity, but because they were not contiguous to his other estates, and were run-rigged with the lands of the proprietor of Overhall. He married first, Mary, daughter of George Gordon of Rothney ; she lived only to have one child, who did not long survive her. He married, secondly, Margaret, daughter of Patrick Dun of Tarty, and had issue—

1711. I. Alexander, his successor, born 1711.

II. Patrick, who died young.

III. Anne, who also died young.

1747. John Leslie died in 1747, aged sixty-four, and was succeeded by his son, Alexander Leslie, eighth Laird of Warthill.

Alexander Leslie, Eighth Laird of Warthill.

ALEXANDER LESLIE,

EIGHTH LAIRD OF WARTHILL.

Alexander Leslie, eighth Laird of Warthill,
1730. married, in 1730, when he was nineteen years of age, Helen, daughter of George Seton of Mounie, of the family of Pitmedden, and had issue—

I. John, who died in infancy.

II. George, who died in his seventeenth year.

Alexander Leslie, Eighth Laird of Warthill.

III. Alexander, who succeeded as ninth laird of Warthill.

IV. Seton, accidentally drowned in his eighth year.

V. Patrick, who went to sea, and was never heard of afterwards. Had he appeared, he would have been heir to Seton of Mounie, and to the paternal estate of Warthill.

VI. Bissel, who died young.

VII. Anne, who died unmarried in 1780. 1780.

VIII. Margaret, who also died unmarried.

IX. Mary, married to George Leslie, seventh laird of Little Folla, whose eldest surviving son, William, succeeded as tenth Laird of Warthill.

X. Jane, married to James Allan, Mains of Waterton, and had several children.

XI. Helen, who died young.

Alexander Leslie, eighth Laird of Warthill, died in 1764, aged fifty-three; and was succeeded by his eldest surviving son Alexander Leslie, ninth Laird of Warthill. 1764.

ALEXANDER LESLIE,

NINTH LAIRD OF WARTHILL.

Alexander Leslie, Ninth Laird of Warthill.

Alexander Leslie, ninth Laird of Warthill, married Isabella, daughter of Mr. Milne in Fraserburgh, but died without issue 16th January 1799. His brothers being all dead, the succession devolved on William Leslie his nephew, the son of his third sister, Mary, who was married to George Leslie, seventh Laird of Little Folla. 1799.

CHAP. III.

William Leslie, Tenth Laird of Warthill.

WILLIAM LESLIE,

TENTH LAIRD OF WARTHILL.

1770. William Leslie, born 29th June 1770, was the eldest surviving son of George Leslie, seventh Laird of Little Folla, by his wife Mary, third, but eldest married daughter of Alexander Leslie, eighth Laird of Warthill. He was also the lineal male descendant of the family of Warthill, being the direct male heir of William Leslie, first Laird of Little Folla, second son of William Leslie, third Laird of Warthill. He succeeded as tenth Laird of Warthill on the death of his uncle Alexander,
1799. ninth laird, 16th January 1799. He married,
1813. 16th January 1813, Jane, third daughter of Dr. Patrick Davidson, minister of Rayne, and had issue—

I. William, his successor.

1815. II. Patrick, born 25th September 1815. He went to New South Wales, and afterwards returned home. He married Catherine, third daughter of the Honourable Hannibal Macarthur of Vineyard, New South
1840. Wales, 9th September 1840; and has a son, Norman
1841. William, born 11th June 1841, who is married, and has issue.

III. Walter Stevenson Davidson, born 11th December
1818. 1818. He went to New South Wales, and afterwards returned home. He married Caroline Robinson, sister of Matilda Rose, wife of William Leslie, eleventh Laird of Warthill.

IV. George Farquhar Leslie, who also went to New
1820. South Wales. He was born 19th August 1820, and died without issue.

CHAP. III.

William Leslie, Tenth Laird of Warthill.

V. James, born 5th December 1824; died 8th October 1829.

VI. Thomas Coats. He was a partner in the house of Dent and Company, China. He married Henrietta Marion, daughter of Sir Robert Horn Dalrymple Elphinstone, Baronet, of Logie Elphinstone, but died without issue.

VII. Maryanne, married, 2d August 1836, to Patrick Davidson of Tillichetly, and had issue— 1836.

I. Duncan Davidson, born 5th August 1843. 1843.

II. Jane Anne, married to Sir Francis Outram, Bart.

III. Frances Mary; besides seven other children.

VIII. Catherine.

William Leslie, tenth Laird of Warthill, was succeeded by his eldest son William Leslie, eleventh Laird of Warthill.

WILLIAM LESLIE,

ELEVENTH LAIRD OF WARTHILL.

William Leslie, Eleventh Laird of Warthill.

William Leslie, eleventh Laird of Warthill, born 16th March 1814, was a partner in the house of Dent and Company, China, but retired from it on his accession to the estate of Warthill. He represented the county of Aberdeen in parliament, having been elected in opposition to the Honourable Arthur Gordon, on the accession of Lord Haddo, the sitting member, to the earldom of Aberdeen, in 1860. He retired from parliament, having accepted the stewardship of the Chiltern

1814. 1860.

CHAP. III.

William Leslie, Eleventh Laird of Warthill.

Hundreds in 1866. He married Matilda Rose Robinson, and has issue—

I. William Douglas.
II. Mary Rose.
III. Jane Emma Matilda.
IV. Florence Matilda.
V. Catherine Evelyn.
VI. Caroline.

THE FAMILY OF LESLIE OF LITTLE FOLLA.

Leslie of Little Folla.

The family of Leslie of Little Folla is descended from the Warthill and Wardis branches of the family of Leslie, Barons of Balquhain.

I. William Leslie, first Laird of Little Folla, was the second son of William Leslie, third Laird of Warthill, by his wife Margaret Gray. He got the lands of Little Folla from his father in
1611. 1611. The lands of Little Folla were bought by William Leslie, third Laird of Warthill, from Gordon of Tillichoudie, his son-in-law. In buying these lands William Leslie met with great opposition from the Raits, who were the tenants of the lands, but by the influence of his friends, particularly of the Baron of Pitcaple, he succeeded in concluding the purchase. In revenge, the Raits cut deep pots in the back of the little moss, commonly called the kitchen-pots, with a design to mar the marsh between Meikle Warthill and Little Folla, which pots—says the manuscript

CHAP. III.

Leslie of Little Folla.

history of the family, dated 1741, are not filled up to this day.

William Leslie, first Laird of Little Folla, married Marjory, daughter of William Crichton, brother of Viscount Frendraught. The marriage took place at Glack, where Marjory was staying with her mother, who, after William Crichton's death, had married Elphinstone, Laird of Glack. On William Leslie's settlement at Folla with his wife, the manuscript history says they suffered much from incantation or witchcraft. "Who were the authors of this, God only knows, although there wanted not suspicion." The issue of the marriage was—

I. JAMES, who succeeded as second Laird of Little Folla.

II. MARGARET, married to James Thomson.

III. ELIZABETH, married to Robert Burnet.

IV. MARJORY, married to Patrick Adam.

William Leslie married, secondly, a daughter of Leith of Harthill, but had no issue by her. He died in 1657, and was succeeded by his son— 1657.

II. JAMES LESLIE, second Laird of Little Folla, who was born in 1630. He married Isabella Milne, a worthy and virtuous woman, daughter of Alexander Milne of Monkshill, and had issue— 1630.

I. WILLIAM, born 1651, who succeeded as third Laird of Little Folla. 1651.

II. GEORGE, born 1655, married Isabella Cheyne, daughter of William Cheyne of Kaithen. He succeeded his brother as fourth Laird of Little Folla. 1655.

III. JAMES, born 1661, married Janet Rait, daughter of John Rait, portioner of Meikle Folla, and had issue—

CHAP. III.

Leslie of Little Folla.

I. GEORGE, who got from his uncle, William Leslie, third Laird of Little Folla, money with which he bought the lands of Kinbruin and Rothienorman, and was the founder of the family of Leslie of Rothie, of whom hereafter.

IV. JANET, married, first, to Alexander Wood, and, secondly, to George Milne, her cousin.

James Leslie married, secondly, Agnes, daughter of Mr. Innis, merchant in Aberdeen. He was not very fortunate in this second marriage. He got into pecuniary difficulties, and his second son, George Leslie, procured for him from his father-in-law, William Cheyne of Kaithen, the sum of 1100 merks, in consideration of which James Leslie disponed the shadow half of Little Folla to his said son, George Leslie, and his heirs. By this second marriage James Leslie had issue—

I. ALEXANDER, died unmarried.

II. WALTER, went abroad, and died unmarried.

III. STEPHEN, who died unmarried.

IV. MARJORY, who also died unmarried.

James Leslie, second Laird of Little Folla, died
1693. in 1693, aged sixty years, and was succeeded by his eldest son—

III. WILLIAM LESLIE, third Laird of Little Folla, who, having finished his academical studies, went to Ireland, and was provided with the church living of Aquareagh, in the county of Fermanagh.
1684. In 1684 he was styled of "Buttler Newtoune in the county of Fermanagh, Clerk." He remained in Ireland till he was upwards of sixty-three

CHAP. III.

Leslie of Little Folla.

years of age, when, finding himself declining, and longing to be buried in the sepulchre of his fathers, he returned and settled at Little Folla, the place of his nativity, in 1714. Having amassed a large sum of money, he got in wadsett Roger's Seat and Kinbruin in 1715, and made over all his substance to his nephew, George Leslie, son of his youngest brother James, in consequence of a disagreement with his second brother George, who, when his late father James, second Laird of Little Folla, was in want of money, got his father-in-law, William Cheyne of Kaithen, to give him 1100 merks, for which James disponed to George Leslie, his son, the shadow half of Little Folla, as has been related. William Leslie resented this division of the paternal inheritance so much, that he left all he could to his nephew George, leaving to his brother George, his heir of entail, only the lands which were entailed. The Rev. William Leslie, third Laird of Little Folla, was never married. He died in August 1722, and was succeeded by his brother—

1714. 1715. 1722.

IV. George Leslie, fourth Laird of Little Folla, who was previously in possession of the shadow half of Little Folla, and succeeded to the sun half of the same on the death of his brother. George Leslie married Isabella Cheyne, daughter of William Cheyne of Kaithen, and had issue—

I. William, his successor.

CHAP. III.

Leslie of Little Folla.

II. JOHN, who succeeded his brother as sixth Laird of Little Folla.

III. Agnes, died unmarried.

IV. MARGARET, also died unmarried.

V. JANET, married to Robert Farquhar, Mains of Law.

George Leslie, fourth Laird of Little Folla, 1730. died 21st June 1730, aged seventy-five years, and was succeeded by his eldest son—

V. WILLIAM LESLIE, fifth Laird of Little Folla. There were a few rigs of Temple Land in the township of Little Folla, of a different holding, which were not included in the entail, and which had been disponed by the Rev. William Leslie, third laird, to his youngest brother James, and his heirs. William Leslie, fifth laird, bought these rigs of land from his cousin, George Leslie of Rothie, son and heir of James Leslie. William Leslie, fifth Laird of Little Folla, after taking his degree as Master of Arts, was for some time schoolmaster at Auchterless, from whence he went to Ireland to his uncle, the Rev. William Leslie, third laird, rector of Aquareagh. After some years spent there he returned to Scotland, and got himself ordained, and then returned to Ireland to assist his uncle. He got a settlement in Ireland, but could not swallow the state oath, 1710. so he eventually returned to Scotland in 1710, and settled as pastor of the Episcopal congregation at Ellon, where he remained till the rebellion in 1715. 1715, when he was ejected and his chapel was burnt down—the Episcopal clergy being looked upon at that period as disaffected to the government, and more particularly so after the rebellion, when they were much harassed. William Leslie continued to preach to some few adherents in his own room at Little Folla, till his death, 31st July 1743, in his sixty-fourth year. He was never married, and was succeeded by his brother— 1743.

VI. JOHN LESLIE, sixth Laird of Little Folla, born in 1697. He married Elizabeth Gordon of Cults, and had issue— 1697.

I. GEORGE, his successor.
II. WILLIAM, died without issue.
III. JOHN, who also died without issue.

John Leslie had also seven other children, who all died without issue. He died 25th April 1783, aged eighty-six years, and was succeeded by his eldest son— 1783.

VII. GEORGE LESLIE, seventh Laird of Little Folla, who married Mary Leslie, third daughter of Alexander Leslie, eighth Laird of Warthill, who, on the death of her brother, Alexander Leslie, ninth Laird of Warthill, became heir-female to Warthill. They had issue—

I. WILLIAM, born 29th June 1770, who succeeded his father as eighth Laird of Little Folla, and his uncle Alexander as tenth Laird of Warthill. 1770.
II. GEORGE, who died unmarried.
III. A Daughter.

CHAP. III.

Leslie of Little Folla.

George Leslie, seventh Laird of Little Folla, sold the lands of Folla to Mr. Gordon of Cocklarachie, and these lands were bought back again by his son, William Leslie, tenth Laird of Warthill, to which property he succeeded on the death of his uncle, Alexander Leslie, ninth Laird
1799. of Warthill, 16th January 1799, in right of his mother, Mary Leslie, eldest married daughter of Alexander Leslie, eighth Laird of Warthill. William Leslie was also the lineal male representative of the Warthill family, through his father, who was the direct male descendant of William, second son of William Leslie, third Laird of Warthill. George Leslie, seventh Laird of Little
1807. Folla, died in 1807, when the family merged in that of Warthill.

Leslie of Rothie.

THE FAMILY OF LESLIE OF ROTHIE.

The family of Leslie of Rothie is descended from the Little Folla, Warthill, and Wardis branches of the family of Leslie, Barons of Balquhain.

I. George Leslie, first Laird of Rothie, was the eldest son of James Leslie, third son of James Leslie, second Laird of Little Folla. James Leslie, third son of James Leslie, second Laird of Little Folla, married Janet Rait, daughter of John Rait, portioner of Meikle Folla, and had issue—

I. George, who became first Laird of Rothie.

II. John.
1711. III. William. } Both died without issue in 1711.

Leslie of Rothie.

James Leslie and his eldest son George were declared heirs by the Rev. William Leslie, third Laird of Little Folla, to all his unentailed property, in consequence of the Rev. William Leslie having taken umbrage because George Leslie, his next brother, had got from his father, James Leslie, second Laird of Little Folla, the shadow-half of the lands of Little Folla, in consideration of having procured for the said James, the second laird, the sum of 1100 merks to relieve him in his embarrassments. On the death of the Rev. William Leslie, third Laird of Little Folla, his nephew, George, obtained the reversionary right of Roger's Seat and Kinbruin, and a considerable sum of money, with which he purchased the lands of Upper Rothie or Rothie Norman, Longman's Wells, and other lands, in 1723; and to these he added the lands of Crannie, Cranabog, and Mill of Barnes, in 1728, and became the founder of the family of Leslie of Rothie. He married Margaret, daughter of James Gordon of Chapeltown, and had issue—

1723.

1728.

I. James, his successor.

II. Margaret, married to Hugh Gordon of Muggiemoss, and had a son who died aged fourteen years.

III. Elizabeth.

Margaret Gordon died in 1737. Her husband, George Leslie, denuded himself of the estate of Rothie in favour of his son James, on his marriage in 1760, and died in 1781.

1737.

1760-81.

CHAP. III.

Leslie of Rothie.

II. JAMES LESLIE, second Laird of Rothie, married, in 1760, Jane Gordon, second daughter of William Gordon, Laird of Badenscoth, in right of whom he succeeded to the half of the lands of Badenscoth—the said Jane, and her elder sister, Catherine, wife of Alexander Forbes of Blackford, being co-heiresses of Badenscoth on the death of their only brother, James Gordon, without issue, in
1778. 1778. James Leslie of Rothie bought the other half of Badenscoth from his wife's sister, Mrs. Catherine Forbes of Blackford, and thus the estate of Badenscoth was united to that of Rothie.
1761. James Leslie also purchased, in 1761, the feu-duty and superiority of the lands of Rothienorman from the Earl of Rothes. James Leslie of Rothie had issue—

I. JAMES, his successor.
II. GEORGE, who succeeded his brother as fourth Laird of Rothie.
III. JOHN, who died at sea, without issue.
IV. WILLIAM, who died in India, without issue.
V. JONATHAN, some time a merchant in Dublin. He died without issue at Badenscoth.
VI. ROBERT, who succeeded as fifth Laird of Rothie.
VII. MARY.
VIII. GRACE.
IX. CATHERINE.
} All died unmarried.

James Leslie, second Laird of Rothie, died in
1794. 1794, and was succeeded by his eldest son—

III. JAMES LESLIE, third Laird of Rothie. He built the present house of Rothie, about three

Leslie of Rothie.

miles west of the parish church of Fyvie, and also the house of Kinbruin, about a mile south-west of Rothie. He was never married. Being of a capricious disposition, he executed a deed of entail in 1821, entailing his whole property on his next brother, George, and his heirs-male, with remainder to his youngest brother, Robert, and his heirs; whom failing, to Jonathan Forbes, youngest son of John Forbes of Blackford, and his heirs-male; whom failing, to the said Jonathan's next elder brother, and his heirs-male, and so on, ascending to the elder brothers successively, till it reach the one in possession of the Blackford estate, when the succession devolves to the Warthill family, beginning with the youngest son of William Leslie, tenth Laird of Warthill, and ascending in like manner. James Leslie in this entail passed over his own brother Jonathan Leslie. He died in 1823, and was succeeded by his next brother— 1823.

IV. George Leslie, fourth Laird of Rothie, who laid out the grounds about the mansion-house of Rothie with great taste, and ornamented them with thriving plantations. He had a great turn for agricultural pursuits, and farmed to a great extent, thereby greatly improving the estate. He paid great attention to the breeding of cattle, so that his cattle and sheep were of a superior description, and were very much admired. Indeed,

CHAP. III.

Leslie of Rothie.

from his long experience, he turned his cattle out better than most people, and was most successful in gaining prizes at the agricultural shows. He was an upright and worthy gentleman, universally respected, beloved, and esteemed, and he was of a benevolent and hospitable disposition. It was long the custom of the Rothie family to have a large party of neighbours to dinner on Auld Yule day, 5th January. During fifty-four years, George Leslie of Rothie, and William Leslie, tenth Laird of Warthill, met, with only two exceptions, annually at Rothie on that day, and cherished their friendship at the festive board. After a lingering illness, George Leslie of Rothie died
1842. unmarried 12th January 1842, and was succeeded by his brother—

V. Robert Leslie, fifth Laird of Rothie, according to the deed of entail executed by his
1821. eldest brother in 1821, in preference to his elder brother, Jonathan Leslie. Robert Leslie of Rothie married Barbara Niven, daughter of Robert Niven of Bruckhills, but had no issue. At his death, in
1861. 1861, the estate of Rothie, according to the dispositions of the entail, went to Lieutenant-Colonel Jonathan Forbes, 78th Highlanders, youngest son of John Forbes of Blackford. He assumed the name and arms of Leslie after the paternal name of Forbes, and he is the present proprietor of the estate of Rothie. It may be remarked that

CHAP. III.

Leslie of Rothie.

though James Leslie, second Laird of Rothie, left six sons and three daughters, all of whom, except two, attained the goodly age of threescore years and upwards, yet not one solitary descendant exists, and his property of Rothie, after having been held by three of his sons successively, has passed from the family of Leslie.

THE FAMILY OF LESLIE OF BUCHARN.

Leslie of Bucharn.

THE family of Leslie of Bucharn is descended from the Wardis branch of the family of Leslie, Barons of Balquhain.

I. ANDREW LESLIE, first Goodman of Bucharn, was the fourth son of John Leslie, second Baron of Wardis, and his eldest son by his fourth wife, Agnes Gordon of Haddo. He married Violet Menzies, daughter of Thomas Menzies of Pitfoddles, Provost of Aberdeen from 1525 to 1535, 1525-35. and by her had twelve sons, named after the twelve Apostles, and six daughters. Of these children there is record only of the following :—

I. ANDREW, who succeeded to the lands of Bucharn.

II. BARTHOLOMEW, who married, first, Marjory Dun of Kettle, and had a son, Robert, and a daughter, Isabella. He married, secondly, Elizabeth Garioch of Carstairs, by whom he had two sons, Alexander and William.

III. PHILIP, who went to France, and was progenitor of the Leslies of Clisson there, of whom hereafter.

II. ANDREW LESLIE, second Goodman of Bucharn, succeeded on the death of his father.

CHAP. III.

Leslie of Bucharn.

He married Jane Keith, daughter of the Laird of Pettendrum, a son of the Earl Marischal, and had issue—

I. Alexander, his successor.

II. George, of Hillbrae, who married Marjory Annand of Pitgavney, and had three sons, William, Andrew, and Alexander, who all died without issue; and two daughters, Jane and Margaret.

III. William, a merchant in Elgin. He bought the Glen of Rothes, to be holden of the Earl of Rothes. By his first wife he had a son, Andrew, who was a bailie in Elgin, and married Margaret Hay, by whom he had a son, James. William Leslie married, secondly, Margaret, daughter of John Innes of Auchluncart, and had a son, George, and four daughters.

Andrew Leslie, second Goodman of Bucharn, had other three sons and two daughters, but of them there is no record. He was succeeded by his eldest son—

III. Alexander Leslie, third Goodman of Bucharn, who seems to have sold the property of Bucharn; at least the property of Bucharn soon went out of the family of Leslie.

Leslie of Clisson.

THE FAMILY OF LESLIE OF CLISSON.

The family of Leslie of Clisson, in France, is descended from the Bucharn and Wardis branches of the family of Leslie, Barons of Balquhain.

I. Philip Leslie, the son of Andrew Leslie, first Goodman of Bucharn, who was the fourth son of John Leslie, second Baron of Wardis, went to

Leslie of Clisson.

France, and entered the army, and was promoted by Count Lavalle Montmorencie to be captain in the Legion of Picardy. He was styled Sieur de Vergene, and married Margaret de Lavalle Montmorencie, daughter of Count Arthur de Lavalle Montmorencie, and by her had issue—

I. CHARLES, his heir, first Lord of Clisson.

This branch of the family of Leslie was established in France, and formed matrimonial connections with some of the most illustrious and noble families in that country. Philip Leslie, Sieur de Clisson, was succeeded by his son—

II. CHARLES LESLIE, first Lord of Clisson, who was also a captain in the Legion of Picardy. He married Anne de Clisson, daughter of James, Sieur de Clisson et de la Touche, Governor of the Castle of Enghein, and by her had issue—

I. NICHOLAS, his heir.

III. NICHOLAS LESLIE, second Lord of Clisson, was a captain in the Legion of Normandy. He married Magdalen de la Periere, daughter of John de la Periere, knight, Sieur de la Periere et de la Rosch, a captain of cavalry, and had a son—

I. PETER, his heir.

IV. PETER LESLIE, third Lord of Clisson, was a captain in the Swiss Legion. He married Anne Letar de Beauvais, daughter of William de la Grandemaison, and had issue—

I. FRANCIS, his heir.

CHAP. III.

Leslie of Clisson.

II. PETER, who married Dorothy de Buzelet, and had a son, Peter, who died young.

V. FRANCIS LESLIE, fourth Lord of Clisson, was held in great esteem in France. He was Knight of Ricardiere, Bersilieure, and Sabouson, a captain in the Royal Marines, and a councillor of the Most Christian King. He married Perina Sevault, by whom he had issue—

I. NICHOLAS, a prior.

II. CHARLES, a canon.

III. FRANCIS, a captain in the Bourbon Legion.

IV. A SON, who was in the Legion of Auvergne, and was Inspector of the Troops in Belgium.

Francis Leslie, fourth Lord of Clisson, was
1740. alive in 1740.

The family of Leslie, Lords of Clisson in France, bear the same arms as the Leslies in Scotland—viz. three buckles on a green belt, the field argent; but ordinarily they write the name Lele or Leloy.

Leslie of Glasslough.

THE FAMILY OF LESLIE OF GLASSLOUGH.

THE family of Leslie of Glasslough in Ireland is descended from the Wardis branch of the family of Leslie, Barons of Balquhain.

George Leslie of Crichie, second son of William Leslie, fourth Baron of Wardis, by his wife, Janet
1570. Innes, married, in 1570, Marjory, daughter of John Leslie of Kincraigie, in the parish of Tarland, and had issue—

Leslie of Glasslough.

I. JOHN LESLIE, founder of the family of Leslie of Glasslough.

II. GEORGE.

III. HENRY, who married, and had a son, the Right Rev. John Leslie, D.D., Bishop of Dromore, who was translated to the See of Clogher in 1671, and had a daughter, Jane, married to the Rev. Charles Leslie. 1671.

IV. JANET, married to Alexander Leslie.

I. The Right Rev. JOHN LESLIE, D.D., eldest son of George Leslie, by his wife Marjory Leslie, was born about 1571. The earlier part of his education 1571. he received at Aberdeen, the latter part at Oxford. He afterwards travelled into Spain, Italy, Germany, and France, and acquired such a proficiency in the languages of all these countries, excepting the last, that he spoke them with the fluency of a native. He remained twenty-two years abroad, and was present at the siege of Rochelle. He also accompanied the Duke of Buckingham on the expedition to the isle of Rhé. He stood high in favour with King Charles I., who made him a privy-councillor. He was made Bishop of Orkney, whence he was removed to the See of Raphoe in Ireland in 1633. 1633. There he built a handsome palace, which he afterwards held out against Oliver Cromwell. He went abroad after the execution of Charles I., and remained abroad till after the Restoration, when he returned to England, and in 1661 he was 1661. translated to the See of Clogher. He married Catherine Cunningham, heiress of Glasslough, and had issue—

I. JOHN, born 19th June 1639; died 18th January 1641.

II. ALEXANDER, born 19th February 1643; died 28th December 1645.

1645. III. JOHN, born 5th January 1645; married Miss Hamilton, and died without issue.

1647. IV. GEORGE, born 22d December 1647; died 18th May
1650. 1650.

1649-50. V. ALBERT, born 23d April 1649; died 22d May 1650.

1650. VI. CHARLES, born 17th July 1650; succeeded to the estate of Glasslough.

1651. VII. MARY, born 15th August 1651; died on the 19th of the same month.

1655. VIII. JANE, born 9th October 1655; married to R. Sanderson.

The Right Rev. Dr. John Leslie of Glasslough,
1671. Bishop of Clogher, died in September 1671, upwards of one hundred years old, being then the oldest bishop in the world, having filled that dignified station for fifty years. He was succeeded in the estate of Glasslough by his sixth, but only surviving son—

II. The Rev. CHARLES LESLIE, who commenced his education at Enniskillen, and was admitted a fellow-commoner in Trinity College, Dublin, in
1664-71. 1664. After the death of his father in 1671, he came over to England, and entered himself in the Temple at London, and for some years he studied the law. Finding this an uncongenial pursuit, he
1680. relinquished it, and applied to divinity. In 1680
1687. he was admitted into Holy Orders, and in 1687 became Chancellor of the Cathedral Church of Connor, and also acted as a justice of the peace.
1688. At the Revolution, in 1688, he was deprived of his

Leslie of Glasslough.

preferment because he refused to take the oaths to King William. He followed the fortunes of James II., and when Ireland was disturbed in 1689 he removed with his family to England, where he employed himself in writing political pamphlets to serve the cause which he had embraced. He also wrote many controversial works against Catholics, Quakers, Jews, Deists, and Socinians, which gained him considerable reputation as a champion of the Church of England. His political pamphlets gave such offence to the ruling party that he found it necessary to quit the kingdom in 1713, when he went to Bar le Duc, and took up his residence by invitation with the Chevalier de St. George, whom he accompanied into Italy in 1716, after the unsuccessful rebellion in England in 1715. There he remained till 1721, when he found his situation so disagreeable that he determined to return to his native country. He married Jane Leslie, and had issue— 1713. 1716. 1715-21.

I. Robert, his successor.

II. Henry, who went abroad, and married a Spanish lady, but died without issue. He acquired the lands of Pittigo, which he left to his nephew, Charles Powell Leslie of Glasslough.

The Rev. Charles Leslie of Glasslough died at Glasslough, 13th April 1722, and was succeeded by his eldest son— 1722.

III. Robert Leslie, third of Glasslough, who married, 1730, Frances, daughter of John Rogerson, 1730.

CHAP. III. — *Leslie of Glasslough.*

Chief-Justice of the court of King's Bench in Ireland, and had issue—

I. Charles Powell, his successor.

II. Annabella, married to Robert Leigh of Rose Garland.

1744. He died 17th December 1744, and was succeeded by his son—

IV. Charles Powell Leslie, fourth of Glasslough, who married, first, 22d May 1765, Prudence Penelope, daughter of Arthur Hill Trevor, first Viscount Dungannon, and had issue— (1765.)

I. Charles Powell, his successor.

II. The Right Rev. John Leslie, D.D., Bishop of Dromore 1812, translated to Elphin in 1820; married, 1st August 1808, Isabella, daughter of the Honourable and Right Rev. Thomas St. Lawrence, Bishop of Cork and Ross, and had issue— (1812-20. 1808.)

I. Rev. Charles, married, first, 8th April 1834, the Honourable Frances King, third daughter of Viscount Lorton, and, secondly, 22d August 1837, Louisa Mary, second daughter of Major-General the Honourable Sir Henry King, K.C.B., and had issue. (1834. 1837.)

II. John.

III. Thomas.

IV. Arthur.

V. Frances Anne Prudentia.

VI. Emma, married, 4th July 1837, to the Rev. Nicolas Toke of Godinton. (1837.)

VII. Charlotte.

VIII. Isabella.

IX. Harriet.

III. Cecil Alexander, died unmarried.

IV. Anne.
V. Frances.
VI. Julia.
VII. Charlotte.
} All died unmarried.

Charles Powell Leslie married, secondly, Maryanne, daughter of the Rev. Joshua Tench of Bryanstown, and had issue—

I. The Rev. EDWARD LESLIE, married Margaret, daughter of the Rev. Mr. Higginson of Lisburne.

II. EMILY JANE, married to the Rev. John Hallward, Vicar of Assington in Sussex.

III. HARRIET, married to the Rev. William Hallward, Rector of Minden in Suffolk.

IV. MARYANNE, died unmarried.

V. ISABELLA, married to Anthony Cliffe of Belview in Wexford.

Charles Powell Leslie of Glasslough was member of parliament for the county of Monaghan during five successive parliaments, till 1800, when he died, and was succeeded by his eldest son— 1800.

V. CHARLES POWELL LESLIE, fifth of Glasslough, who represented the county of Monaghan in parliament during seven successive parliaments. He was High Sheriff of Monaghan in 1788, and was colonel of the Monaghan Militia. He married, first, Anne, daughter of the Rev. Dudley Charles Ryder of Dublin, and had issue— 1788.

I. ALICIA MARIA.

II. CHARLOTTE, died unmarried.

III. ANNE, married to John Gurdon of Assington in Sussex.

Charles Powell Leslie married, secondly, Christiana, daughter of George Fosbery of Clorane, and had issue—

I. CHARLES POWELL, his successor, born 13th September 1821. 1821.

CHAP. III. *Leslie of Glasslough.*

II. JOHN, who married.
III. THOMAS.
IV. CHRISTIANA, married, in 1843, to the Rev. Lord John Beresford.
V. PRUDENCE PENELOPE.
VI. JULIA.
VII. EMILY.

Charles Powell Leslie died 15th November
1831. 1831, and was succeeded by his eldest son—

VI. CHARLES POWELL LESLIE, sixth of Glasslough, member of parliament for the county of Monaghan.

Leslie of Tarbet.

THE FAMILY OF LESLIE OF TARBET.

THE family of Leslie of Tarbet in Ireland is descended from the Wardis branch of the family of Leslie, Barons of Balquhain.

I. JAMES LESLIE of Milton, fourth son of William Leslie, fourth Baron of Wardis, by his wife, Janet Innes, married Magdalen Erskine of Pittodrie, and had issue—

I. JOHN.
II. JAMES, a clergyman in the Established Church in Ireland.

1620. II. JAMES LESLIE of Milton died in 1620. His eldest son, John Leslie, married Catherine Cunningham, and had issue—

I. The Rev. Dr. JOHN LESLIE.
II. CATHERINE, married to Archdeacon Hamilton.

Leslie of Tarbet.

III. John Leslie died 26th December 1648. His son, the Rev. Dr. John Leslie, married Marian Galbraith, and had issue—

I. John, who was killed.
II. James.
III. George.
IV. Elizabeth.
V. Isabella.
VI. Letitia.
VII. Catherine.

IV. The Rev. Dr. John Leslie died in 1700. His second son, James Leslie, married Sarah Kelly, and had issue— 1700.

I. John.
II. The Right Rev. James, Bishop of Limerick.
III. George.
IV. Robert, married Sophia Babbington.

V. The Right Reverend James Leslie, Bishop of Limerick, married Joyce Lysters, and had issue—

I. Sir Edward Leslie of Tarbet.
II. Richard Leslie, Archdeacon.
III. Elizabeth.
IV. Joyce.
V. Barbara.
VI. Eliza.
VII. Maria.
VIII. Catherine.
IX. Martha.

VI. Sir Edward Leslie of Tarbet married Anne Cave, and had issue—

I. Catherine Laura, married to Lord D. Gordon Hallyburton, who died without issue in 1841. 1841.

CHAP. III.

Leslie of Kincraigie.

THE FAMILY OF LESLIE OF KINCRAIGIE.

The family of Leslie of Kincraigie is descended from the family of Leslie, Barons of Balquhain.

I. William Leslie, first Laird of Kincraigie, was the second son of Sir William Leslie, fourth Baron of Balquhain, by his first wife, the Honourable Elizabeth Fraser, daughter of Hugh, first Lord Lovat. He got from his father the lands of Craigtowie, and he bought the lands of Kincraigie from his brother, Alexander Leslie, fifth Baron of
1470. Balquhain, in 1470. He married Miss Ross of Achlossan, and by her had—

I. William, his successor.

II. William Leslie, second Laird of Kincraigie, married Bessie Strachan, daughter of Robert Strachan of Dalhousie in Angus, and had issue—

I. Alexander, his successor.
II. Patrick of Lochtilloch.
III. James of Kirktown of Knokinglews.
IV. A Daughter, married to Mr. Leichton in the Mearns.

III. Alexander Leslie, third Laird of Kincraigie, obtained an attestation by a notary-public that he had presented himself at the pier of Loch Canmor in Cromar, to have presence of the Earl of Huntly, that he might ask release of his lands of Kincraigie recognosced in the Earl's hands; that the Earl sent Master John Irving to the

CHAP. III.

Leslie of Kincraigie.

said Alexander Leslie, saying that he could not have presence of the Earl at that time, but that the Earl would give an answer to the notary; that the notary being admitted to the Earl's presence, asked release of the said lands of Kincraigie in name and behalf of the said Alexander Leslie, offering to do homage in his name; that the Earl appointed the said Alexander Leslie to show the charters by which he claimed the said lands at a court to be holden at Cluny on the 27th November next ensuing, when justice should be done to him—dated 7th November 1529. He also obtained another attestation by a notary-public, that, in the court of the Earl of Huntly, held at Cluny by Thomas Davidson his bailie, Alexander Leslie of Kincraigie had asked release, as from his overlord, of his lands of Kincraigie, offering the homage used and wont, but that the Earl's bailie had refused the release so sought—dated 20th January 1530. These difficulties with the Earl of Huntly were surmounted, though the account of the transactions regarding them does not seem to have been preserved. Alexander Leslie was engaged with John Leslie of Balquhain in the slaughter of Alexander Forbes. He married Margaret Gordon, daughter of George Gordon of Hallhead, and had issue—

See App. No. XLIX.

See App. No. L.

I. George, his successor.

II. John of Durno, married, first, Jean Gordon of Braco, and had—

CHAP. III.

Leslie of Kincraigie.

I. John, killed in Holland.

II. James, killed at the battle of Innerkethin.

III. Andrew, married, first, Elizabeth Leith of Newton, secondly, Jean Forbes of Abersnithack.

John Leslie of Durno married, secondly, Miss Patterson, but had no issue by her.

Alexander Leslie, third Laird of Kincraigie,
1554. died 6th June 1554, and was succeeded by his eldest son—

IV. George Leslie, fourth Laird of Kincraigie, who, as son and heir-apparent of Alexander Leslie of Kincraigie, obtained a grant from Queen Mary of the goods of John Strachan in Kincraigie forfeited by his absenting himself from the Queen's host at Roslin Muir, at the first siege of St. Andrews, at the raid of Langholm, and at
See App. No. LI. the siege of Haddington; 18th July 1548. He also obtained a charter from George, Earl of Huntly, Lord Gordon and Badenoch, Chancellor of the whole realm of Scotland and Lieutenant of the North, of the lands of Kincraigie in the lordship of Tough, dated at Aberdeen, 14th April
1549. 1549; which charter was confirmed by King James VI. by a charter dated at Stirling, 26th
See App. No. LII. February 1594. He married a daughter of Patrick Leith of Likliehead, but does not seem to have had any issue by her. He married, secondly, Margaret Dunbar, and by her had issue—

I. PATRICK, his successor.
II. ALEXANDER, who died young.
III. ISABELLA, married to Alexander Leslie, son of William Leslie, first Laird of Warthill.
IV. MARGARET, married to Alexander Anderson in Bonniton.
V. ELIZABETH, married to Walter Mearns, Mill of Inveramsay.

George Leslie died in March 1562, and was succeeded by his eldest son— 1562.

V. PATRICK LESLIE, fifth Laird of Kincraigie, who, being a very handsome man, was called Bonnie Patrick. He married Jane, daughter of John Leslie, eldest son of John Leslie, eighth Baron of Balquhain, and had issue—

I. GEORGE, his successor.
II. JOHN, married Marjory Strachan of Tipperty, and had issue—
I. WILLIAM, who went to the Barbadoes, where he was dean and vicar to the Archbishop of Canterbury for the island.
II. PATRICK, an Episcopal clergyman. He was deposed by the Covenanters. At the Restoration he was made rector of Monaghan in Ireland. He married, first, Miss Forbes of Kintore, and by her had a son, John. He married, secondly, Miss Smith of Aberdeen.
III. MARJORY, married in 1570 to George Leslie of Crichie, second son of William Leslie, fourth Baron of Wardis, and progenitor of the Leslies of Glasslough in Ireland. 1570.
IV. ISABELLA, married, first, to John Forbes of Tough, and, secondly, to William Guthrie, brother of the Laird of Guthrie.

CHAP. III.

Leslie of Kincraigie.

Patrick Leslie of Kincraigie died in 1611, and was succeeded by his eldest son—

VI. GEORGE LESLIE, sixth Laird of Kincraigie, who married Magdalen Wood of Bonnytown, and had issue—

I. GEORGE, his successor.
II. JOHN, married Margaret Gordon of Braco, and had issue—
  I. GEORGE.
  II. JAMES.
  III. ALEXANDER.
  IV. WILLIAM.
  V. JANE.
  VI. ISABELLA.
III. JAMES, married Miss Irvine, and had issue—
  I. GEORGE.
  II. JOHN, married Miss Gray of Schivas.
  III. JAMES of Byth.
IV. WILLIAM, married Miss Gordon of Cotton, niece of Gordon of Cluny, and had two sons and two daughters.

George Leslie of Kincraigie was succeeded by his eldest son—

VII. GEORGE LESLIE, seventh Laird of Kincraigie, who married Lucretia Abercrombie of Birkenbog, and had issue—

I. PATRICK, his successor.
II. ALEXANDER.
III. JAMES.
IV. JOHN, minister of Cushnie in Mar. He died unmarried.

V. WILLIAM, lived in Huntly, and married Miss Gordon of Auchanachie.

VI. GEORGE.

George Leslie, seventh Laird of Kincraigie, besides these six sons, had five daughters. He was succeeded by his eldest son—

VIII. PATRICK LESLIE, eighth Laird of Kincraigie, who at his succession found the estate of Kincraigie very much reduced and encumbered with debt, but, being a frugal gentleman and an excellent manager, he greatly retrieved his fortune. He married Jane, daughter of William Forbes of Corsindae, and had issue—

I. GEORGE, his successor.

II. JOHN, who was bound as an apprentice to a merchant in Aberdeen, but gave up his apprenticeship and entered the army.

III. WILLIAM, a Presbyterian teacher, it is said, at Tough, and deposed for beating some merchants at Barthol Fair at Kincardine, and for maltreating his servant, and also because his wife sold cloth at the fair.

IV. CHRISTIAN, married without her father's consent to a man Donaldson, and had a son and a daughter. The son went out to the plantations in America, to Jamaica it is said, and there acquired a large fortune, and died unmarried, leaving his fortune to his sister, who lived in Aberdeen, married to George Simpson, a cooper who therewith bought the lands of Hazelhead, three miles south-west of Aberdeen; and her son, Donaldson Simpson, was alive and in possession of the land in 1781. 1781.

Patrick Leslie of Kincraigie died in 1696, and was succeeded by his eldest son— 1696.

CHAP. III.

Leslie of Kincraigie.

IX. GEORGE LESLIE, ninth Laird of Kincraigie, a promising young man, who, after he had finished his course at college, went to Holland and studied the law. He went to London, and entered as attorney there. Afterwards, by his father's advice, he returned to Scotland, and was an advocate in Edinburgh. He was served heir to

1705. his father Patrick Leslie, 2d November 1705.

He married, first, a daughter of Dr. Hay, and had a son—

I. JOHN.

His first wife died soon after the birth of her son. He married, secondly, when advanced in life, a daughter of Bailie Brand of Edinburgh. This lady acquired great influence over him, and he was entirely governed by her, and became estranged from his son John, who had taken orders in the Episcopal Church, and had obtained a living in the north of Ireland, through the influence of his relatives, the Leslies of Glasslough. John Leslie remained in Ireland till the death of his father, when he returned to Scotland to claim the patrimonial estate of Kincraigie, which he found in the possession of his stepmother's family, to whom his father had devised it, having taken the steps necessary according to Scotch law for that purpose, although, except under peculiar circumstances, entails can lawfully be barred only with great difficulty. John Leslie was obliged to compromise matters with his stepmother and

CHAP. III.

Leslie of Kincraigie.

her family, and relinquished his claim for £5000, a large sum in those days. With this money he returned to Ireland, and purchased from Sir James Colquhoun the manor and castle of Rosamonil and Corkee, to which he gave the name of Kincraigie. He had several sons, of whom the three eldest succeeded successively to the estate of Kincraigie in Ireland. The eldest reduced the estate greatly by his extravagance. He died without issue, and was succeeded by his next brother, who also died without issue, and was succeeded by his next brother, Charles. John Leslie had a fourth son, Matthew, a man of excellent character, who was rector of the parish of Kilmacronan. He had four sons, one of whom was a doctor in Cork, and fourteen daughters, one of whom married Mr. Paterson in the north of Ireland, and another married James Grove, and had twenty-one children.

Charles Leslie of Kincraigie in Ireland had a son who succeeded him, and had a son, Charles Leslie, the present proprietor of the estate.

"The estate of Kincraigie in Scotland," says the old manuscript history of the family, "is gone from the name of Leslie after they had enjoyed it for the space of 230 years, and it is now purchased by one Alexander Achindachy, a person risen from the very dunghill, being of very mean, not to say worse parents. After he had been a servant to one Jamieson, a Popish

CHAP. III.

Leslie of Kincraigie.

priest, he fell in about the Earl of Dunfermling's house, and after the said Earl's death at St. Germains, he became so intimate with the Countess of Dunfermling that she not only made him her chamberlain while she lived, but made over all her effects to him after her death. He is now a man of great substance, and his daughter is married to John Elphinston of Glack, the blind baggage (money) of this world having such a prevailing with some, as to make them deaf as well as blind. His only son, George Achindachy, is married to Isabel, daughter of William Gordon of Rothnie, whose head (as it was truly said of Richard Cromwell) is not like to fill his father's
1741. bonnet." This manuscript history is dated 1741.

Leslie of New Leslie.

THE FAMILY OF LESLIE OF NEW LESLIE.

THE family of Leslie of New Leslie is descended from the family of Leslie, Barons of Balquhain.

I. GEORGE LESLIE, first Laird of New Leslie, was the second son of Sir William Leslie, fourth Baron of Balquhain, by his second wife, Agnes Irvine of Drum. He married Comney Constantia Ramsay, daughter of the Baron of Dalhousie, and had issue—

I. WALTER, his successor.

II. ALEXANDER, first Laird of Kininvie, of whom hereafter.

1526. III. JANET, married, in 1526, to Alexander Leslie, third Baron of that Ilk.

Leslie of New Leslie.

IV. A Daughter, married to Benton of Cocklarachie.

V. A Daughter, married to Alexander Forbes of Finzeacht.

II. George Leslie was succeeded by his eldest son, WALTER LESLIE, second Laird of New Leslie, who married Beatrice Bisset, daughter of the Laird of Lessendrum, and had issue—

I. GEORGE, his successor.

II. HENRY of Largie, who married Janet Keith of Aquhorsk, and had a son, Walter Leslie of Largie, who married Elizabeth Spence of Boddam, and had a son, John Leslie, who married Julia, daughter of Alexander Anderson of Dumbanen, and was basely slain by the Laird of Ardlogie while he was sowing oats, leaving several sons, one of whom was William Leslie, a canon of St. Quentin.

III. JOHN of Pitblanie, who was slain at the battle of Pinkie, 1547. 1547.

IV. WILLIAM of Lentusch, who married Margaret Galloway, and had a daughter married to Adam Morrison.

V. MICHAEL, who lived at the Mill of Williamston, and held the Mill of Pitmeden and a plough of the land of Newton of Dury. He married, and had issue—

I. ANDREW, who married a daughter of Walter Leslie, second son of Alexander Leslie, fourth Baron of that Ilk, by his wife Christian Leslie, heiress of Leslie, and had two sons; the younger of whom had a son, William Leslie, who married Miss Duncan, and had two sons—John, who died at Dantzig, and George Leslie, who was provost of Aberdeen in 1685, and married Christian Walker, 1685. and had five sons—John, James, George, Gilbert and Alexander, and three daughters—Isabella, married to Cruickshank of Berriehill, the second married to Alexander Davidson of Newton, and the third, Sarah, married to Cruickshank of Banchory.

II. MICHAEL.

CHAP. III.

Leslie of New Leslie.

VI. Elizabeth, married to William Caddel.
VII. Annabella, married to Duncan Gordon.
VIII. Christian, married to the Laird of Dyce.
IX. Jane, married to the Laird of Ardmannethie.
X. A Daughter, married to Robert Gordon.

III. Walter Leslie was succeeded by his eldest son, George Leslie, third Laird of New Leslie, who married Margaret Dunbar of Grangehall, and had issue—

1547. I. George, who was slain at the battle of Pinkie, 1547.
II. William, who succeeded as fourth Laird of New Leslie.
III. Michael, who married, first, Jane Maitland; secondly, Janet Cruickshank, relict of William Leslie, first Laird of Warthill, when she was upwards of sixty years old; and, thirdly, Jane Udny of Udny.
IV. George.
V. Andrew, who entered a religious order in France.
VI. James, who died abroad without issue.
VII. Alexander, who died young.

George Leslie, third Laird of New Leslie, had also five daughters, who were all married. He was succeeded by his eldest surviving son—

IV. William Leslie, fourth Laird of New Leslie, who married, first, Margaret Cowie or Colville, daughter of James Cowie or Colville of Newburgh in Lindores, and got with her in feu the lands of Inch and Christiskirk. By her he had a son—

I. Andrew, his successor.

He married, secondly, Elizabeth Forbes, daughter of Forbes of Barnes, and by her had—

I. John, who died without issue.

II. GEORGE, who married Marjory Leith of Mountgerrie.
III. A Daughter, married to John Steven.
IV. MARGARET, married, first, to Alexander Leslie in Inverurie, and, secondly, to James Milne.
V. A Daughter, married to James Spence, Vicar of Insch, son of Spence of Boddam.

V. William Leslie was succeeded by his eldest son, ANDREW LESLIE, fifth Laird of New Leslie, who married Janet Leslie, a daughter of John Leslie, Bishop of Ross, and by her had issue—

I. JOHN, his successor.
II. GAVIN, who entered a religious order in France. Others say that he married in France. He was canon of the cathedral church of Rouen.
III. WILLIAM, who died young.
IV. A Daughter, married to William Gordon of Tilliangus.
V. A Daughter, married to Michael Lang at Mill of Auchindoir.
VI. A Daughter, married to Norman Leslie in Lankmuir.
VII. A Daughter, who died unmarried.

Andrew Leslie of New Leslie was served heir to his uncle Michael Leslie, formerly in Little Warthill, and portioner of Rothmuriel, 5th January 1595.* He was succeeded by his eldest son— 1595.

VI. JOHN LESLIE, sixth Laird of New Leslie, who was the last who was publicly baptized according to the Catholic ritual in the parish church of Leslie. He went to France in his youth for his education. He was served heir to his father Andrew Leslie, in the lands of Insch, with the

* *Retours Abbreviate*, No. 8426, D. 19.

CHAP. III.

Leslie of New Leslie.

mill and multures of the town of Flunderis, Christskirk, Largieinche, Eddirlick, the brew-house of Insch, the lands of Eddirlick and Christs-kirk, within the regality of Lindores; the Kirk-lands of Christskirk of Rothmurriell, with the teinds, being part of the patrimony of the vicarage of Kinnethmount; the Templar lands of Roth-murriell or Christskirk, with the teind-sheaves, and the office of bailiary of these lands; the shady half of the town and lands of Drumrossie and Rothnayis, the Dalhairbog, and Dalblakboig, with the half of the mill and common pasture in the forest of Bennachie; the lands of New Leslie, within the barony of Leslie and regality of the Garioch; and the teind-sheaves of the towns and lands of Christskirk, Kirklands, and Temple Croft, of the town and lands of Eddirlick, and of the town and lands of the shady half of Rothnays and Drumrossie, in the parishes of Kinnethmount, Premnay, and Insch, and regality of Garioch, 23d
1623. January 1623.*

John Leslie, younger of New Leslie, grandson and heir to John Leslie, Bishop of Ross, con-stituted Mr. Gavin Leslie, canon of the cathedral kirk of Rouen in France, his procurator for up-lifting and receiving the debts contained in the bishop's latter will and testament, and also the debts owing the same bishop, in name of pension or otherwise, in Italy, Spain, France, Flanders, or

* *Inquisitiones Speciales Vicecomitatus de Aberdeen*, No. 178.

elsewhere, and to receive from Sir Philip Dayala, counsellor to the King of Spain, or from whoever had it, the bishop's original testament. The procuratory was extended in Latin under the Privy Seal of the town of Aberdeen.*

John Leslie of New Leslie and others in the Garioch seem to have resisted the king's authority, and Sir Robert Gordon, brother of John, Earl of Sutherland, got a commission from the Privy Council, by order of the king, to apprehend them as rebels. They were taken prisoners and carried to Edinburgh.

John Leslie ruined his estates by his prodigality. He sold the lands of New Leslie, in 1649, to John 1649.
Leith of Edingarioch, who sold the lands of Kirktown of Rayne, and bought the lands of New Leslie, Peill, Syde, Arnbog, and others; and his son, James Leith, afterwards built on the lands of Peill the house of Leith-hall, now the residence of his descendants, the Leith-Hays of Leith-hall.

John Leslie married Miss Ramsay, and had issue—

I. GEORGE, his successor.
II. A Daughter, married to Mr. Gordon of Swelton.
III. A Daughter, who became an Ursuline nun. She was alive in 1692. 1692.
IV. BRIDGET, also a nun.
V. MARIA, who was abbess of a convent at Mons in Hainault.

---

* *Records of Aberdeen*, 6th August 1599. Gordon's *Scots Affairs*, vol. i. pref. xiii. note.

CHAP. III.

Leslie of New Leslie.

VII. George Leslie, only son of John Leslie, sixth Laird of New Leslie, finding that all the family property was spent and gone, went abroad and entered the Society of Jesus. He afterwards returned to Scotland, where he was provincial of the Society of Jesus, and superior of the Scotch missions. He lived thirty years in Scotland, chiefly at Balquhain, under the name of Johnston.
1687. He died in 1687, and with him ended the line of the family of Leslie of New Leslie.

Leslie of Kininvie.

THE FAMILY OF LESLIE OF KININVIE.

The family of Leslie of Kininvie is descended from the New Leslie branch of the family of Leslie, Barons of Balquhain.

I. Alexander Leslie, first Laird of Kininvie, second son of George Leslie, first Laird of New Leslie, by his wife, Comney Constantia Ramsay, got, or bought from the Earl of Athole the lands of Kininvie in Balveny, in the parish of Mortlach, in Banffshire, and built a mansion-house there. In his youth he travelled in France and Germany, He married Marian Calder, daughter of Alexander Calder or M'Pherson of Napferson, and had issue—

I. Walter, his successor.

II. Alexander of Edenville, of whom hereafter.

III. George of Drummuir, progenitor of the Earls of Leven, of whom hereafter.

Leslie of Kininvie.

IV. WILLIAM of Rudderie, of whom hereafter.

V. LEONARD, Abbot of Cupar. At the Reformation he became a Protestant, and married, and had issue—

I. LEONARD, who was parson of Rothes, and married Jane Armstrong, and had issue two sons, Leonard of Chapel-hill, and William.

II. GEORGE of Murthlack in Athole.

III. A Son, who married Mary Grant of Elchies, and had—

I. LEONARD, a gallant gentleman, a captain in the army, who was killed in Ireland.

II. ISABELLA, married to Stephen Bruntfield, a merchant.

III. MARGARET, married to Mr. Scott, a merchant in Edinburgh.

IV. ANDREW, an advocate in Edinburgh, who married Agnes Blackhall.

VI. JOHN of Caldwells, who married, first, Margaret Stewart of Ardbrake, and, secondly, Helen Munro of Foulis, and had issue—

I. ALEXANDER, who died young.

II. JOHN, his successor, called the Vicar, who was an industrious man, and acquired a considerable fortune. He married Miss Hay, daughter of the Laird of Mains or Meine, and had an only daughter, who sold the property of Caldwells to Ferquhard Leslie, third son of William Leslie of Rudderie.

Alexander Leslie, first Laird of Kininvie, and his heirs, got a charter from Norman Leslie, Master of Rothes, son and heir of George, Earl of Rothes, with the consent of the said Earl, and of his spouse, Agnes Somerville, of all the lands of Conrack, Clayhols, and Fishertown, in the shire of Elgin, to be holden in fee and heritage for ever

CHAP. III.

Leslie of Kininvie.

of the said Norman and his heirs, for payment of a 1d. Scots, upon the ground of the said land at Whitsunday if demanded allenarlie; dated at
1540. Ballinbreich, 27th April 1540.

II. Alexander Leslie was succeeded by his eldest son, WALTER LESLIE, second Laird of Kininvie in
1549. 1549. Walter Leslie went to France in his youth, and when he was twenty-one years of age he was a captain in the guards of the King of France, as appears by his patent still extant. He married Catherine Grant of Ballindalloch, and had issue—

I. ROBERT, his successor.

II. WILLIAM, a learned scholar. He died without issue.

III. WALTER, who went to Denmark, and married there; and many persons of considerable note in that country were descended from him, as appears by letters
1739. written from thence in 1739.

IV. MARIAN, married to Sir James Stewart of Culcovie in Ross, from whom are descended the Stewarts of Culcovie, of Auchmedies, of Ardbrake, of Newtown; the Innises of Auchluncart; and the Grants of Largie and of Garthmore.

V. JANE, married to Mr. Gordon of Clunymore.

VI. ISABELLA, married to Mr. Grant of Tulligorum.

VII. A Daughter, married to Ferquhard Cumming of Lochtervandish.

1562. Walter Leslie died in 1562, and was succeeded by his eldest son—

III. ROBERT LESLIE, third Laird of Kininvie, who married Elizabeth Gordon of Beldorny, and had issue—

I. JOHN, his successor.

II. A Daughter, married to Duncan Maconnachie of Dell.

III. A Daughter, married to Alexander Leslie of Drumfarrick.

Robert Leslie was a very excellent gentleman, and was much esteemed by his neighbours. He improved his estates, and brought them into good condition. He died at an advanced age in 1609, and was succeeded by his son— 1609.

IV. JOHN LESLIE, fourth Laird of Kininvie, who married, first, Mary Gordon, daughter of the Laird of Haddo, progenitor of the Earls of Aberdeen, and had two sons, who both died young, and one daughter married to Gordon of Buckie. He married, secondly, Margaret Ogilvie of Milton, and had issue—

I. JOHN, named Hardsoever, Goodman of Ardfour. He married Jane Stewart, daughter of the Laird of Boggie, by whom he had several children, who all died young. He died before his father.

II. ALEXANDER, who succeeded to the estate of Kininvie.

III. GEORGE, minister at Cullen.

IV. NORMAN, a minister in the Merse.

V. DAVID, died while studying at Aberdeen.

VI. ROBERT, also died a student at Aberdeen.

VII. ISABELLA, married to James Sharp of Banff Castle, Sheriff-Clerk of Banffshire, and had issue—

I. JAMES SHARP, born 6th May 1618, Regent of St. Leonard's College, St. Andrews; Minister of Crail, Minister of New College, St. Andrews; Archbishop of St. Andrews, and Primate of Scotland; murdered 3d May 1679. 1618. 1679.

II. ROBERT SHARP of Banff Castle, Sheriff-Clerk of Banffshire.

CHAP. III.

Leslie of Kininvie.

III. Sir William Sharp of Stronghall, Cash-keeper to Charles II.

VIII. Jane, married to John Forbes of Keithmore.

IX. Margaret, married to Walter Hacket of Carnelone.

V. John Leslie was succeeded by his eldest surviving son, Alexander Leslie, fifth Laird of Kininvie, who married Anne, daughter of William Innis of Tombreachach, and had issue—

I. John, his successor.

II. George.

III. Isabella.

John, sixth Earl of Rothes, having redeemed the lands of Conrack, Clayhols, and Fishertown, for 300 merks, from John Leslie, fourth Laird of
1621. Kininvie, 19th May 1621, made a contract with Alexander Leslie, fifth Laird of Kininvie, to infeft him in the said lands for the sum of £1500 Scots, and an annual rent of £50 Scots—13th April
1626. 1626. John, Earl of Rothes, obtained a decreet from the Lords of Session against Alexander Leslie of Kininvie, ordaining letters of horning for payment of £203 Scots, resting-due for feu-
1628-32. duties for 1628 and 1629, dated 19th July 1632.

VI. Alexander Leslie was succeeded by his eldest son, John Leslie, sixth Laird of Kininvie, who married Helen Grant, daughter of Grant of Bellenton, and had issue—

I. Alexander, his successor.

II. Robert, who married Christian Gordon of Auchlyne.

III. James, who bought the estate of Kininvie from his brother Alexander.

IV. JOHN, who married Helen Grant of Auchannachy.

V. PETER, who studied law at Edinburgh. He died without issue.

VI. HELEN, married to Mr. Grant of Nevie.

VII. JANE, married to Leslie, Laird of Drumdollo.

VIII. ELIZABETH, married to Adam Harper, minister at Boharn.

IX. FANNY, married to William Sharp, an Episcopal clergyman in Edinburgh.

VII. John Leslie was succeeded by his eldest son, ALEXANDER LESLIE, seventh Laird of Kininvie, who, having engaged in trade, suffered great losses, and his estate of Kininvie being much burdened with debt, he sold it to his brother, James Leslie. He married a daughter of Archbishop Sharp of St. Andrews, and, it is said, had a son, Alexander.

"Mortlach," according to the description given by the Rev. George Gordon, "is situated in Banffshire, in the province of Moray, about fifty miles to the north of west from Aberdeen. King Malcolm II. gave a charter to the first Bishop of Mortlach in 1010. The see was transferred to 1010. Aberdeen in 1139. A part of the barony of Kin- 1139. invie lies in this parish, which is, and for centuries has been, in the possession of a branch of the ancient family of Balquhain, and of which James Leslie, Esq. of Kininvie, the only resident heritor, is the present laird (1793), an excellent farmer 1793. himself, and a kind landlord to his tenants, and a most hospitable gentleman. The house of

CHAP. III.

Leslie of Kininvie.

Kininvie stands upon the east side of the rivulet Fiddoch, and is environed with natural woods. The scenery is very romantic of hill and dale, woods and water,—Glenfiddoch, the Craig of Baldorny with the old castle, the Giant's Chair, and the cascade of the Linen Apron, or the water of Dullan. The church is of venerable antiquity, being built about the eleventh century. The walls are of extraordinary solidity, without any magnificence of architecture. The windows are long narrow slits, 6 feet high, and only about 11 inches wide outside, but sloped inwards through the thick walls, to out 10 feet wide inside. There is only one effigie remaining, which is a figure lying at full length over the door which leads from the choir to the Leslie Aisle, or burying-ground. There is no inscription, but tradition reports it as a Leslie, a predecessor of the Kininvie family, who was a celebrated person of marvellous gallantry."

The present representative of the family, and the proprietor of the estate of Kininvie, is George A. Young Leslie, Esq., a deputy-lieutenant and magistrate of Banffshire.

Leslie of Edenville.

THE FAMILY OF LESLIE OF EDENVILLE.

The family of Leslie of Edenville is descended from the Kininvie and New Leslie branches of the family of Leslie, Barons of Balquhain.

CHAP. III.

Leslie of Edenville.

I. Alexander Leslie, first Goodman of Edenville, was the second son of Alexander Leslie, first Laird of Kininvie, by his wife, Marian Calder. He was a prudent and virtuous gentleman. He got the lands of Edenville, and married Jane Stewart of Ardbrack, and had issue—

I. James, his successor.
II. Norman, of Nether Clunie.
III. Jane, married to Farquhar Cumming of Rathnen in Strathavon.

II. Alexander Leslie was succeeded by his eldest son, James Leslie, second Goodman of Edenville, who married Janet Harvey of Elrick, and had issue—

I. John, his successor.
II. Alexander, a captain. He went to Russia, and died without issue.
III. Elspet, married to James Grant, son of Grant of Bellentum.
IV. Marjory, married to James Stewart of Easter Caldwell.

III. James Leslie was succeeded by his eldest son, John Leslie, styled of Aberlour, third Goodman of Edenville. He married Bessie Calder or Caddel of Asloune, and had issue—

I. Alexander, who died without issue before his father.
II. John, who succeeded his father.
III. Margaret, married to Robert Anderson, a doctor in Elgin.

IV. John Leslie was succeeded by his only surviving son, John Leslie, styled of Parkbog,

CHAP. III.

Leslie of Edenville.

fourth Goodman of Edenville. He married Isabella Gordon of Munimore.

The lands of Edenville are in the parish of Aberlour, on the river Spey, and forms part of the lordship of Balveny.*

Leslie of Drummuir.

THE FAMILY OF LESLIE OF DRUMMUIR.

THE family of Leslie of Drummuir is descended from the Kininvie and New Leslie branches of the family of Leslie, Barons of Balquhain.

I. GEORGE LESLIE, first Laird of Drummuir, was the third son of Alexander Leslie, first Laird of Kininvic, by his wife, Marian Calder. He got the lands of Drummuir from his father. He was a virtuous, learned, and gallant gentleman. He married Margaret Stewart of Culcovie, and had issue—

I. ALEXANDER, his successor.
II. GEORGE, progenitor of the Earls of Leven.

II. ALEXANDER LESLIE, second Laird of Drummuir, held the lands of Urquhall or Urchwall in Athole. He married Sybil Stewart of Grandtully, and had issue—

I. GEORGE, his successor.
II. LEONARD.
III. MARIAN, married to Mr. Munro of the family of Foulis.

* Shaw's *History of Moray*, p. 29.

CHAP. III.

Leslie of Drummuir.

III. George Leslie, third Laird of Drummuir, married Margaret Innis of Auchluncart, and had issue—

I. John of Towie, who died without issue.

George Leslie married, secondly, Elizabeth Finnie of Coupeshill, and had—

I. George, who was killed at the battle of Worcester, 1651. 1651.

II. Walter, who entered the French service.

III. Adam, who married Jane Fraser, and had two daughters.

IV. Lauchlan, who was factor to the Earl of Leven. He married, first, an English lady in London, and lived much respected at Inch Leslie in Fife. He married, secondly, Catherine Leslie, daughter of Robert Leslie of Fairy, with whom he got a considerable portion.

V. Robert, who lived at Balgonie.

VI. William.

THE FAMILY OF LESLIE, EARLS OF LEVEN.

Family of Leslie, Earls of Leven.

The family of Leslie, Earls of Leven, is descended from the Drummuir, Kininvie, and New Leslie branches of the family of Leslie, Barons of Balquhain.

George Leslie, second son of George Leslie, first Laird of Drummuir, acquired the lands of Balgonie. He was captain of the castle in Blair of Athole in the reign of King James VI., and was held in great esteem as a brave soldier. He married Sybil Stewart of Ballathan, and had issue—

CHAP. III.

Family of Leslie, Earls of Leven.

I. JOHN, who entered the French service, and was a captain in the Life Guards of the King of France. He returned to Scotland, and lived with his sisters at Newtown in Fife.

II. GEORGE, who went to Germany, entered the army, and attained the rank of Colonel. He was killed at a siege, leaving a daughter, who was married in London to the Laird of Newhall.

III. DAVID, who died a student at Douai.

George Leslie had also several daughters, with whom their brother John lived at Newtown in Fife, after he retired from the French service. Besides these, he had also a natural son, Alexander Leslie, afterwards created Earl of Leven. After the death of Sybil Stewart, George Leslie married Alexander's mother to legitimatise him, who was then a general.

Alexander Leslie betook himself early to the profession of arms. He was a captain in the regiment of Horatio, Lord Vere, in Holland, and assisted the Dutch against the Spaniards. He acquired the reputation of being a very good officer during this campaign. He then entered the service of Gustavus Adolphus, King of Sweden, who raised him to the rank of lieutenant-general,
1628. and field-marshal. In 1628 he was sent to take command of Stralsund, and successfully resisted the siege of that place by Wallenstein, the Imperial general, who was obliged to retire. In
1630. 1630, General Leslie drove the Imperialists out of the Isle of Rugen. He continued in the Swedish

CHAP. III.

Family of Leslie, Earls of Leven.

service, after the death of Gustavus Adolphus, under Queen Christina, with great glory and renown, till 1639, when he was invited to Scotland, by the Covenanters, to take the command of their army. He accepted the invitation, and joined with the Scotch covenanting nobles in requesting the assistance of the King of France, as appears by the following letter addressed to Louis XIII., King of France, in 1639:— 1639.

Sir—Your Majestie being the refuge and sanctuary of afflicted princes and states, wee have found it necessary to send this Gentleman, Mr. Collvill, to represent unto your Majestie the candor and ingenuity, as well of our actions and proceedings, as of our intentions, which we desire to be engraved and written to the whole world with a beame of the sunne, as well as to your Majestie. We therefore most humbly beseech you, sir, to give faith and credit to him, and to all that he shall say on our part, touching us and our affaires, being most assured, sir, of an assistance equall to your wonted clemencie heretofore, and so often shewed to this nation, which will not yeeld the glorie to any other whatsoever to be eternally Sir, Your Majesties most humble, most obedient, and most affectionate servants,

ROTHES, MONTROSE, LESLY, MAR,
MONTGOMERY, LOUDON, FORRESTER.*

With regard to Leslie's signature to this letter, Lord Hailes, in his *Memorials of Charles I.*, says, "The subscription of General Leslie is so awkward and mis-shapen that it confirms the tradition of his being absolutely illiterate. It is reported that once upon a march, passing by a house, he said,

* Gordon, *Scots Affairs*, vol. iii. p. 8.

CHAP. III.

Family of Leslie, Earls of Leven.

'There is the house where I was taught to read.' 'How, General!' said one of his attendants; 'I thought that you had never been taught to read;' 'Pardon me!' replied he, 'I got the length of the letter G.'"

Spalding, in his *Memorialls of the Trubles, Anno* 1639, writes as follows concerning General Leslie:—

1639.

"Now about this tyme, or a little befoir, thair cam out of Germany fra the warrs, home to Scotland, ane gentleman off bass birth borne in Balveny, who had servit long and fortunatly in the Germane warris, and callit to his name Felt Marshall Leslie his Excellence. His name indeid wes Alexander Leslie, bot by his valour and good lok attaned to this title his Excellens, inferiour to none bot to the King of Swaden, wnder whome he servit amongis all his cavallierie. Well, this Felt Marschall Leslie haueing conquest fra nocht, honour and welth in gryte aboundance, resoluit to cum hame to his native countrie of Scotland, and sattill him self besyde his chief, the Erll of Rothass, as he did indeid and coft fair landis in Fyff; bot this Erll foirseing the truble quhairof himself wes one of the principall beginneris, took hold of this Lesly, who wes both wys and stowt, acquent him with the plot, and had his advyss for furtherance thairof to his pouer. And first he devysis cannon to be cassin in the Potterraw by one Capitane Hammiltoun; he began to dreill

Family of Leslie, Earls of Leven.

the Erllis men in Fyf; he causit send to Holland for ammvnitioun, pulder and ball, in gryte abounddans; for moskat, carrabin, pistoll, pik, suord, cannon, cartow, and all vther sort of necessar armes fit for old and young soldieris. He causit send to Germanye, France, Holland, Denmark, and vther countreis, for the most expert and valiant capitanes, livetennantis, and wnder officiares, who cam in gryte numberis vpone hope of bloodie war, thinking (as thay war all Scottis soldiouris that cam) to mak wp thair fortunis vpone the rwin of our kingdome; bot the Lord did vtheruaies blissit be his holie name."*

General Leslie took the castle of Edinburgh, without the loss of a single man, in 1639. He 1639.
commanded the Scottish army at Dunse Law in May 1639. On the pacification of Berwick in June following, the Scottish and English armies were disbanded without proceeding to hostilities. But the pacification was of short duration. In 1640 another army was raised in Scotland, and 1640.
General Leslie was appointed commander-in-chief. He marched into England in August 1640, and attacked and routed the Royal army at Newburn on the 28th of that month; and obtained possession of Newcastle, Tynemouth, Shields, and Durham. Peace was restored by the treaty of Ripon. The articles of peace were ratified by

* Spalding's *History of the Trubles in Scotland*, vol. i. p. 130.

CHAP. III. *Family of Leslie, Earls of Leven.* parliament in 1641, and General Leslie was created Lord Balgonie and Earl of Leven, by patent to him and his heirs whomsoever, 11th October 1641.

1642. In 1642 the Earl of Leven was appointed general of the Scottish forces raised for suppressing the rebellion in Ireland, and he went over to that kingdom, from whence he was re-
1643. called by parliament in 1643, to take the command of the Scottish army. The army, which consisted of 21,000 men, assembled at Berwick, crossed the
1644. Tweed in January 1644, joined the Parliamentary forces, and defeated the Royalists at Marston Moor, 2d July 1644.

Afterwards, the Earl of Leven, being dissatisfied with Cromwell's measures, withdrew from the Parliamentary party, and showed some inclination to join the Royalists. When an army was raised
1648. for the rescue of Charles I. in 1648, the command was offered to the Earl of Leven, but he declined
1649. it. He sat in parliament in 1649, and served as
1650. a volunteer at the battle of Dunbar, in 1650. When forces were raised to accompany Charles II. into England, the Earl of Leven had a meeting with several noblemen to concert measures for furthering that enterprise. They met at Eliot in Angus, and were surprised by a detachment from
1651. the garrison of Dundee, 28th August 1651, and were carried prisoners to the Tower of London. At the intercession of Christina, Queen of Sweden,

CHAP. III.

Family of Leslie, Earls of Leven.

the Earl of Leven was released, his sequestration taken off, and no fine imposed on him. He returned to Scotland in May 1654, and from thence he went to Sweden to thank the Queen for her intercession.

Alexander, Earl of Leven, acquired great landed property. He bought the property of Balgonie in the parish of Markinch, on the banks of the river Leven in Fife. He much enlarged the mansion-house, and laid out new gardens, and enclosed a large park on both banks of the Leven. The property formerly belonged to the ancient family of Sibbald. Sir Andrew Sibbald of Balgonie, who died in the reign of James IV., left an only daughter, Helen, heiress of his estates. She married Robert de Lundin, a younger son of the Baron of Lundin. The ancient baronial castle of Balgonie stands on a steep bank overhanging the Leven. The old part consists of a donjon or keep, 80 feet high, and 45 feet by 36 feet in length and breadth. The basement storey is dimly lighted by a narrow slit in the massive walls; it and the storey above are both vaulted. The summit has projecting battlements with turrets at each angle, the roof being flat and laid with slabs of freestone. On the roof is a lodge or watch-tower, with a sloping roof. Besides the additions made to it by the first Earl of Leven, one of his successors added another wing on the foundations of former structures, thus forming

CHAP. III.

Family of Leslie, Earls of Leven.

two sides of a quadrangle, the other two sides being formed by a strong wall. The main entrance to the court is an arched gateway flanked by two towers. Over the arch was a chamber which communicated with the main tower or keep by a passage through the walls. The castle was formerly surrounded on three sides by an earthen rampart and deep fosse, the inaccessible nature of the position on the side next the river requiring no other defence.
1823. In 1823 the estate of Balgonie was sold by David, tenth Earl of Leven and seventh Earl of Melville, to James Balfour of Whittingham, for £104,000.

Besides the estate of Balgonie, Alexander, first Earl of Leven, acquired the property of Inchmartin, in the Carse of Gowrie, which he bought
1650. from the Ogilvies in 1650, and to which he gave the name of Inch Leslie. Charters were granted to Sir Alexander Leslie of Balgonie, major-general in Lower Saxony, to his wife and son, of the barony of Balgonie, and other lands, in the counties of Berwick, Fife, and Roxburgh, 6th
1635. July 1635; to Alexander, Earl of Leven, and Alexander Lord Balgonie, his son, of the lands of Eastnisbet, and of the barony of Balgonie, united into the Lordship of Balgonie, 18th November
1641. 1641; to Alexander, Earl of Leven, his son, and his grandson, of the same Lordship, 31st July
1643. 1643; and to Alexander, Earl of Leven, and

Family of Leslie, Earls of Leven.

his spouse, of the barony of Inch Leslie, 3d June 1650.

Alexander, first Earl of Leven, married, first, Agnes Renton of Billy, and had issue—

I. Gustavus, who died without issue before his father.

II. Alexander, Lord Balgonie, who married Lady Margaret Leslie, only daughter of John, sixth Earl of Rothes, and sister of John, Duke of Rothes; and by her, who married, secondly, Francis, second Earl of Buccleuch, and, thirdly, David, second Earl of Wemyss, had issue—

I. Alexander, who succeeded his grandfather as second Earl of Leven.

II. Catherine, married to George, Earl of Melville.

Alexander, Lord Balgonie, died before his father, in 1643. 1643.

III. Lady Anne, married, first to Hugh, Master of Lovat, who died in 1643, secondly, to Sir Ralph Delaval of Seaton-Delaval, Baronet. 1643.

IV. Lady Margaret, married to James, Viscount Frendraught.

V. Lady Mary, married to William, third Lord Cranstoun.

VI. Lady Barbara, married to Sir John Ruthven of Dunglass.

VII. Lady Christian, married to Walter Dundas of Dundas.

Alexander, first Earl of Leven, married, secondly, Frances, daughter of Sir John Ferrers of Tamworth, relict of Sir John Packington of Westwood, and died 4th April 1661. He was succeeded by his grandson, Alexander, second Earl of Leven, son of Alexander, Lord Balgonie, who died in 1643. 1661. 1643.

II. Alexander, second Earl of Leven, married Lady Margaret Howard, daughter of the Earl of Carlisle, and had issue—

CHAP. III.

Family of Leslie, Earls of Leven.

I. LADY MARGARET, who succeeded as third Countess of Leven.
II. LADY CATHERINE, who succeeded as fourth Countess of Leven.

Alexander, second Earl of Leven, executed an entail of his estates, 13th February 1663, and made a resignation of his honours and estates in favour of himself and the heirs-male of his body, with remainder to the eldest heir-female of his body, or of the bodies of his heirs-male, without division, provided that the said heir-female should marry a gentleman of the name of Leslie, or one that should assume the name of Leslie; whom failing, to the second son of John, seventh Earl, afterwards Duke of Rothes, and the heirs-male of his body; whom failing, to the second son of George, Earl of Melville, and Lady Catherine Leslie, his spouse, daughter of Alexander, Lord Balgonie, and to the heirs-male of the body of the said second son; whom failing, to the second son of David, second Earl of Wemyss, and Lady Margaret Leslie, daughter of John, sixth Earl of Rothes, and relict of Alexander, Lord Balgonie, and of Francis, Earl of Buccleuch, and the heirs-male of the body of the said second son; whom failing, to the heirs-male whomsoever of the said Earl of Leven, the entailer; whom failing, to his heirs and assigns whomsoever.

1663.

Alexander, second Earl of Leven, died 15th July 1664, and having no male issue, was succeeded by his elder daughter—

1664.

III. MARGARET, third Countess of Leven, in terms of the entail, dated 13th February 1663. A royal charter, proceeding on the entail and resignation made by Alexander, second Earl of Leven, was granted 7th September 1665.* This 1665.
charter bears that the king was willing that the Countess Margaret, notwithstanding that her father, Alexander, second Earl of Leven, died before a charter and precept could be obtained, on his resignation of the honours and estates of Leven in favour of the heirs mentioned in the deed of entail, should yet inherit the honours and estates. This charter, given at Edinburgh, did not proceed upon the sign-manual, and is not warranted by the king. It was passed only in common form, by the Treasurer and Barons of the Exchequer, upon a simple escheat, without the doquet of the Secretary of State countersigned by him, and the superscription of the King.*

Margaret, third Countess of Leven, married, in 1674, the Honourable Francis Montgomery of 1674.
Giffen, second son of Hugh, seventh Earl of Eglinton, but died the same year in minority, without issue. She was succeeded by her sister.—

IV. CATHERINE, fourth Countess of Leven, who was never married. She died in 1676, and, 1676.
according to the terms of the entail of 1663, the 1663.

---

* *Registrum Magni Sigilli*, lib. lxvi. No. 23.
† Riddell on *Peerage and Consistorial Law*, vol. i. p. 57.

CHAP. III.

Family of Leslie, Earls of Leven.

title and estates of Leven devolved on David, second son of George, Earl of Melville, by his wife, Lady Catherine Leslie, daughter of Alexander, Lord Balgonie.

V. DAVID, fifth Earl of Leven, did not assume
1682. the title till 1682, after the death of John, Duke of Rothes, the title being kept in abeyance, as the second son of the Duke of Rothes would have been a nearer heir of entail than the second son of the Earl of Melville. The Lords of Session decided that as the Duke of Rothes might yet have sons, the succession should in the interim merge in the king as *pater patriæ.* Charles II.,
1677 by a grant under the Privy Seal, 27th May 1677, assigned the rents of the Leven estates to George, Earl of Melville, father of David, the heir in abeyance, who was then a minor. On the death
1681. of the Duke of Rothes in 1681, without male-issue, David Melville entered into possession of the Leven estates, and was served heir to his
1682. mother, Lady Catherine Leslie, 26th April 1682.

David Melville, fifth Earl of Leven, took the name and arms of Leslie on his accession to the title. In his youth he went to Germany and served in the army of the Duke of Brandenburg.
1688. He returned home after the revolution of 1688, and was made governor of the Castle of Edinburgh by William III. He was also appointed colonel of a regiment and a Privy Councillor.

In 1703 he was appointed Major-General of the forces in Scotland. In 1704 he was appointed General of the Ordnance, and, 2d March 1706, he was made Lieutenant-General and Commander-in-Chief of the forces in Scotland. He was one of the commissioners for the union of Scotland and England in 1707; and in the same year he succeeded his father as second Earl of Melville— 1707.
his elder brother Alexander, Lord Raith, having died in 1695, before his father, without issue. 1695.

David, fifth Earl of Leven and second Earl of Melville, married, in 1691, Lady Anne Wemyss, 1691.
eldest daughter of Margaret, Countess of Wemyss, sister of David, third Earl of Wemyss, and had issue—

I. George, Lord Balgonie and Raith, who died before his father, in August 1721, having married in 1716 1721.
his cousin-german, Lady Margaret Carnegie, eldest daughter of David, fourth Earl of Northesk, by Lady Margaret Wemyss, second daughter of Margaret, Countess of Wemyss, and by her had issue—

I. David, who succeeded his grandfather as Earl of Leven and Melville.

II. Anne, born 7th April 1721, died unmarried. 1721.

II. Alexander, who succeeded his nephew, David, as Earl of Leven and Melville.

III. Lady Mary, married to William, second Earl of Aberdeen, and had a daughter, Anne, Countess of Dumfries.

David, fifth Earl of Leven and second Earl of Melville, died in May 1728, aged sixty-eight 1728.
years, and was succeeded by his grandson—

CHAP. III. VI. DAVID, sixth Earl of Leven and third Earl of Melville, who died in June 1729, aged twelve years, and was succeeded by his uncle—

Family of Leslie, Earls of Leven.

VII. ALEXANDER, seventh Earl of Leven and fourth Earl of Melville, who was a member of the
1719. Faculty of Advocates in 1719, and was appointed
1734. one of the Lords of Session 11th July 1734. He was elected one of the Representative Peers of
1747. Scotland in 1747. He married, first, in 1721, Mary, eldest daughter of the Honourable Colonel John Erskine of Carnock, son of David, Lord Cardross, by whom he had—

I. DAVID, his successor.

He married, secondly, Elizabeth, daughter of David Monypenny of Pitmilly, and had issue—

I. ALEXANDER, a lieutenant-general in the army. He married a daughter of Walter Tulideph of Tulideph, and had a daughter, Mary-Anne, married, 15th June
1787. 1787, to John Rutherford of Edgarstown.

II. LADY ANNE, married to George, second Earl of Northesk.

III. LADY ELIZABETH, married to John, second Earl of Hopetoun.

IV. LADY MARY, married to James Walker of Innerdovat.

Alexander, seventh Earl of Leven and fourth
1754. Earl of Melville, died 2d September 1754, and was succeeded by his eldest son—

VIII. DAVID, eighth Earl of Leven and fifth
1722. Earl of Melville, born 4th March 1722. He
1747. married at Edinburgh, 29th July 1747, Willhelmina, posthumous daughter of William Nisbet of

Dirleton, with whom he lived upwards of fifty years, and had issue—

I. Alexander, his successor.

II. William, who was killed in an engagement with the Americans at Princetown, in New Jersey, 3d January 1777, while serving under Lord Cornwallis. 1777.

III. David, a Major-General, married, 16th January 1787, Rebecca, daughter of the Rev. John Gillies, D.D., and died without issue 21st October 1838. 1787. 1838.

IV. John, a Lieutenant-General, born 20th November 1759; married, 13th September 1816, Jane, eldest daughter and heir of T. Cuming, Esq., and assumed the surname of Cuming. He died without issue in 1824. 1759-1816. 1824.

V. George, born 21st April 1766; married, 27th November 1802, Jacomina Gertrude, only daughter of William Jacob van der Graaff, and died 8th March 1812, leaving a daughter, Mary Christina. 1766. 1802. 1812.

VI. Lady Jane, married to Sir John Wishart Belsches Stuart, Baronet, of Fettercairn.

VII. Lady Mary Elizabeth, married to James, fifth Lord Ruthven. She died in 1820. 1820.

VIII. Lady Charlotte, died unmarried in 1830. 1830.

David, eighth Earl of Leven and fifth Earl of Melville, died in 1802, and was succeeded by his eldest son— 1802.

IX. Alexander, ninth Earl of Leven and sixth Earl of Melville, born 7th November 1749. He married, 11th August 1784, Jane, daughter of John Thornton of Clapham, and by her, who died 13th February 1818, had issue— 1749-84. 1818.

I. David, his successor.

II. John Thornton, born 18th December 1786, succeeded as Earl of Leven and Melville on the death of his brother, in 1860. 1786. 1860.

CHAP. III.

Family of Leslie, Earls of Leven.

III. William Henry, born 1788, placed on the Bengal Civil Establishment in 1805.

IV. Robert, a clergyman. He died 24th October 1826.

V. Alexander, of Branston Hall, born 18th June 1800. He married, 19th October 1825, Charlotte, daughter of Samuel Smith, and has issue— 1825.

- 1829. I. Alexander, born 25th July 1829.
- 1831. II. William David, born 9th January 1831, and 1839. died in 1839.
- 1833. III. Henry, born 14th October 1833, and died in 1840. 1840.
- 1835. IV. Charles, born 21st February 1835.
- 1838. V. Frederick Abel, born 18th September 1838.
- 1842. VI. Arthur Henry, born 12th March 1842.
- VII. Marianne.
- VIII. Charlotte Elizabeth.
- IX. Caroline.
- X. Lucy Sophia Emily.

1794-1824. VI. Lady Lucy, born 1794; married, 14th July 1824, to Henry Smith, nephew of Lord Carrington.

1796. VII. Lady Jane Elizabeth, born 1796; married, 13th 1816. October 1816, to Francis Pym, Esq. of the Hazels, 1848. Bedfordshire. She died in 1848.

1822. VIII. Lady Mary-Anne, married, in 1822, to Abel Smith, Esq., M.P. for the county of Hertford. She died in 1823. 1823.

Alexander, ninth Earl of Leven and sixth 1820. Earl of Melville, died 22d February 1820, and was succeeded by his eldest son—

X. David, tenth Earl of Leven and seventh 1785. Earl of Melville, born 22d June 1785, who was a captain in the navy. He married Elizabeth Anne, daughter of Sir Archibald Campbell, Baronet, of 1863. Succoth, and by her, who died in 1863, had issue—

1831-57. I. Alexander, Viscount Balgonie, born 19th November 1831; died without issue, before his father, in 1857.

II. David Archibald, born 14th October 1833; died without issue.

III. David Alexander, born in January 1836; died without issue.

IV. Lady Elizabeth Jane, born in 1825; married, in 1858, to Thomas Robert Brook Leslie Melville Cartwright, Esq., son of the late Sir Thomas Cartwright, G.C.H., of Aynho, Northamptonshire, and has issue. 1858.

V. Lady Anne Maria, born 1826; married, 1865, to Sir William Stirling Maxwell of Pollok and Keir, Baronet, and has issue. 1826-65.

VI. Lady Susan Lucy. Appointed, in 1866, Lady of the Bed-chamber to the Princess Christian. 1866.

VII. Lady Emily Eleanor, born 1840; married, 1864, to John G. C. Hamilton, Esq., of Dalzell, and has issue. 1840-64.

David, tenth Earl of Leven and seventh Earl of Melville, died in 1860, and having no surviving male issue, he was succeeded by his brother— 1860.

XI. John Thornton, eleventh Earl of Leven and eighth Earl of Melville, born 18th December 1786, who married, first, Harriet, daughter of Samuel Thornton, Esq., of Albury Park, Surrey, and by her, who died 26th July 1832, he had issue— 1786. 1832.

I. Alexander, Viscount Kirkaldy, his heir, born 11th January 1817. 1817.

II. Alfred John, born 5th June 1828; died without issue. 1828.

III. Lady Emily Maria, born 1815; married, 1858, to Robert Williams, Esq., of Bridehead, Dorsetshire. 1815-58.

IV. Anna Maria, who died in 1836. 1836.

V. Lady Harriet Rosa.

VI. Lady Julia, born 1829. 1829.

VII. Lady Adelaide Harriet, born in 1831. 1831.

The Earl of Leven and Melville married,

CHAP. III. *Family of Leslie, Earls of Leven.*

secondly, 23d April 1834, Sophia, fourth daughter of Henry Thornton, Esq., M.P., and has issue—

I. RONALD RUTHVEN, born 19th December 1835.

1839-61. II. NORMAN, born 5th February 1839; married, 1861, Georgina, daughter of William Shirley Ball, Esq., of Abbeylara, County Longford, and has issue.

1845-62. III. ERNEST, born 20th January 1845; died 1862.

1843. IV. LADY CLARA SOPHIA, born 1843.

1848. V. LADY FLORENCE LUCY, born 1848.

Leslie of Rudderie.

RECORDS OF THE FAMILY OF LESLIE OF RUDDERIE.

THE Leslies of Rudderie are descended from the Kininvie and New Leslie branches of the family of Leslie, Barons of Balquhain.

I. WILLIAM LESLIE, first Laird of Rudderie, was the fourth son of Alexander Leslie, first Laird of Kininvie, by his wife Marian Calder. He married, first, Isabella, daughter of Stewart of Culcovie, and had issue—

I. ROBERT, his successor.

II. WILLIAM, of Conrack, who married Isabella Harvey of Elrick, and had issue—

I. WILLIAM, a Jesuit; entered the Scotch College
1608. at Rome in 1608, and died rector of the Scotch college at Douai, an exemplary and pious man.

II. ALEXANDER, who succeeded his father in the lands of Conrack. He married Miss Gordon of Corsnellat, and had issue—

I. WILLIAM, a learned man, attached to Cardinal Barberini in Rome. He was much commended for his

Leslie of Rudderie.

zeal and charity. He had charge of the Archivesof the Congregation of Propaganda. He died 23d April 1707. 1707.

II. JOHN of Tullachallum, who married Jane Stewart of Tannachie.

III. WALTER, a priest on the Scotch mission.

IV. ALEXANDER, also a priest on the Scotch mission.

III. JOHN, a Jesuit. He came to the Scotch mission in 1628, and died 23d May 1635. 1628-35.

IV. ANDREW, also a Jesuit. He was imprisoned at Aberdeen in May 1647, and afterwards removed to Edinburgh. Through the influence of the French ambassador he was released in July 1648, and was ordered to quit the realm, under penalty of death should he venture to return. Afterwards he was rector of the Scotch College at Rome. 1647. 1648.

V. JAMES, died at Douai.

VI. ELIZABETH, married to William Innis of Tombreachie.

VII. ISABELLA, married to John Baillie of the Leyes, son of the Laird of Dounian.

III. FERQUHARD, who bought the lands of Caldwells from the daughter of John Leslie, the vicar, son of John Leslie of Caldwells, and grandson of Alexander Leslie, first Laird of Kininvie. Ferquhard Leslie was a remarkably witty and cheerful gentleman. He married Marian Caddel of Assvaulie, and had a son, William, who died young, and a daughter, Elizabeth, married to Alexander Gordon of Achanachie. He married, secondly, Violet Innis of Auchluncart, and had a son, Walter, his successor, who married Beatrix Duff of Drummuir, and a daughter, Violet, married to Ogilvie of Glassack, by whom she had two sons, Walter and James Ogilvie, both ministers.

IV. LAUCHLAN, of Miltown of Balveney, and Tulloch, who married Janet Baillie of Dounian, and had issue—

CHAP. III.

Leslie of Rudderie.

I. ALEXANDER, a writer to the Signet in Edinburgh. He married, first, Margaret Scott, daughter of the city-treasurer, and had a daughter, married, first, to John Ellis, and, secondly, to William Russel. He married, secondly, Jane Lindsay, but had no issue by her.

II. WILLIAM, of Miltown, a very frugal gentleman. He married, first, Catherine Grant of Blairfindie, and had two daughters—Elizabeth, married, first, to James Grant of Tomdon, and, secondly, to John Grant of Knockandrich; and Mary, married to William Gordon, son of Gordon of Clysterum. He married, secondly, Marjory Grant of Abbachy, and had other two daughters—Margaret, the elder, married to Walter Grant of Arndilly, and the younger died unmarried.

III. LAUCHLAN, who died without issue.

IV. JOHN, of Achray, who married Margaret Innis of Edingeith, and had two sons, who died young; and two daughters—Jane, married to Alexander Baillie of Arnidele, and Isabella, married to Walter Ogilvie of Blerack.

V. GEORGE, who was sheriff-clerk of Inverness. He married Elizabeth Mackenzie of Seddie, but had no issue.

VI. WALTER of Tulloch. He married Elizabeth Leslie of Haughs or Haches, and had issue, a son, John, who, after being long a bachelor, married Miss Ross of Clova, and died soon afterwards without issue. Walter Leslie of Tulloch married, secondly, Christian, daughter of Alexander Douglas, sheriff-principal of Banffshire, and had issue—

I. GEORGE, of North Leslie, who married Christina Gordon of Aberlour, and had two sons, James and John.

Leslie of Rudderie.

He married, secondly, Helen Gordon of Park, and had a son, George. By the death of his brother John, and of his uncle Adam, and his children, he succeeded to a fortune of £20,000 Scots.

II. ADAM, who died young.

III. LAUCHLAN.

IV. A Daughter, married to Ogilvie of Ardoch.

V. ELIZABETH.

VI. ISABELLA.

VII. ADAM, who married Helen Laurie, daughter of Bailie Laurie, and had three children, George, Alexander, and Janet, who all died without issue. Adam Leslie was succeeded by his nephew George Leslie, son of his brother, Walter Leslie of Tulloch.

VIII. MARGARET, married to James Anderson of Colnach.

IX. ISABELLA, married to Grant of Arndilly.

William Leslie, first Laird of Rudderie, married, secondly, Jane Leslie of Aikenway, and had issue—

I. DUNCAN, who married Catherine Hepburn of Inverlochie, and had two sons, George and Walter, and one daughter, all young and unmarried in 1695. 1695.

II. JOHN.

III. ARCHIBALD.

William Leslie had also several other daughters. He was succeeded by his eldest son—

II. ROBERT LESLIE, second Laird of Rudderie, who married Miss Grant of Gartimbeg, and had a son, Alexander, his successor.

CHAP. III.

Leslie of Rudderie.

III. Alexander Leslie, third Laird of Rudderie, married, first, Miss Grant of Bellentoun, and had a son, Duncan. He married, secondly, Miss Ogilvie of Ardloche, and had a son, Walter Leslie of Collergreen, who married Elizabeth Milne.

Leslie of Pitcaple.

THE FAMILY OF LESLIE, BARONS OF PITCAPLE.

The family of Leslie, Barons of Pitcaple, is descended from the family of Leslie, Barons of Balquhain.

David, First Baron of Pitcaple.

DAVID LESLIE,

FIRST BARON OF PITCAPLE.

David Leslie, first Baron of Pitcaple, was the eldest son of Sir William Leslie, fourth Baron of Balquhain, by his third wife, Euphemia Lindsay, only child and heiress of William Lindsay of Cairney, second son of David, first Earl of Crawford, by Janet, daughter of King Robert II. Sir William Leslie, fourth Baron of Balquhain, resigned into the hands of the king the lands of Harlaw, Rasinet, the barony of Pitcaple, and others, in favour of David Leslie, his eldest son of a third marriage procreate betwixt him and
1457. Euphame Lindsay—5th March 1457.* Hence

* Nisbet's *Heraldry*, vol. ii. part iv., Append. p. 73; and *Collections on Shires of Aberdeen and Banff;* Spalding Club, p. 530, *note.*

David, First Baron of Pitcaple.

David Leslie and his successors were styled Barons of Pitcaple. The castle of Pitcaple, the residence of the family, is situated on the bank of the river Urie, in the parish of Chapel of Garioch, on the north side of the hill behind Balquhain Castle, and is about two miles distant from that ancient seat of the Balquhain family.

David Leslie, first Baron of Pitcaple, granted a charter to Robert Culan, burgess of Aberdeen, of an annual rent of four merks Scots, from the half of the lands of Crechmond, with the mill, in the regality of the Garioch, 16th April 1472. He left no lawful issue, but he had an illegitimate daughter, Bessie, married, first, to Gilbert Menzies of Findon, from whom she was separated, and, secondly, to the Laird of Landro, in the Mearns. David Leslie was slain in Edinburgh, and was succeeded by his brother, James Leslie, second Baron of Pitcaple.

See App. No. LIII.

1472.

JAMES LESLIE,

SECOND BARON OF PITCAPLE.

James, Second Baron of Pitcaple.

James Leslie, second Baron of Pitcaple, was the second son of Sir William Leslie, fourth Baron of Balquhain, by his third wife, Euphemia Lindsay of Cairney. He succeeded to the barony of Pitcaple, and other lands, on the death of his elder brother, David, first Baron of Pitcaple, after 1472. He married Elizabeth Seton, daughter of the Baron of Meldrum, and had issue— 1472.

CHAP. III.

James, Second Baron of Pitcaple.

I. DAVID, his successor.

II. JAMES of Rosseviot, who was tutor or guardian to his nephew.

III. WALTER, parson at Monymusk. He had a son—

I. ROBERT, an advocate in Edinburgh, who purchased the lands of Innerpestry, and part of the barony of Kinnaird, and died in 1537, having had issue—

1537.

I. ANDREW, an advocate. He had a daughter married to James Brown, besides other children, who died young.

II. —— LESLIE, parson of Mortlach. He married Miss Monypenny of Pitmille, and had two sons—Robert, who died at Venice, and William, who died at Cullen.

III. JOHN, parson at Kinnoul.

IV. A daughter, married to Thomas Hamilton, father of Sir Thomas Hamilton, first Earl of Haddington.

Walter Leslie married, secondly, Lady Elizabeth Stewart, daughter of the Earl of Athole, and had issue—

I. ANDREW, who married, and had issue—

I. JOHN, a priest, commonly called Sir John the priest.

II. GEORGE.

II. A Daughter, who was Prioress at Elcho.

James Leslie, second Baron of Pitcaple, was succeeded by his eldest son—

David, Third Baron of Pitcaple.

DAVID LESLIE,

THIRD BARON OF PITCAPLE.

DAVID LESLIE, third Baron of Pitcaple, was served heir to David Leslie, his father, in the

CHAP. III.

David, Third Baron of Pitcaple.

lands of Pitcaple, and the mill, in twenty-two bovates of the lands of Rosseviot, in the half of the lands and mill of Crechmond, in an eighth part of the lands of Ardoyne, a third part of the lands of Harlaw, three-quarters of the lands of Alehouse of Legatsden, excepting the sixteenth part of these lands, and in an annual rent of four merks Scots from the lands of Crechmond, in the regality of the Garioch, 27th October 1506. He 1506.
got a charter of confirmation to him and his heirs, under the charter of the deceased David Leslie, first Baron of Pitcaple, of the lands of Pitcaple, and the mill, with the patronage of the chaplainry of Pitcaple at the altar of the Blessed Virgin Mary, in the chapel of Garioch; twenty-two bovates of the lands of Rosseviot, the half of the lands and mill of Crechmond, an eighth part of the lands of Ardoyne, a third part of the lands of Harlaw, three-quarters of the lands of Alehouse of Legatsden, excepting the sixteenth part of these lands, and an annual rent of four merks from the lands of Crechmond,—the said lands all united into one free barony of Pitcaple; dated at Edinburgh, 14th August 1511.

See App. No. LIV.

See App. No. LV.

David Leslie, third Baron of Pitcaple, married and had a son—

I. ALEXANDER, his successor.

He died before January 1534. 1534.

CHAP. III.

Alexander, Fourth Baron of Pitcaple.

ALEXANDER LESLIE,

FOURTH BARON OF PITCAPLE.

ALEXANDER LESLIE, fourth Baron of Pitcaple, obtained an instrument of sasine in the barony of Pitcaple and others, four merks of annual rent from the lands of Crechmond, and the right of patronage of the chaplainry of Pitcaple, 19th January 1534. He was witness to a bond of manrent between Hector Maclean of Dowert, and George, Earl of Huntly, 10th December 1536.* Margaret Forbes, Lady of Wardis, in the absence of Alexander Leslie of Duncanston, fiar of Wardis, renounced her conjunct infeftment in the lands of the Haugh of Myltone of Durno, called the Swerd Haugh, on the east side of the Urie, in favour of Alexander Leslie of Pitcaple, 27th September 1538; and, on the same day, the said Alexander Leslie of Duncanston granted a charter of the said lands to the said Alexander Leslie of Pitcaple, for a certain sum of money. John Leslie, fiar of Balquhain, with the consent of John Leslie of Syde, his father, and of Walter Leslie, burgess of Aberdeen, his curators, and William Leslie, liferenter, seventh Baron of Balquhain, granted to Alexander Leslie of Pitcaple a charter of the lands of Harlaw, extending to four bovates of land, of two bovates of the lands of Rosseviot,

See App. No. LVI.

1536.

1538.

* Gordon Papers ; *Spalding Club Miscellany*, vol. iv. p. 200.

Alexander, Fourth Baron of Pitcaple.

with part of the lands of Legatsden, lying in the barony of Balquhain and regality of the Garioch, 20th August 1541. A charter of confirmation of the same passed the Great Seal 11th September 1541; and sasine followed 22d September 1541. 1541.
Andrew Chalmers of Strathechin granted a charter to Alexander Leslie of Pitcaple, and Margaret Gordon, his spouse, and their heirs-male, of a fourth part of the lands of Rosseviot and Legatsden, for a certain sum of money 2d March 1546, 1546.
and a charter of confirmation of the same passed the Great Seal 30th October 1549. Alexander 1549.
Forbes of Auchintoul granted a charter to Alexander Leslie of Pitcaple, and Margaret Gordon, his spouse, of a third part of the shadow half of the lands of Aquhorsk, in the barony of Leslie, 3d June 1555. Alexander Leslie of Pitcaple signed 1555.
a bond for the Queen's service, headed by George Earl of Huntly, Lieutenant of the North, in 1568.* 1568.

Alexander Leslie, fourth Baron of Pitcaple, married Margaret Gordon of Achanachie, and had issue—

I. WALTER, married Miss Gordon of Strathdon, and had issue—

I. JANET, married to William Strachan of Lesmundy.

II. ELIZABETH, married to Alexander Panton, a son of Pitmeden

Walter Leslie died before his father

* Gordon Papers; *Spalding Club Miscellany*, vol. iv. p. 156.

CHAP. III.

Alexander, Fourth Baron of Pitcaple.

II. WILLIAM, married Marjory Rowan, daughter of William Rowan, a bailie in Aberdeen, and had issue—

I. DUNCAN, who succeeded his grandfather as fifth Baron of Pitcaple.

II. A Daughter, married to Williams of Westerdisblair.

William Leslie also died before his father.

III. JAMES, who got the lands of Daviot from his father. He married Janet Arbuthnot, daughter of the Laird of Netherdulan, and had—

I. ELIZABETH, married to George Watt, Mill of Pitcaple.

II. a daughter married to Allan Gordon, Sheriff of Aberdeen, and factor for the Earl of Huntly's woods.

IV. ROBERT, who got from his father the lands of Auld Craig, two ploughs of the lands of the manor of Pitcaple, a third part of the shadow-lands of the manor of Pitcaple, with the tower, mill, and mill-lands, three ploughs of the town and lands of Rosseviot, and two ploughs of the lands of Harlaw,
1567. 2d August 1567 ; and a charter of confirmation of the
1572. same passed the Great Seal 1st March 1572. He also obtained the lands of Tocher in wadsett. William Leslie, burgess of Inverurie, and his spouse, granted
1580. a bond of reversion, 21st September 1580, acknowledging the sunny half of the town and lands of Harlaw, lying in the barony of Pitcaple and parish of Logydurno, to be redeemable from them by Robert Leslie of Auld Craig on consignation of the sum of 1000 merks Scots in the hands of Andrew Leslie of New Leslie, or William Leslie of Wardis, for payment of which sum Alexander Leslie of Pitcaple, father of the said Robert Leslie, became bound. Robert Leslie married Jane Meldrum, daughter of Alexander Meldrum of Meiklefolla, and had issue—

I. ALEXANDER, who got from his father the wadsett of the lands of Tocher. He died without issue.

II. GEORGE, went to France, and on the death of his father succeeded to the lands of Auld Craig

CHAP. III.

Alexander, Fourth Baron of Pitcaple.

and others in the shire of Daviot, being served heir to his father 11th May 1602.* He married Christian Leslie, daughter of John Leslie, fifth Baron of Wardis, by whom he had a daughter, Marjory, married to Robert Couts, son of the Laird of Wester Coull. George Leslie of Auldcraig killed George Leith of Freefield. He was a man of undaunted courage and great strength; and although none of the Leiths dared to attack him, yet after many wanderings he was obliged to quit the country, after slaying several of the Leiths who were continually watching an opportunity of avenging Freefield's death. There is a song called "Leslie among the Leiths," or "Auld-Craig's Guise," set to a chivalrous tune, no doubt composed to commemorate the feud in which Auldcraig acted a conspicuous part. On leaving Scotland, George Leslie went to Germany, and entered the Imperial service, where he died with the rank of captain. Robert Leslie of Auld Craig had also two daughters, married to Robert Stewart of Laithers and William Leslie of Dyce.

V. John, who got the lands of Daviot after the death of his brother James. He married Christian Arbuthnot of Lentusch, but had no issue.

VI. Elizabeth, married to Alexander Abercrombie of Birkenbog.

VII. Isabella, married to Alexander Leslie of Dyce.

VIII. Marjory, married to James Elphinstone of Glack, in 1559. 1599.

IX. Mary, married to Arthur Forbes of Meikle Wardis, fourth son of Alexander, Lord Pitsligo, in 1620. 1620.

Alexander Leslie, fourth Baron of Pitcaple, was succeeded by his grandson—

* *Inquisitiones Speciales Vicecomitatus de Aberdeen*, No. 85.

CHAP. III.

Duncan, Fifth Baron of Pitcaple.

DUNCAN LESLIE,

FIFTH BARON OF PITCAPLE.

DUNCAN LESLIE, fifth Baron of Pitcaple, obtained a charter under the Great Seal, of the barony of Pitcaple, dominical lands of the same, with the tower, fortalice, manor-place, mill, mill-lands, and pertinents of the same; the right of patronage of the chaplainry of Pitcaple in the chapel of Garioch, with the croft belonging to the same; the lands and town of Rosseviot, with the new manor-place of the same; the alehouse croft called Legatsden; the Black Inches; the sunny half of Harlaw, with the two crofts belonging to the same; eight bovates of the lands of Ardoyne, with the mill, and common pasturage in the forest of Bennachie; the sunny half of the lands of Crechmond, Romblekendill, Ardeherauld, and Ardibuk,—which lands and barony of Pitcaple had been resigned into the hands of the king by Alexander Leslie, fourth Baron of Pitcaple, in favour of his son Robert Leslie of Auld Craig, uncle of the said Duncan Leslie, and which the said Robert had again resigned in favour of Duncan Leslie, fifth Baron of Pitcaple, 30th
1588. August 1588. Duncan Leslie of Pitcaple granted a charter of the barony of Pitcaple to his spouse, Agnes Gordon, daughter of John Gordon of Cluny, for her lifetime, and to John Leslie, his son and apparent heir, and his legitimate heirs-male; with

Duncan, Fifth Baron of Pitcaple.

remainder to Alexander Leslie, his next son, and his legitimate heirs-male; whom failing, to Patrick Leslie, his next son, and his heirs-male, 16th May 1600.

Duncan Leslie married Agnes Gordon, daughter of John Gordon of Cluny, and had issue—

I. William, who died young.
II. John, who succeeded as sixth Baron of Pitcaple.
III. Alexander, married Miss Gordon, and had issue—
   I. Thomas, a captain.
   II. Margaret, married in Holland. Her father went to Holland to live with her there, and was called by her children "gleed uncle."
IV. Patrick.
V. A Daughter, married to John Meldrum of Reidshill, who was executed at Edinburgh for the burning of the House of Frendraught.

JOHN LESLIE,

SIXTH BARON OF PITCAPLE.

John, Sixth Baron of Pitcaple.

John Leslie, eldest surviving son of Duncan Leslie, fifth Baron of Pitcaple, succeeded as sixth baron on the death of his father.

Duncan Leslie of Pitcaple granted a charter to his second son John Leslie, and his legitimate heirs-male, with remainder to his third son Alexander Leslie, and his legitimate heirs-male, failing whom, to the said Duncan Leslie, the granter, and his heirs, of a third part of the sunny side of the town and lands of Rothmeis, and a third part of the lands of Keltiswall, in the parish of Rayne, at an annual rent of £20 Scots, on condition that

CHAP. III.

John, Sixth Baron of Pitcaple.

if William Leslie, eldest son of the said Duncan Leslie, should die without legitimate heirs-male, then John Leslie and his heirs should be bound to renounce the said lands in favour of his brother Alexander Leslie, and his heirs; dated 8th December 1593. John Leslie of Pitcaple got a charter of the Mains of Balquhain 28th June 1610; of the Kirktown of Daviot, 25th February 1619; of the lands of Pitbee and Knockallochy, with the mill, the lands of Aquhorties, Craigmyln, and others, 27th August 1625. He obtained a precept of *clare constat*, as heir of his father Duncan Leslie in the town and lands of Aquhorsk, from George Leslie of that Ilk, 10th July 1627.

1593. 1610. 1619. 1625. *See* App. No. LVII. 1627.

It was in the time of John Leslie, sixth Baron of Pitcaple, that the mysterious burning of the House of Frendraught happened, and in which the Pitcaple family were concerned. The following is an account of the circumstance:—

William Gordon of Rothiemay sold certain lands to James Crichton of Frendraught, but a dispute arose regarding some salmon-fishings appertaining to the lands, which was decided by law in favour of Crichton. This irritated Gordon so much that he assembled a number of disorderly men, and endeavoured to waste the lands of Frendraught. Crichton obtained a commission from the Lords of Council to apprehend Rothiemay and his associates. For this purpose, being joined by his friends, Sir George Ogilvie of Banff,

John Sixth Baron of Pitcaple.

George Gordon, his own uncle, and James Leslie, second son of John Leslie, Laird of Pitcaple, John Meldrum of Reidshill, and others, he proceeded, 1st January 1630, towards Rothiemay. Gordon advanced to meet them: a conflict ensued in which he was defeated and mortally wounded, and he died three days afterwards; and on the other side George Gordon was mortally wounded, and John Meldrum was badly wounded. After the feud continued for some time the affair was amicably settled by the intermediation of the Marquis of Huntly, with two commissioners from the Lords of Council—Sir Robert Gordon and Sir William Seton. But John Meldrum, conceiving that Crichton had not rewarded him sufficiently for his past services, and for his wound in the above feud, and that he had delayed to grant him what he required, came one night and carried off two of Crichton's best horses. Crichton accused Meldrum of theft, and obtained a commission to apprehend him. John Meldrum had married a sister of John Leslie, Laird of Pitcaple, and was then lying concealed in Pitcaple's bounds. On Crichton coming to search for him on Pitcaple's lands, he met James Leslie, Pitcaple's second son, who expostulated with him regarding Meldrum. Crichton took this in good part, as James Leslie had been his friend in his former feud when Gordon of Rothiemay was killed. But Robert Crichton, a relation

CHAP. III.

John, Sixth Baron of Pitcaple.

of Frendraught, argued the affair so warmly with Leslie, that from words they came to blows. Robert Crichton drew out a pistol, and shot James Leslie through the arm, and the latter was carried home for a dead man. Frendraught returned home much enraged at his relation. "By this," says the old chronicler, "we see that those who were parties in shedding another's blood, are now by the ears, and made the avengers of another's quarrel."

On this occurrence many families of the name of Leslie confederated against Crichton, and took up arms in the quarrel. Crichton represented to the Marquis of Huntly, and to the lieutenant, the Earl of Moray, how much he was grieved for what had happened to James Leslie. Huntly summoned the several chiefs of parties, and endeavoured to effect a reconciliation. But Pitcaple and his friends would listen to no terms until it was known whether James Leslie would die in consequence of his wound. So the several parties departed, and the Marquis detained Frendraught with him at the Bog of Gight two days. On learning that the Leslies had assembled, and were lying in wait for Frendraught on his return home, Huntly sent his son, the Viscount Melgum, and the Laird of Rothiemay, to escort his guest back to the House of Frendraught. Crichton and his wife, Lady Elizabeth, insisted on Lord Melgum remaining that night at Frendraught, and

John, Sixth Baron of Pitcaple.

they entertained him and Rothiemay, and his followers, with every demonstration of kindness, showing themselves happy to have now acquired such friends who had formerly been their foes. But this happiness was but momentary, for that same night the Tower of Frendraught, in which Viscount Melgum was lodged, was burnt, and he and Rothiemay, with six attendants, were burnt to death, 8th October 1630. 1630.

The origin of this unhappy occurrence was attributed to various causes, according to the feelings of the different parties then existing in the kingdom:—some casting aspersions on Crichton, as if he had wilfully destroyed his guests who had come to defend him, and others ascribed it to an accidental fire; while many suspected it to have been done by the adherents of the Leslies, as it was said that John Meldrum and Alexander Leslie, Pitcaple's brother, had been heard to threaten that they would burn the House of Frendraught. There does not seem to have been any ground for the suspicion against Frendraught himself, for, besides the improbability of the matter, he lost by the fire a large sum of money, a quantity of silver-plate, many valuable deeds, and all his papers.

In November 1630, John Meldrum and some 1630.
others of Pitcaple's followers and adherents were apprehended on suspicion of being concerned in the plot, and were carried to Edinburgh, and

CHAP. III.

John, Sixth Baron of Pitcaple.

tried before the Lords of the Council. They all denied the deed, and were remanded to prison, where John Meldrum remained till 1633, when he was brought to trial by reason of his having confessed that the evening before the House of Frendraught was burnt, he had said to Sir George Ogilvie of Banff, and to George Baird, bailie of Banff, when they were earnestly persuading him to a reconciliation with Crichton, that he could not be reconciled to the Laird of Frendraught unless it were instantly done, because Frendraught would be burned before next morning, which actually happened. Meldrum acknowledged having used these words, but denied that he was accessory to the burning of the house. The jury found him guilty, and he was hanged and quartered at Edinburgh, continuing to the last to deny his guilt. There was, however, an impression on men's minds that he was guilty. There were also two men of James Grant's party apprehended at Inverness, who made a confession concerning this affair, and were executed at Edinburgh, when they charged John Meldrum and Alexander Leslie, Pitcaple's brother, with having made use of some such words as John Meldrum admitted having spoken to Sir George Ogilvie.

John Leslie of Pitcaple, perhaps apprehensive that his estates might suffer by these troubles, made over his property to Sir Gilbert Ramsay of Balmain, the father of Agnes Ramsay, wife of

John, Sixth Baron of Pitcaple.

John Leslie, younger of Pitcaple, and Sir Gilbert Ramsay got a charter of the barony of Pitcaple 24th December 1634.

John Leslie, sixth Baron of Pitcaple, married Marjory Cheyne, daughter of John Cheyne of Pitfichie, and had issue—

I. John, his successor.

II. James, of Aquhorsk, who got from his father a charter of the lands of Aquhorties, 3d September 1625. He married Margaret Hay, daughter of Sir Patrick Hay of Meigens, and gave her a liferent-charter of the lands of Aquhorties, 5th October 1527. He was a colonel in the Guards, and was killed at the battle of Worcester, leaving issue— 1625. 1527.

- I. John, who succeeded his father in the lands of Aquhorsk. He married, first, M. Seton, widow of the Baron of Crombie, by whom he had no issue. He married, secondly, Miss Forbes of Pitfluig, by whom he had issue—
  - I. John.
  - II. Christian.
- II. Alexander, married Miss Lundie, daughter of James Lundie of Glaswier, minister of Kinnoul, and had several children. He was killed by Thomas Ogilvie in the Mearns.

John Leslie, sixth Baron of Pitcaple, died in 1640, and was succeeded by his eldest son, John Leslie, seventh Baron of Pitcaple. 1640.

JOHN LESLIE,

SEVENTH BARON OF PITCAPLE.

John, Seventh Baron of Pitcaple.

John Leslie, seventh Baron of Pitcaple, got a charter from his father to him and Agnes Ramsay,

CHAP. III.

John, Seventh Baron of Pitcaple.

his future spouse, of the lands of Harlaw, Temple Croft, Rosseviot, Newplace, Legatsden, and the Mill of Pitcaple, dated 9th December 1619. He also granted a bond obliging himself not to use any diligence against John Leslie, eleventh Baron of Balquhain, his person or estate, for £8000
1630. Scots, due to him by bond, 1st February 1630. John Leslie, younger of Pitcaple, John Forbes of Leslie, and others, made a representation to the Covenanting nobility against the blockade of the
1639. harbour of Aberdeen, 31st May 1639.

John Leslie married Agnes Ramsay, second daughter of Sir Gilbert Ramsay of Balmain, and had issue—

I. Alexander, his successor, and several daughters, one of
1650. whom married William Leith of Harthill in 1650, and had three sons—Patrick, George, and William Leith—of whom the two latter signed a disposition, 17th De-
1679. cember 1679. Another daughter married James Horn of Westhall, sometime a minister in Elgin.

When the Marquis of Montrose was taken prisoner in the north, he was brought to Pitcaple
1650. in April 1650, on his way south. Agnes Ramsay, wife of John Leslie, seventh Baron of Pitcaple, and cousin to Montrose, offered him her assistance to escape, but he resolved to stand his trial at Edinburgh, where he was executed 21st May
1650. 1650. The room in which he was confined at Pitcaple was called Montrose's room.

1650. In the month of July 1650, Charles II. sailed from Holland, and landed at Garmouth on the

Spey, from whence he proceeded to rest at the Bog of Gight, now called Gordon Castle. When on his journey southward he sent notice to John Leslie of Pitcaple that he would dine with him. Pitcaple received this notice while he was attending St. Sair's fair, and hearing that the king was attended by a considerable number of followers, he was apprehensive that his stock of wine would not be sufficient. Therefore he bought all the claret exposed for sale in the market, to aid in entertaining the royal party. When the king crossed the Urie near the castle of Pitcaple, he was struck with the luxuriance of the crop, and observed that it reminded him of dear England. The farm to which this remark was applied has ever since been called England.

John, Seventh Baron of Pitcaple.

John Leslie, seventh Baron of Pitcaple, was a lieutenant-colonel, and was engaged in the battle of Worcester, where he received a wound of which he died in 1651. He was succeeded by his son— 1651.

ALEXANDER LESLIE,

EIGHTH BARON OF PITCAPLE.

Alexander, Eighth Baron of Pitcaple.

Alexander Leslie, eighth Baron of Pitcaple, got a disposition of the Mill of Pitcaple, with the multures thereof, from his uncle, Sir Gilbert Ramsay of Balmain, 18th December 1652; also of the lands and Mains of Pitcaple, 1652. with the fortalice, the croft of land called England,

CHAP. III.

Alexander, Eighth Baron of Pitcaple.

the town and lands of Pitbee, and croft at the Chapel of Garioch, in the parish of Logydurno, with commonty and common pasturage in the moss and forest of Bennachie, and the liberty of casting, winning, and bringing peats and fuel in and from the said moss to the said lands, used
1656. and wont, 21st October 1656. He granted a disposition of the above lands to Elizabeth Leslie, his spouse, in liferent, and to his eldest son, John, and his lawful heirs-male, in fee, with remainder to his second son, Alexander Leslie, 6th Janu-
1657. ary 1657. He obtained a disposition of the teinds of the said lands from John, Earl of Louden, 4th February, and registered in the books
1659. of Exchequer 11th February 1659. Alexander Leslie of Tullos, fourteenth Baron of Balquhain, made a contract, dated 29th June and 3d July
1669. 1669, with Alexander Pitcaple, Elizabeth Leslie, his spouse, and John Leslie, their eldest son, for the sale to them of the lands of Pitbee, the croft at Chapel of Garioch, and the reversion of the lands of Pitbee Hauch, to be held by them in the same manner as the same were held by the deceased John Leslie elder, and John Leslie
1625. younger, of Balquhain, in the year 1625.

Alexander Leslie married Elizabeth Leslie, daughter of Leonard Leslie, Laird of Haches, and had issue—

I. JOHN, who got a charter of the lands of Pitcaple and
1657. others, 6th January 1657, but died without issue before his father.

CHAP. III.

Alexander, Eighth Baron of Pitcaple.

II. ALEXANDER, born 23d January 1656; succeeded as ninth Baron.
III. CHARLES, died in Holland.
IV. DAVID, also died in Holland.
V. WILLIAM, a Jesuit.
VI. WALTER, also a Jesuit.
VII. JANET, married to David Dunbar of Kirkhill. A decreet of adjudication was issued, at the instance of Patrick, Count Leslie, fifteenth Baron of Balquhain, against Alexander Leslie, ninth Baron of Pitcaple, charged to enter heir to the deceased Alexander Leslie of Pitcaple, his father, in the lands of Pitcaple. One of the debts mentioned in the adjudication was due to Janet Leslie, sister of the said Alexander Leslie younger, and spouse of David Dunbar of Kirkhill, 7th November 1682. 1682.

Alexander Leslie, eighth Baron of Pitcaple, died before 1679, when Elizabeth Leslie, his relict, 1679. assigned to Alexander Leslie of Pitcaple, her son, a bond by John Leslie of Aquhorsk, obliging himself to convey to her the teind right of the lands of Pitbee and others. He was succeeded by his son—

ALEXANDER LESLIE,

NINTH BARON OF PITCAPLE.

Alexander, Ninth Baron of Pitcaple.

ALEXANDER LESLIE, ninth Baron of Pitcaple, with William Erskine of Pittodrie, executed a bond, binding himself to obey peaceably the government of King William and Queen Mary, December 1689. 1689. He married Marjory, eldest daughter of Patrick, Count Leslie, fifteenth Baron

CHAP. III. *Alexander, Ninth Baron of Pitcaple.* of Balquhain. The marriage-contract is dated 20th June 1681, and was signed before John Leslie of Aquhorsk, and Alexander Leslie, younger of Kininvie, witnesses. Patrick, Count Leslie of Balquhain, gave a discharge to Alexander Leslie of Pitcaple of the sum of £3936 : 10 : 10 Scots, and that because the said Alexander had discharged James Leslie, eldest son of the marriage between him and the deceased Marjory Leslie, daughter of the said Patrick, Count Leslie, of the sum of £2330 : 13 : 6 Scots, part of the sum of £5596 : 13 : 4 Scots, with which he had burdened the fee of his said son. The discharge by Patrick, Count Leslie, was signed before John Leslie of
1709. Middletoune, 20th October 1709. By Marjory Leslie, Alexander Leslie had issue—

I. JAMES, his successor.

He married, secondly, Henrietta Irvine of Drum, and had issue—

I. GEORGE, a lieutenant in the navy, died without issue.

II. JOHN, in holy orders.

1693. III. ALEXANDER, a Jesuit, born 7th November 1693; was admitted into the noviciate of the Society of Jesus
1713. 12th November 1713; made his profession 2d
1729. February 1729. He served on the Scotch mission
1747. till 1747, when he went to Rome, and died there
1760. about 1760. He edited the *Mozarabic Missal*, pub-
1755. lished at Rome in quarto in 1755, and he wrote a treatise on the Legions of Rome. His friend, Father Thorpe, says, that in looking over Father Leslie's papers, he observed what he had too much honour to make known during his life—namely, that he had a

principal hand in compiling those works which made Father Azevedo's name so famous throughout Italy, and which gained him so much favour from his Holiness.

Alexander, Ninth Baron of Pitcaple.

IV. CHARLES, a goldsmith in Dublin, where he married, but died without issue.

V. JANE, born 1700, who succeeded her brother James in the barony of Pitcaple. 1700.

VI. ISABELLA.

VII. TERESA, who was agent for her brother James when he was absent in France.

VIII. AGNES, born in 1710. 1710.

IX. ANNE, married to Alexander Cumming of Alathan.

Alexander Leslie, ninth Baron of Pitcaple, was succeeded by his eldest son—

SIR JAMES LESLIE,

TENTH BARON OF PITCAPLE.

Sir James, Tenth Baron of Pitcaple.

SIR JAMES LESLIE, tenth Baron of Pitcaple, in his youth had gone abroad and had entered the French service, in which he attained the rank of brigadier-general, and was made a Knight of St. Louis, and Commandant of the Royal Swedish Regiment.

On the death of Ernest Leslie, eighteenth Baron of Balquhain, without male issue, in 1739, 1739.
the direct line of heirs-male of the Scotch branch of the family of Leslie, Barons of Balquhain, failed, all the heirs-male in Scotland being sons or grandsons of the daughters of Patrick, Count Leslie, fifteenth Baron of Balquhain. As has been related at length in the records of Anthony,

CHAP. III.

Sir James, Tenth Baron of Pitcaple.

Count Leslie, nineteenth Baron of Balquhain, this event occasioned a dispute regarding the succession to the Balquhain estates. Sir James Leslie of Pitcaple considered himself entitled to succeed to them in right of his mother, Marjory Leslie, the eldest daughter of Count Patrick Leslie. Count Charles Cajetan Leslie, and his sons, Counts Leopold and Anthony Leslie, in Germany, considered themselves entitled to succeed as the direct heirs-male of Count Patrick Leslie, in right of their father and grandfather, Count James Ernest Leslie, Count Patrick's eldest son. Count Charles Cajetan Leslie endeavoured to dissuade Sir James Leslie from asserting his claim, and offered to give him the management of the Balquhain estates on advantageous terms. But Sir James Leslie determined to pursue his claim in the Court of Session, and in the meantime he returned from France, and took possession of the Balquhain estates. After a lengthened litigation, the Court of Session pronounced in favour of Sir James Leslie's claims, 11th February
1741. 1741. But the Counts Leslie carried the case by appeal to the House of Lords, who reversed the decision of the Court of Session, and pronounced in favour of the claims of Anthony, Count Leslie, second son of Charles Cajetan, Count Leslie, 29th
1742. April 1742. Consequently, Anthony, Count Leslie, became nineteenth Baron of Balquhain, and Sir James Leslie was obliged to relinquish his

Sir James, Tenth Baron of Pitcaple.

possession of the Balquhain estates, and an execution of arrestment was issued, 11th November 1742, at the instance of Charles Cajetan, Count Leslie, and Anthony, Count Leslie, his second son, in the hands of Mrs. Teresa Leslie, sister to Sir James Leslie of Pitcaple, for the sum of £2000 sterling, the amount of the wrongous intromissions of the said Sir James Leslie with the rents of Balquhain from Martinmas 1739 to Whitsunday 1742. 1739. 1742.

Sir James Leslie, tenth Baron of Pitcaple, died without issue, 12th March 1757, and his brothers being all dead without issue, or in holy orders, and so excluded from the succession, he was succeeded by his eldest sister— 1757.

Jane Leslie, married to John Lumsden, Professor of Divinity in the University and King's College, Aberdeen, and had two daughters, who succeeded her as co-heiresses in the estate of Pitcaple, which they sold to Henry Lumsden, a lawyer in Aberdeen, whose grandson is now in possession of the estate.

RECORDS OF THE FAMILY OF LESLIE OF CULTS.

Leslie of Cults.

The family of Leslie of Cults was descended from the family of Leslie, Barons of Balquhain.

I. Malcolm Leslie, first Laird of Cults, was the illegitimate son of Sir Andrew Leslie, third

CHAP. III.

Leslie of Cults.

Baron of Balquhain, by the Fair Maid of Strathdon. Sir Andrew Leslie had a feud with the Forbeses, and made an incursion with a large body of retainers up to Strathdon, and devastated the lands, and carried off the daughter and heiress of the Baron of Cray, chief of the Clan Allan, and who was called the Fair Maid of Strathdon: others say that the lady whom Sir Andrew Leslie carried off was a daughter of Sir James Stewart of Inveravon, also called the Fair Maid of Strathdon. It seems certain that, by one or other of these ladies, Sir Andrew Leslie had a natural son, Malcolm Leslie, to whom he gave the lands of Cults. Malcolm Leslie of Cults is a witness to a charter of half of the lands of Westhall, granted by Alexander Ramsay of Westhall
1453. to his brother, Edward Ramsay, 26th May 1453.*
Malcolm Leslie of Cults had two sons—

I. ANDREW, parson of Slisk. He had a daughter, Mary, married to John Gordon of Essie, by whom she had Duncan Gordon of Knower, Alexander Gordon of Knockespock, William Gordon, Bridge of Gight, and several other sons, from whom are descended the Gordons of Cairnborrow, of Buckie, of Crimond, and of Crawley.

II. ALEXANDER of Auching.

II. ALEXANDER LESLIE of Auching was bailie of the lands of Frendraught for Dunbar, Earl of Moray, and his daughter Lady Elizabeth. He married Marian Cruickshank, daughter of Alex-

* *Registrum Episcopatus Aberdonensis*, vol. i. p. 260.

Leslie of Cults.

ander Cruickshank of Auchenden, or Auching, by whom he had issue—

I. George of Erlifield, who got from his father the lands of Little Crannie in heritage, and also several wadsetts. He was bailie to William Leslie, seventh Baron of Balquhain. He was engaged in the battle of Flodden, in which he received a wound, and died in consequence after his return home. He had a son, Andrew, who was parson at Fetternear and Oyne, and a daughter, Elizabeth, married, first, to William Tarbet, and, secondly, to William Thain.

II. Berald, parson of Rothes and vicar of Elgin. He was tutor to the Earl of Rothes, the Baron of Balquhain, and several other noblemen and gentlemen. He was buried in the Chanonrie kirk of Elgin, with his brother Gavin, as their monuments testify.

III. Malcolm, who was taken prisoner during the feuds between the Leslies and the Forbeses in 1526, and 1526.
was carried behind a man on horseback to Druminnor, where he was basely slain at the instigation of the Laird of Lentusch. He left a son, George, who was killed at the battle of Pinkie in 1547. 1547.

IV. Gavin, of whom presently.

V. Margaret, married to John Leslie, second son of George Leslie, first Laird of Ackenway, 25th May 1529. 1529.

Alexander Leslie of Auching died in 1500. 1500.
His fourth son—

III. Gavin Leslie, was an eminent lawyer, and was greatly accomplished, having travelled much in England, the Low Countries, Italy, and France. After finishing his studies in France, he was made a licentiate Doctor of Laws. He was Judge Official, or Commissary, of the Diocese of

CHAP. III.

Leslie of Cults.

Moray. He married Miss Ruther, daughter of the Laird of Gormack, by whom he had a son—

1526. I. John Leslie, who became Bishop of Ross, born in 1526.

1554. Gavin Leslie died 16th March 1554. His son,

John Leslie, Bishop of Ross.

IV. John Leslie, who is called by Buchanan a priest's giett—*i. e.* the spurious son of a priest—as, according to some authorities, his father Gavin was in priest's orders, and consequently was never married, Miss Ruther being only his concubine. A dispensation or legitimation under papal
1538. authority was granted, 19th July 1538, by Alexander Sutherland, official of Moray, in favour of John Leslie, therein designed as John Lesley, scholar in Moray, enabling him, notwithstanding the defect of his birth, to receive holy orders.* John Leslie was educated at the University of Aberdeen, and gave early indications of
1544. extraordinary genius. In 1544, when he was eighteen years of age, he was nominated by the magistrates and council of Aberdeen to a prebend, and to the office of organist and teacher of the song-school, with an income of £20 a-year.
1546. In 1546 the bishop of Aberdeen made him an
1550. acolyte in the cathedral of Aberdeen. In 1550 he was appointed canon of Aberdeen and Ellon, prebendary of Aberdeen, and vicar of Dyce. In

* Keith's *Scottish Bishops*, first edition, p. 115.

† *Book of Bonaccord*, p. 124.

John Leslie, Bishop of Ross.

1553 he was appointed canonist in King's College, Aberdeen.* He went to France, and studied canon and civil law at Poictiers, Toulouse, and Paris, and took his degree as Doctor of Laws, and lectured in the schools of law. In 1558 he received holy orders, and was appointed official of the diocese of Aberdeen. In 1559 he was inducted into the parsonage of Oyne.

1558.

1559.

About this time the doctrines of the Reformation began to spread, and great animosities and debates arose among all ranks of people. A solemn disputation between the Catholics and the Reformers was agreed to. We find that in 1560, the Rev. John Leslie, official of Aberdeen, licentiate in both faculties of law, and Mr. Alexander Anderson, the principal of the college, with others, were ordered by the Lords of the Congregation to go to Edinburgh, to meet and discuss points of faith with John Knox, John Willox, and others. But nothing was settled by the discussion. Dr. Leslie was detained in Edinburgh, and was ordered not to preach again.

The troubles in Scotland daily increasing, both parties thought it necessary to invite Queen Mary home from France. Dr. Leslie was sent to France by the Catholic party, and particularly by the Earls of Huntly and Athole, to offer their services to the queen. Lord James Stewart, Queen Mary's natural brother, was sent by the

* *Fasti Aberdonenses*, Appendix, p. lxxx.

CHAP. III.

John Leslie, Bishop of Ross.

Reformers to offer their services. Dr. Leslie made such despatch that he arrived at the French Court several days before Lord James Stewart. Queen Mary set out for Scotland, and embarked at
1561. Calais 20th August 1561, and arrived at Leith six days afterwards. Dr. Leslie accompanied her.

1562. In 1562, Dr. Leslie was appointed professor of canon law in the University and King's College, Aberdeen. Soon afterwards he was appointed one of the Senators of the College of Justice, an ordinary Lord of Session, and a privy councillor.
1564. In 1564 he received the Abbey of Lindores in
1565. commendam. In 1565, on the death of Henry Sinclair, Bishop of Ross, Dr. Leslie was appointed to the bishopric of Ross.

The Bishop of Ross, observing that the laws of Scotland were becoming obsolete and ill kept from not being collected into one body, urged Queen Mary to appoint a commission to collect, amend, and correct all the laws. The queen accordingly appointed a commission for this purpose, and to the care and industry of the commissioners, and especially of the Bishop of Ross, we owe the first impression of the *Laws of Scotland*,
1566. printed at Edinburgh, 1566, commonly called the "Black Acts of Parliament,"—so called because they were printed in the black or Saxon character.

The Bishop of Ross joined Queen Mary after
1568. her escape from Lochleven. In 1568 he was sent as one of her commissioners to meet the

John Leslie, Bishop of Ross.

commissioners of Queen Elizabeth at York, to defend the Queen of Scotland against the calumnies of her rebellious subjects. The bishop proved himself most faithful to his queen on this and on other occasions, and acted as her agent and ambassador at several courts, never ceasing, while she lived, to act for her with great earnestness and much labour. When Mary was detained a prisoner by Queen Elizabeth, she sent the Bishop of Ross to Elizabeth to represent the injustice which was done to her. A particular account of what the Bishop of Ross did to further Queen Mary's liberation, taken from his own writings, is preserved in manuscript in the Advocates' Library at Edinburgh.

The Bishop of Ross, finding that Queen Elizabeth paid no attention to his representations, endeavoured by secret transactions to procure the escape of Queen Mary, and forwarded the project of a marriage between the unfortunate queen and the Duke of Norfolk, which being discovered, the duke was condemned for high treason, 16th January 1572, and was executed in June following. 1572.
The Bishop of Ross was summoned before the English council. He pleaded the privileges of an ambassador, but without avail. He was sent a prisoner to the Isle of Ely, and afterwards to the Tower of London. He was set at liberty in 1573, and was banished from England. He re- 1573.
tired to the Netherlands, where he published a

CHAP. III.

John Leslie, Bishop of Ross.

treatise in Latin upon afflictions and tranquillity of mind, for the use of his mistress, the Queen of Scots. Afterwards he went to France, and solicited the kings of France and Spain, and the German princes, to interest themselves for Queen Mary. But, finding that all these acted very
1575. slowly in the affair, in 1575 he went to Rome to urge the Pope to use his influence with the princes of Europe in the Queen's behalf. While
1578. at Rome, in 1578, he published his *History of Scotland* in Latin, written in a polished and nervous style. This work is entitled *De Origine Moribus et Rebus Gestis Scotorum.* He visited
1579. different countries after leaving Rome, and, in 1579,
1580. he was made Vicar-General of Rouen. In 1580 he published in Latin at Rheims several treatises in vindication of Queen Mary; amongst others, an answer to those who opposed her title to the succession to the crown of England; a treatise to show the advantages that would result to Scotland and England from the union of the two crowns; and an answer to those who opposed the government of women. He was appointed coadjutor to the Archbishop of Rouen, but was prevented by the troubles of the times from enjoying this preferment.

When the sorrowful tidings of the execution of Queen Mary reached Brussels, where the Bishop of Ross was then residing, the circumstances and inhumanity of her untimely end filled him with such horror that he retired to a monastery of the

CHAP. III.

John Leslie, Bishop of Ross.

canons-regular of the order of St. Augustine at Gertrudenberg, about two miles from Brussels, where he spent the remainder of his days in great devotion. He died in June 1596, aged seventy years, and was buried in the monastery under a monument erected to his memory by his nephew, John Leslie, and bearing the following inscription :—

"Sola Virtus."

"Joannes Leslaeus, Episcopus Rossensis, Scotus, ex illustri familia Leslaeorum, omnis generis scientiarum cultissimus, orator ad Regem Gall. Franciscum II. Consiliarius Mariae, P. M. Scotorum Reginae, Catholicae religionis propugnator, post immensos pro avitâ fide labores, presertim in Regno Scotiae restituenda; post defensam in Anglia Mariam Reginam; post varia summâ cum laude gesta, tranquilissime excessit Bruxel. prid. kalend. Junii, A.D. MDXCVI. Aetatis suæ 70. 1596.

"Avunculo grato ne superesset ingratus, Joannes Leslaeus, Nepos, haeres moestus posuit et pro eodem anniversarium p. p. fundavit in hoc coenobio Gertrudenbergensi prid. kal. Junii celebrandum. Natalem Locum et Diem scimus, sepulchri nescimus."

An old manuscript history of the Leslie family states, but on what authority does not appear, that John Leslie, Bishop of Ross, had three daughters—Janet, married to Andrew Leslie of New Leslie; a second, married to Richard Irvine; and a third, married to Cruickshank of Tillymorgan.

CHAP. III.

Leslie of Crichie.

RECORDS OF THE FAMILY OF LESLIE OF CRICHIE.

THE family of Leslie of Crichie was descended from the family of Leslie, Barons of Balquhain.

I. WILLIAM LESLIE, fourth Baron of Balquhain, had several natural children by Mary Meldrum, daughter of Sir Thomas Meldrum of Fyvie. One of these was Patrick Leslie, who got from his father the lands of Logydurno. He married Miss Spence of Boddam, and had issue—

I. WILLIAM, first Laird of Crichie.

II. WALTER of Steenbridge, who had a son, Henry Leslie of Buchanston, who had a son, James Leslie, who sold the lands of Buchanston to Mr. Horn of Horn and Westhall.

III. PATRICK, progenitor of the Leslies of Iden, of whom hereafter.

1490 Patrick Leslie of Logydurno died about 1490. His eldest son—

II. WILLIAM LESLIE, first Laird of Crichie, married Miss Bisset of Lessendrum, and had issue—

I. ALEXANDER, his successor.

II. WILLIAM of Balcairn or Baccarn, who married a daughter of Richard Udny of Minnas, and had issue—

I. JOHN, second Laird of Balcairn, who married, first, Miss Forbes of Abersnithack; and secondly, Jane Wood, relict of James Leslie of Peterstone, and mother of George Leslie, Father Archangel, the Scottish Capuchin. He had two sons—Francis, a captain, who died without issue; and William, who married Margaret Forbes, and had two sons, George and William. CHAP. III.

Leslie of Crichie.

III. James, who lived in Aberdeen, and was bailie to the Baron of Balquhain. He married Agnes Hunter, and had issue—

I. Thomas, a burgess in Aberdeen. He married Miss Mercer, and had a son, Gilbert, who had two sons—

I. Gilbert, a schoolmaster, and the author of several works.

II. James, a Doctor of Medicine, Principal of Marischal College, Aberdeen, in 1661; who, by his first wife, Miss Lumsden, Ruthrieston, had a son, John, and two daughters—Marjory, married to Robert Bruce, and Anne, married to John Forbes, son of the Laird of Corse. By his second wife, a daughter of Provost Gray of Aberdeen, he had three daughters—Elizabeth, married to George Peacock, and Catherine and Magdalen. He married, thirdly, Margaret Bennet, and died in 1678. 1661. 1678.

IV. John, of Segget, who married, and had two sons—Alexander in Dorlethen, and William in Whitehaugh.

V. Robert of Courtestoune.

William Leslie, first Laird of Crichie, died in 1520, and was succeeded by his eldest son— 1520.

III. Alexander Leslie, second Laird of Crichie, who married, and had issue—

I. William, his successor.

II. Walter, who married Miss Macintosh, and had two sons.

III. George, who died without issue.

CHAP. III.

Leslie of Crichie.

Alexander Leslie, second Laird of Crichie, died in 1560, and was succeeded by his eldest son—

IV. WILLIAM LESLIE, third Laird of Crichie, who, according to some authorities, married Miss Affleck, Shethin; and, according to others, Miss Auchinach, daughter of the Laird of Shethin. He sold the lands of Crichie to George Leslie, second son of William Leslie, fourth Baron of Wardis. He died in 1620, leaving several sons, one of whom was—

1620.

V. GENERAL SIR ALEXANDER LESLIE of Auchintoul, born in 1566. He went to Russia, and entered the Muscovite service. After many eminent military achievements, he attained the rank of general, and was appointed Governor of Smolensko. At this period there were three colonels and many captains and subaltern officers of the name of Leslie in the Muscovite service, besides General Sir Alexander Leslie. He was twice married, and had two sons—John, a lieutenant-colonel, and Theodore. He died in 1661, aged ninety-five years.

1566.

1661.

Leslie of Iden.

RECORDS OF THE FAMILY OF LESLIE OF IDEN.

THE family of Leslie of Iden, or Eden, is a branch of the family of Leslie, Barons of Balquhain.

One account states that Arthur Leslie, third son of William Leslie, ninth Baron of Balquhain,

Leslie of Iden.

and who was drowned in the Don, near Fetternear, by the falling of his horse while crossing the river, left a son, Patrick, who also had a son Patrick, who was the progenitor of the family of Leslie of Iden. But there is no mention in any record of the marriage of this Arthur Leslie, and it seems certain that he died unmarried. Another account, which is more probable, states that the progenitor of the family of Leslie of Iden was Patrick Leslie, third son of Patrick Leslie of Logydurno, a natural son of William Leslie, fourth Baron of Balquhain, by Mary, daughter of Sir Thomas Meldrum of Fyvie.*

I. Patrick Leslie, third son of Patrick Leslie of Logydurno, by his wife, a daughter of Spence of Boddam, was a merchant in Aberdeen. He married Miss Ankret, daughter of John Ankret, burgess of Aberdeen, and had issue—

I. Alexander, who died young.
II. Walter, who also died young.
III. Patrick, of whom presently.
IV. A Daughter, married, it is said, to John Leslie, Baron of Balquhain.
V. A Daughter.

II. Patrick, third son of Patrick Leslie, by his wife, Miss Ankret, was a burgess of Aberdeen. He married Miss Innes of Auchintoul, and had a son, also called Patrick.

---

* See Family of Leslie of Crichie.

CHAP. III.

Leslie of Iden.

III. This Patrick Leslie, the fourth of the name, was also a burgess of Aberdeen. He married Isabella Seton, and had issue—

I. Sir Patrick Leslie, first Laird of Iden.

II. John, who married Miss Henry, daughter of Alexander Henry, burgess of Aberdeen, and had three sons—John of Colpnay, James, and Thomas.

IV. Sir Patrick Leslie of Iden was Lord Provost of Aberdeen at different periods from
1634-47. 1634 to 1647. He received the honour of knighthood, and bought the lands of Iden from the Meldrums. He married, first, Jean, daughter of John Leslie, tenth Baron of Balquhain, and had issue—

I. Patrick, who married the Honourable Miss Fraser, daughter of Lord Saltoun of Philorth, and had a son, who died without issue at Breda. Patrick Leslie and
1680. his wife died in London in 1680.

II. John, who married Miss Galloway of Aberdeen, and had three sons—John, Alexander, and George; and four daughters—Jean, married to George Keith of Crichie, provost of Aberdeen, Isabella, married to Mr. Stewart of Colpnay, Helen, and Anne.

III. Alexander, who died young.

IV. Isabella, married to Alexander Gordon of Lesmore.

V. Mary, married to Alexander Lumsden of Ruthrieston.

Sir Patrick Leslie of Iden married, secondly, Isabella, daughter of John Cheyne, bailie in Aberdeen, and had two sons—

I. George, his successor in the lands of Iden.

II. Walter, who died unmarried in Poland.

Sir Patrick Leslie of Iden was a man of great

repute, and he figured much in the troublesome times of the Covenant, being a rigid Covenanter. He died in 1660. He was succeeded by his eldest son of his second marriage— CHAP. III. *Leslie of Iden.* 1660.

V. GEORGE LESLIE, second Laird of Iden, who married Miss Gordon of Park, and had issue—

I. A Son, who succeeded him.

II. WILLIAM, a merchant in Aberdeen, who married, and had a daughter, Jane, married in Edinburgh, 22d November 1703, to Alexander Tytler, writer in Edinburgh, eldest son of John Tytler, merchant in Aberdeen, by his wife Barbara Skene, daughter of the Laird of Skene. By Alexander Tytler, who was born 1st January 1678, and died 16th December 1743, Jane Leslie had issue— 1703. 1678. 1743.

I. ALEXANDER TYTLER, born 2d October 1704; died without issue in Jamaica. 1704.

II. WILLIAM TYTLER of Woodhouselee, born 12th October 1711. He married Anne Craig, daughter of James Craig of Dalnair, and had two sons—Alexander Fraser and Patrick. Alexander Fraser Tytler, the elder son, was one of the senators of the College of Justice, by the title of Lord Woodhouselee, and he married Anne Fraser, daughter and heiress of William Fraser of Belnain, and by her he acquired the lands of Belnain. He had three sons—William Fraser Tytler of Belnain, James Fraser Tytler of Woodhouselee, and Patrick Fraser Tytler, the historian of Scotland; and two daughters—Anne Fraser Tytler, and Jane Fraser Tytler, married to James Baillie of Reolick. The eldest son, William Fraser Tytler of Belnain, married Margaret, only daughter and heiress of George Grant of Burdsyards, 10th March 1801, and had five sons and six daughters. 1711. 1801.

CHAP. III.

Leslie of Iden.

VI. George Leslie, second Laird of Iden, was succeeded by his eldest son, Mr. LESLIE, third Laird of Iden, who married, and had issue—

I. GEORGE, his successor.
II. ALEXANDER.
III. HELEN.
IV. SOPHIA.
V. MARY.

VII. GEORGE LESLIE, fourth Laird of Iden,
1710. married, in 1710, Margaret Leslie, sixth daughter of Patrick, Count Leslie, fifteenth Baron of Balquhain, and had a daughter, Elizabeth. George Leslie of Iden having sent to King's College, Aberdeen, as a present, a curious manuscript on vellum relating to the cathedral church of Aberdeen, containing the necrologie thereof, and other valuable papers, a letter of thanks was ordered to be written to him by the university
1727. authorities, 12th December 1727.* This manuscript, called in the index a Registrum Chartarum, was written by Alexander Galloway, parson of Kinkell, who, according to an entry therein by
1552. another hand, died 6th October 1552. George Leslie sold the lands of Iden, situated in the parish of King Edward, on the banks of the Deveron, between Turriff and Banff, to Duff of
1740. Braco, before 1740, in which year he died. His wife, Margaret Leslie, commonly called Lady
1744. Kinnares, died 3d February 1744.

* *Fasti Aberdonenses*, p. 445.

CHAP. III.

Leslie of Iden.

The lands of Iden, now called Eden, are in the possession of Mountstuart Elphinstone Grant Duff, Esq. of Eden.

RECORDS OF GEORGE LESLIE,

COMMONLY CALLED THE SCOTCH CAPUCHIN, OR FATHER ARCHANGEL.

George Leslie, Father Archangel.

GEORGE LESLIE, commonly called the Scotch Capuchin, or Father Archangel, was the son of James Leslie of Peterstone, by his wife Jane Wood, who, after her husband's death, married, secondly, John Leslie, second Laird of Balcairn, of the family of Leslie of Crichie. George Leslie became a Capuchin monk, and was employed on the Catholic mission in Scotland. He seems to have published some controversial works, as Mr. Andrew Logie, parson of Rayne and archdeacon of Aberdeen, wrote an answer to him under the title "Cum bono Deo Raine from the clouds, upon a Choicke Angel (in reference to George Leslie's name in religion, Father Archangel), or a returned answere to that common quaeritur of our adversaries, 'Where was your church before Luther?' digested into several meditations according to the difference of points. Extorted off the Author for stilling the incessant and no lesse clamourous coassation of some Patmicke Frogges, against the lawfulnesse of our calling, &c. &c. Aberdene,

CHAP. III.

George Leslie, Father Archangel.

Imprinted by Edward Raban, dwelling upon the Market Place at the Towne's Arms, 1624. Dedicated to Sir Alexander Gordon of Clunie." Prefixed to this work are three commendatory poems, one in Latin by David Wedderburn, and another in English by Thomas Cargill. From the third, which is anonymous, we learn that the work was written in answer to Father Archangel.*

Father Archangel is briefly mentioned by Dempster in his *Historia Ecclesiastica Gentis Scotorum*, pp. 43, 44. His name also occurs in the following list of Catholic priests and adherents of the Catholic church in the north-eastern counties of Scotland, drawn up at the beginning of the reign of Charles I. about 1625, and preserved among Sir James Balfour's manuscripts in the Advocates' Library, Edinburgh :—

1625.

I. "The names of priestis and traffecting seminaries in the Dyoceis of Aberdene and Murraye.

"Father Stevin ; a most busie and dangerous traffequer—Mr. John Ogilvie—Father Stitchell —Father Higgets—Capucian Leslie—commonly called Archangel—Mr. William Leslie, commonly called the Capitane—Mr. Andro Leslie—Mr. John Leslie—Thrie Christies, quherof one is called principall of Dowye—Doctor William Leslie, doctor of Physick, a seditious traffequer and reasoner, who under pretence of administration of physick, is a most dangerous seducer, and is suspect to have receavit ordours.

* Gordon's *Scots Affairs*, vol. iii. p. 246, *note*.

George Leslie, Father Archangel.

II. "The names of resaitteris of seminaries and Jesuites that are excommunicat and lyes at the horne in the Dyocie of Aberdene onlie.

"Mr. Alexander Irwing, burges of Aberdene, the avowed resaitter of seminaries, and the most pernicious and peirt infecter in the north. Walter Leslie, in Aberdene, alledgeit to be a seminarie himself. John Gordoun, Laird of Craig, younger, a most scandalous example and sedulous seducer, cloaking all his insolencies and contempt of laws with ane exemption from his lait Majestie, ance already banished from the Kingdom. Mr. Robert Bisset of Lessendrum, bailyie to the Marquis of Huntlie, a most pestiferous seducer, a public reasoner and railer. Alexander Leslie, brother to the Laird of Petcapell.

III. "The names of resaitteris of seminaries and Jesuites that as yet are nocht excommunicat nor denounced bot most of thame under processe with resorteris and convoyeris of thame.

"The Erle of Errol—The Lord of Aboyne—Laird Delgatie—Laird of Geicht—John Turin, Laird of Foverne—William Hay of Fetterletter—Gordon of Blelack—Patrick Gordoun of Kincraigie—Mr. Gordoun of Abergeldie—James Gordoun of Letterfurie—William Leslie, brother to George Leslie, the Capucian—Patrick Christiesone in Fetterneir, and others.

"These are the names of the most scandalous and irregular onlie of the adversars of the treuth, surceasing to sett doun the great number of otheris (and speciallie of the female sex) that hes maid the lyk defectioun from the treuth." *

* Maidment's *Analecta Scotica*, vol. ii. pp. 52-55, Edinburgh, 1837; Miscellanies of the Spalding Club, vol. ii. preface p. lv.; and Gordon's *Scots Affairs*, vol. iii. p. 246.

CHAP. III.

George Leslie, Father Archangel.

Among a number of papers brought from the Scotch College at Douai, and now in the collection of the late Right Rev. James Kyle, D.D., Bishop of Germanicia, and Vicar-Apostolic of the northern district of Scotland, there is a letter from Father William Christie, a Jesuit, dated at Douay, 29th
1653. December 1653, in which Father Christie states that George Leslie, afterwards styled the Capuchin,
1608. entered the Scotch College at Douai in 1608, and
1623. came to the mission in Scotland in 1623; that he was a very zealous man, but that little more could be said regarding him; that he died in his mother's poor house just over the river Dee, opposite the hill of Aboyne, and was buried in an old ruinous church between that and Huntshall; that the period of his death was not correctly ascertained; that Father Christie believed the book entitled *The Scotch Capuchin* was a pure romance, not written by Mgr. Rinuccini, Archbishop of Fermo, but that he conjectured that it was written by Father Andrew Leslie, a Jesuit.

The history of Father Archangel, published in Italian under the name of Jean Baptiste Rinuccini, Archbishop of Fermo, and translated into French by Francis Barrault, procureur de la doctrine Chretienne, and of which a second and improved
1682. edition was published at Paris in 1682, is of such an extraordinary and romantic character, that it has cast considerable discredit on the subject of the memoir. As the *Laurus Leslæana* remarks,

George Leslie, Father Archangel.

in this little work more attention seems to have been paid to exhibit the eloquence of the writer than to the truth of the circumstances narrated. It is probable that during the residence of Father Archangel at the Capuchin convent at Fermo in Italy, he related to his brethren his adventures in Scotland; and that these adventures were afterwards written down by men ignorant of Scotch names, places, and manners, and then published under the name of Rinuccini, Archbishop of Fermo, who was afterwards papal nuncio in Ireland. However, the truth of all that is really important in this history of the Scotch Capuchin is fully confirmed by a letter written by Father Archangel himself to Colonel Sempill, concerning the missions in Scotland, dated at Paris, 20th January 1630. There can be no doubt of the truth of the statements made in this letter, as they were made to one who had constant communications with Scotland, and to whom the parties mentioned were well known, and who took a great interest in the Catholic missions in Scotland. A Spanish translation of the original letter is preserved in the Scotch College at Valladolid in Spain. The original was written in English, and, with a Spanish translation, was given to the Spanish government, who then took a warm interest in the Scotch Catholics. This original is probably still in the Spanish archives, which have been carefully arranged and preserved. The

1630.

CHAP. III.

George Leslie, Father Archangel.

following is a copy of an English translation made from the Spanish translation of the original in English. The Spanish translator has misspelled many names, which leaves us in ignorance of many persons named in the letter, and in doubt about others :—

"The manner I have conversed with heretics and the method I have practised in Scotland for these last six years in converting souls, will shortly be published and dedicated to his Holiness—at least, I have been advised to do so by some of those who, flying from the calamities and persecutions in our country, have taken refuge in France. I am more inclined to dedicate it to your Excellency. I have therefore omitted to give it a foreign appearance for many just reasons. I shall send to your Excellency some books of it just published, by which you will see the method I have employed in my vocation in the country.*

"I wrote three other treatises in Scotland; two on the vocation of ministers, and one in reply to the reasons which induced a certain noble lady to apostatise from the Catholic faith to the Protestant. These treatises have disposed many to follow the Catholic faith, and many learned persons are of opinion that they should be published, and I could not dedicate them to any person more worthy than your Excellency, whose zeal for the conversion of souls and love of the servants of our faith are so well known. Know therefore that the best and most beautiful signs of a nobleman is to serve and fear God, and to take care of religion, as Livy says, and this your Excellency does in your own person by the ardent desire which you have to serve the Holy Roman Church, and to save souls in your country, as is proved by the pension which by the care and solicitude of your Excellency is so liberally distributed among the

* This probably refers to his controversial works, to one of which, Mr. Andrew Logie, parson of Rayne, wrote an answer, as has been related.

CHAP. III.

George Leslie, Father Archangel

laborers of the Church, and for which benefit I thank your Excellency with all my heart, and I shall continue to petition our Lord that he may reward it. I therefore wish that this dedication may serve to commemorate the piety and charity which your Excellency has shown towards me and others who dedicate themselves to the conversion of souls in our country. And as these treatises are part of my labors in very perilous and dangerous times, I would be sorry to see them perish in the cradle. In the meantime I beseech your Excellency to be pleased to continue the pension which you gave me while I was on the mission, to pay the expense of publication, and because when I return to Italy I propose getting them published at Venice if your Excellency will aid in the expense.

"For two reasons I return to Italy; first, because the government of our missions has been changed. Formerly all depended on a General who sent those of every nation to labor in their own country of which they were subjects. But now a French father, named Joseph, through the influence of Cardinal Richelieu, obtained from his Holiness the government of all the missions of our order in the east and west. Before this Father became Governor, we had twelve houses of our order in Turkey and Persia, governed by a learned and active gentleman called Father Pacifico; but immediately on Father Joseph becoming Governor in France, he recalled Father Pacifico and all the Italians and Spaniards who were in those places, leaving in his place a French superior, who now admits only Frenchmen in those countries; so that by this change only Frenchmen are admitted into the missions of the east and west, as likewise in England and Scotland.

"The second reason for my journey to Italy is to exculpate myself from some calumnies which have been imputed to me before the congregation of the Propagation of the Faith. To these calumnies I shall oppose all the Catholic ladies and gentlemen who, flying from the persecution, have arrived in these parts, for the many conversions which God has made by means of me afford no trace of those vile

CHAP. III.

George Leslie, Father Archangel.

things which they impute to me; for God has used me as an instrument for the conversion of my stepfather, of my mother and brothers, and of all the family; for the conversion of Alexander Leslie of Afford, of his wife and sons; of John Gordon of Deuthdies, of his wife and sons; of Mr. Regower, aged eighty years, and of his sons; of the Baron of Aquhorties, Leslie, and of his wife; of the Baron of Kirkadi, and of his wife, who made her first confession to Father Steven of the Company; of the Baron of Pitcaple; of the Baron of Cluny, Gordon, whose father for this cause sought to kill me; of three entire families in the hills of Badenoch; of the Laird of Brunthill, Hays, who carried the standard when the Earl of Errol commanded the advanced guard in the battle of Glenlivat, against the Earl of Argyle; of the Laird of Littlehill, Leith. In Angus I converted the eldest son of Viscount Oliphant, and one of his nephews, and two daughters-in-law of the Baroness of Monorgan, who died within eight days, having received all the sacraments. In the village of Fowlis I converted two whole families. In the southern parts of Scotland I converted the Viscountess Herries, and the Baroness of Locharby, and three gentlemen of the name of Maxwell. I converted to a good life the Baron of Lochinvar, who died in my arms, and this nearly cost me my life. In the west of Scotland I converted a daughter and two sons of the Earl of Abercorn, and some servants. In Edinburgh I converted Baron Ridhall Hamilton, and another gentleman and his wife, who doubting the truth of the mass, heard a voice saying three times, "Rise, rise, rise, go to mass." I must omit innumerable other persons, both men and women, for there is not a corner in all the kingdom where I have not left the seed of Faith, thanks be to God, the Fountain of all good.

"This is a summary of the souls I converted in Scotland, and well known by all those acquainted with me. But now, who are those who calumniate me? Are they perhaps heretics? No; for these do not frequent the court of Rome. Are they secular Catholics? No; because none

CHAP. III.

George Leslie, Father Archangel.

of these would venture to say that they ever saw in me any trace of levity. Are they perhaps priests? I say they are; but let them come to particulars, and specify the conversions which they have made, and we shall see if theirs can compete with mine. But enough of this disagreeable matter.

"With regard to the present persecution in Scotland, it continues and increases every day, to the great detriment of the Faith and of souls. It is distressing to see the number of Catholics who, driven from their country, arrive at this part of France, where it would appear that Christian charity is dead, for men sneer at their necessities, rather than think of remedies. There is at Paris a Baroness, widow of the late Baron Crilton Maxwell, whom, after a long imprisonment, they have banished from the kingdom. Her daughters, beautiful girls, remain in Scotland, excommunicated by the ministers, and although the Queen of England has recommended her to the Queen-mother, nothing has been done for her, because charity seems banished from the court of France. I therefore beg to recommend her to your Excellency, because she is a learned, virtuous, and noble lady. There is also a Scotch gentleman named George Mortimer, a most honourable man, and zealous in the service of God and of his country. He has given me the means to pay for publishing my narrative. May I request you to acknowledge his assistance. I have written this to your Excellency in a very humble and common style, because I know I speak with the common Father of all. Supplicating our Lord to multiply your years,

Your Excellency's most obliged
servant and poor relation,

FR. ACHANGEL LESLIE, Capuchin."

Paris, 20th January 1630. 1630.

The following is a summary of the life of George Leslie, Father Archangel, the Scotch

CHAP. III.

George Leslie, Father Archangel.

Capuchin, published first in Italian, professing to be written by Jean Baptiste Rinuccini, Archbishop of Fermo, about 1650, and translated into French by Francis Barrault, procureur de la doctrine Chretienne, and of which a second

1682. edition was published at Paris in 1682.

In that place where Scotland is divided by many mountains, on the coast of the German Sea, the city of Aberdeen lies. James, Count Leslie, and Jane Wood, his wife, persons no less noble than rich, dwelt in Aberdeen. At the end of the first year of their marriage they had a son, George, whom they brought up a Calvinist. Count James Leslie died soon afterwards, and left his son George his heir, and by his testament he provided that the boy should be bred at Paris. Jane Wood, after the death of her first husband, Count James Leslie, married the Baron of Torrey, and her son, George Leslie, being in his eighth year, was sent to Paris with a noble equipage, and a train suiting his rank. He was intrusted to the care of a wise and judicious preceptor, and was recommended above all things to be steadfast in the Protestant religion. He applied to his studies, and became acquainted with two brothers of an illustrious family, who gained his confidence, and who spoke to him on subjects of controversy, and introduced him to their father. The result was that George Leslie was convinced of the errors in which he had been brought up, and at length he

CHAP. III.

George Leslie, Father Archangel.

became a convert to the Catholic faith. His preceptor, having discovered this change of religion, sent an account of it to Aberdeen. His mother wrote to him a letter threatening to disown him for her son, to abandon him to beggary, to deprive him of his estates, and to blot out his name from the genealogical tree of the family. Threats having no effect, she tried entreaties, but in vain. Then she recalled the preceptor, and withdrew all supplies of money from her son, whom she renounced.

George Leslie, thus disowned by his mother, was received by the father of his two companions, and was treated by him as a son. When he was sixteen years of age he accompanied his friends on a tour through Italy. At Rome he became acquainted with Ange de Joyeuse, a Capuchin monk, known in the world as Count de Bouchage, and was greatly edified by his conversations with him. George Leslie resolved to become a Capuchin, and offered himself to the general of the order, Jerom de Castel-Ferrato. But the general doubted whether he could, consistently with certain bulls of the Pope, receive the son of heretics into the order. George Leslie obtained an audience with the Pope, Paul V., who dispensed him from the objection raised by the general of the Capuchins, and he was received into the order as a novice. He went through his noviciate in an exemplary manner, and made his religious

CHAP. III.

George Leslie, Father Archangel.

profession, assuming the name of Brother Archangel. He then applied himself to philosophy and theology, and after finishing his studies he began to preach.

His mother was much troubled on learning that he had become a Capuchin. She sent her eldest son by her second marriage, the young Baron of Torrey, to induce him to quit the order, and to return to Scotland, and promised that if he would do so, he would be permitted to enjoy his paternal inheritance of Monymusk. The two brothers met at Urbino. Frederick Maria de Rovere, Duke of Urbino, received the young Baron of Torrey with great demonstrations of esteem, and sought to convert him to the Catholic faith. With the aid of the Capuchins he succeeded, and the conversion was celebrated with much rejoicing. The two brothers now resolved if possible to convert their mother to the Catholic faith, and to sow the seed of the true religion throughout Scotland. For this purpose the Baron of Torrey returned home first, but his mother, having learned his change of religion, cursed him, and commanded him to leave the castle.

George Leslie, Father Archangel, was appointed court-preacher to Mary de Medicis, Regent of France; and when Gregory XV. succeeded Paul V., he appointed Father Archangel chief of the Catholic missions in Great Britain. It happened that an ambassador from Spain to the court of

George Leslie, Father Archangel.

London was then at Paris, appointed to negotiate a marriage between the Infanta and the Prince of Wales, and he wished to have an English interpreter. Father Archangel undertook the office, in order that, disguised as a layman, he might more easily perform his mission. The Spanish ambassador was so much pleased with him that on quitting England he made him a present of a fine horse.

Father Archangel sent for his brother, the Baron of Torrey, from Scotland, that he might concert with him the proper measures for the success of his mission. Then he set out for Scotland, and wrote a letter in his own name to his mother, and dated it from Urbino, and recommended the bearer of it as a gentleman of great worth, and his particular acquaintance. When Father Archangel arrived at Monymusk, his mother was busied, with her two daughters-in-law, in embroidering a silk bed for her eldest son, should he return from Italy. Archangel presented his letter, and his mother read it with some displeasure. Yet she welcomed the stranger, as did also her youngest son, Edward, and a great feast was prepared. Archangel remained undiscovered for five days, when his mother recognised him, and great joy prevailed in the castle of Monymusk. The Baron of Torrey, who had been sent away, was recalled to share the happiness of the family. The news of the safe return of George

CHAP. III.

George Leslie, Father Archangel.

Leslie went through the town, and the old lady received a thousand visits of congratulation. The fame of the event so long wished for reached even to Aberdeen. Fires of rejoicing were lighted on the battlements of the castle of Monymusk, and the inhabitants of the town discharged their culverins, and let off many sky-rockets, which seemed as the aerial messengers of their gratitude. The lady told her son that this day of joy repaid all the affliction that she had experienced, and all the tears that she had shed for twenty-five years, and she was willing to leave him undisturbed in the religion which he had chosen, and that she looked for the like privilege from him.

Archangel began to preach in the forests and mountains, where he collected what auditors he could. His success was great. In eight months he converted four thousand persons in the neighbourhood of Monymusk and Aberdeen, and he would have converted the whole country if he had not been recalled soon afterwards. What he had most at heart was the conversion of his mother. In this he was at last successful. She, her daughter-in-law, her youngest son, and all the officers and servants of the castle, were converted and received into the Church. A hall in the castle was turned into a chapel, and the divine offices were celebrated in the castle of Monymusk with the utmost solemnity and splendour. After two years spent in Scotland, Father Archangel re-

George Leslie, Father Archangel.

tired to England, in consequence of a proclamation published at Aberdeen commanding all Catholic priests to quit Scotland within a certain time under pain of death. His mother was excommunicated for contumacy for not attending the Protestant church, and all her goods and property were confiscated. She was obliged to retire to a small house, where she lived on the little she could earn by spinning. Archangel resolved to pay her a visit. He disguised himself as a peasant, and as he drew near Monymusk he gathered some herbs, and pretending to be a gardener, he went forward and cried them about the streets. The guards stopped him at the gates of the town, but he gained admittance. Not knowing where his mother lived, and being afraid to ask questions of any one, he passed three times through Monymusk, crying, "Buy my greens." At last his mother came out of a miserable hovel and cried, "Here, gardener." Archangel was deeply affected at seeing his mother dressed like a servant-maid, and reduced to the necessity of buying vegetables for herself. He made himself known to her, but they were almost immediately interrupted by the king's commissaries, who were in search of priests, and he was obliged to return to England.

On his return to England, Archangel received letters from the General of the Capuchins informing him that he was accused of having trans-

CHAP. III.

George Leslie, Father Archangel.

gressed the rules of the mission, and advising him to return to Italy to justify himself. Archangel took the advice, and went to Cremona, where he attended those who were attacked by the plague, which at that time devastated Italy. He was fully acquitted of the charges brought against him, and Pope Urban VIII. granted him permission to return to Scotland, but his superiors thought it proper that he should remain for some time in Italy. He was made Guardian or Superior of the convent of Mount George, in the arch-diocese of Fermo, of which Mgr. Jean Baptiste Rinuccini was then archbishop.

After some time, Father Archangel and Father Epiphanes were appointed to the mission in Great Britain, and they set out on their journey. They passed through Paris, and embarked at Calais. They suffered shipwreck on a rock near the Isle of Wight. Some of the passengers were saved, but most of the crew of the vessel perished. Archangel converted two of his fellow-passengers. When they arrived at St. Calpin, Archangel laid aside his name of Leslie, lest his family should be known, and he assumed the name of Wood, which was his mother's name. Meeting a young Scotch gentleman at the inn, Archangel asked him whether there were many Catholics in Scotland since the persecution. He was answered that formerly there were many Catholics, even of

CHAP. III.

George Leslie, Father Archangel.

the first families, but that the king, by severe edicts, had expelled them all, and had confiscated all their estates, and that there was only one Catholic family now remaining, and it was established in the large town of Monymusk. To it the king, by an instance of bounty altogether singular, had lately restored all its estates which had been forfeited, and for gratitude for the services done to him by that family, he tolerated it alone in the exercise of the Catholic religion. This young Scotch gentleman proved to be Archangel's youngest brother Edward, and from him he also learned that the court of France had interposed its good offices in favour of the family of Monymusk, and that King Charles I. had restored to it the possession of all its estates. From his brother Archangel also learned the account of his mother's death. She had heard that Archangel was about to return to Scotland, and she grew impatient to get some account of him. She walked every day on the road leading from England to Monymusk and Aberdeen, and, having met some merchants on their return from a fair at London, she learned from them that there had been a great tempest in the German Sea, and that many ships had perished, and particularly one in which were some priests. The old lady immediately concluded that her son Archangel was drowned. A slow fever seized her, and she died nine days afterwards.

CHAP. III.

George Leslie, Father Archangel.

Father Archangel and his brother Edward, and Father Epiphanes, waited on the king at Newport, and were confirmed in their immunities. They then went to Scotland, where Archangel was so successful in his mission that the king was angry, and revived all the proclamations against Catholics, and commanded Archangel and his brothers to be sent to court. Archangel lost no time in setting out for England. He employed himself in preaching by the way. In the neighbourhood of the city of Torphichen he had a conference with a considerable number of gentlemen, and converted the eldest son of Baron Cluny, an Englishman of quality. When he was on the frontiers of England he fell ill of a fever, occasioned by excessive fatigue. A Jesuit, who happened to be in the neighbourhood, performed the last offices to him, and closed his eyes when he died. There was a mountain not far distant, which hardly any man dared to approach, by reason of a constant noise of a pack of hounds in full cry, accompanied with the hallooing of men and the sound of horses galloping. Yet the confidence which the faithful had in the merits of Archangel inspired them with resolution enough to carry his body up to that mountain, where they buried it.

The Archbishop of Fermo concludes his history of Father Archangel with some arguments to prove that Archangel should be held as a saint. In particular, he observes that if there be saints

CHAP. III.

George Leslie, Father Archangel.

whom the voice of the people alone, commonly called the voice of God, has canonised, no one better deserves that honour than George Leslie of Monymusk.

From the authentic facts known concerning George Leslie, Father Archangel, the Scotch Capuchin, and already related, we are enabled to trace the origin of some of the errors contained in his Life, purporting to have been written by the Archbishop of Fermo. It is necessary now to point out another error in the archbishop's work. George Leslie is described as the son of Count James Leslie of Monymusk. This is a mistake, as it has been shown that he was the son of James Leslie of Peterstone, by his wife Jane Wood. There was no Count Leslie for a considerable time after Father Archangel was born. The first Count of the name of Leslie was Count Walter, son of John Leslie, tenth Baron of Balquhain, created a Count of the Holy Roman Empire by the Emperor Ferdinand III., 15th March 1637. He died in 1667 without issue, 1637-67.
and was succeeded by his nephew, James, second Count Leslie, who died in 1694. Neither of these 1694.
Counts lived in Scotland, and they were the only Counts of the name who could have been contemporaries of Father Archangel.

Then this so-called Count James Leslie is described as proprietor of Monymusk. This also is a mistake. Earlier than the thirteenth century

CHAP. III. — *George Leslie, Father Archangel.*

Monymusk was church property. In the pontificate of Innocent III., 1198-1216, a commission was granted to the Bishop of St. Andrews to examine and reform the monastery of Kildey of Monymusk.* Monymusk remained in the possession of the church till the Reformation, when it became the property of Duncan Forbes of Corsindae, who succeeded his father, Duncan Forbes, second son of James, second Lord Forbes. Duncan Forbes pulled down the monastery of Monymusk, and made use of the materials to build the present mansion-house of Monymusk. He got a charter under the Great Seal, "Duncano Forbes de Monymusk," of the lands of Coclaro-
1554-87. quhie, 1st December 1554. He died in 1587, and was succeeded by his eldest son, William
1618. Forbes of Monymusk, who died before 1618, and was succeeded by his eldest son, William Forbes, who was created a Baronet by Charles I., by patent "Domino Willelmo Forbes de Monymusk,"
1626. 2d April 1626. He was succeeded by his eldest son, Sir William Forbes, second Baronet, who was succeeded by his son, Sir John Forbes, third Baronet, who was succeeded by his son, Sir William Forbes, fourth Baronet, who got a charter from Charles II. "Domino Willelmo Forbes de
1661. Monymusk," 22d July 1661.† Monymusk re-
1710. mained in the possession of the Forbeses till 1710,

* *Registrum Episcopatus Aberdonensis*, p. 264.
† Douglas's *Baronage*, p. 39.

George Leslie, Father Archangel.

when it was purchased by Sir Francis Grant of Cullen, who was succeeded by his eldest son, Sir Archibald Grant of Monymusk, and in this family the estate of Monymusk has remained till the present time. Thus there never was a family of Leslie of Monymusk.

It is unnecessary to point out the many other evident errors in the archbishop's work. As has been mentioned, it is not at all certain that the Archbishop of Fermo was the author of the Life of Father Archangel. From the want of dates, and the general style of the book, it seems to have been written as a pious romance, fo undedprobably on the narrations given by Father Archangel of his adventures in Scotland to his Capuchin brethren during his stay in Italy. This view seems to be corroborated by the fact that the work was dramatised and published in Rome in 1673, under 1673.
the title "Il Cappuccino Scozzese in Scena, con la seconda parte, e sua morte, non ancor mai piu stampata. Data in luce dal Signor Francesco Rozzi d'Alatri. In Roma, per il mancini, 1673."

DUGUID

Duguid, First Baron of Auchinhove.

FIRST BARON OF AUCHINHOVE.

THE first person of the name of Duguid of whom any record is found, is Robert Duguid, who is witness to a deed of resignation made by Thomas Strachan of Glenkindy of all right and title which

CHAP. III.

Duguid, First Baron of Auchinhove.

he had to the lands of Snowdoun, in the barony of Craigy, in the county of the Mearns, in favour of Patrick Grey, Dominus de Broxmouth, dated at Dundee 16th May 1406.*

1445. Duguid married Elizabeth of Balcarne, Auchinhove, and Warthill, about 1445, as is proved by a charter granted by King James III., dated at Edinburgh, 5th March 1470. They had a son, Robert Duguid, who succeeded his mother in the lands of Auchinhove. Duguid, the husband of Elizabeth, heiress of Balcarne, Auchinhove, and Warthill, died before August 1478, at which period it appears that Elizabeth of Balcarne was married to Alexander Hay.

See App. No. LVIII.

1478.

See App. No. LIX.

Robert Duguid, Second Baron of Auchinhove.

ROBERT DUGUID,

SECOND BARON OF AUCHINHOVE.

ROBERT DUGUID succeeded his mother, Elizabeth of Balcarne, in the lands of Auchinhove, Warthill, and Blalok, as is proved by a charter granted to him by King James III., dated at Edinburgh, 5th
1470. March 1470. In this charter the king grants and confirms to Robert Duguid, son and heir of Elizabeth of Balcarne, all and each the lands of Auchinhove, Warthill, and Blalok, with their pertinents, lying in the county of Aberdeen, which lands belonged to the said Elizabeth by hereditary

* *Miscellany of Spalding Club*, vol. v. p. 254.

CHAP. III.

right, and which she had spontaneously resigned into the king's hands.

Robert Duguid, Second Baron of Auchinhove. 1478.

Robert Duguid of Auchinhove disponed the lands of Balcarne in favour of Alexander Seton of Meldrum, 25th August 1478, as appears by the Burgh Records of Aberdeen. On that day Alexander Seton of Meldrum, and Robert Duguid of Auchinhove, produced in the Burgh Court, held by the bailies of Aberdeen, an instrument relating to the lands of Balcarne, by which Elizabeth of Balcarne, mother of the said Robert Duguid, had resigned to the said Robert Duguid, her son, the said lands of Balcarne, and had given them to him in feu and freehold; and Alexander Hay, now the husband of the said Elizabeth of Balcarne, had ratified and confirmed the said instrument by solemn oath, in open court, before the bailies of Dundee. Alexander Seton then petitioned the bailies of Aberdeen to have the said instrument transferred to him, which they did in due form, and signed with their seal.

See App. No. LIX.

Robert Duguid married Agnes Forbes of Brux, by whom he had a son, Robert, who succeeded him as third Baron of Auchinhove about 1500.

1500.

CHAP. III.

Robert Duguid, Third Baron of Auchinhove.

ROBERT DUGUID,

THIRD BARON OF AUCHINHOVE.

ROBERT DUGUID was retoured heir to his father, Robert Duguid, second Baron of Auchinhove, in
1501. 1501. He obtained sasine of the lands of Auchinhove, Warthill, and Blelack, with the mill
1513. thereof, in 1513, and of the lands of the two Auchinhoves, Warthill, Blelack, Tulloch, and the
1529. mill thereof, 18th January 1529. A commission under the Privy Seal was granted to the Sheriff
1533. of Aberdeen in 1533, on the complaint of Robert Duguid of Auchinhove against Alexander Irvine of Drum, for encroaching upon the lands of Warthill, Auchinhove, and Greencoats, and it was found that Robert Duguid had the right to the said lands. Robert Duguid of Auchinhove was frequently on the assize at Aberdeen from 1503 to 1536.* He entered into a bond of manrent with George, Earl of Huntly, 1st November 1536. *See* App. No. LX.

Robert Duguid, third Baron of Auchinhove, married a daughter of Alexander Irvine of Drum, by whom he had a son, William, who succeeded
1537. him. He died in 1537.

* *Records of Aberdeen*, lib. Actorum Curiæ Vicecom. de Aberdeen; and *Antiquities of Aberdeen*, vol. ii. p. 11.

WILLIAM DUGUID,

FOURTH BARON OF AUCHINHOVE.

William Duguid, Fourth Baron of Auchinhove.

William Duguid, son of Robert Duguid, third Baron of Auchinhove, succeeded as fourth Baron on the death of his father in 1537. He obtained 1537.
a precept furth of the Chancery for infefting him in the lands of Auchinhove, Wartle, Greencoats, Bleiack, and Tulloch, with the mill, dated 6th February 1538. Sasine followed thereon 19th 1538.
May 1538.

William Duguid married, first, Janet Leslie, daughter of John Leslie, eighth Baron of Balquhain, about 1545. He married, secondly, in 1545.
1575, Janet Forbes, second daughter and co- 1575.
heiress of Sir William Forbes of Pitsligo. This marriage is authenticated by a charter by which William Duguid granted the lands of Warthill to Janet Forbes, his spouse, 14th September 1575, 1575.
who, previous to her marriage with him, had been served heir-portioner to her father, Sir William Forbes of Pitsligo, 22d June 1574.* 1574.

It would appear that William Duguid married, thirdly, Agnes Ross, as in a court held at Aberdeen, 31st July 1595, there was an act of re- 1595.
moving at the instance of Alexander Duguid against Agnes Ross, designed the relict of William

* See *Registrum Magni Sigilli*, lib. xxxiv, No. 64; and Douglas's *Peerage*, vol ii. p. 368.

CHAP. III.

William Duguid, Fourth Baron of Auchinhove.

Duguid of Auchinhove. This is further confirmed by the proceedings of an assize-court held at Aberdeen, 4th April 1597, for the trial of Margaret Ogg for witching Agnes Ross, Lady Auchinhove. The second charge in the "Dittay or accusation against Margrat Og, spous to Johne Robbie, in Mariewell for hir being a vitche and sorcerar, and vsing the craft thereof, be the inspiratioun of the Devill, thir dyvers yeris bygane," is as follows :—

"Secundlie. Thou art indyttit as a notorious witche, for the bevitching of vmquhill Agnes Ross, Lady Auchinhuiff, in maner folowing, to vit: The said vmquhill Agnes hauing bocht a showder of muttoun fra Johne Duged, at the Mylne of Auchinhuiff, in the moneth of Merche, fourscoir fyftene yeris; and the said vmquhill Agnes having brocht the said schulder to the houss of Beatrix Robbie, thy dochter, compartner with the in all thy devilische practizes, quhair the said vmquhill Agnes tareit all that nicht, thow and thy said dochter tuik out thrie grippis out of the middist of the said schulder, and causit rost the same vpon the morne, quhilk being rostit, and the said vmquhill Agnes eating thereof, scho instantlie contractis a deidlie disease, quhairin scho continowit be the space of thrie quarteris of a yere, the ane halff of the day birning as giff it had bene in a fyrie fornace, and the vther halff of the day melting avay in a cauld sweyt, quhill scho at last departis this lyff. And this thou can nocht deny, for the said vmquhill Agnes, immediatlie befoir hir depairture, left hir dead on the, and thy said dochter. Testefeit be the said John Duged."

The same charge was made against Beatrix Robbie, daughter of Margaret Og. The trial took place

1597. at Aberdeen, 24th April 1597, before John Leslie,

CHAP. III.

William Duguid, Fourth Baron of Auchinhove.

tenth Baron of Balquhain, Sheriff of Aberdeen; Thomas Leslie, his deputy; Alexander Rutherford of Robislaw, Provost of Aberdeen, and a jury, among whom were Robert Duguid, fifth Baron of Auchinhove, and John Duguid, at the Mill of Auchinhove, who pronounced the following verdict:—

"The haill assyis, for the maist pairt, convictis and fyllis Margaret Oig in sex pointis of dittey, for wichecraft and socerie, contenit in thair ditteyis.

"The haill assyis, for the maist pairt, findis that Beatrix Robie is ane suspitious persone, dochter to Margaret Og convict for wichecraft, in that scho hes resortit in hir motheris companie, and that scho is nocht of ane gude lyf and conversatioun, and therefor referrit hir ponishment to the modificatioune and discretioune of the justice. To be baneist the shirrefdom of Aberdene.

"The justice, be reasoun of the convictioun of Issobel Ritchie in four poyntis of vytchcraft and sorcerie, and of the convictioun of Mergerat Og, in sex poyntis of vytchcraft and sorcerie contenit in hir dittay, and of the convictioun of Helene Rogie, in sex poyntis of vytchcraft contenit in hir dittay, and of the convictioun of Issobell Oge, of twa poyntis of hir dittay be the assyis aboue writtin, ordanit the saidis four personnis to be haid owt betuixt the hillis, et efternowne, bund to ane staik, virreit thairat quhill thai be deid, and thaireaftir brint in asches; and that was gevin for dome, be the mouth of Hutcheoun, adiudicator and dempster."*

William Duguid, fourth Baron of Auchinhove, died before 23d June 1593, leaving a son, Robert, who succeeded him as fifth Baron of Auchinhove. 1593.

* *Miscellany of the Spalding Club*, vol i. pp. 142-155.

CHAP. III.

Robert Duguid, Fifth Baron of Auchinhove.

ROBERT DUGUID,

FIFTH BARON OF AUCHINHOVE.

ROBERT DUGUID succeeded his father, William Duguid, as fifth Baron of Auchinhove, as is proved by the retour of the service of Robert Duguid as heir to his father William Duguid in the lands of Auchinhove, Wartle, Greencoats, and
1593. Tulloch, 23d June 1593. Sasine followed thereon 10th September 1593.

Robert Duguid married Janet Forbes, daughter of Robert Forbes of Echt, during the lifetime of his father, when he was styled younger of Auchinhove. Robert Duguid, younger of Auchinhove, was divorced *a vinculo*, from his wife, Janet Forbes, for adultery committed with Elizabeth
1583. Mitchell in 1583. He was afterwards, however, contracted in marriage with Marjory Gordon, as then held, incompetently; but the king, James VI., feeling some indulgence towards him on account of his extreme youth (*minime etatis existens*), was induced to pass a remission and dis-
1589. pensation in his favour 29th July 1589, wherein, after pardoning the offence in a criminal view, he dispenses with the material objection arising from the survivance of Janet Forbes, his former spouse, and specially declares the marriage he was now to solemnise to be *adeo fidele in omnibus respec-*

tibus ac si eandem (Marjory Gordon) *in primam uxorem duxisset;* that is, to be as binding as if he had married Marjory Gordon as his first wife. The grant, moreover, has an express legitimation of the future issue, to the same effect and as fully as if they had been born of the said Robert's first wife.*

CHAP. III. *Robert Duguid, Fifth Baron of Auchinhove.*

Robert Duguid granted procuratory for resigning the lands of Auchinhove and others in favour of himself and Marjory Gordon, his spouse, and William Duguid, his son, 6th November 1594, and obtained a charter of the same. A precept furth of the Chancery was issued for infefting him in the said lands, 15th March 1595, and sasine followed thereon 10th April 1596.† 1594. 1595. 1596.

By Marjory Gordon, Robert Duguid had issue—

I. WILLIAM, his successor.

II. ROBERT, styled portioner of Ruthven. He married Marian Forbes in 1611, by whom he had a son, Robert Duguid, who went to Poland about 1639, and was alive in 1669, as is proved by a birth-breve sworn before the magistrates of Aberdeen, 16th June 1669. 1611. 1639-69. *See* App. No. LXI.

Robert Duguid, fifth Baron of Auchinhove, died about 1614, and was succeeded by his eldest son, William Duguid, sixth Baron of Auchinhove. 1614.

---

* Riddell on *Peerage and Consistorial Law*, vol. i. p. 394.
† Inventory of Auchinhove Deeds.

CHAP. III.

William Duguid, Sixth Baron of Auchinhove.

WILLIAM DUGUID,

SIXTH BARON OF AUCHINHOVE.

William Duguid, eldest son of Robert Duguid, fifth Baron of Auchinhove, by Marjory Gordon, his spouse, succeeded as sixth Baron of Auchinhove on the death of his father, to whom he was
1614. served heir 1st July 1614.*

At a Sheriff-court, held at Aberdeen, 1st Nov-
1633. ember 1633, to tax the incomes of all persons holding annual rents and wadsetts, "Johne Farquhar in Norum, declarit that thair wes restand to him be William Duiged of Auchinhuif v^c merkis.†" William Duguid of Auchinhove, with certain of his servants, was taken prisoner by the famous freebooter Gilderoy, Patrick M'Gregor, who kept him captive till he got a bond for 200 merks as his ransom, as was proved at the trial of Gilderoy and his accomplices at Edinburgh,
1636. 27th July 1636.

See App. No. LXII.

Alexander Irvine of Drum, 26th October 1616, made a contract with William Duguid of Auchinhove, whereby he disponed to him the lands of Tillylair and Greencoats, with the multures of the said lands, lying within the lordship of Mar and sheriffdom of Aberdeen. A charter in terms of the said contract was executed on the same day, and was registered in the books of Council

* *Inquis. Retour. Abbrev.* folio 224, No. 592.

† *Miscellany of the Spalding Club*, vol. iii p. 88.

CHAP. III.

William Duguid, Sixth Baron of Auchinhove.

and Session 1st November 1624. Alexander Irvine of Drum executed a procuratory for resigning the said lands, and the instrument of resignation following thereon is dated 19th June 1618. A charter of confirmation under the Great Seal was granted 20th June 1618, and sasine followed thereon 11th September 1618. 1618.

The Lords of Council and Session issued a decreet of transumpt, at the instance of William Duguid of Auchinhove, against Alexander Irvine of Drum, 29th July 1618; transuming a charter 1618. under the Great Seal, granted to Alexander Irvine, of the lands of Coul and pertinents, lying in the barony of O'Neil and sheriffdom of Aberdeen, dated 19th February 1494. 1494.

To an action of reduction raised by the Earl of Mar against his vassals in 1634, William Duguid 1634. of Auchinhove pleaded that he and his predecessors had been infeft in his lands, holding of the king, for the space of two hundred years, which lands were designed to lie in the sheriffdom of Aberdeen only, but not within the earldom of Mar or lordship of the Garioch. But in reply, the Earl offered to prove them parts and pendicles of the earldom of Mar, which reply the Lords sustained to be proven by public and authentic writs and evidents.* Soon after this, William Duguid got his lands of Auchinhove erected into a barony. On the 13th February 1643 he resigned the said 1643.

* *Antiquities of the Shires of Aberdeen and Banff*, vol. ii. p. 40.

CHAP. III.

William Duguid, Sixth Baron of Auchinhove.

lands in favour of himself, his spouse, M. Forbes, and Francis Duguid, his eldest son; and on the same day obtained a charter under the Great Seal of the mains and mosses of Auchinhove and Boglochs, and the fishings thereof; Auchinhove, with the mill and multures thereof; the lands of Warthill, Tulloch, Osnythrods, Blelack, and the bogs of the same; Corntown, and the bog thereof; Greencoats, Badmyle, and Marywell, with the outlets, parts, and pendicles, all lying within the sheriffdom of Aberdeen, united into one free barony called the barony of Auchinhove.

1656. William Duguid of Auchinhove purchased from George Forbes of Corse, in 1656, that part of the barony of O'Neil, lying in the parish of Lumphanan, consisting of Easter and Wester Kincraigie and pendicles.*

William Duguid, sixth Baron of Auchinhove, married M. Forbes, eldest daughter of Robert Forbes of Barnes, of the Monymusk family, by whom he had a son, Francis, who succeeded him.

1656. He died in 1656.

FRANCIS DUGUID,

SEVENTH BARON OF AUCHINHOVE.

Francis Duguid, Seventh Baron of Auchinhove.

Francis Duguid, son of William Duguid, sixth Baron of Auchinhove, by his wife, M. Forbes, succeeded as seventh baron on the death of his father

1656. in 1656.

* *Collections for Shires of Aberdeen and Banff*, p. 607.

CHAP. III.

Francis Duguid, Seventh Baron of Auchinhove.

George Forbes of Corse executed a contract, dated 1656, whereby he disponed to Francis Duguid of Auchinhove the lands of Easter and Wester Kincraigie, with pendicles, Knowhead, Killoch, and Bogloch, lying within the parochin of O'Neil and sheriffdom of Aberdeen, and he executed a charter of the said lands, to be holden *de me*, in favour of the said Francis Duguid. Sasine followed thereon 9th July 1657; regis- 1657.
tered at Aberdeen 12th August 1657, and in the books of Council and Session 17th February 1671. 1671.
Francis Duguid of Auchinhove got a charter of confirmation, under the Great Seal, of the said lands, 12th January 1672. Franciscus Duguid 1672.
de Auchinhove, Haeres Willelmi Duguid de Auchinhove Patris, was retoured heir, 2d July 1673.* Francis Duguid of Auchinhove was 1673.
retoured heir to his father, William Duguid of Auchinhove, in the lands of Coul, called Greencoats and Tillylair, with pendicles, 2d July 1673; 1673.
and George Nicholson of Clunie, Sheriff-clerk of Aberdeen, gave a commission to Francis Fraser, notary-public, Sheriff-clerk-depute, to take sasine in favour of Francis Duguid upon the precept of infeftment contained in the said retour on the said lands. Sasine followed 19th October 1673; re- 1673.
gistered at Aberdeen, 1st November 1673.

Francis Duguid obtained a charter under the

* *Lib. Retour.* vol. xxxi. fol. 253, No. 414.

CHAP. III.

Francis Duguid. Seventh Baron of Auchinhove.

Great Seal, of the barony of Auchinhove, comprehending the mains, manor-place, boglochs, and fishings, 5th September 1673; sasine followed thereon 30th May 1674.

Francis Duguid, seventh Baron of Auchinhove, married Elizabeth Seton, by whom he had a son,
1675. Francis, who succeeded him. He died in 1675.

Francis Duguid, Eighth Baron of Auchinhove.

FRANCIS DUGUID,

EIGHTH BARON OF AUCHINHOVE.

FRANCIS DUGUID, son of Francis Duguid, seventh Baron of Auchinhove, by his wife, Elizabeth Seton, succeeded as eighth baron on the death of his father, to whom he was retoured heir 30th
1675. April 1675.* A precept was issued furth of the Chancery for infefting Francis Duguid in the lands and barony of Auchinhove, 14th May 1675. George Nicholson of Clunie, Sheriff-clerk of Aberdeen, gave a commission to James Anderson, notary-public, for giving sasine to Francis Duguid in the lands and barony of Auchinhove, lying within the parishes of Lumphanan, O'Neil, and
1675. Aboyne, 19th May 1675; registered in the Sheriff-court books, Aberdeen, 7th October 1675.

Francis Duguid, younger of Auchinhove, entered as a student at King's College, Aberdeen,
1664. under Robert Forbes, in 1664.†

Francis Duguid of Auchinhove, and Alexander

* *Lib. Retour.* vol. xxxii. fol. 242, No. 426.

† *Records of the University and King's College, Aberdeen*, p. 481.

CHAP. III.

Francis Duguid, Eighth Baron of Auchinhove.

Chalmers of Balnacraig, were appointed commissioners to make up the list of pollable persons within the parochin of Lumphanan. In this list are contained the following entries:—

The Laird of Auchinhove his valuatione, as greatest heritor in the said parioshin is . .	£808	13	4
The hundreth pairt whereof, payable by the tennents is aucht pound one shilling and ninepence, *inde*	£8	1	9
Imprimis, The Laird of Auchinhove his valuatione in the said pariochin being above £500, is layable for £12 of poll, and the generall poll of 6s., both is	£12	6	0
Item, His ladie, her generall poll is . .	0	6	0
Item, Robert, Alexander, Patrick, James, Francis Dugids, his children, their poll is	9	0	0
Item, Margrat and Jean Dugids, his daughters *in familia*, their general poll is .	0	12	0
Item, George Gordon, his servant, his fee per annum 40 merks, the fortieth pairt whereof is 13s. 4d., and the generall poll of 6s., both is	0	19	4
Item, Thomas Millne, his servant, his fee 25 merks per annum, the fortieth pairt whereof is 8s. 4d., and the generall poll of 6s., both is	0	14	4
Item, John Duguid, his servant, his fee per annum is 25 merks, the fortieth pairt whereof is 8s. 4d., and the generall poll of 6s., both is	0	14	4
Item, Patrick Sutor, his servant, his fee per annum is 25 merks, the fortieth pairt whereof is 8s. 4d., and the generall poll of 6s., both is	0	14	4
Item, John Duncan, his servant, his fee per annum 25 merks, the fortieth pairt whereof is 8s. 4d., and the generall poll of 6s., both is .	0	14	4

CHAP. III.

Francis Duguid, Eighth Baron of Auchinhove.

Item, Arthur Ross, his servant, his fee per annum is 25 merks, the fortieth pairt whereof is 8s. 4d., and the generall poll of 6s., both is	£0	14	4
Item, James Forbes, his servant, his fee per annum 20 merks, the fortieth pairt whereof is 6s. 8d., and the generall poll of 6s., both is	0	12	8
Item, Andrew Massie, his servant, his fee per annum 20 merks, the fortieth pairt whereof is 6s. 8d., and the generall poll of 6s., both is	0	12	8
Item, Anna Gordon, his servant, her fee per annum 20 merks, the fortieth pairt whereof is 6s. 8d., and the generall poll of 6s., both is	0	12	8
Item, Anna King, his servant, her fee per annum 20 merks, the fortieth pairt whereof is 6s. 8d., and the generall poll of 6s., both is	0	12	8
Item, Elspet Gibb, his servant, her fee per annum is 20 merks, the fortieth pairt whereof is 6s. 8d., and the generall poll of 6s., both is	0	12	8
Item, Elspet Hood, his servant, her fee per annum is 20 merks, the fortieth pairt whereof is 6s. 8d., and the generall poll of 6s., both is	0	12	8
Item, Grisell and Agnes Hoods, his servants, their fees per annum 40 merks, the fortieth pairt whereof is 13s. 4d., and the generall poll of 6s., both is . . .	1	5	8
Item, Jean Middletone, his servant (no fee) her generall poll is	0	6	0
	£32	2	8

The said Laird of Auchinhove, being possessor of a considerable pairt of the lands, his proportione of the

CHAP. III.

valuatione is £5 : 8 : 5, but he being classed in a higher capacity is not layable for the samen." *

Francis Duguid, Eighth Baron of Auchinhove.

In the parish of Aboyne, "Francis Duguid of Auchinhove, his valuation in the said parochin is £100 : 4 : 6. The hundreth part whereof, payable be the tennents, is £1 : 0 : 1."†

Francis Duguid of Auchinhove married, and had issue—

I. Robert, his successor.
II. Alexander.
III. Patrick.
IV. James.
V. Francis.
VI. Margaret.
VII. Jane.

Francis Duguid, eighth Baron of Auchinhove, died in 1698, and was succeeded by his eldest son, Robert, ninth Baron of Auchinhove. 1698.

ROBERT DUGUID,

NINTH BARON OF AUCHINHOVE.

Robert Duguid, Ninth Baron of Auchinhove.

Robert Duguid, eldest son of Francis Duguid, eighth Baron of Auchinhove, succeeded as ninth baron on the death of his father, to whom he was served heir 7th February 1698.‡ Sasine followed 14th May 1698. 1698.

Robert Duguid of Auchinhove granted a bond over the lands of Auchinhove in favour of George,

* *List of Pollable Persons within the Shire of Aberdeen*, vol i. p. 116. † *Ibid* p. 67. ‡ *Lib. Retour.* vol. xl. fol. 21, No. 505.

CHAP. III.

Robert Duguid, Ninth Baron of Auchinhove.

1699. Earl of Aberdeen, dated 21st June 1699, and registered at Edinburgh 5th March 1711. A charter thereon under the Great Seal followed, dated 15th September 1699, written to the seal, and registered 3d November 1699, and sealed on the following day.

1700. The Sheriff of Aberdeen issued a precept to Robert Duguid for his taxed duties and other duties in the *capias securitatem*, for his infeftment upon his retour, dated 13th June 1700. The Sheriff of Aberdeen granted a commission to Alexander Chalmers and Francis Moir for taking judicial resignation of Teresa Leslie or Duguid of five ploughs of land, and her judicial renunciation of her liferent interest in the same in favour of Francis Farquharson of Finzean, 6th

1700. July 1700; registered at Aberdeen, 28th July 1700.

1703. Robert Duguid granted a disposition of the lands of Auchinhove, comprehending the mains, manor-place, boglochs, and fishings of the same, in favour of Sir Thomas Forbes, styled of Auchinhove, dated 7th July 1703. An instrument of resignation of the said lands was executed by Robert Duguid in favour of the said Sir Robert

1704. Forbes, 4th February 1704, who on the same day obtained a charter of the same under the Great Seal. Sasine followed thereon, 25th March 1704; registered at Aberdeen, 1st April 1704.

William Duguid granted a heritable bond for

CHAP. III.

Robert Duguid, Ninth Baron of Auchinhove.

the sum of ten thousand pounds Scots of principal, upon the Mains of Auchinhove, and the lands of Melikle and Little Tillylair, in favour of Robert Duguid, 23d February 1709; also a heritable bond for the sum of ten thousand merks of principal, upon the foresaid lands of Tillylair, in favour of Teresa Leslie or Duguid, same date. Teresa Leslie or Duguid obtained a decreet of adjudication against William Duguid, adjudging the lands of Tillylair, 15th February 1710; and 1710.
Robert Duguid obtained a decreet of adjudication against the said William Duguid, adjudging the lands of Meikle and Little Tillylair, 10th June 1714. The Earl of Aberdeen obtained a 1714.
decreet of adjudication against Robert Duguid of Auchinhove and Sir Robert Forbes, adjudging the lands of Auchinhove, 15th February 1712. 1712.
Robert Farquharson of Finzean obtained a decreet of sale of the lands and barony of Auchinhove, excepting the East and West Mains of Auchinhove, with the mill, and the lands of Meikle and Little Tillylair, 27th July 1727, which decreet of sale 1727.
was disponed by the said Robert Farquharson of Finzean in favour of John Farquharson of Invercauld, 5th March 1728, who again disponed it in 1728.
favour of Francis Farquharson, younger of Finzean, 25th February 1730. 1730.

Robert Duguid of Auchinhove, and Patrick Duguid, his son, executed a bond for six thousand pounds Scots of principal, in favour of James,

CHAP. III.

Robert Duguid, Ninth Baron of Auchinhove.

Count Leslie, seventeenth Baron of Balquhain, 18th June 1730. Robert Duguid, with the consent of Teresa Leslie, his spouse, of Patrick Duguid, his eldest son, and of Mary Duguid, his daughter, disponed and assigned the heritable bond for ten thousand pounds Scots, secured upon the Mains of Auchinhove and the lands of Meikle and Little Tillylair, granted to him by William Duguid, with the decreet of adjudicaton obtained thereon, to James, Count Leslie of Balquhain, as security for the foresaid bond for six thousand pounds Scots, and the annual rents due thereon,
1730. 18th June 1730; which disposition and assignation was duly ratified by Teresa Leslie on the same day.

Robert Duguid of Auchinhove married Teresa Leslie, third daughter of Patrick, Count Leslie, fifteenth Baron of Balquhain, by his first wife, Elizabeth Douglas. Their marriage-contract is
1699. dated 18th November 1699; and Teresa Leslie got a charter under the Great Seal, of her liferent
1699. provision, 22d December 1699. He had issue—

I. PATRICK, his successor, who became twenty-first Baron of Balquhain.

1711 II. ALEXANDER, born 1711. Was a clergyman at Aber-
1747-88. deen in 1747, and died at Elgin 1788.

1713. III. JOSEPH, born 1713. In holy orders. Died at Edin-
1775. burgh 12th February 1775.

IV. JAMES, married to M. Brodie, by whom he had a daughter, Kitty, who was married to George Ferguson. He had also a natural son, Joseph Duguid, who claimed the estates of Auchinhove and Balquhain from his uncle, Patrick Leslie Duguid, in 1775, as being the nearest Protestant heir of entail. CHAP. III.

V. Mary, married first to Mr. Gordon of Tillychoudie, and secondly to Mr. Irvine in Elgin.

VI. Another Daughter, married to Captain John M'Gregor.

Robert Duguid, Ninth Baron of Auchinhove.

Robert Duguid, ninth Baron of Auchinhove, died in 1731, and was succeeded by his eldest son, 1731.
Patrick, who also succeeded to the Balquhain estates on the death of Peter Leslie Grant, twentieth Baron of Balquhain, in 1775, when he 1775.
became twenty-first Baron of Balquhain, and assumed the name and arms of Leslie.

NOTE TO CHAPTER III.

NOTE—WARDIS. *See* Page 273.

Note. THE name of Wardis or Wardhouse is said to be derived from the circumstance of King Gregory of Scot-
893. land, who died in 893, having built a castle as a royal residence, with a vitrified fort, on the top of the beautiful green hill of Dunodeer, situated in the upper part of the lordship of the Garioch, in the parish of Insch, a mile from the Kirktown, where King Gregory died. The ruins of the castle remain to this day. King Gregory also erected a fortified building at the foot of the heights, to guard and protect the entrance and the road up to this stronghold, and this tower or outpost received the name of the King's Wardhouse. It is also said that this name of Dunodeer is descriptive of the local situation of the castle, and the purpose for which it was intended, being derived from the Celtic *Dun-aud-iridh,* signifying a fort on the acclivity of a hill (see Kennedy's *Annals,* p. 6). Others say the name is derived from *dun,* a hill, and *ereith,* a signal. The mansion-house of Wardis was situated in a valley, which was beautifully diversified with natural woods, and the gardens surrounding the house were exceedingly rich. The ancient castle of Meiklewardis stood in a narrow valley to the west of the Hill of Dunodeer. The only remaining vestige of it is the fosse by which it was sur-

Note.

rounded, although it is not many years since the ruins of the walls were removed. Young Patrick Leith of Harthill, having obtained a commission from the Marquis of Montrose, who was then raising troops in the cause of King Charles I., found that he had no horses to mount his troop. Hearing that Forbes of Craigievar was lying at Inverurie with his troop, Patrick Leith went there in the night with a party of his friends, and made the whole troop prisoners, and mounted his own men on their horses, and joined Montrose in a few days afterwards. Montrose highly commended the conduct and courage of the young gentleman, and entrusted him with the defence of the castle of Meiklewardis, which was besieged by General Middleton. The castle was taken, and Patrick Leith was made prisoner, and suffered death for his loyalty, being beheaded at Edinburgh, 20th October 1647, when he was scarcely twenty-five years old. 1647.
He was reckoned one of the handsomest youths in the country, and he suffered, like a true and faithful loyalist, with great firmness and constancy.—(Macfarlane's *Geographical Collections.*)

APPENDIX.

APPENDIX No. I. *Appendix I.*

SIR WILLIAM LESLIE, FOURTH BARON OF BALQUHAIN.

CHARTER of the Lands of Selby and Lochtillok in the Garioch, granted by ALEXANDER STEWART, Earl of Mar and Lord of the Garioch, to Sir WILLIAM LESLIE, fourth Baron of Balquhain—1433. 1433.

ALEXANDER STEWARTUS Comes de Mar et de Garviauch dilecto fratri nostro Andree Stewarto militi ballivo nostro comitatus de Garviauch hac vice specialiter constituto salutem Sciatis quod concessimus hereditarie dilecto nostro Willelmo de Lesley de Balchane totas et integras terras nostras de Selby et de Lochtillok cum pertinenciis jacentes in comitatu nostro de ly Garviauch infra vicecomitatum de Aberdene. Quare vobis precipimus et mandamus quatenus eidem Willelmo de Lesley vel suo certo actornato latori presencium saisinam et possessionem hereditarie dictarum terrarum cum pertinenciis juste liberare faciatis et sine delacione secundum formam tamen et tenorem carte nostre talliatus de terris baronie de Balchane quam inde habet. Datum sub sigillo nostro apud castrum nostrum de Kyndrumy decimo die mensis Decembris Anno Domini millesimo quadringentesimo tricesimo tercio (10th December 1433). 1433.

Original in Balquhain Charter-room. Charter No. 666.

APPENDIX.

Appendix II.

APPENDIX No. II.

Sir William Leslie, Fourth Baron of Balquhain.

Confirmation by King James II. of a Charter granted on 27th March 1460, by Alexander Leslie, first of that Ilk, to his Kinsman, William Leslie, fourth Baron of Balquhain, of the Lands of Bracach, the Quyltis, and the Milton of Knockenlewis, and the Drummis, in the Barony of Leslie, in the Regality of

1460. the Garioch—A.D. 1460.

Jacobus Dei gratia Rex Scotorum .... Sciatis nos quamdam cartam Alexandri Lesly de eodem factam et concessam dilecto nostro Willelmo Lesly de Balquhan militi ... ad plenum intellexisse . Omnibus hanc cartam visuris vel audituris Alexander de Lesly dominus Ejusdem salutem in Domino sempiternam . Noveritis me dedisse concessisse et hac presenti carta mea confirmasse dilecto consanguineo meo Domino Willelmo Lesly de Balquhan militi totas et integras terras de Bracach le Quyltis et le Mynlton of Knokynblewis et le Drummis cum pertinentiis jacentes in baronia de Lesly in regalitate de Garviache infra vicecomitatum de Aberdene Que quidem terre cum pertinentiis fuerunt dicti Willelmi hereditarie et quas . . . in manus meas apud Edinburgh coram subscriptis testibus per fustem et baculum et suos procuratores ad hoc legittime constitutos et suas literas patentes . . . simpliciter resignavit . . . Tenendas . . . dicto Domino Willelmo Lesly militi pro toto tempore vite sue et post ipsius Domini Willelmi decessum Alexandro Lesly filio suo inter ipsum et quondam Agnetem de Irwyn sponsam suam legittime procreato et heredibus masculis de corpore dicti Alexandri legittime procreandis Quibus forte deficientibus Georgio de Lesly fratri germano dicti Alexandri et heredibus masculis de corpore ipsius Georgii legittime procreandis . quibus forte deficientibus veris legitimis et propinquioribus heredibus dicti Domini

Willelmi quibuscunque de me et heredibus meis in feodo et hereditate imperpetuum . . . . Faciendo inde annuatim . . . . servicia de dictis terris debita et consueta . . . In cujus rei testimonium presenti carte mee sigillum meum est appensum apud Edinburgh vicesimo septimo die mensis Marcij Anno Domini millesimo quadringentesimo sexagesimo Testibus reuerendis in χρ̄o patribus et dominis Dominis Georgeo episcopo Brechinensi cancellario Scocie / Thoma episcopo Aberdonensi / nobilibus dominis Jacobo domino Levyngston / Patricio domino de Grahame / Andrea domino Avandalie / Andrea Lundy, Magistro Alexandro Lummisden rectore de Flisket Johanne de Cockburn cum multis aliis . Quam quidem cartam . . . . pro perpetuo confirmamus Saluis nobis juribus et serviciis de dictis terris ante presentem confirmacionem nobis debitis et consuetis In cujus rei testimonium presenti carte nostre confirmacionis magnum sigillum nostrum apponi precepimus . Testibus reuerendis in χρ̄o patribus Georgeo episcopo Brechinensi cancellario nostro / Thoma episcopo Aberdonensi / et consanguineis nostris Jacobo domino Levingston magno camerario nostro / Patricio (domino de Grahame) Andrea domino Avendalie / et Magistro Johanne Arous archidiacono Glasguensi nostri se (creti sigilli) custode apud Edinburgh quarto die mensis Aprilis Anno Domini millesimo qu (adringentesimo) sexagesimo / et anno regni nostri vicesimo quarto.

APPENDIX. II. 1460. 1460.

Registrum Magni Sigilli, lib. v. No. 102.

APPENDIX No. III.

Appendix III.

William Leslie, Seventh Baron of Balquhain.

Obligation entered into by William Leslie, seventh Baron of Balquhain, and John Leslie, second Baron of Wardis, not to molest the Town of Aberdeen—12th February 1527. 1527.

Apud Abirdene XII° Februarii, Anno 1527. The quhilk day, in presens of our souerane lordis justice, and com-

APPENDIX III.

ponitouris Willeame Leslie of Buchquhane, and Jhone Leslie of Warderis, obleist thame conjunctlie and seueralie to our souerane lordis the kingis grace for thame selfis, thair kyne frendis, men tenentis, seruandis, adherentis, and part-takaris, and all that thai may lat, that thai nor nane of thame sall nocht molest, wex, inquiett, nor trouble the prouest, bailzeis, counsaill, communitie, and inhabitaris the burgh of Abirden, or ony ane of thame, ony manner of way in tyme cumming in thair personis, landis, or gudis, utherwais than law will, vnder the pane of twa thousand pundis, to be aplyit to our souerane lordis use; and gif it sall happen ony of the forsaid lairdis of Buchquhane and Warderis, thair kyne frendis, men seruandis, adherentis, and part-takaris, to mak ony truble or molestatioun to ony of the inhabitaris of the said burgh, ether within the samyn or outwith, the saidis lairdis of Buchquhane and Warderis deliuerand the persone or personis makand the said brak or truble to the prouest or bailleis of the said burgh, to the effect that justice may be done on thame, sall nocht incur the panis forsaidis. Extractum de libro adjornalis S.DN. regis per me Nicolaum Craufurd de oxen gangis clericum justiciarie ejusdem generalem sub meis signo et subscriptione manualibus.

Extracts from the *Burgh Records of Aberdeen*, vol. i. p. 115; Spalding Club.

Appendix IV.

APPENDIX No. IV.

William Leslie, Seventh Baron of Balquhain.

1530.

Obligation anent the Lands of Cultercullane and Pettemwk, between William Leslie, seventh Baron of Balquhain, and John, Lord Forbes—1530.

Obligation by William Leslie of Balquhane to Johnne lord Forbess who had infeft him in the lands of Cultercullane and Pettemwk and in twenty-four shillings of

APPENDIX. IV.

annual rent furth of the alehouse of Fudess in fulfilment of a decreet-arbitral given at Aberdeen on the 11th of February 1527, and registered in the books of Council and Session; and for security and keeping kindness and eschewing of trubliss and inconvenientis to ryss betuix them; the said lands and annual rent to remain with the said William Leslie "gif the said Johne lord Forbess or ony wthir of his pairt takkaris or assistaris makis ony new braik or dois ony harm to me or my sone othiris of our pairt takkaris or assistaris;" and if the doer of the skaith be not delivered up to the law within forty dayis or fugitate, in that case the said Lord his "pairt takkaris and assistaris sall hald him perpetually out of thair rowmiss and bundis and treulye assist and tak pairt with me my pairt takkaris and assistaris that gettis the skaith faithfully but fraude or gyle and never to help the faltar in the law nor by the law quhilk gif they do not the said landis to be brukit be me my airis and assigneis as said is:" the said William Leslie binding himself, notwithstanding his infeftment in the lands, to take up no profit of them till the fault be made, but all mails and profits to remain with the Lord Forbes as the decreet-arbitral and charter made thereon more fully bear. Witnesses—George, Earl of Huntlie; Robert, Abbot of Kinloss; Alexander Irwin of Drum, knight; Gilbert Keyth of Trowpe; Johne Gordoune of Potare; Alexander Gordone of Strathdowne: the judges arbiters—John, Lord Erskine; Archibald of Douglace of Kilspindie, treasurer to the king; William Scot of Balvery, knight; Gilbert Keith of Trowpe; and Walter Scot. At Aberdeen, xxii February j^{m}ccccxxix. 1529.

Antiquities of the Shires of Aberdeen and Banff, vol. iii. p. 115; Spalding Club. Original in Charter-chest at Castle Forbes.

APPENDIX.

Appendix V.

APPENDIX No. V.

William Leslie, Seventh Baron of Balquhain.

Charter by King James IV. to William Leslie, seventh Baron of Balquhain, of the Lands of Balquhain; the Nethertown and Oldtown of Knockinlews; four Bovates of the Lands of Harlaw; the Lands of Selbie, Lochtilloch, Whitecross, and Knockallochy, with the Mill; two Bovates of the Lands of Ressavate; two Parts of the Lands of Wardis Flemyng, and of Wraes; the Lands of Syde, with the Mill and Alehouse; the Lands of Seggyden and Erlesfield, in
1511. the Regality of the Garioch—A.D. 1511.

Jacobus Dei gracia Rex Scotorum . . . Sciatis nos . . . . confirmasse dilecto nostro Willelmo Leslie de Balquhane omnes et singulas terras de Balquhane le Nethertoun de Knockinblew le Auldtoun de Knockinblew quatuor bouatas terrarum de Harlaw terras de Selvye Lochtilloch Quhitecors et Knokalloquhy cum molendino eiusdem duas bouatas terrarum de Ressavate binam partem terrarum de Warderis Flemyng binam partem terrarum de Wrais terras de Syde cum molendino le *Alehouse* eiusdem terras de Seguyden et Erlisfeild cum pertinenciis jacentes in regalitate de Garuiach et infra vicecomitatum de Abirdene Quequidem terre . fuerunt dicti Willelmi prius hereditarie et quas ipse . . . in manus nostras apud Edinburgh . . . resignavit . . . Insuper pro bono gratuitoque seruicio nobis et successoribus nostris per prefatum Willelmum et heredes suos impenso et impendendo . . . . creamus omnes et singulas terras suprascriptas in vnam meram et liberam baroniam Baroniam de Balquhane perpetuis futuris temporibus nuncupandam et maneriem de Balquhane principale messuagium eiusdem baronie existere ordinamus . . Tenendas . . . dicto Willelmo et heredibus suis in antiqua infeodacione predecessoribus ipsius Willelmi pro eorum heredibus per Comites de Mar pro tempore existentibus data et confecta per nostrum predecessorem bone memorie Jacobum primum confirmata contentis de nobis et successoribus nostris in feodo et hereditate imperpetuum .... Reddendo inde annuatim ... unam communem sectam in curiis vicecomitis nostri de Abirdene unacum wardis releuiis et maritagiis cum contigerint .... In cujus rei testimonium presenti carte nostre magnum sigillum nostrum apponi precepimus .... apud Edinburgh vicesimo nono die mensis Julii Anno Domini millesimo quingentesimo vndecimo et regni nostri vicesimo quarto. 1511.

APPENDIX V.

Antiquities of Shires of Aberdeen and Banff, vol. iii. p. 376; Spalding Club. From *Registrum Magni Sigilli*, lib. xvii. No. 95, MS. in General Register House, Edinburgh; and Balquhain Charters, No. 1.

APPENDIX No. VI.

Appendix VI.

William Leslie, Seventh Baron of Balquhain.

Charter by King James V. to William Leslie, seventh Baron of Balquhain, and Elizabeth Ogilvie, his Wife, of the Lands of Syd, with the Mill, Erlisfeild, Segateden, and the Wrays, in the Earldom of Mar and Lordship of the Garioch—A.D. 1514. 1514.

Jacobus Dei gracia Rex Scotorum ... Sciatis nos cum auisamento et consensu carissime matris nostre Margarete Regine Scocie nostre tutricis testamentarie ... confirmasse dilectis nostris Willelmo Leslie de Balquhane et Elizabeth Ogiluy, ejus sponse ac eorum alteri diucius viventi in coniuncta infeodacione totas et integras terras de Syd cum molendino earundem terras de Erlisfeild Segateden et le Wrays cum suis pertinenciis jacentes in comitatu de Mar dominio de Garviauch infra vicecomitatum nostrum de Abirdene Quequidem terre ... fuerunt dicti Willelmi

APPENDIX VI. hereditarie et quas .. idem ... in manibus prefate carissime matris nostre tanquam nostre tutricis testamentarie nostro nomine ... simpliciter resignauit ... Tenendas et habendas .... dictis Willelmo Leslie et Elizabeth Ogiluy ejus sponse et eorum alteri diucius viventi in coniuncta infeodacione et heredibus inter ipsos legitime procreatis seu procreandis quibus deficientibus legitimis et propinquioribus heredibus dicti Willelmi quibuscunque de nobis et successoribus nostris Scotorum Regibus in feodo et hereditate imperpetuum ... Faciendo inde annuatim ... jura et seruicia ... debita et consueta . In cujus rei testimonium presenti carte nostre magnum sigillum nostrum apponi precepimus ... Apud Striueling septimo die mensis
1514. Aprilis anno Domini millesimo quingentesimo decimo quarto, et regni nostri primo.

Antiquities of Shires of Aberdeen and Banff, vol. iv. p. 529 ; Spalding Club. From *Registrum Magni Sigilli*, lib. xix. No. 45, MS., General Register House, Edinburgh.

Appendix VII.

APPENDIX No. VII.

William Leslie, Seventh Baron of Balquhain.

Charter by King James V. to William Leslie, seventh Baron of Balquhain, and Marjory Keith, his Wife, of the Lands of Erlisfeild, Segydene, and the Wrayis,
1522. with the Mill of the Syde—A.D. 1522.

Jacobus Dei gracia Rex Scotorum ... Sciatis nos cum consensu carissimi consanguinei et tutoris nostri Johannis ducis Albanie etc . regni nostri protectoris et gubernatoris ... confirmasse dilectis nostris Willelmo Leslie de Balquhane et Mariorie Keith eius sponse et eorum alteri diucius viuenti in coniuncta infeodacione ... totas et integras terras de Erlisfeild Segydene et le Wrayis cum molendino de le Syde et suis pertinentiis jacentes infra vicecomitatum nostrum de Aberdene Quequidem terre . . fuerunt dicti

Willelmi hereditarie et quas . . . idem . . . in manibus prefati carissimi consanguinei et tutoris nostri nomine nostro . . . . simpliciter resignauit . . . Tenendas et habendas . . . . prefatis Willelmo Leslie et Mariorie Keith ejus sponse et eorum alteri diucius viventi in coniuncta infeodacione et heredibus inter ipsos legitime procreatis seu procreandis quibus forte deficientibus legitimis et propinquioribus heredibus dicti Willelmi Leslie quibuscunque de nobis et successoribus nostris in feodo et hereditate imperpetuum . . . Faciendo inde annuatim . . . jura et seruicia . . . debita et consueta In cujus rei testimonium huic presenti carte nostre magnum sigillum nostrum apponi precepimus . . . apud Edinburgh decimotercio die mensis Februarii Anno Domini millesimo quingentesimo vicesimo primo et regni nostri nono. 1521-2.

APPENDIX. VII.

Antiquities of the Shires of Aberdeen and Banff; Spalding Club, vol. iv. p. 229. From the *Registrum Magni Sigilli*, lib. xx. No. 92, MS., General Register House, Edinburgh ; and Balquhain Charters, No. 840.

APPENDIX No. VIII.

Appendix VIII.

John Leslie, Eighth Baron of Balquhain.

Band by John Leslie of Syde to George, Earl of Huntly,—1541. 1541.

Be it kend till all men be thir present lettres, me Johnn Lesly of Syid, sone and apperand air to Villeame Leslie of Bolquhane, to be bundyne and oblest, and be the fayth and trewtht in my body bindis and oblesis me, in the straightest forme and styill of obligatioun, to ane noble and michty lord, George erll of Huntly, lord Gordone and Badzenoch, &c. That forsamekle as my said lord hes gevin to me the soume of four hundretht merkis numerit usuale Scottis monee &c. tharfor I the said John Lesly, be the tennour heirof, becumis leil, trew, anefald man and

APPENDIX VIII.

seruand to my said lord, and sall witht my kyn, freyndis, seruandis, allys, tenentis, parttakeris, and all that I ma purchace, serue, gang and ryid, &c., contrar and aganis all levand or de may, the kingis grace and George erll of Rothes, in his avin propir actioun, allanerly excepit &c. In witnes of the quhilkis, to thir my present letteris of obligatioun, and band of seruice and manrent, subscriuit witht my hand, my propir seill is affixit at Abirdene, the last day of Julii, the yeir of God ane thousand five hun-
1541. dretht fourty ane yeiris, befor thir vitnes, honorabill men, Alexander Irwyng of Drwm, Willyam Woyd of Bonetown, William Leslie of Balquhayne, Alexander Irwing of Cowll, James Gordon of Colquhodilstane, Robert Carnegye of Kynnard, witht uthers diuerss.

JHON LESLY of the Syid.
G. GORDONE.

Gordon Papers; Spalding Club Miscellany, vol. iv. p. 205.

Appendix IX.

APPENDIX No. IX.

JOHN LESLIE, EIGHTH BARON OF BALQUHAIN.

REMISSION by King JAMES V. to JOHN LESLIE, eighth Baron of Balquhain, ALEXANDER LESLIE of Kincraigie, and JOHN KEITH, for the Slaughter of ALEXANDER
1527. FORBES, otherwise called SPANGARE—1527.

JAMES be the grace of God King of Scottis to all and sindry oure justices shireffis justice clerkis crowneris and thair deputis aldermen provestis and ballies of burrowis and all otheris oure liegis and subditis quham it efferis . . . greting wit ye ws of oure speciale grace with auise of oure thesaurar to haue respet and be thir our lettres in the law and by the law specialie respettis Johne Leslie son and apperand aire to Williame Leslie of Buchquhane Alexander Leslie of Kincraigy and John Keith for the slauchter of vmquhile Alexander Forbes alias Spangare ane of the

murtheraris of vmquhile Alexander Seytoun of Meldrum quhilk vmquhile Alexander Forbes was slane on sudantie and in spoliatioun of ane pure man duelland on the Bishop of Abirdenis land and for all actioun and cryme that may folou thairupon and for all otheris actionis crymes transgressionis and offensis quhatsumeuir committit and done be thame or ony of thame in ony tyme bigane vnto the day of the date heirof tressoun in oure persone murthure fire revesing of wemen and commone thift exceptan to be vnhurt vnharmyt vnarrestit vnattachit vnfolowit vnpersewit vnvexit and vndistrublit in thair personis landis or gudis be you or ony of you oure officiaris liegis and subditis foresaidis during the tyme of thir oure lettres—vnder all the hieast pane charge and offenss that ye and ilkane of you may committ . and inrin agane oure Maiestie in that part Thir oure lettres of speciale respett for the space of nynetene yeris nixt to cum eftir the date of the samyn to indure . Gevin vnder our priue sele at Abirdene the nynt day of Februar the yeir of God $j^{m}v^{c}$ tuenty sevin yeris and 1527.
of oure regne the fiftene yeire.

Per Signaturam manu S.D.N. Regis subscriptam.

Antiquities of Shires of Aberdeen and Banff, vol. iii. p. 377 ; Spalding Club.

APPENDIX IX.

APPENDIX No. X.

Appendix X.

JOHN LESLIE, EIGHTH BARON OF BALQUHAIN.

CONTRACT between WILLIAM, Lord Forbes, JOHN LESLIE, eighth Baron of Balquhain, and THOMAS MENZIES of Pitfoddles, for the Settlement of their Feuds—A.D. 1551. 1551.

AT Grantulie the xxvii day of Februar the yeir of God ane
thousand five hundred and fifty ane yeris in presens of ane 1551.
potent and nobel lord George erll of Huntlie luftennent of the north it is . . . contractit and faithfullie oblegit betwixt

APPENDIX X.

Williame lord Forbes and Johne Leslie of Balquhane for thameselffis kyn freindis seruandis assisstiris pairttakkeris on that ane pairt and James Gordoun of Methlyk in name and behalf of Thomas Menzes of Pittfoddilis he oblesand for him himselff his kyn freindis seruandis assisstiris and pairttakkeris on that vther pairt eueschuing all eilestis offencis displesure . . . standand betwixt thame and in special of the slauchteris happenit betwixt Maister Thomas Dauedson Maister Walter Leslie and otheris ther complices and pairttakkeris baitht of the slauchteris mutilatioun gif ony be hurting blude drauing and woundis and otheris whatsomeuir . . . to the effect following that is to say for till euischew griter inconvenience and commond weill of the haill cuntreth the saydis Lord Forbes for his kyn freindis seruandis and all personis perteining to him that it is offended to hes oblesit him for thame and in likwayiss the sayd Johnn Leslie of Balquhane oblesand him for himself his kyn freindis seruandis and all personis perteining to him that it is offended to and als the sayd James Gordoun of Methlyk in name of the sayd Thomas Menzes for his kyn freindis seruandis and all other personis perteining to him that it is offended to hes submittit the decisioun of all the premises to my sayd Lord Luftennent Williame Lord Forbes and Johnn Leslie of Balquhane all three coniunctly in ane voce as gugis arbitrateris and amicable componituris quha sal convein God willing in the cathedrall Kirk of Aberdene on Monunday the ellevint day of April . . . followand the date of ther presentis at nyne hours befor nowne and sal deliuer thair finall sentence and amicable compositioun within xxiiii. houris thairefter and as thai deleuer the saydis partiis sal fulfill and for securitie and guid rewile to be had in the mydtyme and that Thomas Menzeis of Pitfoddellis Gilbert Menzeis Mr. Thomas Menzeis Alexander Menzeis Robert Menzeis and William Menzeis sonis to the sayd Thomas Menzeis Dauid Menzeis and Gilbert Menzeis brether to the sayd Thomas Menzeis his brothers sone Patrik Menzeis Gilbert Menzeis and Gilbert Menzeis seruandis to the said Patrik / Maister

APPENDIX X.

George Johnstoun Alexander Waus younger lard of Mane Thomas Nicholsoun Dauid Mar bailyie Alexander Knowis Maister Andro Herwy Williame Herwy his brother James Litster Patrik Malisoun Jhone Crawfurd son to Andro Crawfurd / James Spens Robert Middiltoun Patrick Middiltoun seruandis to the sayd Thomas Menzeis / Jaspart Bard Alexander Kempt Thomas Burrol Jhone Boyd Andro Beney Henrie Laying William Jamesoun masoun Thomas Shand and Coling Pertaweill sal be harmless and skaithless of all bodelie harme to Sonday callit Dominica in Albis inclusiue the said William Lord Forbes and Johnn Leslie of Balquhane obleiss thame for thameselffis kyn freindis seruandis assisteris or pairttakkeris respectiue ilk ane for thair awn sae mony as the sayd Thomas betuix this and Twysday nixt cummes deleueris in bill subscriuit with his hand to Mr. Robert Lumisden and otheris quhom thai ma lat that the foresaydis Thomas Menzeis of Pitfoddelis and personis forsaydis sal be harmless and skaithless to the said Sonday under the pane of periure infame and inhabilite and refound to our Souerane Lady hir tutor and thesaurar the soume of ane thousand lib . Scottis money tanquam interesse habentium in case the sayd Thomas or ony of the forsaydis personis get or incur ony bodelie harme or skaitht in thair personis be ony way as sayd is and to euischew all sic eilestis my Lord Luftennent forsayd ordanis quhat tyme my Lord Forbes the Lard of Balquhane his son the Lard of Wardderis or his sone Arthure Forbes or Maister Duncan Forbes happynis to be in Aberdene the Prouest beyng adwertesit he sal cause his sone and seruandis that was present at the forsayd displesure as is allegit that is to say Robert Menzeis Mr. George Johnstoun young Lard Mane Mr. Andro Herwy John Crauford Robert Middiltoun Patre Middiltoun Jaspert Bard Alexander Kempt younger Tom Burrol Jhone Boyd Gilbert Menzeis Hewbrand Menzeis Alexander Gilbert to euischow frae all oppin conventioun or passing upoun the get induring the tyme forsayd and als the sayd Thomas Menzeis sal gif to Mr. Duncan Forbes his brether freindis seruandis assisteris

APPENDIX X. and pairttakkeris ane sufficient assurance for sae mony personis as he vill gif in bill to the sayd Sonday in Albis ilk person under the panis forsaydis quhilk assurance shall be deliuerit to Mr. Duncan Forbes betuix this and Twysday nixt be requirand the same and the saydis prouest to assure for the Middiltounis as well as for his awin seruandis induring the forsayd tyme . In witness of the quhilks my saydis Lord Luftennent Lord Forbes and Johne Leslie of Balquhane hes subscriuit thir presentis with thair handis day and place forsayd and sic like quhen the Middiltounis happenys to be in the toune or thair special freindis the said Maister Duncan beyng advertesit he sal cause Johne Tullidaf Williame Jak to euischow frae all opin conventioun or passing upoun the get induring the tyme forsayd.

GEORGE erll off Huntlie   JON LESLIE of Balquhane.
WILLIAM Lord Forbes.   JAMES GORDOUNE

Antiquities of Shires of Aberdeen and Banff, vol. iii. pp. 277-279 ; Spalding Club. From original in Pitfodels Charter-chest.

Appendix XI.

APPENDIX No. XI.

JOHN LESLIE, EIGHTH BARON OF BALQUHAIN.

LEASE of the Church-lands called Kirktowne of Rayne, by THOMAS MYRTOUN, Archdeacon of Aberdeen, to JOHN
1543. LESLIE, eighth Baron of Balquhain—7th June 1543.

CARTA assedationis terrarum ecclesiasticarum que vocantur Kirktowne de Rayne cum lye Ailhouscroft a Thoma Myrtoun Archidiacono facta Johanni Leslye et heredibus suis masculis . Reddendo xxij marcas unacum duplicatione dicti feudi in introitu cuiuslibet heredis ac reseruando unam acram terre vicinam ecclesie pro edificatione unius mansionis pro residentiis Archidiaconi . Data apud Aber-
1543. dene vij Junii . A.D. M.D.XLIII.

Registrum Episcopatus Aberdonensis, vol. i. p. 420.

APPENDIX No. XII.

Appendix XII.

John Leslie, Eighth Baron of Balquhain.

Lease of half of the town of Leddintusche, granted by William Gordon, Bishop of Aberdeen, to John Leslie, eighth Baron of Balquhain—7th February 1549. 1549.

Carta assedationis ab episcopo facta Johanni Leslie de Balquhane dimidietatis ville de Leddintusche extendentis ad octo bouatas terrarum pro terminis in suo rentali decursuris . Reddendo inde annuatim tres libras sex solidos et octo denarios quatuor bollas et tres firlotas farrine et brasii per medium cum bato cuilibet bolle brasii duas quartas unius marte unum mutonem duodecim capones duodecim gallinas domesticas unam aucam domesticam unam bollam anenarum cum pabulo et viginti denarios pro bondagio cum arragiis carragiis aliisque seruitiis solitis . Prouiso quod dictus Johannes Leslie suique heredes ecclesiam ac orthodoxam fidem quantum in eis est defendant . Data apud Canoniam Aberdonensem vij Februarii A.D. M.DXLIX. 1549.

Registrum Episcopatus Aberdonensis, vol. i. p. 444.

APPENDIX No. XIII.

Appendix XIII.

John Leslie, Eighth Baron of Balquhain.

Lease of the Barony and Shire of Fetternear, granted by William Gordon, Bishop of Aberdeen, to John Leslie, eighth Baron of Balquhain—22d October 1550. 1550.

Assedatioun maid be ye bischop to Johne Leslie of Balquhane of ye baronye and schire of Fetterneir and of ye toun of Bonyngtoun lyand within ye baronye of Rayne for nynten yeiris. Payand heirfor yeirlie sevynten pundis

APPENDIX XIII. sax schillingis aucht penneis usuall monye of Scotland, togidder with thre pundis money forsaid for ye fisching of ye same or ane barroll salmond in ye optioun of ye occupyoiris aucht schillingis aucht penneis for bondage thre chelder aucht bollis beir with ane pecc to ilk boll. Ane mutoun threttein dusane pultre and for ye saidis landis and toun of Bonnyntoun with ye pendikillis and pertinentis thairof tuenty pundis money forsaid twa martis sex mutones twanty aucht bollis meill and malt equalie with ane pecc to ilk boll malt sex dusoun capones sex dusoun pultre aucht bollis aittis with ye stray ten schillingis for bondage with arrage carrage and utheris
1550. dew seruice. At Aberden, xxij October M.D.L.

Registrum Episcopatus Aberdonensis, vol. i. p. 451.

Appendix XIV.

APPENDIX No. XIV.

William Leslie, Ninth Baron of Balquhain.

Decreet anent the Multures of the Mill of Fintray, by William Leslie, ninth Baron of Balquhain, Sheriff of
1565. Aberdeen—1565.

Curia vicecomitatus de Abirdene tenta in pretorio eiusdem duodecimo die mensis Januarii Anno Domini millesimo
1564-5. quingentesimo sexagesimo quarto per honorabilem virum Vilhelmum Leslie de Balquhane vicecomitem de Abirdene Jacobum Leslie et Georgium Bissat eius deputatos . . . pro tribunali sedentes. Sectis vocatis et curia legitime affirmata. The said day in the actioun and caus persewit be Willeame Wod of the Myln of Fintray agains Dauid Chalmer off Balbathane anent the clame of the Knaivschip off Heddirvik and Balbathane and cotter mvltyr and Knaivschip of Cragorthie and the pleucht of Weistir Fintray awand to the said Williame be the said Dauid and his tennentis occupears of the toun and landis above writtin . . . The shireff witht consent of baytht the saidis parteis absoluit the said Dauid and

his tennentis of all mvlturis Knavschippis and wthiris dewiteis awand of the saidis landis be the said Dauid and his tennentis in ony tymes bipast preceiding the day and daitt of thir presentis to the said William and decernit and ordanit the said Dauid his airis and assignais tennentis and possessouris of the landis aboue writtin to ansuir and obey the said William and his airis assignais possessouris of the said myln in all tymes cumming of the Knaveschip of Heddirvik and Balbathan and cotter mvlter Knavschip of Cragorthie and the pleucht of Weistir Fintray pertenyng to the said Dauid wsit and wont the tyme of obtenyng of the said William infeftment of the said myln and immediatlie obefor wsit and wont conforme to the said infeftment and this done in jugement witht consent of baytht the saidis pairteis and oblegit thame thair airis executouris and assignais to obserwe this appontment in all tymes cumming . . . and athir of the saids pairteis dischargis wtheris *hinc inde* off all maner of clames . . . preceiding the day and daitt of thir presentis and siclyik the said Dauid and Johne Wod sone to the said Williame hes dischargit wthiris in lyik maner to stand at amite and kyndnes as friendis in tymes cumming and sicklyik the said Williame of his avin confessioun . . . oblegis him to desist . . . fra all forthyr occupatioun or laboring of the auchtane part of the waist medowe of Fintray pertenyng heritablie to the said Dauid and that in all tymes cumming . . . Quhilkis premissis done in jugement as said is the shireff witht consent of the parteis forsaids decernit to have the strynthe of ane decreit judiciall To the quhilk the said shireff interponit his auctorite as efferis . . . Extractum de Libro Actorum curie vicecomitatus Aberdonensis per me scribam ejusdem subscriptum.

Ita est Mr. Andreas Leslie scriba curie vicecomitatus Aberdonensis ad hec sua manu.

A. Leslie.

Antiquities of Shires of Aberdeen and Banff, vol. iii. p. 424 ; Spalding Club. From the original in Charter-chest at Skene House.

APPENDIX

Appendix XV.

APPENDIX No. XV.

William Leslie, Ninth Baron of Balquhain.

Feu-Charter by William Gordon, Bishop of Aberdeen, to William Leslie, ninth Baron of Balquhain, of the Bishop's shire or barony of Fetternear, and Salmon-fishing in the Don, &c.; of the lands of Talzeaucht in the shire of Fetternear, the lands of Bonyngtoun, with the mill, &c., the lands of Lowesk, the third part of the town and lands of Ledintusch, the lands of Custestoun in the shire of Rayne, and the lands of Auchlyne, with the mill and haugh of Bogy or Blairdinny, in the shire of Clatt—A.D 1566.

1566.

Omnibus hanc cartam visuris . . . Willelmus . . . Aberdonensis Episcopus salutem . . . Quia regni Scotie retro principes diuersi in parliamentis suis cum tribus regni sui statibus . . . terras regias et prelatorum aliorumque dominorum temporalium . . . ceterorumque quorumcunque . . . in . . . feodifirmam perpetuam . . . dimittendas fore decreuerunt . . . Noveritis igitur nos cum . . . consensu . . . canonicorum Capituli ecclesie nostre Cathedralis Abirdonensis . . . ac etiam pro nonnulis pecuniarum summis . . . monete . . . Scotie per Willelmum Leslie de Balquhan modernum extendentibus in toto ad summam decem mille librarum . . . necnon propter varias et diuersas gratitudines et benemerita per quondam Johannem Leslie de Balquhane et dictum Willelmum Leslie ejus filium nobis nostre ecclesie cathedralis antedicte presidenti et canonicis eiusdem in hoc turbulento reipublice ecclesiastice statu et tempore impensa et precipue quia dicti quondam Johannes et Willelmus honesto comitatu ac famulis et consanguineis eorundem stipati continuam residentiam fecerunt hoc tempore transacto apud nostram ecclesiam cathedralem ad nostram et nostri capituli instantiam et supplicationem et seipsos promptos paratos et strenuos exhiberunt in defensione nostre ecclesie sedis et cleri inibi residentis instante etiam seuissima et grauissima seditione persecutione dicte nostre ecclesie et sedis per Catholice fidei hostes vndique grassantis aliisque . . . auxiliis seruitiisque . . . assedasse . . . et ad feodifirmam . . . perpetuam hereditarie dimisisse . . . prefato Willelmo Leslie de Balquhane heredibus suis masculis et assignatis quibuscunque . . . terras schiram seu baroniam nostram de Fetterneir cum toto hospitio turre et fortilicio eiusdem cum piscaria salmonum super aqua de Done pratis molendino forresta ac croftis aliisque pendiculis et pertinentiis terras de Talzeaucht jacentes infra schiram de Fetterneir . . . terras nostras de Bonyngtoun cum molendino multuris fabrina et crofto fabrine eiusdem necnon . . . terras nostras de Lowesk ac etiam tertiam partem ville et terrarum de Ledintushe . . . terras nostras de Custestoun jacentes infra schiram de Rayne terras de Auchlyne cum molendino ejusdem ac lie *hauch* seu crofta de Bogy alias Blairdynny vocata jacentes infra schiram de Clatt cum earundem molendinis multuris sequelis terris molendinariis fabrilibus brasinis . . . et pertinentiis earundem universis jacentes infra vicecomitatum de Abirden Tenendas . . . de nobis et successoribus nostris Abirdonensibus episcopis in feodifirma ac emphiteosi et hereditate imperpetuum . . . Reddendo inde annuatim . . . nobis successoribus nostris Abirdonensibus episcopis nostrisve aut eorundem camerariis pro prefata baronia (seu) schira de Fetterneir cum toto hospitio turre et fortilicio eiusdem molendino multuris foresta . . . aliisque . . . pertinentiis eiusdem . . . summam septemdecim librarum sex solidorum octo denariorum monete Scotie tres celdras septem bollas ordii cum bato cuilibet bolle vel octo libras pro qualibet celdra ad rationem vnum mutonem vel sex solidos octo denarios pro eodem tridecim duodenas gallinarum domesticarum vel quatuor solidos pro qualibet duodena vnam bollam auenarum vel quadraginta denarios pro eadem pro gressuma annuatim tres libras nouem solidos quatuor denarios pro bondagiis octo solidos octo denarios pro piscaria salmonum vnum barillum salmonum vel tres libras pro eodem pro seruitiis eiusdem baronie decem solidos et quinque solidos quatuor denarios in augmentationem nostri rentalis .

APPENDIX XV.

Pro terris de Bonyngtone cum . . . pertinentiis . . . viginti quatuor libras sexdecim solidos duas martas vel quadraginta solidos pro qualibet marta sex mutones vel sex solidos octo denarios pro quolibet mutone viginti octo bollas farine et brasii per medium cum bato cuilibet bolle brasii vel decem solidos pro qualibet bolla sex duodenas caponum vel octo solidos pro qualibet duodena sex duodenas gallinarum domesticarum vel quatuor solidos pro qualibet duodena octo bollas auenarum cum pabulo vel quadraginta denarios pro qualibet bolla monete antedicte Pro terris de Lowesk . . . quatuor libras nouem bollas duas firlotas farine quatuor celdras vnam bollam duas firlotas brasii cum bato cuilibet bolle vel octo libras pro qualibet celdra sexdecim capones vel octo denarios pro qualibet pecia tres duodenas gallinarum domesticarum vel quatuor solidos pro qualibet duodena Pro tertia parte de Ledintushe . . . quatuor libras quatuor bollas tres firlotas farine et brasii per medium cum bato cuilibet bolle brasii vel decem solidos pro qualibet bolla dimedietatem vnius marte vel viginti solidos pro eadem vnum mutonem vel sex solidos octo denarios pro eodem duodecim capones vel octo solidos pro eisdem duodecim gallinas domesticas vel quatuor solidos pro eisdem vnum aucam vel duodecim denarios pro eadem vnam bollam auenarum cum pabulo vel quadraginta denarios pro eadem Pro bondagiis et servitiis dictarum terrarum de Bonyngtoun Lowesk Ledintushe . . . octodecim solidos quatuor denarios vnacum servitiis de dictis terris debitis et consuetis et in augmentationem rentalis nostri decem solidos monete suprascripte Pro dictis terris de Custestone . . . pro firma quinque libras sex solidos octo denarios pro gressuma viginti vnum solidos quatuor denarios nouem bollas duas firlotas farine et brasii per medium cum bato cuilibet bolle brasii vel decem solidos pro qualibet bolla vnam martam vel quadraginta solidos pro eadem duos mutones vel sex solidos octo denarios pro qualibet pecia viginti quatuor capones vel octo solidos pro qualibet duodena viginti quatuor gallinas domesticas videlicet quatuor solidos pro qualibet duodena duas bollas auenarum cum pabulo vel quadraginta denarios pro qualibet bolla pro bondagiis et seruitiis quinque solidos et in augmentationem nostri rentalis tres solidos quatuor denarios . . . Pro prefatis terris de Auchlyne pro firma earundem tredecim libras sex solidos octo denarios pro gressuma quinquaginta tres solidos quatuor denarios vnam martam vel quadraginta solidos pro eadem quatuor mutones vel sex solidos octo denarios pro qualibet pecia quatuor aucas vel duodecim denarios pro qualibet pecia viginti quatuor gallinas domesticas vel quatuor solidos pro qualibet duodena viginti quatuor gallinas murales vel quatuor solidos pro qualibet duodena viginti quatuor capones vel octo solidos pro qualibet duodena quatuor bollas auenarum cum pabulo vel quadraginta denarios pro qualibet bolla pro bondagio sex solidos octo denarios pro crofto fabrine predicto tredecim solidos quatuor denarios in firma Pro gressuma eiusdem duos solidos octo denarios sex gallinas domesticas vel quatuor denarios pro qualibet pecia pro servitiis dictarum terrarum et crofti tredecim solidos quatuor denarios et pro augmentatione rentalis nostri sex solidos octo denarios Pro terris de Talzeauch . . . quatuor libras pro quarta parte vnius marte decem solidos vnum mutonem vel sex solidos octo denarios pro eodem nouem *lie pultre* vel quatuor denarios pro qualibet pecia nouem gallinas murales vel quatuor denarios pro qualibet pecia vnam bollam auenarum cum pabulo vel quadraginta denarios pro eadem pro bondagio viginti denarios pro seruitiis dictarum terrarum sex solidos octo denarios pro augmentatione rentalis tres solidos quatuor denarios Pro *lie hauche* et crofto de Bogy alias Blairdynny vocato . . . viginti quatuor solidos pro bondagiis et seruitiis viginti denarios pro augmentatione rentalis eiusdem tres solidos quatuor denarios monete regni Scotie . . Prestando tres sectas ad tria placita capitalia . . annuatim in curiis nostris capitalibus apud Pallacium nostrum Abirdonense tenendis Et tenentes ac occupatores suprascripte baronie et terrarum in exercitibus Regiis et regni balliuo nostro principali sufficienter armati juxta morem patrie seruire tenebuntur Necnon quilibet heres aut assignatus predictus in suo primo anno introitus ad prefatas terras . . . et pertinentias earundem vniuersas

APPENDIX XV.

antedictas postquam venerit ad legitimam etatem nobis et successoribus nostris antedictis fidelitatis et homagij juramentum prestabit quod nos et successores nostros sedem nostram Abirdonensem decanum canonicos eiusdem nostras personas res et bona necnon Cristianam et orthodoxam fidem pro posse . . . defendet . . . Saluis tamen per omnia supremis dominis Regi et Regine nostris seruitiis de premissis baronia terris . . . et pertinentiis vniuersis suprascriptis debitis et consuetis . . . In cuius rei testimonium huic carte nostre manu nostra subscripte sigillum nostrum rotundum vnacum subscriptionibus manualibus presidentis et canonicorum dicti nostri capituli . . . vnacum eorum sigillum commune in signum eorum consensus . . . sunt appensa apud civitatem nostram Abirdonensem octauo die mensis Junii Anno Do-
1566. mini Millesimo quingentesimo sexagesimo sexto coram hiis testibus Magistro Roberto Lumisden de Cloway cht Alexandro Forbes de Auchanasy Alexandro Paip Magistro Johanne Robertsoun . . .

Villelmus Episcopus Abirdonensis.
Alexander Setone cancellarius Abirdonensis.
Patricius Myrtoun thesaurarius Abirdonensis.
Alexander Andersone de Mvrthlik.
Joannes Leslie de Vne subscribo.
M. Robertus Merser de Banquhorie Devynik.
Cuthbertus Reid de Dwlmaok.
G. Hay of Rothwen.
Joannes Elphynstoun de Inuernochty.
Thomas Burnett de Methlik subscribo.
Jacobus Gordoun de Lonmay.
Andreas Leslie de Ellone.
Jacobus Forbes rector ejusdem.
Willelmus Cabell de Tulynessill.
Joannes Colison succentor Abirdonensis.

Antiquities of Shires of Aberdeen and Banff, vol. iii. pp. 377 381 ; Spalding Club. From original in Charter-chest at Fetternear.

Appendix XVI.

APPENDIX No. XVI.

WILLIAM LESLIE, NINTH BARON OF BALQUHAIN.

CONFIRMATION by Pope CLEMENT X., to ALEXANDER ABERCROMBIE of Fetternear, of the Charter granted by WILLIAM GORDON, Bishop of Aberdeen, to WILLIAM LESLIE, ninth Baron of Balquhain, of the Barony of Fetternear and other Lands, dated 8th June 1566; 1566.
Confirmation dated 20th September 1670. 1670.

AD Perpetuam Rei Memoriam. Militantis ecclesiae regimini meritis licet imparibus per ineffabilem diuinae sapientiae, atque clementiae abundantiam prepositi, illa quae a Praelatis, et personis ecclesiasticis ad fidei Catholicae bonorumque et jurum ecclesiasticorum conseruationem in fauorem personarum eiusdem fidei tuendae zelo praeclarisque in ecclesiam meritis conspicuarum prouidi atque salubriter facta esse dicuntur, ut firma semper atque inviolabilia persistant libenter dum id a nobis petitur apostolici muniminis praesidio constabilimus. Exponi si quidem nobis nuper fecit dilectus filius Alexander Abercambri baro de Balquehane Scotus, quod dudum cum tunc in humanis agens Baro Guillelmus Lessleius auus decem millia librarum monetae Scotiae tunc existentibus Episcopo et Canonicis ecclesiae Aberdonensis in subuentionem ciuitatis Aberdonensis, et ecclesiae huiusmodi tunc temporis propter ciuium dissensiones et excitatas ab orthodoxae fidei hostibus persecutiones in augustias redactae erant praestitisset, et non solum ipse Guillelmus sed etiam quondam Baro ejus genitor qui ad instantiam et preces dicti Episcopi et Canonicorum in dicta Ciuitate ut ad illius defensionem eo promptiores essent habitare elegerant ciuitatem predictam ab huiusmodi fidei orthodoxae hostibus longo tempore personaliter armata manu suisque semper expensis egregie et fideliter defendissent, et praeservassent iidem Episcopus

APPENDIX XVI.

et Canonici pecuniarum huiusmodi in ecclesiae utilitatem, et fidei Catholicae tuitionem erogatarum necnon seruitiorum a memoratis Joanne et Guillelmo laudabiliter praestitorum contemplatione eundem Guillelmum aliqua grati animi significatione prosequi cupientes capitulariter congregati de communi consensu, maturaque prius desuper habita deliberatione vocatis omnibus interesse habentibus, ac seruatis omnibus solemnitatibus ad huiusmodi alienationes a statutis et consuetudinibus regni Scotiae requisitis Baroniam de Fetternir cum arce, terris, piscandi jure, molendinis et aliis pertinentiis suis ipsi Guillelmo eiusque descendentibus masculis inperpetuum infeudarunt ea lege ut dictus Guillelmus eiusque descendentes pro tempore feudatarj fidem Catholicam Romanam profiterentur, et quisquis eorum, homagium et fidelitatem pro tempore existentibus Episcopo et Canonicis dictae ecclesiae Aberdonensis iuraret, ac nonnullos annuos Canones pro numero terrarum et locorum infeudatorum proportionatim impositos pro vna in die festo Pentecostes, et altera ratis partibus in festo Sancti Martini ipsis Episcopo et Canonicis persoluerent sub poena caducitatis eo ipso incurrenda si eosdem Canones huiusmodi in terminis non soluissent, ac sub aliis conditionibus prout in publico desuper die octava Junii
1566. MDLXVJ confecto instrumento uberius dicitur contineri. Cum autem sicut eadem expositio subiungebat dictus Alexander qui (ut asserit) orthodoxae fidei candorem in se conseruat illibatum et uti prefati Guillelmi successor dictam Baroniam de presenti pacifice possidet licet de validitate infeudationis huiusmodi quae centum et amplius annorum possessione roborata est minime dubitet, illam tum que firmius subsistat apostolicae confirmationis nostrae robore communiri summopere desideret Baroniamque predictam si (quod non timetur) dicta infeudatio nullitatis initio laboraret ad assertum modernum Episcopum Aberdonensem haereticum deueniret. Nos dicto Alexandro gratiam facere volentes eumque a quibusuis excommunicationis suspensionis et interdicti, aliisque ecclesiae sententiis, censuris et poenis a jure, vel ab homine quauis occasione, uel causa latis

APPENDIX XVI.

si quibus quomodolibet innodatus extiterit ad effectum presentium tantum consequendum harum serie absoluentes, et absolutum fore consentes. Supplicationibus eius nomine nobis super hoc humiliter porrectis inclinati de venerabilium fratrum nostrorum S.R.E. Cardinalium negotiis et consultationibus Episcoporum et Regularium praepositorum qui dilectum filium Rectorem Collegij Scotorum de vrbe audiuerunt consilio veris existentibus narratis infeudationem predictam cum conditionibus restrictiuis et annua pensione supra expressis auctoritate apostolica tenore presentium confirmamus et approbamus, illique inuiolabilis apostolicae firmitatis robur adjicimus, ac omnes et singulos juris et facti defectus siqui desuper quomodolibet interuenerint supplemus Salua tum semper in praemissis auctoritate congregationis eorundem Cardinalium decetero necnon easdem presentes literas firmas et efficaces existere et fore suosque plenarios et integros effectus sortiri et obtinere ac dicto Alexandro et aliis ad quos spectat et pro tempore spectabit in omnibus et per omnia plenissime suffragari sicque in praemissis per quoscumque judices ordinarios et delegatos et causarum palatii apostolici auditores iudicari et definiri debere ac nullum et inane quidquid secus super his a quoquam quauis auctoritate scienter vel ignanter contigerit attentari. Nonobstantibus felicis recordationis Pauli ij et aliorum Romanorum Pontificum Praedecessorum nostrorum de rebus ecclesiae non alienandis, aliisque constitutionibus et ordinationibus apostolicis ac quatenus opus sit dictae ecclesiae Aberdonensi etiam juramento confirmatione apostolica, vel quauis firmitate alia roboratis statutis et consuetudinibus, priuilegiis quoque indultis et literis apostolicis incontrarium praemissorum quomodolibet concessis confirmatis et innouatis. Quibus omnibus et singulis illorum tenores Presentibus pro plene et sufficienter expressis et insertis habentes illis alias in suo robore permansuris ad praemissorum effectum hac uice dumtaxat specialiter et expresse derogamus caeterisque contrariis quibuscumque. Datum Romae apud Sanctam Mariam maiorem sub annulo piscatoris die xx Septembris MDCLXX 1670.

APPENDIX XVI.

Pontificatus nostri Anno Primo.

Collections on the Shires of Aberdeen and Banff, pp. 542-544; Spalding Club. From original charter in Balquhain Charter-chest.

Appendix XVII.

APPENDIX No. XVII.

William Leslie, Ninth Baron of Balquhain.

1554. Charter by Queen Mary, A.D. 1554, confirming a Charter of Sale by John Leslie, eighth Baron of Balquhain, to his son, William Leslie, and Janet Forbes, his Wife, of the fourth part of the east half of the west town of Syde, in the Regality of the Garioch—A.D. 1550 and 1554.

Maria Dei gracia Regina Scotorum . . . Sciatis nos quandam cartam . . . venditionis factam per Johannem Leslie de Buchquhane dilectis nostris Willelmo Leslie filio dicti Johannis et Jonete Forbes eius coniugi . . . ad plenum intellexisse sub hac forma. Omnibus hanc cartam visuris vel audituris Johannes Leslie de Buchquhane eternam in Domino salutem Noveritis me . . . vendidisse . . . dilecto filio meo Willelmo Leslie et Jonete Forbes sue sponse . . . totas et integras terras meas quarte partis orientalis dimidie occidentalis ville de Syde jacentes infra regalitatem de Garveauch et vicecomitatum de Abirdene . . . Tenendas et habendas . . . prefatis Willelmo et Jonete in coniuncta infeodacione et eorundem alteri diucius viuenti eorundemque heredibus masculis inter ipsos legitime procreatis seu procreandis quibus forte deficientibus heredibus meis masculis quibuscunque de suprema domina nostra Regina et suis successoribus . . . in feodo et hereditate imperpetuum . . . Reddendo inde annuatim . . . seruicium warde et releuij et seruicium regium solitum et consuetum . . . In cujus rei testimonium sigillum meum proprium presentibus manu mea subscriptis est appensum Apud Abirdene decimoseptimo die mensis Januarij anno Domini millesimo quingentesimo quinquagesimo presentibus ibidem honorabilibus viris Thoma Menzes de Petfoddelis Gilberto Menzes eius filio Magistris Waltero Leslie et Thoma Dauidsoun notariis publicis cum diuersis aliis Quamquidem cartam . . . pro perpetuo confirmamus . . . In cujus rei testimonium huic presenti carte nostre confirmationis magnum sigillum nostrum apponi precepimus . . . Apud Edinburgh penultimo die mensis Junii Anno Domini millesimo quingentesimo quinquagesimo quarto et regni nostri duodecimo.

APPENDIX XVII. 1550. 1554.

Antiquities of Shires of Aberdeen and Banff, vol. iv. p. 531; Spalding Club. From *Registrum Magni Sigilli*, lib. xxxii. No. 619, MS. General Register House, Edinburgh.

APPENDIX No. XVIII.

Appendix XVIII.

John Leslie, Tenth Baron of Balquhain.

Laird of Balquhanis Band of Seruice, 1603.

1603.

Be it kend till all men be thir presentis, me John Leslye off Balquhane to be bund and obleist, and be the fayth and treuthe in my bodye bindis and oblisses me, in the strattest forme and styill of obligatioun, to ane nobill and mychtie lord, George, marquess off Huntlye, erlle of the Enzie, lord Gordon and Badzenocht, &c. that forsamekle as my predicessouris lardis of Balquhane hes bene dependaris and seruandis to the hous of Huntlye, and that be vertew of thair bande of manrent and seruice, and that the said George now marquess of Huntlye is villing to except me, and wse me in the place of my predicessouris, &c. I bynd and obleiss me to be leill, trew, efauld, and faithfull man and servant to my said lord marques, &c. contrair and aganis all leiffand, the kingis grace and authoritie onlye except, &c. In witness of the quhilk to thir my present obligatioun and band of seruice and manrent, subscryuit witht my hand, my propir seill is affixit at Huntlye, the

APPENDIX XVIII.

xxi day of Marche, yeir of God ane thowsand sex hundretht and thre yeiris, befoir witnessis, Normound Leslye. And inlyikmaner the saidis Marquess obleissis him, in streatest forme of obligatioun, to do for the said Jhon Leslye of Balquhane, he beand freind and serwand as said is, in all his actionis that he hes ado, lyik as ane lord aucht to do for his speciall freind and serwand &c. vitnes day, yeir, and place aboue vretin.

GEORGE marquis of Huntlye.
Normound Leslye, *vitnes*. JHONE LESLIE of Balquhane.

Gordon Papers ; *Spalding Club Miscellany*, vol. iv. p. 255.

Appendix XIX.

APPENDIX No. XIX.

JOHN LESLIE, TENTH BARON OF BALQUHAIN.

YOWNG FRENDRAWCHT his LETTRE to the LAIRD of BALQUHYNE.

HONORABILL and luffing brother, my werraye hartlye commendatioun rememberitt: The Laird of Drum and I hes resaued ane lettre fra my Lord Erroll with sic particullar pointis, quhairbye we persaue his lordschip iwill instructitt att the present; be quhayis informatioun we can nocht direcklie juge, bot douttis nocht bot God with tyme will bayth interpreit tham and wss (I meane ewerye ane in thair awin collowris). Trewe itt is, brother, that from the beginning of this mater the laird of Drum, your selff and I, hes coniunctlye and efaldlye delt heirin, as luffing and indifferent freindis to thame baytht, but respect of partie, or perrell wnto our selfis, respecting alwayis thair weillis and concord as our cheif contentment: quhilkis, nowe yitt as abefoir, I am maist asseured is your, the laird off Drum, and myne awin onlye intentioun, quhowsoever iwill disposed personis sall enterpreitt ather of ws; for we all thre knowis perfytlye, that incais sum iwill disposit persoun or personis haid nocht interruppitt our luffing and freindlye intentioun, my Lord Errol of his lordschipis awin naturall inclinatioun, haid newer recleamed from ws, (being sa indifferentlye chosin). Thairfoir, brother, as ye haiff from the beginning delt be ws and we be yow, as thre distinct personis haiffing bot ane mynd and ane onlye intentioun, vill nowe maist eirneslie request yow for till concur with ws in the end, as we sall with yowe, for effectuing of sa guid a purpois: quhairintill we sall haiff contentment with honnour, in perfyting ane mater sa weychtie committit till our charge, being sa longe lingared be noble men off our rank and abowe befoir this tyme. And althocht bayth thir noble men be miscontentitt for the present, or the day thrie yeir at farrest, thaye will blisse our bairnis, incais we be nocht present in persoun to receawe thankis. To conclud: we luik asseuredlie that quhowfar ye haiff gain with ws att the beginning of this mater, ye will also end and conclud with ws: seing by yow we concluditt nathing, and thatt quhowsoewer ather off the erlis will interpreitt ws, we mon as our foirbearis, leiff and die as coniunct freindis, and with God his helpe leiff ane introductioun till our posteritie. In the meantyme, quhow rasche soewer my Lord Erroll interpretis the lard Drum or me to be in this particullar tuiching his lordschip and Ludquharne, we haiff delt and yitt sall dell quhat in ws lyis to satisffeye my Lord Errol his lordschipis desyir, prowyding we cut nocht my Lord Merschael his lordschipis thrott: and to that effect will desyr yow to meitt ws the morne be tene howris, quhair we sall abyd your cumming, at Stirwelin hill, and thair att lengtht we sall ressoun forder nor we cane presently wreitt. Sua resting thairto I committ yow maist hartlye to the protectioun of the Almychtie. Innervgye this Sonday

Youris maist luffing brothir,

J. CRYCHTOUN.

To the rycht honorabill and his maist luffing brother
The Laird Balquhane.

Erroll Papers; *Spalding Club Miscellany*, vol. ii. pp. 287, 288.

APPENDIX.

Appendix XX.

APPENDIX No. XX.

John Leslie, Tenth Baron of Balquhain.

1602.

The Laird of Drwm and Yowng Frendracht thair Letter to Balquhine of the tent of Julij MDCII conserning the Erllis of Errol and Mershall.

Rycht honorabill and hairtlie beluffed brother, Efter our hairtliest commendatiouns, pleisse heirwith to resaiff ane copie of the decreitt we ar to consent in the blank betuix the Erlis off Erroll and Marschell; quhilk we haiff formit for our ingyn in termis leist offensiue to Erroll, quhairbe ye mycht the mair hairtelie join with us (as we stand nothe in doubt bott off duetie ye vill) in this mater tuiching sa neirlie thair veilfairis and concord and our honesteis. And sa it sall pleisse yow to reid the same and to retourn itt vith the berar towardis ws, and to certefe ws off your consent be your letter heirto as is sett doun: for seing we are joinit in all deuteis we desyr nothe we suld devyd in this wthervayis we vilbe forcit, fering our schame and thir nobill men thair onquyetnes, to pronunce be our selffis: albeitt we visse vthervayis, that we suld gang coniunctlie togidder, seing no iust reson to distract ws. Attour, itt sall pleisse you, for clering off this mater betuix my Lord Erroll and Ludquharn, to resaiff on the bak off the said decreitt the very just copie of George Hay his band; quhairbe ye vill aiselie considder that the Erle of Marschall can na vayis releiff him selff off the perrell of his bandis to Ludquharn and Alexander Keyth, bott be your randering off that band or discharge grantit to Erroll be Ludquharn, or be my Lord his decreitt to be pronuncit in final conclusioun off thais ilestis; quhairin seing we find your part sum thing heauie, in respect ye procurit that discharge and on quhilk conditionis ye knaw best, wald ather conseill you to mak that be dischargit bak to Erroll, or then we will be forcit off reson to conclude in sentence vith Marschell: and na thing mair nor ye condescendit to your selff seing Marschell hes no other band of thairis to releiff him be, and to bind him to them in ane mater vthervayes concludit we think itt nothe the best. Itt sall pleisse you, Sir, to meitt ws on Mononday, be nyn houris befoir noun, on the ground: quhair ye sall be partner or witnesse of the conclusion in that erand, as ye pleisse: and quhosoevir ye be dispositt vill pray your presence maist hartlie as ye sall heff ouris at command. And sa our humbill dutie rememberit to my Lord and Laydie, thair committis you maist hartle to God, this x off Julij 1602. 1602.

APPENDIX XX.

Youris luffing brether at pouer assured

A. IRWIN off Drum.

J. CRYCHTOUN.

To the Richt Honnorabill
The Laird off Balquhyn.

Erroll Papers; *Spalding Club Miscellany*, vol. ii. pp. 288, 289.

APPENDIX No. XXI.

Appendix XXI.

JOHN LESLIE, TENTH BARON OF BALQUHAIN.

CHARTER by King JAMES VI. A.D. 1597, confirming a Charter of Sale by JOHN LESLIE, tenth Baron of Balquhain, to Sir THOMAS GORDON of Cluny, of the Lands and Mill of Syid, with the Peil, and the Customs of St. Rule's Fair, Ailhous Croft of Syd, Arnbrig, Erllisfeild, Seggydene, Kirkhill, and Mostoun, in the parish of Kinethmont—A.D. 1595. 1597. 1595.

JACOBUS Dei gratia Rex Scotorum . . . Sciatis nos quandam cartam . . . factam per Joannem Leslie de Balquhane hereditarium proprietarium et fuedifirmarium terrarum subscriptarum . . . dilecto nostro Thome Gordoun de Cluny militi . . . ad plenum intellexisse sub hac forma Omnibus hanc cartam visuris vel audituris Joannes Leslie de Balquhane dominus hereditarius et emphitesta terrarum respective subscriptarum eternam in Domino salutem

APPENDIX XXI.

Noueritis me . . . pro perimpletione certe mee partis cuiusdam contractus inter Dominum Thomam Gordoun de Cluny militem ab una et me parte ab altera de data presentium . . . confecti . . . vendidisse . . . et ad perpetuam feudifirmam dimississe . . . prefato Domino Thome Gordoun de Cluny militi heredibus eius masculis et assignatis quibuscunque omnes et singulas terras meas de Syid molendinum granarum terras molendinarias astrictas multuras eiusdem cum *lie Peill* eiusdem cum colmeto fori vulgo nuncupati *Truelfair* eidem incumbenti Ailhous Croft de Syd et Arnbrig terras de Erllis Feidill et Seggydene jacentes in parochia de Kinethmont baronia de Balquhane et vicecomitatu de Abirdene Necnon et terras de Kirkhill et *lie outtsetis* eiusdem vocatas Mostoun jacentes in parochia de Kinethmont et vicecomitatu antedicto . . . Et in speciale warrantum predictarum terrarum . . . omnes et singulas terras meas de Logydurnocht Newlandis Cragtowie Cragmylne Nethertoun de Knokinblewis et nouum molendinum jacentes in parochiis de Logydurnocht Oyne et Invervrie respective et infra vicecomitatum de Abirdene . . . Tenendas et habendas . . a me heredibus meis et assignatis de Balquhane dominis de supremo domino nostro Rege . . . in feodo et hereditate imperpetuum . . . Reddendo inde annuatim . . . pro predictis terris de Syde molendino . . . et *lie Peill* cum colmeto fori vulgo nuncupati *Truelfair* antedicto Erllisfedell et Seiggydene summam septem librarum . . . et pro predictis terris de Kirkhill cum pertinentiis summam sex librarum sex solidorum et octo denariorum Et pro predictis terris datis pro warranto . . . summam sedecim librarum . . . In cujus rei testimonium huic presenti carte mee . . . manu mea subscripte sigillum meum est appensum Apud Fetterneir decimo nono die mensis Junii Anno Domini millesimo
1595. quingentesimo nonagesimo quinto Coram his testibus Joanne Gordoun de Biruko Jacobo Gordoun et Alexandro Bisset seruitoribus dicti Domini Thome Alexandro Middeltoune seruitore Magistri Johannis Chene de Fortrie Magistro Roberto Davidsoun seruitore Magistri Alexandri Irwing aduocati scriba presentis carte et Johanne Leslie apparente

de Balquhane Quamquidem cartam . . . pro perpetuo confirmamus . . . In cuius rei testimonium huic presenti carte nostre confirmationis magnum sigillum nostrum apponi precepimus . . . Apud Falkland vicesimo quarto die mensis Julii Anno Domini Millesimo quingentesimo nonagesimo septimo et regni nostri tricesimo. 1597.

APPENDIX XXI.

Antiquities of the Shires of Aberdeen and Banff, vol. iv. pp. 532, 533. From the *Registrum Magni Sigilli*, lib. xli. No. 304, MS. General Register House, Edinburgh.

APPENDIX No. XXII.

Appendix XXII.

John Leslie, Tenth Baron of Balquhain.

Charter by King James VI. to John Leslie, tenth Baron of Balquhain, and Jean Erskine, his Wife, of the Barony of Fetternear, the office of Constable of the place and chief messuage of the Bishopric of Aberdeen, and an Annual Rent of One hundred and twenty-six pounds and ten pence, from the Lands of Auchlyne, Talzeaucht, Blairdinny, Bonyngton, Casteltoun, and Louesk, in the parishes of Clatt and Rayne, for the support of the office of Constable—A.D. 1602. 1602.

Jacobus Dei gratia Rex Scotorum Omnibus . . . Salutem Sciatis nos post nostram perfectam etatem viginti quinque annorum completam et omnes nostras reuocationes tam generales quam speciales et post actum dissolutionis factum in parliamento annexationis omnium terrarum temporalium quorumcumque beneficiorum huius regni ad coronam vt cum eadem in perpetuum remaneat tanquam pars patrimonii eiusdem cum auismento et consensu fidelis et dilecti nostri consiliarii Magistri Joannis Prestoun de Fentounbarnis collectoris generalis et thesaurarii augmentationum dedisse. . . et ad feudifirmam . . . perpetuam dimisisse . . . Joanni Leslie de Balquhane et Jeanne Erskine sue sponse in coniuncta infeodatione et heredibus masculis et assignatis

APPENDIX XXII.

dicti Joannis Leslie quibuscumque hereditarie . . . terras et schyram seu baroniam de Fetterneir cum omnibus . . . earundem pendiculis . . . necnon dedisse . . . dicto Joanni Leslie de Balquhane suis heredibus masculis et assignatis antedictis hereditarie . . . officium Constabularii loci et principalis messuagii Episcopatus de Abirdene in canonia eiusdem locati et edificati cum hortis pomeriis domibus edificiis pratis graminibus pastura et . . . pertinentiis . . . necnon summam annuum feodum centum et viginti sex librarum decem denariorum monete leuandum de terris subscriptis videlicet de terris de Auchlyne Tailzeacht Blairdynnie Bonetoune Casteltoun et Luesk jacentibus in parochiis de Clatt et Rayne respectiue infra vicecomitatum de Abirdene ad duos anni terminos . . . pro annua sustentatione guardia et custodia officii Constabularii dicti messuagii tanquam annuum feodum eiusdem Quequidem terre molendina officium Constabularii aliaque supraspecificata ad patrimonium dicti Episcopatus Abirdonie . . . perprius pertinuerunt . . . Necnon volumus . . . quod vnica sasina . . . capienda apud turrim et fortalicium de Fetterneir erit sufficiens sasina pro . . . predictas terras turre fortalicio officio Constabularii et aliis suprascriptis . . . Tenendas . . . predictas terras schyram seu baroniam de Fetterneir cum . . . pertinentiis earundem . . . necnon . . . officium Constabularii loci et principalis messuagii Episcopatus Abirdonie cum . . . pertinentiis . . . necnon predictum annuum feodum . . . in feudifirma feodo et hereditate respectiue imperpetuum de nobis et nostris successoribus superioribus earundem . . . Reddendo inde annuatim . . . nobis et successoribus nostris pro dicti officio Constabularii loci et principalis messuagii dicti Episcopatus de Aberdene cum dictis . . . pertinentiis ac pro annua deuoria centum viginti sex librarum et decem denariorum monete . . . vnum denarium monete huius regni super solo et fundo dicti messuagii ad Festum Pentecostes nomine albe firme . . . necnon . . . soluendo nobis et successoribus nostris Camerariis . . . aut aliis pro tempore jus habentibus pro predictis terris et schyra seu baronia de Fetterneir cum . . . pertinentiis summam quinquaginta quatuor librarum octo solidorum monete antedicte tanquam antiquam feudifirmam et in augmentationem rentalis nostri viginti sex solidos et octo denarios . . . necnon reddendo tres sectas ad tres curias capitales tenendas per nostros balliuos apud Palacium nostrum de Abirdene . In cujus rei testimonium huic presenti carte nostre Magnum Sigillum nostrum apponi precipimus Testibus predilectis nostris consanguineis et consiliariis Joanne Marchione de Hammiltoun Comite Arranie domino Evan et Joanne Comite de Montrois domino Grahame etc. Cancellario nostro Georgio Mariscalli Comite domino Keyth etc. regni nostri Mariscallo dilectis nostris familiaribus Consiliariis Dominis Jacobo Elphingstoun de Barnetoun nostro secretario Richardo Cokburne juniore de Clerkingtoun nostri secreti sigilli custode militibus Magistro Joanne Skene nostrorum rotulorum registri ac consilii clerico Domino Joanne Cokburne de Ormestoun milite nostre justiciarie clerico et Magistro Willelmo Scott . nostre cancellarie directore apud Pertham decimo die Mensis Maii Anno Domini Millesimo Sexcentesimo secundo et regni nostri trigesimo quinto. 1602.

Antiquities of Shires of Aberdeen and Banff, vol. iii. pp. 381-383; Spalding Club. From original in Balquhain Charter-chest.

APPENDIX No. XXIII.

Appendix XXIII.

ANTHONY, COUNT LESLIE, NINETEENTH BARON OF BALQUHAIN.

SUMMONS issued at the instance of PETER LESLIE GRANT, Claimant of the Balquhain Estates, 9th September 1756. 1756.

GEORGE, &c. OUR WILL IS, and we charge you, that ye lawfully summon, warn, and charge Captain John Grant, late of Ballindalloch, in the service of the States-

APPENDIX XXIII.

General, James Leslie of Pitcaple, Charles Cajetan, Count Leslie, only son of James Ernest, Count Leslie, Antonius, Count Leslie, Carolus, Count Leslie, Count Leslie, Count Leslie, Count Leslie, and Count Leslie, all lawfull sons of the said Charles Cajetan, Count Leslie, and the said Charles Cajetan, Count Leslie, as curator and administrator-in-law to his said sons, in manner following—viz. if they be within that part of Great Britain called Scotland, personally, or at their dwelling-places, upon twenty-one and six days' warning, for first and second Diets, and if they be forth thereof, by open Proclamation at the Market-cross of Edinburgh, pier and shore of Leith, upon sixty and fifteen days' warning for first and second Diets, to compear before the Lords of our Council and Session at Edinburgh, or where it shall happen them to be for the time, the and days of next to come, in the hour of cause, with continuation of days, to answer at the Instance of Our Lovit Peter Grant, eldest son of the said Captain John Grant, late of Ballindalloch, in the service of the States-General, in the action and cause after-mentioned—viz. THAT WHEREAS the now deceased Patrick, Count Leslie of Balquhain, designed in the Deed of Tailzie after mentioned Patrick Leslie of Balquhain, by his Bond and Deed of Tailzie, dated the
1692. 8th day of November 1692 years, and registrate in the
1698. Register of Tailzies the 25th day of February 1698 years, reciting that he had the undoubted right of Succession to Count James Leslie, his eldest brother, failing Heirs of his body, in his lands and estate in Germany, and that he was Proprietor of the lands and others therein and after mentioned, lying within Scotland: and that he judged it rational, equitable, and honourable, that the said two estates should be kept distinct and separate, and that the same should be inherited and possessed by his Heirs of Tailzie severally, and without conjunction, according to the division and order of succession, therein and after mentioned; and also reciting, that in Prosecution thereof,

APPENDIX XXIII.

he had sufficiently secured and provided James Leslie, his eldest lawful son of his first marriage, in the said lands and estate in Germany, and in his right of succession to the same after the death of the said Count James Leslie his brother, as a competent provision to him ; and that it was just and necessary, that George Leslie, his eldest lawful son of his second marriage, and his other heirs of tailzie after mentioned, should be also settled and secured in his lands and estate in Scotland, as a provision to him and them, in manner after mentioned: THEREFORE, the said Patrick Count Leslie bound and obliged him and his heirs to resign, and made and constitute procurators for resigning ALL and HAILL the lands and barony of Balquhain, comprehending therein the Mains of Balquhain, the lands of Newton of Balquhain, Cowbyres, Boguingus, and Croft thereof, with the Castle, Tower, Fortalice, and Mannor-place of Balquhain, Houses, Biggings, Yards, Orchards, together with the Mill, Mill-lands, Multures, Sequels, Annexis, Connexis, Dependencies, Outsets, Insets, Tenants, Tenandries, and Service of free Tenants thereof, together also with the Commonty, common Pasturage Foggage, Fewel, Feal and Divot, in and through the Forest of Bannachie, with all and sundry other Parts, Pendicles, Liberties, Privileges, righteous Pertinents of the said lands, and others used and wont, as the samen were possessed by the deceased John Leslie of Balquhain elder, and his Predecessors and Authors, and their Tenants, lyand within the Parishin of Logiedurno and Sheriffdom of Aberdeen: ALL and HAILL the Town and Lands of Auldtown and Nethertown of Knockenglewes, with Multures thereof, Houses, Biggings, Yards, Tofts, Crofts, Meadows, Mosses, Privileges, and Pertinents whatsomever pertaining thereto, in the Parochin of Inverurie, Regality of Garioch, and Sheriffdom foresaid: And ALL and HAILL the Town and Lands of White Corsland, Tulloss, with the Mill of White Corse, Mill-lands, Multures, Knaveships, Houses, Biggings, Yards, Tofts, Crofts, Outsets, Muirs, Marishes, Meadows, Commonties, Annexis, Connexis, Dependencies, Parts, Pendicles, and Pertinents thereof whatsomever, lying

APPENDIX XXIII.

within the Parochin of Logiedurno, Regality and Sheriffdom foresaid, with full power to the said Tenants of Balquhain, Auldtown and Nethertown of Knockenlewes, of casting, winning, and carrying away Peats and Turfs in all Time coming, in and forth of the Mosses of Fetterneer, by Ways and Passages used and wont: AND LIKEWISE, with full power of winning and taking away from and forth the said Mosses of Fetterneer, yearly, for serving the Uses of the Families in the Mannor-place of Balquhain, in all time coming, all erected, created, and united in an haill and free Barony, called the Barony of Balquhain: ALL and SUNDRY the Lands and others underwritten, viz. ALL and HAILL the East Plough of Lands of the Town and Lands of Whiterashes, sometime occupied by Thomas Simpson, with Houses, Biggings, Yards, Mosses, Muirs, Meadows, Commonties, Common Pasturage, Annexis, Connexis, Dependencies, Parts, Pendicles, Mills, Multures, Teind-sheaves and Pertinents thereof whatsomever; as also, the West Plough of Land of the Samen Town and Lands of Whiterashes, sometime occupied by Patrick Reid, with the Houses, Biggings, Yards, Mosses, Muirs, Meadows, Commonties, Common Pasturage, Annexis, Connexis, Dependencies, Parts, Pendicles, Mills, Multures, Teind-sheaves, sequels and haill Pertinents thereof, all lying within the Parochin of Turreff and Barony of Delgatie, and Sheriffdom of Aberdeen foresaid: and likewise a Plough of Land of the Town and Lands of Wrae, lately occupied by John Stevenson, with Houses, Biggings, Yards, Mosses, Muirs, Meadows, Commonties and Common Pasturages, Annexis, Dependencies, Parts, Pendicles, Mills, Multures, Sequels, and haill Pertinents, lying within the Parochin of Turreff, Barony and Sheriffdom foresaid: ALL and HAILL the Plough of Land of the Lands of Ashoagill, astricted Multures, Sequels, and Knaveships thereof used and wont: and particularly with the astricted Multures, Sequels, and Knaveships of the two Ploughs of Land of Hiltoun, with the Pertinents, Crofts, four Ploughs of Land at Ashoagill, the Plough of Land of Sketteetie, the Plough of Land of

Claymires, the Plough of Land of Brae, two Ploughs of Land of Whiterashes, with the Multures, Knaveships, and Sequels of all other Lands and Crofts astricted to the said Mill, together with the haill Houses, Biggings, Yards, Orchards, Tofts, Crofts, Mosses, Muirs, Meadows, Annexis, Connexis, Dependencies, Parts, Pendicles, Teind-sheaves, and Pertinents, and with Salmond-fishing in the Water of Dovern, and Privileges thereof, if it has any, in so far as it concerns the Plough of Land of the said Lands of Ashoagill, Mill and Mill-lands thereof, lyand within the Barony of Delgatie, Parochin of Turreff, and Sheriffdom of Aberdeen foresaid. AND LIKEWISE, of ALL and HAILL the Town and Lands of Largie and Lanshberrie, the Lands of Meiklenwards, comprehending therein the Lands of Meiklewards, Over and Nether Boriscocks, and Brankstones and Miretoun, with the Mill of Meiklewards, Mill-Croft thereof, Mill-lands, Multures, Knaveships, and Sequels thereof, together with the Teind-sheaves of the said lands, and all and Sundry the Mannor-places, Houses, Biggings, Yards, Orchards, Tofts, Crofts, Mosses, Muirs, Marishes, Meadows, Commonties, Pasturages, Outsets, Insets, Annexis, Connexis, Dependencies, Parts, Pertinents, and Pendicles whatsomever lying within the Parochin of Inch and Sheriffdom of Aberdeen foresaid: AS ALSO of ALL and HAILL the Town and Lands of Middletown of Knockinglewes, with the Multures, Sequels, and Knaveships, thereof with Liberty to the Tenants and Possessors of the said Lands of Middletown, to transport Corns from the said Mills to the Mill of Whitecross, called the Bog-mill, to the Ways and Passages most commodious, holding off Corn-lands and hained Grass, through the lands of Glaschoe, Houses, Biggings, Yards, Tofts, Crofts, Annexis, Connexis, Dependencies, Muirs, Meadows, Parts, Pendicles, Tenants, Tenandries, Service of free Tenants, and Pertinents of the said Lands whatsomever, together with the Teind-sheaves of the Samen Lands, lying, bounded, and marched as after following, viz. beginning at the Cairn at the West-nook of Alexander Duncan's yard, called the March Cairn, which

APPENDIX XXIII.

divides the Lands of Oldtown of Knockinglewes at the South, and the Town of Knockinglewes at the North, passing therefrae West and South-west, as it is cairned, marched and propted with Stones to ane great Cairn on the Head of the Blackhill, which divides the said Oldtoun at the South, and the Middletoun at the North, and therefrae passing South-west thereby frae Cairn to Cairn, as it is propted, while it come to an Cairn called the March Cairn at the High King's Gate, and therefrae direct West, keepand the said Gate, till it come to a March-stone, called William's Cross, and therefrae keepand the Gate West, till it come to an Cairn, called the Caylies Cairn: and therefrae direct North, till it come to a Cairn, now called Arthur's Cairn: and therefrae direct North, till it come to a Cairn called Saint Katherine's Cairn: and North till it come to a Cairn called Cairnwall: and therefrae, till it come to a Cairn called Cairnpaip: passing therefrae direct East, keeping the Lands Ends, till it come to an Cairn, called Cairn Clerk: passing therefrae East, keeping the Lands Ends of the said Lands of Middletoun, till it come to an Cairn, at the North-end of a Stone-dyke, called Cairndyke: passing therefrae North-east, till it come to an Cairn, called Cairnwyllie: passing therefrae North, keeping the West side of the March-ridge of the Greens, till it come to an Cairn, at the North end of the said Ridge: passing therefrae North-east till it come to ane Bush, called the Sauchen Bush, which is the March, dividing the Land of Balquhain at the North, the Land of Glaschoe at the West, the Lands of Middletoun at the East, and the South Parts, passing therefrae direct East keeping East the Burn, as it runs to an Ford, called the Chapel Ford: and therefrae South and South-east, till it come to an Cairn at the Chapel Fauld-dyke: and therefrae South-east, Cairn by Cairn, as they are propted, till it come to the Head of the Bank-dyke, at the Head of the White Loan Croft: passing therefrae South-East, till it come to an Meikle March-stone, which divides the Lands of Middletoun at the South, and the Nethertoun at the North: passing therefrae direct

North, down to an Stone-bank, betwixt the Bullruge of the Middletoun and the Bauckridge of the Nethertoun, and to an March-stone, at the end of the said Bauckridge, direct East, till it come to two set March-stones, at the side of the Road : and therefrae direct North, keeping the said Road, till it come to an Stone at the West side of the Hill of Nethertoun : and therefrae East be two Rigg-heads : and therefrae North frae Stone to Stone, till it come to an Stone at the Head of the March bauck, which divides the Nethertoun at the West, and the Middletoun at the East, and therefrae direct East, keeping the March bauck which divides the Middletoun at the South, and the Nethertoun at the North, till it come to the end of the March-rigg of Middletoun : and therefrae South and South-east directly, till it come to the Head of the Mary Stone-dyke, and keeping the Dyke foresaid, East and North-East, till it come to an March Cairn at the end of the said Dyke in the Myne : and thereafter direct East to another Cairn, keeping the said Myne ; and thereafter till it come to the West nuick of the Lampenley of Conglas : and therefrae keeping the Strype East and South-East, till it come to the South-East nuick of the West-fauld : and therefrae keeping the Loneing Dyke West and South-west, till it come to the said March Cairn at the Head of the said Alexander Duncan's Yard, where the said Marches began : together with the Loneings to the Hill of Bannochie, lying within the Parish of Garioch and Sheriffdom of Aberdeen. AND ALSO, ALL and HAILL the Piece of Ground of Moss, called Hackney Moss, marched and meithed as the Samen Marches are set down by William Orum in Blairdaff, Alexander Thomson in Fetterneer, Alexander Ferguson there, and William Peirrie in Deuckries, viz. beginning at the uppermost of the round Hillocks standing on the Burn-side, and going from that South-east, towards the Bell Craigie, as the saids persons has already marched and carried the Samen : and from the Bell Craigall, within the Naish or hard Ground, having liberty and power to lay their peats and fewel on the Naish and hard ground, where they please,

APPENDIX XXIII.

till they come to the Redford: and from the Redford, keeping the Burn, till it come to the uppermost Wind-hillock, where the first March-Stone is at the West end of the same. AND LIKEWAYS, of ALL and HAILL the Sun and Shadow-halfs of the Mains and Mannorplace of Auquhorties, and Croft of Land, called Laird's Croft, and piece of Land called Deans Sun, and Shadow-half of the Town and Lands of West and East Netherbiggin, and Sun and Shadow-halfs of the Milltown of Auquhorties and Bograxes, and Mill of Auquhorties, Mill-land, astrict Multures, Sucken, Sequels, and Knaveships thereof, with Houses, Yards, Orchards, Inclosures, Parts, Pendicles, and Pertinents thereof, lying in the Parochin of Inverurie, and Sheriffdom of Aberdeen foresaid: and in special Warrandice thereof: ALL and HAILL the Town and Lands of Balcairn, with Houses, Biggings, Yards, Tofts, Crofts, Outsets, Insets, Mosses, Muirs, Meadows, Commonties, Common Pasturage, Liberty of Moss, Fewel, Feal and Divot, Parts, Pendicles, and Pertinents thereof belonging thereto, used and wont, lying in the Parochin of Bethelnie and Sheriffdom of Aberdeen, as the Samen were possessed by William Duncan, William and Patrick Finlays, and their subtenants, with the Teind-sheaves of the said Warrandice Lands, above written: AND ALSO, of ALL and HAILL the Town and Lands of Knockinbaird, Mill thereof, Mill-lands, Multures, Sucken, Sequels and Knaveship thereof: the Town and Lands of Scotstown, with Houses, Biggings, Yards, Tofts, Crofts, Outsets, Insets, Mosses, Muirs, Meadows, Commonties, Common Pasturage, Annexis, Connexis, Dependencies, Parts, Pendicles, and Pertinents thereof whatsomever, by and within the Parochin of Inch, Regality and Lordship of Garioch, and Sheriffdom of Aberdeen foresaid, with the Teinds, great and small, Parsonage and Vicarage thereof: AND LIKEWAYS, of ALL and HAILL the Town and Lands of Greenhall and Marieheadless, with the two Crofts belonging thereto, and all other Pendicles of the same, with the Houses, Biggings, Yards, Tofts, Crofts, Outsets, Insets, Mosses, Muirs, Meadows, Commonties, Common Pasturage,

APPENDIX XXIII.

Annexis, Connexis, Parts, Pendicles, and Pertinents of the said lands whatsomever, by and within the Parochin of Inch, Regality and Lordship of Garioch, and Sheriffdom foresaid, with the Teinds, great and small, Parsonage and Vicarage thereof. AND IN LIKE MANNER, ALL and HAILL the Shire or Barony of Fetterneer, containing the particular Towns, Lands, Fishings, and others under written, as proper Parts and Pendicles of the Samen, viz. the Mains of Fetterneer, as it was possessed by the said Patrick Count Leslie himself, and Patrick Cromuire and William Leslie, his Tenants and Sub-tenants, with the Tower, Fortalice, Dwelling-place, Houses, Biggings, Yards, and Orchards of the Samen; ALL and HAILL the Town and Lands of Overtoun and Nethertoun of Fetterneer; the Town and Lands of Kaithnie, with the Wauk-mill of Fetterneer, and the Mill, commonly called the Mill of Whitehaugh, with the Mill-lands, Multures, Sequels, and Knaveships of the Samen, together with the Salmon fishing upon the water of Don pertaining to the Lands and others after specified respective, together with the haill Houses, Biggings, Commonties, Common Pasturage, Yards, Woods, Crofts, Meadows, Moss, Muirs, Marishes, Annexis, Connexis, Dependencies, Outsets, Insets, Tenants, Tenandrice, and Service of free Tenants, haill Parts, Pendicles, and universal Pertinents to the said Lands, Mill, Mill-lands, Fishings, and others above expressed respective, lying of old within the Parochin of Fetterneer, and now within the Parochin of Logiedurno, Barony of Fetterneer, and Sheriffdom of Aberdeen, in the Hands of his immediate lawful Superiors thereof in Favors and for new Infeftments of the same to be made and granted to him, the said Patrick Count Leslie, in Liferent during all the Days of his Lifetime, and the said George Leslie his eldest Son of the second Marriage, procreate betwixt him and Mary Irvine his second Spouse, and the Heirs-male of his body: which failing, to the Heirs-male procreate, or to be procreate of the said Patrick Count Leslie's body, of that or any other Marriage, and the Heirs-male of their bodies; which failing, to the said

APPENDIX XXIII.

James Leslie, his only Son of the first Marriage, and the Heirs-male of his body; which failing, to the Heirs-male procreated, or to have been procreated of the said Count James Leslie his eldest Brother's body, and the Heirs-male of their Bodies: which failing, to Francis James Leslie, only son of the deceased Count Alexander Leslie, youngest Brother of the said Patrick, and the Heirs-male lawfully to have been procreate of his Body; which failing, to the Heirs-female procreated, or to have been procreated of his own Body, and the Heirs-male of their Bodies; which failing, to the Heirs-male of the said James Leslie, his eldest Son of the first Marriage, his Body, and the Heirs-male of their Bodies; which failing to the Heirs-female of the said George Leslie, his eldest Son of the second Marriage, and the Heirs-male of their Bodies; which failing, to the other Heirs of Tailzie and Provision therein mentioned, WITH and under the Reservations, Conditions, and irritant and resolutive Clauses therein mentioned, and herein referred to brevitatis causa: AND PARTICULARLY, it is thereby provided, that if the said George Leslie should happen to succeed to the Lands and Estate in Germany, in that case, he, and the Heirs-male of his Body, should be obliged to dispone the said Lands and Estate of Balquhain, in favours of the other Heirs therein mentioned. AND FURTHER, that in case it should happen any other Heirs-male of the said Patrick's Body to succeed to both the said Estates, in that case, the foresaid Estate of Balquhain, and others above specified, should fall and belong to the next Heir-male to have been procreate of the said Patrick's Body of his then present, or any other Marriage: which failing, to the subsequent Heirs of Tailzie aforesaid, in the Order of Succession above mentioned, to whom, and in whose Favours, the said Heir-male, and the Heirs of his Body, who should succeed to the said Lands and Estate of the said Count Leslie in Germany, should be holden and obliged, by their acceptation of the said Deed of Tailzie, to dispone and resign the said Lands and Estate of Balquhain, and the same should from thence furth be redeemable by

the other and next Heirs-male, to have been procreate of the said Patrick's body of his then present, or any other marriage, and the other Heirs of Tailzie foresaid, from the said Heirs-male, who should succeed to both the said Estates, and his Heirs-male foresaid, by Payment of the sum of ten Merks Scots, as the said Deed of Tailzie, containing a Faculty to alter, and Sundry other clauses in itself at more Length bears. UPON WHICH Deed of Tailzie and Procuratory of Resignation therein Contained, a Charter was expede under the Great Seal of Scotland, of the said haill Lands and Estate (excepting the said Lands of Greenhall and Knockingbaird) in Favours of the said Patrick, Count Leslie, in Liferent, and the said George Leslie, and the Heirs-male of his Body, and the other Heirs of Tailzie and Provision above mentioned, dated the ninth
day of March, 1694 years. AND IN virtue of the precept of 1694.
Seasine contained in the said Charter, they were infeft in the said Estate, conform to the Instrument of Seasine, dated
the Third Day of September 1694, and registrate in the 1694.
Particular Register of Sasines at Aberdeen, the fourth of October thereafter. AS ALSO the said Patrick, Count Leslie, by his other obligation and Deed of Tailzie, dated the
thirteenth Day of July 1700 years, and registrate in the 1700.
Register of Tailzies the thirtieth Day of the said Month and Year, narrating the Deed of Tailzie before mentioned, and subsuming, that after mature Deliberation, he found it expedient and necessary to alter the foresaid Tailzie in the Nomination thereof, and because he had already disponed his Estate in Germany to the said James Leslie, therein designed James Ernest, Count Leslie, his eldest son of the first marriage, therefore, and in Prosecution of the Faculty and Power reserved to him by the said Deed of Tailzie, he obliged himself to resign, and made and constitute Procurators for resigning the said Lands and Barony of Balquhain, and haill other Lands, and others above mentioned, contained in the Deed of Tailzie before recited, and in Favors of himself in Liferent, and the said George Leslie, his eldest son of the second marriage, and the

APPENDIX XXIII.

Heirs-male lawfully to have been procreate of his body; which failing, to the Heirs-male lawfully to have been procreate of the said Patrick Count Leslie's own Body of any other Marriage, and the Heirs-male lawfully to have been procreate of their Bodies: which failing: to the said Charles Cajetan Count Leslie, therein designed, second son lawfully procreate betwixt the said James Ernest, Count Leslie, and Berne Princess of Lichtenstein, his spouse, and the Heirs-male lawfully to have been procreate of his body: which failing, to any other second son procreate, or to have been procreated of the said James Ernest, Count Leslie, his body, of that or any subsequent marriage, and the Heirs-male lawfully to have been procreate of their Bodies: which failing, to any second son lawfully to have been procreate of Joseph Patrick Count Leslie, lawful eldest son of the said James Ernest, Count Leslie his body, and the Heirs-male lawfully to have been procreate of their Bodies; which failing, to any second son lawfully to have been procreate of the Body of Francis Jacob, Count Leslie, only lawful son of the deceased Alexander, Count Leslie, Brother-german to the said Patrick, and the Heirs-male lawfully to have been procreate of their Bodies: which failing, to any second son lawfully to have been procreate of the said Francis Jacob, Count Leslie, his lawful eldest son's body, and the Heirs-male lawfully to have been procreate of their Bodies; which failing, to the said James Leslie, eldest lawful son to Alexander Leslie of Pitcaple, procreate betwixt him and Marjory Leslie, eldest lawful Daughter of the said Count Patrick, and the Heirs-male lawfully to have been procreate of his Body: which failing, to the said John Grant, eldest lawful Son of John Grant of Ballindalloch, procreate betwixt him and Anna Francisca Leslie, the said Count Patrick's second lawful Daughter, and the Heirs-male lawfully to have been procreate of his body: which failing, to James Grant, second lawful Son, procreate betwixt the said John Grant of Ballindalloch, and the said Anna Francisca Leslie, and the Heirs-male lawfully to have been procreated of his Body; which failing, to the Heirs-male lawfully to have been procreate of the Bodies of Teresa, Mary, Margaret, and Jean Leslie, successive, without Division, and the Heirs-male lawfully to have been procreate of their Bodies, respective and successive, as said is, which failing, to any other Heirs-female lawfully to have been procreate of the said Patrick, Count Leslie's own Body, and the Heirs-male lawfully to have been procreate of their Bodies: which failing, to any other Heirs-female lawfully to have been procreate of the said George Leslie, his Body, and the Heirs-male lawfully to have been procreate of their Bodies; which failing, to Mary Leslie, lawful eldest Daughter of the said James Ernest, Count Leslie, and the Heirs-male lawfully to have been procreate of her Body: which failing, to any other Heir-female lawfully procreate or to have been procurate of the said James Ernest, Count Leslie, his Body, and the Heirs-male lawfully to have been procurate of their Bodies; which failing, to any Heirs-female lawfully to have been procreate of the said Joseph Patrick, Count Leslie, his body, and the Heirs-male lawfully to have been procreate of their Bodies: which failing, to any Heir-female lawfully to have been procreate of the Body of the said Charles Count Leslie, and the Heirs-male lawfully to have been procreate of their Bodies: which failing, to any Heir-female lawfully to have been procreate of any lawful Heirs-male of the said George Leslie his body, and the Heirs-male lawfully to have been procreate of their Bodies: which failing, to any Heirs-female lawfully to have been procreate of the said James Ernest, Count Leslie, his body, and the Heirs-male of their Bodies; which failing, to any Heirs-female, lawfully to have been procreate of any lawful Heir of the said Joseph Patrick, Count Leslie, his body, and the Heirs-male lawfully to have been procreate of their Bodies: which failing, to any Heirs-female lawfully to have been procreate of any lawful Heir of the said Charles Count Leslie, his body, and the Heirs-male lawfully to have been procreate of their Bodies:

APPENDIX XXIII.

which failing, to any Heirs-female lawfully to have been procreate of any second lawful son of the said George Leslie his Body, and the Heirs-male lawfully to have been procreate of their Bodies: which failing, to any Heirs-female of any second son of the said James Ernest, Count Leslie, his Body, and the Heirs-male lawfully to have been procreate of their Bodies: which failing, to any Heirs-female lawfully to have been procreate of any lawful second son of the said Joseph Patrick, Count Leslie, his body, and the Heirs-male lawfully to have been procreate of their Bodies: which failing, to any Heirs-female lawfully to have been procreate of any second son of the said Charles, Count Leslie, his body, and the Heirs-male lawfully to have been procreate of their Bodies: which failing, to any Heirs-female lawfully to have been procreate of the said Francis Jacob, Count Leslie, his Body, and the Heirs-male lawfully to have been procreate of their Bodies: which failing, to any Heirs-female lawfully to have been procreate of the said James Leslie his Body, and the Heirs-male of their Bodies: which failing, to any Heirs-female lawfully to have been procreate of the said John Grant his Body, and the Heirs-male of their Bodies: which failing, to any heirs-female lawfully to have been procreate of the said James Grant his body, and the Heirs-male lawfully to have been procreate of their Bodies: which failing, to the eldest Heir-female of the eldest Heirs-female, and the Heirs-male lawfully to have been procreate of their Bodies, And so furth successive nominate as is above appointed and that always haill and entire without Division: which all failing, to the said Patrick, Count Leslie his other Heirs-male whatsoever; and which all failling, to his Heirs and Assignies whatsoever in Fee; AND FURTHER, the said Patrick, Count Leslie, thereby dispensed with, and discharged the condition imposed upon his Heirs of Tailzie succeeding from Germany to his Lands and Estate of Balquhain, whereby they were obliged to come and reside in Scotland within the time therein limited, under an Irritancy of their Right to the said Lands and

Estate: and he thereby allows his Heirs to reside in Germany, or in Scotland, at their pleasure: but providing always, that these, his heirs of Tailzie, who should happen to succeed from Germany in manner above expressed, as well as his other Heirs above nominate in the Order and Course of Succession foresaid; and these also, his other Heirs first specified in the said last Bond of Tailzie, as well as these in Germany, and all of them respective and successive in the course and order of succession above set down, should be bound and obliged; LIKEAS, they, by their acceptation of the said Deed, bound and obliged them respective and successive, to maintain, compleat, fulfil, perform, and closely adhere to, the haill other Clauses, Conditions, Provisions, Restrictions, Limitations, Irritancies, Reservations, and Exceptions, specified and contained in the said registrate Bond of Tailzie, as well, and sicklike in all points, as if the same had been one by one therein at full Length, and per expressum insert and set down, with the Burden whereof (excepting always their Coming to, and Abode in Scotland, as is above expected) the said Deed was made and granted by him, and accepted of by one, or other, and all of them, successive, as aforesaid, allenarly and no otherways; AND the said Patrick, Count Leslie, did thereby dispense with for ever, all Imperfections and Nullities thereof, and declared and appointed the same to be as valid and sufficient, to all Intents and Purposes, anent the Changing of the foresaid Nomination, dispensing with the foresaid Irritancy, and biding by and adhering to the haill other Clauses specified in the foresaid registrate Bond of Tailzie, as if all Writs, Rights, and Clauses requisite and necessary thereanent, either for Resignation, Precept of Seasine, or other securities whatsoever, had been therein solemnly at large, and at full length Incorporated and ingrossed, as the said last Bond of Tailzie, containing also a Faculty to the said Patrick, Count Leslie, to alter, in itself at more Length bears; TO which Procuratory of Resignation contained in the said last Deed of Tailzie, the now deceased Ernest Leslie of Balquhain, the only surviving son of the said

APPENDIX XXIII.

George Leslie, had right as Heir of Tailzie, and Provision served and retoured to his said Father, before the four ordinary Macers of our Court of Session, conform to his
1739. Retour dated the seventeenth Day of July, one thousand seven hundred and thirty nine years: AND thereafter, upon the twenty sixth Day of the said month of July, the said Ernest Leslie expede a Charter of Resignation under the Seal appointed by the Treaty of Union to be kept in Scotland in place of the Great Seal formerly used there, of the said haill lands and Estate of Balquhain, and others before mentioned (excepting Greenhall and Knockinbaird) in favours of himself, and the Heirs-male of his Body, and the other Heirs of Tailzie and Provision above mentioned and contained in the said last
1700. Deed of Tailzie, dated the thirteenth Day of July, one thousand seven hundred years, with and under the haill Conditions Provisions, and resolutive and irritant Clauses contained in the said Deeds of Tailzie, in so far as the same were then subsisting: And in virtue of the Precept of Seasine contained in the said Charter, the said Ernest Leslie was infeft and seased in the said Lands and Estate, conform to an Instrument of Seasine dated the 16th Day of October,
1739. 1739 years, and registrate in the Particular Register of Seasines at Aberdeen, the 20th Day of the said month and year: AND WHEREAS, by the Death of the said Ernest Leslie without issue, the succession of the said Lands and Estate of Balquhain hath devolved upon the said Charles Cajetan, Count Leslie, and that he hath also succeeded to, and possesses and enjoys the said lands and Estate in Germany, and that he is an Heir-male of the Body of the said Patrick, Count Leslie, his Grandfather: AND ALSO, WHEREAS the said Antonius, Count Leslie, on the 29th
1742. Day of June, 1742, obtained an Decreet of Declarator at his Instance, before the Lords of Council and Session, Pursuant to, and in Consequence of a Judgment and Decree of Our House of Peers, WHEREBY the said Lords of Session found and declared, that the said Antonius Count, Leslie, was the next Heir of Tailzie, to whom the said

Estate of Balquhain, in the event which had happened, devolved, and DECERNED and ORDAINED the said Charles Cajetan, Count Leslie, to denude himself of the said estate of Balquhain, in favours of the said Antonius, Count Leslie: AND FOUND, that the said Estate was redeemable by the said Antonius from the said Charles Cajetan, Count Leslie, and the said Leopoldus, Count Leslie, his eldest Son and Heir-male for Payment of the sum of ten Merks Scots money, in terms of the said entail: and he, the said Antonius, Count Leslie, on the 2nd day of August, 1742, was served and retoured Heir of Tailzie and Provision to the said Ernest Leslie of Balquhain, and on the day of obtained Decreet of Adjudication, in Implement, at his Instance, against the said Charles Cajetan, Count Leslie, his Father, adjudging the said Estate of Balquhain to belong to him the said Antonius, and the Abbreviate thereof duly recorded, whereupon the said Antonius procured a Charter of Adjudication in his Favours, under the seal appointed by the Treaty of Union to be kept in Scotland, in Place of the Great Seal formerly used there, dated, and thereupon the said Antonius Count Leslie, was infeft, Conform to an Instrument of Seasine in his Favours, dated and registrate

APPENDIX XXIII.

1742.

AND LIKEWISE, WHEREAS the said Charles Cajetan, Count Leslie, the saids Leopoldus, Antonius, and Carolus, Count Leslies, Count Leslie, Count Leslie, Count Leslie, and Count Leslie, are not only all Aliens, born out of our Allegiance, but that they, and the said Captain John Grant, and James Leslie, are persons professing the Popish Religion, past the age of fifteen, who have omitted to renounce Popery, in the form and manner set down in the Act of Parliament under written: at least, any of the foresaid persons, if within the years of Pupillarity, have been, and are still under the Education of Papists, and thereby, as Aliens and Papists are incapable to succeed to, or take, hold, enjoy, or possess the said Lands and Estate of Balquhain, by which Act

APPENDIX XXIII.

being the 3rd of the 8th and 9th Sessions of the first Parliament of King William, dated 3rd of November 1700, and intitled, Act for preventing the Growth of Popery, it is inter alia enacted, "That in all Time coming, no professed "Papist, who being suspected thereof, shall refuse to purge "themselves of Popery, in the Form and Manner set down "in that Act, should be capable to purchase and enjoy, by "any voluntary Disposition or Deed, that shall be made to "them, or any Person in Trust for their Behoof, any Lands, "Houses, Tenements, Annualrents, or other real Rights or "Tacks of Land or Teinds: but that the said Voluntary "Dispositions and Deeds, with all that shall follow thereon, "shall eo ipso become void and null, to all Intents and Pur-"poses, and the Right thereof remain with the Disponer or "Granter, his Heirs or assigns, sicklike as if the same had "not been made nor granted; AS ALSO, that no Person or "Persons, professing the Popish Religion, past the age of "fifteen years, shall hereafter be capable to succeed as "Heirs to any person whatsoever, nor to bruik or enjoy "any Estate by Disposition or other Conveyance, flowing "from any Person, to whom the said Papist might succeed "as Heir, in any Manner of Way, until the said Heirs "Purge themselves of Popery in Manner therein mentioned: "and if any Person or Persons, educated in the Popish "Religion, shall happen to succeed as Heirs to their Pre-"decessors, or any Conveyance shall happen to be made in "their Favours, from a Person to whom they might succeed "as Heirs, before they attain the said age, then, and in "either of these Cases, they shall be holden and obliged to "purge themselves of Popery before they attain to the said "age of fifteen years: and in these cases, and in either of "them, viz: if the succession devolve to any Papist, after "the age of fifteen years, or any Conveyance shall happen "to be made in their Favour by any Person, whom they "might have succeeded to, or the Right be devolved to "them by succession or other Conveyance, before that age, "and they neglect, or omit to renounce Popery, as aforesaid, "then, and immediately thereafter, their Right and Interest

APPENDIX XXIII.

"in or by the said Succession or Conveyance, shall become "void and null, and shall devolve and belong to the next "Protestant Heir or Heirs, who would succeed, if they, and "all the interveening Popish Heirs were naturally dead: "and it shall be lawful to the said Protestant Heir or Heirs, "to serve Heir to the Defunct, to whom the interveening "Papist might have succeeded, by virtue of this act, and "the Irritancy incurred by the interveening Popish Heir or "Heirs, which Protestant Heir or Heirs shall have Right to "the said Estate, and Profits, Mails and Duties thereof, "from the incurring of the Irritancy, ay and while the "foresaid Person or Persons shall purge themselves of "Popery in manner foresaid; and also, that if the Popish "Heir or Heirs excluded, do not renounce Popery, as "aforesaid within ten years after Irritancy is incurred, not "reckoning the years of minority in the said ten years, "they and their heirs shall for ever be excluded. Providing "always and declaring, that all Estates whatsoever, devolved "in Manner, and for the Causes foresaid, shall be devolved, "transferred, and belong to the succeeding Protestant Heir, "with, and under the Tailzies, Conditions, Irritancies, and "Clauses resolutive contained in the Rights of the said "Estate, as they stand, or shall stand, in the Person of "these to whom they shall succeed on the Grounds, and for "the Reasons foresaid, the same being Consistent with and "agreeable to this Act, and the other Laws of this King-"dom; and for avoiding all Questions anent the next "Protestant Heir, in Case the next Heir or Heirs to the "Persons excluded should happen to be Infants, or within "Pupillarity, it is thereby declared that the next Heir or "Heirs within Pupillarity shall be reckoned Protestant "Heirs, though of Popish Parents, in Case they be under the "Education of Protestants, but if the said Pupil Heir or "Heirs be under the Education of Papists, they shall be "reckoned Popish Heirs, and thereby excluded until they "renounce Popery, as therein directed," AND that the said Peter Grant, Pursuer, is now the nearest lawful Heir of Tailzie, capable to succeed to the said Estates; at least,

APPENDIX XXIII.

that in his Favours the said Charles Cajetan, Count Leslie, stands bound to denude, conform to, and in terms of the condition and provision particularly before recited and contained in the said Deeds of Tailzie; and thereby the said Peter Grant has good and undoubted Right to prosecute the Action of Exhibition, Reduction, and Declarator; THAT IS TO SAY, The Defenders to exhibit and produce before our said Lords of Council and Session, the Deeds of Tailzie, and other writs particularly above mentioned, together with the Charter Chest, and whole Charters, Infeftments, and other Writs and Evidents of and concerning the said Estate, and the same being so exhibited, the said Defenders ought and should be decerned and ordained to deliver the same to the Pursuer: and the foresaid Decreet of Declarator obtained at the said Antonius, Count
1742. Leslie's instance, anno 1742, with his Retour and Decreet of Adjudication in Implement, with the Abbreviate, and Charter and Seasine following thereon, all particularly above narrated, being so exhibited and produced, the same ought and should be reduced and declared Null for the Reasons following, viz., the said Writs last above mentioned are intrinsically void and null, as wanting the substantial solemnities requisite in Law. 2do the said Writs are absolutely null, IN respect they are conceived in favour of Aliens, contrary to the Public Laws of the Kingdom, and, 3tio the said Charles Cajetan, Count Leslie, the said Leopoldus, Antonius, and Carolus, Count Leslies, and the said Count Leslie, Count Leslie, Count Leslie, and Count Leslie, are not only all Aliens, born out of our Alledgeance, but that they and the said Captain John Grant and James Leslie, are persons professing the Popish Religion past the Age of fifteen, who have omitted to renounce Popery in the Form and Manner set down in the Act of Parliament above written: at least any of the foresaid Persons, if within the years of Pupillarity, have been, and are still under the Education of Papists, and thereby, as Aliens and Papists, incapable to succeed to, or take, hold,

enjoy, or possess the said Lands and Estate of Balquhain, AND THEREFORE, and for other Reasons to be proponed at discussing hereof, the said Writs last above mentioned conceived in favours of the said Antonius, Count Leslie, or the other Defenders called, OUGHT and SHOULD be reduced, rescinded, cassed, annulled, decerned, and declared to have been from the Beginning, to be now, and in all Time Coming, Void, Null, and of no Force, Strength, or Effect, and to bear no Faith in Judgment nor outwith the same in Time Coming, AND IT OUGHT and SHOULD be FOUND and DECLARED, that the said Charles Cajetan, Count Leslie, the saids Antonius, Leopoldus, and Carolus, Count Leslies, and the said Count Leslie, Count Leslie, Count Leslie, and Count Leslie, are not only all Aliens born out of our Alledgeance, but that they and the said Captain John Grant and James Leslie are persons professing the Popish Religion past the Age of fifteen, who have omitted to renounce Popery in the Form and Manner set down in the Act of Parliament before recited, at least any of the foresaid Persons, if within the years of Pupillarity, have been, and are still under the Education of Papists, and thereby, as Aliens and Papists, incapable to succeed to, or take, hold, enjoy, or possess the Lands and Estate of Balquhain, AND THAT the said Charles Cajetan, Count Leslie, has succeeded to the said Lands and Estate in Germany, and that he has also succeeded to the said Estate of Balquhain, at least the succession thereof hath now devolved upon him, and that he is an Heir-male of the Body of the said Patrick, Count Leslie: and thereby, and in the Terms and Conditions before recited, contained in the said Deeds of Entail, he stands bound to denude of the said Estate in favours of the next lawful Heir of Tailzie, in the order of succession before mentioned, AND therefore, that the said Peter Grant, Pursuer, is now the nearest lawful Heir of Tailzie, capable to succeed to the said Estate, and, thereby, has the only and undoubted Right to serve himself Heir therein to the said deceased Ernest Leslie agreeable to, and in virtue of

APPENDIX. XXIII.

the Deeds above mentioned, at least that in the terms of the said Deeds, the said Charles Cajetan, Count Leslie, stands bound to denude thereof in his Favours, AND the same being so found and declared, the said Charles Cajetan, Count Leslie, Heir-male, and of Tailzie and Provision to the said Ernest Leslie, at least as lawfully Charged to enter Heir to him, OUGHT and SHOULD be decerned and ordained by Decreet of our said Lords, to obtain himself served, retoured, entered, and infeft in the said Lands and Estate of Balquhain, and others before mentioned, as nearest Heir of Tailzie and Provision to the said Ernest Leslie: and being so served, retoured, entered, and infeft therein, he the said Charles Cajetan, Count Leslie, OUGHT and SHOULD be decerned and ordained to grant, subscribe, and deliver, a valid and sufficient disposition, containing a Procuratory of Resignation, and all other necessary clauses of the said Lands and Estate of Balquhain, and others before mentioned, to, and in favours of the said Peter Grant, Pursuer, and the Heirs-male of his Body, whom failing, to the other substitute Heirs of Tailzie above mentioned, and Contained in the said Deeds of Tailzie, WITH and UNDER the Conditions, Provisions, and irritant and resolutive Clauses therein specified, after the Form and Tenor of the Deeds of Entail, and other writs before specified, and Laws and daily Practice of Scotland, observed in the like Cases, in all points, or else to alledge a reasonable Cause, in the Contrary, why the same should not be so done, with Certification as effeirs,

According to Justice, &c.

1756. Dated and Signet, 9th September 1756.

Appendix XXIV.

APPENDIX No. XXIV.

CHARTER-CHEST OF BALQUHAIN.

NINE days after the death of Count Ernest Leslie, 18th
1739. Baron of Balquhain, viz. 29th November 1739, John Innes

of Tillyfour granted receipt in the Commissary books of Edinburgh for the two keys of Count Ernest Leslie's Charter Chest, to be delivered to the Commissary of Aberdeen, for the interest of all concerned. On the 21st December 1739, Mrs. Teresa Leslie, sister and Factrix to James Leslie of Pitcaple, petitioned the Commissary of Aberdeen that he would go to the House of Fetternear, and seal up the Charter Chest, that the haill writs therein contained might be duly preserved. On the same day the Commissary granted warrant to James Catanach, Advocate in Aberdeen, to go to the House of Fetternear and there seal up the said Charter Chest with the Commissary's seal, in order that the writs therein might be preserved for behoof of Sir James Leslie of Pitcaple, and of all other persons having interest. 1739.

After the House of Lords, 29th April 1742, pronounced judgment in favour of Count Anthony Leslie's claim to the Estate of Balquhain, Thomas Dundas of Fingask, as Factor and Commissioner for the Count, presented a petition, 28th August 1742, to the Commissary of Aberdeen, showing that upon the decease of Count Ernest Leslie of Balquhain, a closet at Fetternear, in which the Charter Chest of the family of Balquhain was lodged, had been sealed up by his Lordship's authority, and that the law proceedings in relation to the succession to the estates being then ended by the judgment of the House of Lords, whereby the estates were declared to belong to Count Anthony Leslie, the said Thomas Dundas was desirous of having the seals of the Court removed, and the keys of the Closet and Charter Chest, in the custody of the Clerk of the Court delivered up to him; and he craved the Commissary to grant warrant to Alexander Innes, his Lordship's Clerk, to remove the seals and to deliver up the keys to him, Thomas Dundas. The Commissary found the petition reasonable, and on the same day granted a warrant in terms of the petition, and Thomas Dundas granted a receipt for the keys in the following terms :— 1742. 1742.

"I, the within designed Thomas Dundas, grants me to "have received from Alexander Innes, Commissary Clerk

APPENDIX XXIV.

" of Aberdeen, the keys of the Charter Chest within men-
" tioned, in terms of the Commissary's warrant thereanent,
" in witness whereof I have written and subscribed these
1742. " presents at Fetternear, 29th August, 1742.

"THOMAS DUNDAS."

Mr. Thomas Mossman, Advocate in Aberdeen, stated that in consequence of a petition from Mr. Thomas Dundas to the Commissary of Aberdeen, a warrant was granted in
1742. August 1742, for getting the Charter Chest, or the keys of it, belonging to the family of Balquhain, and that he, Thomas Mossman, some time afterwards, by desire of Mr. Smith, the Factor, went to Fetternear, and brought away the Charter Chest, which was sent to Edinburgh.

Mr. John Lumsden, Writer in Edinburgh, and his son, John Lumsden, Junior, were employed by Thomas Dundas, Manager for Count Charles Cajetan Leslie, and his son, Count Anthony, as law agents in the process with Sir
1740-42. James Leslie of Pitcaple during the years 1740-1742, and afterwards, and John Lumsden, Junior, admitted that during that period they had in their possession, among other documents belonging to the Estate of Balquhain, the following deeds.

I. The deed of Entail made by Patrick, Count Leslie, in favour of his second son, George Leslie, with remainder to others
1692. therein mentioned, dated 8th November 1692, and
1698. registered 25th February 1698.

II. The disposition and resignation of James Ernest, Count Leslie, of the Estate of Balquhain, in favour of his half-
1695. brother, George Leslie, dated 9th December 1695.

III. The nomination and deed of Entail made by Patrick, Count Leslie, in favour of his second son, George Leslie, and others, dated 13th July 1700 and registered 30th
1700. July 1700.

John Lumsden, Junior, stated that by order of Thomas Dundas he delivered these three deeds, with others, to Walter Stewart, Writer in Edinburgh. Being further called upon oath to exhibit what papers he was possessed of belonging to the Counts Leslie, he exhibited two inventories of writs, deeds and other documents, with a receipt annexed to the first as follows:—

"Edinburgh, 25th March 1745. 1745.

"Received by me, Walter Stewart, Writer in Edinburgh, "by order of Thomas Dundas of Fingask, from John Lumsden, Writer to the Signet, the sixty-seven pieces of writs "contained in this and the seven preceding pages of this "inventory, in order to be new inventoried with the rest "of the writs and other family deeds of the Estate of "Balquhain, and to be returned on demand.

"WALTER STEWART."

These writs, deeds, and documents were fixed on Thomas Dundas by a posterior receipt given by him, 27th December 1750, whereby he not only acknowledged the receipt of the writs contained in that inventory, but declared that these were the whole papers belonging to Count Leslie then in the hands of John Lumsden. 1750.

Peter Grant's title for carrying on his action for evicting the Estate of Balquhain from Count Anthony Leslie, which continued in Court from November 1756 till February 1762, was founded on extracts of the two deeds of Tailzie above mentioned, taken from the Register of Tailzies, and although a most protracted and dilatory defence was made by Thomas Dundas on the part of the Counts Leslie, to gain time, yet it was never pretended that the original deeds of Tailzie were out of his hands till the 10th March 1761, when Peter Grant made application to the Lords of Session, by petition, for having a day fixed to advise the whole cause speedily, the then next summer session. Then, and no sooner, in order to prevent a day being so fixed, a petition was presented to the Lords of Session in behalf of the Counts Leslie, praying that it might be found that no proceedings could be made in the cause until the deeds of Tailzie of the Estate, upon which the action was founded, were produced. Whereupon Thomas Dundas was called upon oath to say what he knew concerning these deeds of

1756. 1762. 1761.

APPENDIX XXIV.

Tailzie, and he deponed that he had never seen them. Thus these two original deeds were then missing. In the law proceedings between the Counts Leslie and Sir James Leslie of Pitcaple, these deeds of Tailzie were produced in Court, and being now lost, Peter Grant presented a petition to the Court of Session praying that it might be declared that the two missing deeds were of the form, tenor, contents, and date of the copies taken from the Register of Tailzies, which was declared accordingly.

1762. After this period, from 1762, the Balquhain family deeds were in the possession of David Orme, writer in Edinburgh, agent for Peter Leslie Grant, twentieth Baron of Balquhain, after whose death they passed into the hands of Mr. Colquhoun Grant, W.S., who was agent for John
1778. Leslie, twenty-second Baron of Balquhain. In 1778 an inventory of writs of the Barony of Balquhain, etc., belonging to John Leslie, Esq. of Balquhain, found in the repositories of the deceased Colquhoun Grant, Clerk to the Signet, was delivered up by Charles Grant, ensign in the 55th Regiment of Foot, his eldest son and general disponee, to Isaac Grant, Clerk to the Signet, agent for the said John Leslie. This inventory contains 1010 writs, charters, and family documents, and fourteen bundles of miscellaneous
1790. papers. In a letter, dated at Edinburgh 10th March 1790, Mr. Isaac Grant wrote to John Leslie, twenty-second Baron of Balquhain—"I have got your writings, and they will require a house to keep them properly. I shall take as good care of them as I can." After the death of Mr. Isaac Grant, a Mr. John Leslie, W.S., Edinburgh, appears to have been agent for the Balquhain estates. In a letter to John Leslie, twenty-second Baron of Balquhain, dated at Edin-
1796. burgh 3d February 1796, he says—"I shall adhere to your instructions in getting your writings and papers agreeable to an inventory which I understand was made of them."
1809. In 1809 Mr. James Mackenzie, W.S., was agent for the Balquhain estates. In a letter to John Leslie of Balquhain, dated at Edinburgh 3d October 1809, he says—"I have got the charter-box containing your titles." After this

period the Balquhain writs, charters, etc., passed into the hands of various agents. In January 1840, Mr. Innes, of Mackenzie and Innes, W.S., Edinburgh, told Colonel Leslie, twenty-sixth Baron of Balquhain, that he was pretty certain that they had a quantity of Balquhain papers in a vault, and that he would have them searched out. But unfortunately Mr. Innes died soon afterwards; and Mr. Mackenzie, on Colonel Leslie applying to him in November 1841, said that the Balquhain papers in his hands had some considerable time previously been sent to Sir Charles Gordon and Mackay, W.S., Edinburgh, in order to be sent to Aberdeen. From the long lawsuits in which the family were engaged, and the frequent change of agents, many ancient charters, writs, and other papers belonging to the Balquhain family, are not now to be found, and no account can be got of them.

APPENDIX XXIV. 1840. 1841.

APPENDIX No. XXV.

Appendix XXV.

Patrick Leslie Duguid, Twenty-First Baron of Balquhain.

Summons issued at the instance of Joseph Duguid against Patrick Leslie Duguid of Balquhain, and his Sons, for the Recovery of the Estate of Balquhain, 30th May 1775. 1775.

George, &ca. Our will is and we charge you that ye lawfully summon warn and charge Patrick Duguid late of Auchinhove now designed Patrick Leslie Duguid of Balquhaine Duguid his the said Patrick Dugud's eldest son Dugud his second son John Dugud his third son and Patrick Dugud his fourth son and Alexander Dugud brother German to him the said Patrick Dugud the elder in manner following if they be within that part of Great Britain called Scotland personally or at their respective dwelling places upon 21 and 6 days warning for the first and second diets and if

APPENDIX XXV.

they be forth thereof by open proclamation at the Merkett Cross of Edinr. Peir and shore of Leith upon 60 and 15 days warning for first and second diets to compear before the Lords of our Council and Session at Edinr. or where it shall happen them to be for the time the and days of next to come in the hour of Cause with Continuation of days to answer at the instance of our Lovite Joseph Dugud only son of the deceased James Dugud who was brother German of the above Patrick Dugud Elder That whereas the said Patrick Dugud has now made up titles in his person to the lands and Barony of Balquhaine as alledged heir of Taillie and provision served and retoured to the now deceased Peter Leslie Grant of Balquhaine who on and Popish acts obtained possession of that estate and stood next infeft therein as nearest and lawful heir of Taillie and provision of the Reformed Protestant religion to his Cousin Ernest Leslie of Balquhaine Esquire And Likewise whereas it is by law established if any person sends another to be educated in the Popish religion or to reside in any religious house abroad for that purpose or contributes any thing to their maintenance when there both the sender and the sent and the contributer are disabled to sue in law or equity and forfeit all their real estate And truth it is That the said Patrick Dugud now of 74 years of age Dugud Dugud and John Patrick and Alexr. Duguds his sons and brother have been educated in Popish Religious houses abroad and are persons professing the Popish religion past the age of 15 who have omitted to renounce Popery in the form and manner set down in the acts of Parlt. underwritten and thereby as being educated in Popish Religious houses abroad and as Papists are incapable to succeed or to take hold enjoy or possess the said lands and estate of Balquhaine And that by the laws and acts of Parlt. of this Realme Particularly the act 71 Parlt. 6 King James 6 Intitled Act anent the youth and others beyond sea suspected to have declined from the true Religion "It is statute and ordained that all

APPENDIX XXV.

"Persons the sons of Noblemen Gentlemen or others pre-"tending the cause of their departure to be for the attain-"ing to the further Knowledge in Letteres sall before their "said departure sute and obtain the King's majesties licence "to that effect containing ane provision that they sall re-"main constant in the profession of the true religion "publicklie preached and by law established within this "Realme and do nor procure nothing to the prejudice "thereof nor of his Hines or his authority under the pain of "Barratrie As Alswa the said persons within the space of "20 days after their returning within this Realme sall pass "to the Bishop superintendent or commissioner of the "Kirks within the Bounds quhere they arrive or happen to "make residence and there offer to make and give the "Confession of their faith according to the true and Chris-"tian Religion preached and be law established within this "Realme Or then within 40 days thereafter devoyde "and remove themselves furth of this Realme quhair-"in gif they failzie that they be admonished and per-"sewed as adversaries of the said true Religion." And by another act being the third of the 8th and 9th sessions of the first Parlt. of King William dated 3rd day of Novr. 1700 Intitled Act for preventing the growth of Popery his Majestie with advice and consent of the Estates of Parlt. revives ratifies and perpetually Confirms the above act 71 Parlt. 6 King James 6th Intitled Act anent the youth and others beyond sea suspected to have declined from the true Religion with all other laws statutes and acts of Parlt. made against Popery and Papists and especially against Jesuits and Seminaries mass Priests and trafficcing Papists and their abode reset and their resetters within this Kingdom as also against all sayers and hearers of Mass and such as shall be present at Mass and all concealers of the same in the whole heads tenor and Contents thereof as if the same were therein fully set down and expressed dispensing with the generality and willing and ordaining the whole acts and statutes to be put to due and vigorous execution in all points And it is inter alia Inacted "That

1700.

APPENDIX XXV.

"in all time coming no professed Papist who being "suspected thereof shall refuse to purge themselves of "Popery in the form and manner set down in that act shall "be capable to purchase and enjoy by any voluntary dis- "position or deed that shall be made to them or any person "in trust for their behoof any lands houses tenements "annual rents or other real rights or Tacks of lands or "Teinds but that the said voluntary Dispositions and Deeds "with all that shall follow thereon shall eo ipso become "void and null to all intents and purposes and the right "thereof remain with the Disponer or granter his heirs or "assignies sicklike as if the same had not been made nor "granted As also that no person or persons professing the "Popish Religion past the age of 15 years shall hereafter be "capable to succeed as heirs to any person whatsoever nor "to bruik or enjoy any Estate by Disposition or other Con- "veyance flowing from any person to whom the said Papist "might succeed as heir any maner of way untill the said "heirs Purge themselves of Popery in manner therein "mentioned and if any Person or Persons shall happen to "succeed as heirs to their predecessors or any conveyance "shall happen to be made in their favours from a Person to "whom they might succeed as heirs before they attain the "said age then and in either of these Cases they shall be "holden and obliged to purge themselves of Popery before "they attain the said age of 15 years or any Conveyance "shall happen to be made in their favour by any Person to "whom they might have succeeded or the right be devolved "to them by succession or other Conveyance before that "age and they neglect or omit to renounce Popery as afore- "said then and immediately thereafter their right and in- "terest in and by the said succession or Conveyance shall "become void and null and shall devolve and belong to the "next Protestant heir or heirs who would succeed if they "and all the intervening Papist heirs were naturally dead "and it shall be lawful to the said Protestant heir or heirs "to serve heir to the defunct to whom the intervening "Papist might have succeeded by virtue of this act and the

APPENDIX XXV.

"irritancy incurred by the intervening Popish heir or heirs "which Protestant heir or heirs shall have right to the "said Estate and profits mails and duties thereof from the "incurring of the Irritancy ay and while the foresaid "Person or Persons shall purge themselves of Popery in "maner foresaid and also if the Popish heir or heirs ex-"cluded do not renounce Popery as aforesaid within Ten "years after the Irritancy is incurred not reckoning the "years of minority in the said Ten years they and their "heirs shall be for ever excluded providing always and de-"claring that all estates whatsoever devolving in maner "and for the causes foresaid shall be devolved transferred "and belong to the succeeding Protestant heirs with and "under the Taillies Conditions Irritancies and Clauses "resolutive contained in the rights of the said Estate as "they stand or shall stand in the Person of these to whom "they shall succeed on the grounds and for the "reasons foresaid the same being Consistent with and "agreeable to the act and the other laws of this "Kingdom." And that the said Joseph Dugud is now the nearest lawful heir of Taillie capable to succeed to the said estate Conform to and in terms of the two deeds of Taillie executed by the deceased Patrick Count Leslie of Balquhaine the first dated the 8th day of Novr. 1692 years 1692.
and registrate in the Register of Taillies the 25th day of Febr^y. 1698 years and the second dated the 13th day of 1698.
July 1700 years and registrate in the Register of Taillies 1700.
the 30 day of the said month and year and thereby the said Joseph Dugud has good and undoubted right to prosecute the action of Exhibition Reduction and Declarator after mentioned That is to say the said Defenders to exhibite and produce before our said Lords of Council and Session all writings contracts settlements and bonds of provision of or concerning the foresaid lands and Barony of Balquhaine or any part thereof or which may any ways affect or incumber the same and Particularly the said Patrick Duguid Elder his Retour dated the day of last with the precept issued forth of

APPENDIX XXV.

1775.

the Chancery for infefting him in the said lands and his seasine dated and recorded in the Particular Register of Seasines for the County of Aberdeen the day of May 1775 years and being so exhibited and produced the same ought and should be reduced and declared null for the reasons following viz$^{t.}$ the said writs are intrinsically null for want of Powers and wanting the substantial solemnities requisite in law Secundo the said writs are absolutely null in respect they are conceived in favours of Patrick Dugud Elder who contrary to the Public laws of the Kingdom was educated in a Popish Religious house abroad and Tertio the saids Dugud and Dugud and the saids John Patrick and Alex$^{r.}$ Duguds are all persons who have not only been educated abroad in Popish Religious houses Contrary to the Public laws of this kingdom as said But they and the said Patrick Dugud Elder are all persons professing the Popish Religion past the age of 15 who have ommitted to renounce Popery in the form and maner set down in the Acts of Parl$^{t.}$ above written and thereby incapable to succeed to or take hold enjoy or possess the saids lands and Estate of Balquhaine And therefore and for other reasons to be proponed at discussion hereof the saids writs ought and should be reduced rescinded cassed annulled decerned and declared to have been from the beginning to be now and in all time coming void null and of no force strength or effect and to bear no faith in Judgment nor out with the same in all time coming And it ought to be found and declared that the saids Patrick Dugud Dugud Dugud and John Patrick and Alexander Duguds are persons who one and all of them have contrary to law been educated in Popish Religious houses abroad and are persons professing the Popish Religion past the age of 15 years who have ommitted to renounce Popery in the form and maner set down in the acts of Parl$^{t.}$ before recited and thereby incapable to succeed to or to take hold enjoy or possess the said lands and Estate of Balquhaine And therefore that the said Joseph Dugud is

APPENDIX XXV.

now the nearest lawful heir of Taillie and provision of the true Reformed Protestant Religion capable to succeed to the said Estate and thereby has the only and undoubted right to serve himself heir therein to the deceased Peter Leslie Grant agreeable to and in virtue of the Deeds of Taillie above mentioned and it ought and should be found and declared by Decreet foresaid that the said Pursuer has right to the rent of this Estate payable by the Tacksman for the last half of Crop 1774 and in time coming After the form and tenor of the said Deeds of Entail and Laws and daily practice of Scotland observed in the like cases in all points or else to alledge a reasonable cause on the Contrary why the same should not be so done with Certification as Effeirs according to Justice dated and signeted 30 May 1775. 1775.

I James Lindsay messenger by virtue of a summons of Reduction whereof the above and the six preceding pages is a full Double raised at the Instance of Joseph Duguid only son of the deceased James Duguid who was brother German of the above designed Patrick Duguid Elder in his Majesty's name and authority Lawfully summon warn and charge you Alexander Duguid Brother German to Patrick Leslie Duguid late of Auchenhove now of Balquhain to compear before the Lords of Councell and Session at Edinburgh or where it shall happen them to be for the time upon the Fifteenth and Twenty second days of November next to come for first and second diets in the hour of cause with Continuation of days to answer at the Instance of the said Pursuer in the matter libelled with Certification as Effeirs This Copie and full Double I give you upon this Nineteenth day of August seventeen hundred and seventy-five years before witnesses. 1775.

James Lindsay, Mess[r].

George, &c. Forasmuch as in the process and action of Reduction and Declarator depending before our Lords of Council and Session at the Instance of Joseph Duguid only

APPENDIX XXV.

son and heir in General served and Retoured to the deceased James Duguid who was Brother German of Patrick Duguid Leslie of Balquhain and his tutor ad litem against the said Patrick Duguid Leslie, James Duguid his eldest son   Duguid his second son John Duguid his third son and Patrick Duguid his fourth son and Alexander Duguid his Brother German It was represented for the Pursuer that since executing the summons the said John Duguid the third son of the said Patrick Leslie Duguid had a son born to him and it would be necessary the son of the said John Duguid and his Tutors and Curators be made parties to the said action and a Diligence was craved for calling them for their Interest upon considering whereof the Lord Justice Clerk ordinary to said action by Interlocutor of the date hereof granted warrand for this our letters at the Instance of the said pursuer and James Laidlaw Writer in Edinburgh his Tutor ad litem for Citing Ernest Leopold Patrick Duguid son to the Defender John Duguid and his Tutors and Curators if he any has for their interest to compear in the said process for their interests to the seventh day of March next as the said Interlocutor bears, Our Will is herefore &c.

I Thomas Adamson Messenger by virtue of letters of Incident Dilligence Dated and Signet the Twenty-first and Twenty-second days of February current raised in the process and action of Reduction and Declarator depending before the Lords of Council and Session whereof what is wrote upon this and the preceeding page is a full double to the wills raised at the Instance of the before named and designed Joseph Duguid against Ernest Leopold Patrick Duguid son of the said John Duguid In his Majesty's name and authority summon warn and charge you the said Ernest Leopold Patrick Duguid to compear before the Lords of Council and Session at Edinburgh upon the seventh day of March next to come In the hour of cause with continuation of days to answer at the Instance of the said Joseph Duguid Pursuer and the said James Laidlaw Writer in Edinburgh his Tutor ad litem in the matters mentioned in the said Letters of Dilligence with certification &c. This I do upon the Twenty-eight day of February Seventeen hundred and seventy-seven years before these witnesses John Coverley and William Kissock both servants to Mr. John Duguid at Terregles. APPENDIX XXV. 1777.

THOMAS ADAMSON.

APPENDIX No. XXVI. *Appendix XXVI.*

JOHN LESLIE, TWENTY-SECOND BARON OF BALQUHAIN.

COPY of the REGISTER written by VIOLET LESLIE, Wife of JOHN LESLIE, twenty-second Baron of Balquhain, on two blank leaves at the beginning of the Missal which was used in the Domestic Chapel at Fetternear.

John Leslie, married to
Violet Dalzell, 14th November 1774. 1774.

1.

Tuesday. Patrick Ernest Leopold, born at Terregles, 28th November 1775. Baptized by Mr. John Pepper. 1775.

2.

Thursday. Amelia Mary, born at Kingswells, 24th April 1777. Baptized by Mr. James Leslie, her uncle. 1777.

3.

Tuesday. Harriet Ann, born at Tullos, 24th November 1778. Baptized by her granduncle, Mr. Alexander Duguid. Died 6th June 1805. 1778. 1805.

4.

Monday. John, born at Tullos, 1st May 1780. Baptized by his granduncle, Mr. Alexander Duguid. 1780.

5.

Friday. Joseph Emmanuel, born 5th October 1781. Baptized by Mr. Alexander Duguid, his granduncle, at Fetternear. 1781.

APPENDIX XXVI.

		6.
1783. 1801.	Thursday.	Teresa Frances, born 27th March 1783. Baptized by Bishop Hay, at Fetternear, Died 31st May 1801.
		7.
1784.	Friday.	James Michael, born 25th April 1784. Baptized by Bishop Hay, at Fetternear.
		8.
1785.	Monday.	Charles Joseph, born 24th April 1785. Baptized by Bishop Hay, Fetternear.
		9.
1786.	Wednesday.	Helen, born 17th May 1786, at Fetternear. Baptized by Bishop Hay.
		10.
1787.	Friday.	Anthony Andrew, born 30th November 1787, at Fetternear. Baptized by Bishop Hay.
		11.
1789.	Saturday.	Violet Winefred, born 18th April 1789, at Fetternear. Baptized by Mr. John Fraser.
		12.
1790.	Saturday.	Margaret Catherine, born 5th June 1790. Baptized by Mr. John Fraser at Fetternear.
		13.
1792.	Sunday.	Edward Henry, born 30th September 1792, at Fetternear. Baptized by Mr. John Gordon.
		14 and 15.
1793.	Monday.	Francis Robert and Louis Xavier, twins, born 14th October 1793, at Fetternear. Baptized by Mr. John Gordon of Aberdeen.

The following deaths are registered by Mrs. Leslie :—

1784. Joseph Emmanuel died at Fetternear 21st December 1784, and was buried in the old chapel.

1801. Theresa Frances Leslie died at Fetternear 30th May 1801, and was buried in the old chapel.

John Leslie left Fetternear 1st December 1803, and left Aberdeen 3d December 1803, in a foreign vessel for Dantzig, which has never since been heard of. APPENDIX XXVI.

Harriet Ann Leslie died at Fetternear 6th June 1805, and was buried in the old chapel. 1805.

Helen Leslie died at Edinburgh 20th December 1811, and was buried in the Canongate Church. 1811.

APPENDIX No. XXVII.

Appendix XXVII.

Walter, First Count Leslie.

Dispositions contained in the Entail executed by Walter, Count Leslie, registered 27th April 1667, the Wednesday after St. Mark's, in the Register Office of the Kingdom of Bohemia at Prague, in the Instrument-Book No. 263, *sub litera* M, p. 26. 1667.

Having received from his present ruling Majesty, Leopold I., the permission to make an Entail or Fidei Commissum familiae perpetuum, I therefore make the following dispositions.

Pro primo. That my Estate Neustadt, which I got as a donation from the Emperor Ferdinand III., with all belonging to it, in the Kingdom of Bohemia;

Pro secundo. The Estate Pettau, in the Dukedom of Styria, which I purchased myself, with all that belongs to it, should be subject to a perpetual entail or Fidei Commissum, and that the succession is to take place in the following manner.

As the Almighty has not blessed me with heirs of my own body, I hereby name, although Cum onere Fidei Commissi, my beloved nephew, James Leslie, eldest son of my brother, Alexander Leslie of Balquhain, in such manner that after my death, all may immediately belong to him—estates, jewels, gold and silver plate, furniture, bonds, &c., that he may enjoy the whole all his lifetime; and after his

APPENDIX XXVII.

lifetime to leave all without the least alienation or diminution, estates, goods, all what I may get, to his eldest son, and failing him, to his grandson; it being understood always conforming to the quality of the Jus primogeniti magistratus or Fidei Commissi; and therefore, all my nephews, the said James Leslie's male descendants, with perpetual exclusion of heirs female, shall succeed hereafter.

Should it happen that my nephew, James Leslie, does not survive me, or that, although he did enjoy my heritage, he might die without male descendants, in that case I institute as heir my brother's second son, Patrick Leslie; and if he be not alive at that time, then his eldest son, or second, or third, each in succession, with all his male descendants after the order and succession, with all the same rights and prerogatives that are mentioned in behalf of my nephew, James Leslie.

Should it ever happen that my brother's line became extinct, and no more male heir existing, then I confer all my Fidei Commiss fortune to the eldest son of Prince Dietrichstein's house (to whom I am related by my wife, and much indebted for many favours), Cum eodem onere fidei Commissi. My heritage shall be united with Prince Dietrichstein's fidei Commiss, and be inherited by the male descendants of the same name and line of the late Prince Maximilian Dietrichstein with perpetual exclusion of the female descendants, they being excluded also in Prince Dietrichstein's fidei Commiss, with the distinction however, that what concerns my present dispositio fideicommissaria et deficiente agnatione, may not extend either to the female descendants of Prince Dietrichstein, or to the Archbishopric of Prague, or to the Archbishopric of Olmutz.

But in the case that all male descendants of the above Prince Dietrichstein's line become extinct, all my heritage shall fall to the descendants of my nephew, James Leslie, without distinction whether they are male or female. Failing them, the other female descendants of his brother shall succeed to the heritage, and so it shall end, and it shall be left to the free will of the first successors of the

APPENDIX XXVII.

female line to dispose the heritage to whom or however they may please.

But as long as any of my brother's descendants of the name of Leslie are in possession of the Fidei Commiss, it is my command and will that, in case the possessor is not a Count, because I might not obtain this dignity for all the branches of the family, he should make application to his Imperial Majesty for the title of Count, and also for permission to wear my arms. Otherwise, he shall be unable to succeed; and in case he does not comply with this injunction within the term of one year, unless unforeseen events prevent him, the next agnate who has the title of Count shall have the right to exclude him from the succession.

In case any of my heirs change his religion or enter into a convent, he shall not make any claim to the Fidei Commiss, and the next in succession shall be heir.

Should, what God forbid, this my Fidei Commiss ever fall to an Idiot, or to one unable to manage any business, he may be considered as not being alive. His maintenance shall be given to him, and the person who would succeed to him after his death, is to get the heritage.

In case the Fidei Commiss should ever become the right of one under age, the person who after his death would have the next claim, is to take the Curatel of the Fidei Commiss, after having first given the necessary security, and taken an exact inventory. He is bound to administer it faithfully, and to endeavour to make the most of it, so that considerable sums of money may be saved and other estates purchased, which latter would not be considered as Fidei Commiss, but as allodial, and used for the maintenance of widows, and for the establishment of the daughters, and the younger brothers who never can succeed.

And in order that the Tutor may have benefit for his trouble, and tutorship, he is to get, in conformity with the Bohemian laws, out of the extrades of my Fidei Commiss fortune the sixth part, which he may enjoy unmolested.

And although I enjoin all my successors (what is like-

APPENDIX XXVII.

wise forbidden by the dispositions fideicommissariae) never to diminish the smallest part of the fidei Commiss, nor to pawn, mortgage, nor to contract any debts on it, yet, because it is necessary that my successors unite themselves with families of high rank and also to establish their daughters, I therefore permit my heirs that at their marriage they may take six thousand florins, never more, as marriage expenses, according to the custom of the country, with one and a half the sum, and then ten thousand florins instead of Dot, and thus altogether twenty-five thousand florins.

He may settle on the widow three thousand florins per annum, besides lodgings: on a daughter six thousand florins, besides her convenient fitting out. All this may be secured on the Fidei Commiss, if there is no allodial fortune.

All my heirs and successors are forbidden to deduct quartum, sive ex S[a.] Trebelliano, sive ex lege falidea, and should any one of my heirs or successors attempt to change this my last will, to alter the clear intent and dispute about it, he shall lose immediately his right, and the next following heir shall succeed.

I enjoin every one of the possessors of the fidei Commiss to take good care of his younger brothers, to give them as much assistance as he can without overburdening the fidei-Commiss, to bring them up in virtuous and noble sentiments, and to assist them in whatever profession and way of living they may incline to.

1692. James, second Count Leslie, in 1692, made an addition to the entail executed by Count Walter, adding to the estate—

The amelioration of Count Walter Leslie's Fidei Commiss estate by the Wine tax; the capital of twenty thousand florins laid out at interest with the Imperial Government in
1688. May 1688, for lessening the burden of the annual taxes; the new gardens planted about the house belonging to the fidei commiss; the immoveable furniture; all the silver plate specified in a paper in the wardrobe; all the tapestries; and all the money belonging to the estate.

APPENDIX No. XXVIII.

Appendix XXVIII.

Alexander Leslie, First Baron of Wardis.

Charter of Sale by Sir William Leslie of Wardis, to his Kinsman Duncan Forbes, son of Alexander Forbes, of the half of the lands of Corbanchory, in the Barony of Cushney, A.D. 1464. 1464.

Omnibus hanc cartam visuris . . . Willelmus de Lesly de Werderis miles Salutem . . . Noueritis me . . . dedisse . . et omnino vendidisse . . . dilecto Consanguineo meo Duncano de Forbes filio Alexandri de Forbes totam et integram dimediam partem terrarum mearum de Corbanchory cum pertinentiis jacentem in baronia de Cusny infra vicecomitatum de Aberdene . . . Tenendam . . . de me heredibus meis et meis assignatis in feodo et hereditate imperpetuum . . . Reddendo inde annuatim . . . mihi heredibus meis et meis assignatis unum denarium usualis monete Scotie . . . nomine albe firme . . . tantum . . . In cuius rei testimonium huic presenti carte mee sigillum meum est appensum apud burgum de Aberdene vicesimo die mensis Julii anno Domini millesimo quadringentesimo sexagesimo quarto coram hiis 1464. testibus Alexandro de Lesly Georgio de Lesly Andrea Glaster de Glak . Alexandro de Skene de eodem Thoma de Forbes Dauysoun et Thoma Monypenny cum diuersis aliis.

Antiquities of the Shires of Aberdeen and Banff, vol. iv. p. 330; Spalding Club.

APPENDIX No. XXIX.

Appendix XXIX.

Alexander Leslie, First Baron of Wardis.

Charter by King James III. to his Familiar Esquire, Alexander Leslie of Wardis, and Isabella Lauder, his Wife, of the lands of Balcomy in Fife—A.D. 1465. 1465.

Jacobus Dei gratia Rex Scotorum . . . Sciatis nos dedisse . . . dilecto familiari scutifero nostro Alexandro de Lesly et

APPENDIX XXIX.

Isabelle de Lawdre sponse sue et eorum alteri diucius viuenti totas et integras terras de Balcolmy cum pertinentiis jacentes infra vicecomitatum nostrum de Fiff . . . Quequidem terre cum pertinentiis fuerunt dicte Isabelle hereditarie et quas eadem Issabella in sua pura et integra virginitate . . . spontanea voluntate in manus nostras . . . simpliciter resignauit . . . Tenendas et habendas . . . dictis Alexandro et Isabelle sponse sue et eorum alteri diucius viuenti et heredibus inter ipsos legittime procreatis seu procreandis dicte Issabelle quibuscunque de nobis heredibus et successoribus nostris in feodo et hereditate imperpetuum . . . In cuius rei testimonium presenti carte nostre confirmacionis magnum sigillum nostrum apponi precepimus . . . Apud Striueline vicesimo septimo die mensis Septembris anno Domini
1465. millesimo quadringentesimo sexagesimo quinto et regni nostri sexto.

Registrum Magni Sigilli, lib. vi. No. 44; in *Antiquities of Shires of Aberdeen and Banff*, vol. iv. p. 516.

Appendix XXX.

APPENDIX No. XXX.

Alexander Leslie, First Baron of Wardis.

Charter of Sale by Alexander Leslie of Wardis, Lord of Balcomy, to Duncan Forbes of Drummellache, of
1469. the lands of Corbanchery, 1469; confirmed by Queen
1545. Mary, 1545.

Maria Dei gratia Regina Scotorum . . . Sciatis nos . . . quandam cartam . . . venditionis factam per Alexandrum Leslie dominum de Balcomy Duncano Forbes de Drummaleche . . . ad plenum intellexisse sub hac forma Omnibus hanc cartam visuris vel audituris, Alexander Leslie dominus de Balcomy salutem in Domino sempiternam Noveritis me . . . vendidisse . . . honorabili viro Duncano Forbes de Drummaleche totas et integras terras meas de Corbanchquere cum suis pertinentiis jacentes in baronia de Cussne infra vicecomitatum de Aberdene . . . Tenendas et habendas . . .

prefato Duncano Forbes heredibus suis et suis assignatis de me et heredibus meis et meis assignatis in feodo et hereditate imperpetuum... cum curiis et curiarum exitibus et eschaetis herezeldis bludewitis et merchetis mulierum ariagiis cariagiis et bondagiis ac dietis... Faciendo inde domino nostro Regi et heredibus suis . . . seruicium forinsecum de dictis terris cum pertinentiis debitum et consuetum Et reddendo mihi et heredibus meis et meis assignatis annuatim vnum par Chirothecarum albarum ad Festum Pasche super solum dictarum terrarum nomine albe firme si petatur Reseruando etiam mihi et heredibus meis et assignatis vnam peciam terre dictarum terrarum de Corbanchquere que vocatur Carnomor ad faciendum seruicium domino meo superiori debitum et consuetum ... In cujus rei testimonium huic presenti carte mee sigillum meum est appensum Apud Aberdene penultimo die mensis Januarii anno Domini millesimo quadringentesimo 1468-9. sexagesimo octauo Testibus honorabilibus viris Henrico Dowglas de Lochlevin milite Magistro Richardo Forbes decano Aberdonensi Domino Henrico de Kingorn Canonico Aberdonensi et Morauiensi Alexandro Skene de eodem Domino Andrea Leslie rectore de Rothes Georgio Leslie fratre meo germano Waltero Andree Jacobo Skene Johanne Dog armigeris et Domino Roberto Leis Capellano et notario publico cum multis aliis Quamquidem Cartam . . . pro perpetuo confirmamus... In cuius rei testimonium presenti carte nostre confirmacionis signum nostrum apponi precepimus . . . Apud Edinburgh vicesimo quarto die Mensis Maii anno Domini millesimo quingentesimo quadragesimo quinto, Et regni nostri tercio. 1545.

Registrum Magni Sigilli, lib. xxxi. No. 22. *Antiquities of Shires of Aberdeen and Banff*, vol. iv. p. 330.

APPENDIX.

Appendix XXXI.

APPENDIX No. XXXI.

Alexander Leslie, First Baron of Wardis.

1473. Charter of Feuferme by King James III. to his Familiar Esquire, Alexander Leslie of Wardis, of the King's Lands of the Thanage of Kintore—A.D. 1473.

Jacobus Dei gracia Rex Scotorum . . . Sciatis nos dedisse . . . et ad feodifirmam dimississe . . . dilecto familiari scutifero nostro Alexandro Lesly de Wardris terras nostras thanagii de Kyntor cum uniuersis annuis redditibus earundem cum pertinentiis jacentes infra vicecomitatum nostrum de Abirdene in augmentationem infrascriptam nostri rentalis de dicto thanagio et pro gratuito et fideli seruicio dicti Alexandri nobis impenso Que terre predicte thanagii cum dictis annuis redditibus cum pertinentiis temporibus retroactis extendebant annuatim ad quadraginta quinque libras vsualis monete regni nostri Tenendas et habendas . . . prefato Alexandro Lesly et heredibus suis de nobis heredibus et successoribus nostris in feodo et hereditate imperpetuum . . . Reddendo inde et soluendo annuatim dictus Alexander et heredes sui reverendo in Christo patri Episcopo Abirdonensi et successoribus suis Episcopis (Abirdonensibus) pro decimo denario dicto Episcopo et ecclesie Abirdonensi de prefato thanagio debito (summam) quatuor librarum et quatuor solidorum dicte monete regni nostri Ac vicecomiti de Forfar et successoribus suis videlicet heredibus quondam Alexandri Ogiluy de Vchtirhous quibuscunque summam trium librarum dicte monete Ac nobis heredibus et successoribus nostris nomine feodifirme quinquaginta libras et viginti duos solidos et octo denarios eiusdem monete ad duos anni terminos Penthecostes videlicet et sancti Martini in hieme per equales porciones tantum pro omnibus aliis seruiciis aueragiis cariagiis et aliis exactionibus quibuscunque que de dictis terris et thanagio et annuis redditibus cum pertinentiis earundem per quos cunque exigi poterunt . . . In cuius rei testimonium presenti carte nostre magnum sigillum nostrum apponi precepimus . . . Apud Edinburgh ultimo die mensis Septembris anno Domini millesimo quadringentesimo septuagesimo tertio et regni nostri decimo quarto . . .

APPENDIX XXXI.

1473.

Antiquities of Shires of Aberdeen and Banff, vol. iv. p. 516. From the *Registrum Magni Sigilli*, lib. vii. No. 62.

APPENDIX No. XXXII.

Appendix XXXII.

ALEXANDER LESLIE, FIRST BARON OF WARDIS.

CHARTER by King JAMES III. mortifying an Annual Rent of Twelve Merks from the Lands of Balcomy in Fife, which failing, from the Lands of Wardis and Quyltpat, in the Sheriffdom of Aberdeen, given by ALEXANDER LESLIE, First Baron of Wardis, for the support of a Chaplain at the Chapel of St. Mary of Garioch, for behoof of the souls of the said ALEXANDER LESLIE, and ISABELLA his Spouse—1474. 1474.

APUD . . . xxviii Novembris, j$^{m.}$ cccc.lxxiv. Rex dedit cartam mortificacionis in forma majori de annuo redditu duodecim mercarum de terris de Balcomy infra vicecomitatum de Fiff quibus deficientibus de terris de Wardris et Quyltpat infra vicecomitatum de Aberdene mortificato per Alexandrum Lesly de Wardris ad sustentacionem unius Capellani annuatim celebraturi ad Capellam Sancte Marie de Garviache pro animabus dicti Alexandri et Isabelle sponse sue etc.

Abbreviatio Registri Magni Sigilli, lib. vii. No. 317. *Antiquities of the Shires of Aberdeen and Banff*, vol. iii. p. 405.

APPENDIX.

Appendix XXXIII.

APPENDIX No. XXXIII.

Alexander Leslie, First Baron of Wardis.

1479. Charter by King James III., A.D. 1479, confirming a Charter by John of Ila, Lord of the Isles, to his Kinsman, Alexander Leslie of Wardis, of the Lands of the Barony of Kynnedward, commonly called the Castletown, and the Lands of Estirtiry, Kynnaroquhy, and Faithly; but reserving to the Granter three merks of the lands of the Castletown, with the Castle-hill, for the service due to the King from the Lands
1478. and Barony of Kynnedward—A.D. 1478.

Jacobus Dei gracia Rex Scotorum . . . Sciatis nos quamdam cartam dilecti consanguinei nostri Johannes de Ila domini Insularum factam et concessam in feodifirma dilecto scutifero nostro Alexandro Lesly de Wardris nostro receptori generali . . . ad plenum intellexisse sub hac forma Omnibus hanc cartam visuris vel audituris Johannes de Ila dominus Insularum salutem in Domino sempiternam Noueritis nos dedisse . . . necnon . . . ad feodifirmam dimittere . . . dilecto consanguineo nostro Alexandro Lesly de Wardris omnes et singulas terras nostras baronie nostre de Kynnedward cum pertinentiis videlicet terras dominicales de Kynnedward vulgariter nuncupatas *le Castletoun* ac terras de Estirtiry Kynnaroquhy et Faithly cum pertinentiis jacentes infra vicecomitatum de Abirdene Reseruatis inde nobis et heredibus nostris tribus mercatis dictarum terrarum de Castletoun cum monte castri eiusdem ad faciendum domino nostro Regi seruicium pro dictis terris de baronia de Kynnedward debitum et consuetum Tenendas et habendas . . . dicto Alexandro Lesly et heredibus suis de nobis et heredibus nostris Dominis Insularum et Baronibus de Kynnedward in feodifirma et hereditate imperpetuum . . . soluendo annuatim . . . nobis et heredibus nostris pro

dictis terris et baronia cum pertinentiis viginti et nouem mercas usualis monete regni Scocie . . . Insuper constituimus . . dictum Alexandrum Lesly balliuum nostrum dictarum terrarum et baronie de Kynnedward cum pertinenciis Tenendum et habendum idem officium balliuatus cum pertinenciis dicto Alexandro Lesly et heredibus suis de nobis et heredibus nostris in feodo et hereditate imperpetuum . . . In cuius rei testimonium presenti carte nostre sigillum nostrum apponi fecimus apud Edinburgh vicesimo secundo die mensis Decembris anno Domini millesimo quadringentesimo septuagesimo octauo Testibus nobilibus et 1478.
prepotentibus dominis Colino Comite Ergadie domino Lorne et Campbell magistro hospicii supremi domini nostri Regis Lachlano Makgilleon de Doward Hectore Makgilleon de Loichbowe Willelmo Mackloid de Glenelg Rory Makloide de Leweis Alexandro McCaus de Ardnamertho et Malcomo Makneile de Geya cum multis et diuersis aliis Quamquidem cartam pro perpetuo confirmamus Saluis nobis heredibus et successoribus nostris juribus et seruiciis . . . debitis et consuetis Et prouiso eciam quod presens nostra confirmacio donacioni de dictis terras cum pertinenciis quam de nobis habet dilecta consanguinea nostra Elizabeth Comitissa Rossie ad vitam sibi Elizabeth in dampnum aut preiudicium non cedat durante toto tempore vite sue In cuius rei testimonium presenti carte nostre confirmacionis magnum sigillum nostrum apponi precepimus . . . apud Edinburgh quarto die mensis Februarii anno Domini millesimo quadringentesimo septuagesimo octauo et regni nostri 1478-9.
decimo nono.

Antiquities of Shires of Aberdeen and Banff, vol. iv. p. 517. From the *Registrum Magni Sigilli*, lib. ix. No. 15.

APPENDIX.

Appendix XXXIV.

APPENDIX No. XXXIV.

Alexander Leslie, First Baron of Wardis.

Charter by King James IV. to his Familiar Servant, Walter Leslie, one of the Marischals of the Household, Son of the deceased Alexander Leslie of Wardis, and Isobel Lauder of Balcomy, his Wife, of the Lands of Balcomy in Fife, resigned by the said
1499. Isobel Lauder—A.D. 1499.

Jacobus Dei gracia Rex Scotorum . . . Sciatis nos dedisse . . . dilecto familiari seruitori nostro Waltero Lesly vni mariscallorum nostri domicilii filio quondam Alexandri Lesly de Wardris inter ipsum et Isobellam Lauder de Balcomy suam sponsam genito totas et integras terras de Balcomy cum pertinenciis jacentes infra vicecomitatum nostrum de Fiffe Quequidem terre . . . fuerunt dicte Isobelle hereditarie et quas eadem in sua pura viduitate . . . in manus nostras . . . simpliciter resignauit . . . Tenendas et habendas . . . dicto Waltero et heredibus suis quibus deficientibus dicte Isobelle et heredibus suis reuersuras de nobis et successoribus nostris in feodo et hereditate imperpetuum . . . Faciendo inde annuatim . . . jura et seruicia . . . nobis debita et consueta In cuius rei testimonium presenti carte nostre magnum sigillum nostrum apponi precepimus . . . apud Striueling primo die mensis Septembris anno Domini millesimo quad-
1499. ringentesimo nonagesimo nono et regni nostri duodecimo.

Antiquities of Shires of Aberdeen and Banff, vol. iv. p. 519. From the *Registrum Magni Sigilli*, lib. xiii. No. 480.

APPENDIX.

APPENDIX No. XXXV.

Appendix XXXV.

JOHN LESLIE, SECOND BARON OF WARDIS.

CHARTER by King JAMES IV. to JOHN LESLIE, Second Baron of Wardis, of the Lands of Balcomy in Fife, resigned by his Brother, WALTER LESLIE—A.D. 1500. 1500.

JACOBUS Dei gracia Rex Scotorum . . . Sciatis nos dedisse . . . dilecto nostro Johanni Lesly de Wardris totas et integras terras de Balcomy cum pertinenciis jacentes infra vicecomitatum nostrum de Fiffe Quequidem terre . . . fuerunt Walteri Lesly fratris dicti Johannis hereditarie et quas idem Walterus . . . in manus nostras . . . simpliciter resignauit . . . Tenendas et habendas . . . dicto Johanni et heredibus suis de nobis et successoribus nostris in feodo et hereditate imperpetuum . . . Faciendo inde annuatim . . . jura et seruicia . . . nobis debita et consueta Reseruato tamen libero tenemento dictarum terrarum de Balcomy cum pertinentiis Isobelle Lawder matri dicti Johannis pro toto tempore vite sue In cuius rei testimonium presenti carte nostre magnum sigillum nostrum apponi precepimus . . . apud Striueling decimoquarto die mensis Februarii anno Domini millesimo quadrigentesimo nonagesimo nono et 1499-1500.
regni nostri duodecimo.

Antiquities of Shires of Aberdeen and Banff, vol. iv. p. 519. From *Registrum Magni Sigilli*, lib. xiii. No. 481.

APPENDIX No. XXXVI.

Appendix XXXVI.

JOHN LESLIE, SECOND BARON OF WARDIS.

CHARTER by King JAMES IV. to JOHN LESLIE of Wardis, in Recompense of certain Sums due by the King's Father to the Father of the said JOHN LESLIE of

APPENDIX XXXVI.

Wardis, the deceased Alexander Leslie of Wardis, when he was the King's Comptroller, of the Office of Bailie of all the King's Lands of the Regality of the Garioch—namely, Glanderstoun with the Mill, Tulyfoure, Duncanstoun, Donydure with the Mill, Rochmuriel, Knokinbard with the Mill, Ardoun, Buchanstoun with the Mill, Harlaw, Mekle Dorno with the Mill, Torreys, Rihill, Warthill, and the Davach of Inverurie with the Mill—the Office of Bailie being

1508. annexed to the Lands of Wardis—A.D. 1508.

JACOBUS Dei gracia Rex Scotorum . . . Sciatis quia pro bono et gratuito seruicio nobis per dilectum nostrum Johannem Leslie de Warderys impenso et in recompensacionem nonnullarum summarum pecuniarum per quondam nobilissimum patrem nostrum cujus anime propicietur Deus quondam Alexandro Leslye de Warderis patri dicti Johannis debitarum tempore quo idem Alexandri eiusdem patris nostri Compotorum Rotulator extiterat in rotulis et compotorum libris suis contentarum fecimus . . . dictum Johannem Leslye balliuum omnium et singularum terrarum nostrarum regalitatis nostre de Gareauche nunc nobis in proprietate pertinentium jacentium infra vicecomitatum nostrum de Abirdene videlicet terrarum de Glanderstoun cum molendino earundem Tulyfoure Duncanistoune Donydure cum molendino earundem Rochmwriell Knokinbard cum molendino earundem Ardovn Buchanistoun cum molendino earundem terrarum de Hairlaw Mekle Durno cum molendino earundem Torreys Rihill Warthill et davate terrarum nostrarum de Inuerowry cum molendino earundem cum omnibus suis pertinenciis Tenendum et habendum dictum officium balliuatus siue ballie . . . cum omnibus eschaetis amerchiamentis bludewitis et proficuis dicti officii . . . de nobis et successoribus nostris Scotorum Regibus in feodo et hereditate imperpetuum . . . Insuper cum predictum officium sit res incorporea et dictus Johannes nullas habet terras sibi cum eodem concessas super quibus dictum officium dependere valeat Nos igitur vniuimus . . . dictum officium terris de Warderis dicto Johanni pertinentibus jacentibus infra regalitatem nostram antedictam ut sit quedam dependencia et pertinencia earundem pro perpetuo infuturum sic quod sasina capienda per heredes ipsius Johannis de prefatis terris de Warderis erit sasina sufficiens et extendet ad dictum officium tanquam dependenciam dictarum terrarum . . . super alique parte dictarum terrarum de Gareauche per deliberacionen virge ut moris est . . . In cuius rei testimonium presenti carte nostre magnum sigillum nostrum apponi precepimus . . apud Edinburgh decimosexto die mensis Junii anno Domini millesimo quingentesimo octauo et regni nostri vicesimo primo. 1508.

Antiquities of Shires of Aberdeen and Banff, vol. iv. p. 521. From the *Registrum Magni Sigilli*, lib. xv. No. 43.

APPENDIX XXXVI.

APPENDIX No. XXXVII.

Appendix XXXVII.

JOHN LESLIE, SECOND BARON OF WARDIS.

CHARTER of FEUFERME by King JAMES IV. to JOHN LESLIE of Wardis, of the Lands of the Thanage of Kintore, namely, the Over Davach and Nether Davach of Kintore with the Mills, the Lands of Crichie, Tavilty, Mekil Kynnaldy with the Mill, Litill Kynnaldy, Petmeddene, Nether Dyce, with the Yearly Rents, the Fishings on the Water of Don, and the Lake and Bogs—A.D. 1508. 1508.

JACOBUS Dei gracia Rex Scotorum . . . Sciatis quia dedimus . . . et hac presenti carta nostra concedimus et ad feodifirmam dimittimus dilecto nostro Johanni Leslie de Warderis totas et integras terras de thanagio de Kintor subscriptas videlicet terras de le Ouer Dawate et Nether Dawate de Kyntor cum molendinis earundem terras de Creiche Tavilty Litill Kynnaldy cum molendino earundem Litill Kynnaldy

APPENDIX XXXVII.

Petmeddene Nethir Dise et annuis redditibus earundem cum Piscariis super aqua de Done infra bondas terrarum predictarum cum lacu et paludibus earundem et suis pertinenciis jacentes infra vicecomitatum nostrum de Abirdene Quequidem terre . . . fuerunt dicti Johannis tanquam heredis quondam Alexandri Leslie de Warderis Patris sui hereditarie per cartam et assedacionem eidem Alexandro et heredibus suis in feodifirma per quondam nobilissimum patrem nostrum cuius anime propicietur Deus in minori etate sua factas in augmentacionem rentalis sui . . . Et quas terras . . . idem Johannes in manibus nostris . . . simpliciter resignauit . . . et pro bono et gratuito seruicio nobis per dictum Johannem impenso et impendendo ac in recompensacionem nonnullarum amplarum summarum pecuniarum per prefatum quondam carissimum patrem nostrum dicto quondam Alexandro Compotori suorum rotulorum pro tempore debitarum de quibus dictus Johannes tanquam heres prefati patris sui pro hoc nouo infeofamento nostro nos tanquam heredem et successorem carissimi Patris nostri antedicti quitteclamauit et exonerauit imperpetuum dedimus . . . et dimisimus . . . ad feodifirmam . . . dicto Johanni . . . predictas terras . . . Tenendas et habendas . . . dicto Johanni et heredibus suis de nobis et successoribus nostris in feodifirma et hereditate imperpetuum . . . Reddendo inde annuatim dictus Johannes et heredes sui reuerendo in Christo Patri Willelmo episcopo Abirdonensi moderno et successoribus suis episcopis Abirdonensibus pro decimis denariis dictis Episcopo et Cathedrali ecclesie Abirdonensi de prefato thanagio debitis summam quatuor librarum et quatuor solidorum vsualis monete regni nostri et Vicecomiti nostro de Forfar et successoribus suis videlicet heredibus Alexandri Ogiluy de Oucterhous quibuscunque summam trium librarum monete predicte ac nobis et successoribus nostris summam quinquaginta vnius librarum duorum solidorum et octo denariorum vsualis monete regni nostri . . . pro omnibus aliis seruitiis oneribus exactionibus et questionibus quibuscunque In cuius rei testimonium presenti carte nostre magnum sigillum nostrum apponi precepimus . . . apud Edinburgh decimo septimo die mensis Junii anno Domini millesimo quingentesimo octauo et regni nostri vicesimo primo.

Antiquities of the Shires of Aberdeen and Banff, vol. iv. p. 520. From the *Registrum Magni Sigilli*, lib. xv. No. 15.

APPENDIX No. XXXVIII.

Appendix XXXVIII.

John Leslie, Second Baron of Wardis.

Precept by King James IV. to infeft John Leslie, Second Baron of Wardis, in the Lands, Rents, and Fishings, of the Thanage of Kintore—A.D. 1508. 1508.

Jacobus Dei gratia Rex Scotorum reuerendo in Christo Patri . . . Willelmo Abirdonensi episcopo nostri secreti sigilli custodi salutem Quia dedimus . . . et ad feodifirmam dimisimus hereditarie dilecto nostro Johanni Leslie de Warderis totas et integras terras thanagii de Kyntor subscriptas videlicet terras de le Ouer Dawate et Nethir Dawate de Kyntor cum molendinis earundem terras de Creichie Tauilty Mekill Kenaldy cum molendino earundem Litill Kenaldy Petmedden Nethir Dise et annuos redditus earundem cum piscaturis super aqua de Done infra bondas terrarum predictarum cum lacubus et paludibus earundem et suis pertinentiis jacentes infra vicecomitatum nostrum de Aberdene Quequidem terre cum molendino et annuo redditibus earundem . . fuerunt dicti Johannis tanquam heredis quondam Alexandri Lesly de Warderis patris sui hereditarie per cartam et assedationem eidem Alexandro et heredibus suis in feodifirma per quondam nobilissimum patrem nostrum . . . in minore etate sua factas in augmentationen rentalis sui . . . et quas terras cum molendino et annuis redditibus earundem idem Johannes in manibus nostris apud Edinburgh . . . simpliciter resignavit . . . Et pro bono et gratuito seruicio nobis per dictum Johannem impenso et impendendo ac in recompensationem nonnullarum ampla-

APPENDIX XXXVIII.

rum summarum pecuniarum per prefatum quondam carissimum patrem . . . dicto quondam Alexandro Compotorum rotulatori pro tempore debitarum . . . ad feodifirmam dimisimus . . . dicto Johanni . . . predictas terras cum molendino et annuis redditibus earundem . . . Tenendas . . . predictas terras . . . de nobis et successoribus nostris in feodifirma et hereditate imperpetuum . . . Reddendo inde annuatim . . . Willelmo Abirdonensi Episcopo moderno et successoribus suis episcopis Aberdonensibus pro decimis denariis dictis episcopo et cathedrali ecclesie Aberdonensi de prefato thanagio debitis summam quatuor librarum quatuor solidorum usualis monete regni nostri et Vicecomiti nostro de Forfair et successoribus suis heredibus quondam Alexandri Ogiluy de Ouchtirhouss quibuscunque summam trium librarum monete predicte ac nobis et successoribus nostris summam quinquaginta unius librarum duorum solidorum et octo denariorum . . . monete regni nostri . . . nomine feodifirme tantum . . . Vobis precipimus . . . quatinus preceptum nostrum sub dicto nostro secreto sigillo pro carta nostra sub nostro magno sigillo dicto Johanni et heredibus suis super premissis conficienda prefati nostri magni sigilli custodi in forma capelle nostre debita dirigatis Datum sub signeto nostro apud Edinburgh decimo septimo die mensis Junii anno regni nostri vicesimo primo (A.D.
1508. 1508.)

Antiquities of Shires of Aberdeen and Banff, vol. iii. p. 233. From a copy in the Archives of the King's College and University, Aberdeen.

APPENDIX No. XXXIX.

Appendix XXXIX.

John Leslie, Second Baron of Wardis.

Charter of Feuferme by King James IV. to John Leslie of Wardis, of the King's Lands of the Garioch, namely, Duncanstoun, Gillanderstoun with the Mill, Donydure with the Mill, Rochmuriell, the Davach of Ardune with the Mill, Dornoch and the Mylnetoun, the Mill of Dornoche, Harlaw, Inverurie with the Davach and Mill, Tullifoure, Torreis, Knokinbarde with the Mill, and Knokinmorgin, in exchange for the Lands of Balcomy with the Manor-place and Rabbit-warrens in Fife—A.D. 1510. 1510.

Jacobus Dei gracia Rex Scotorum . . . Sciatis nos dedisse . . . et ad feodifirmam dimisisse et hac presenti carta nostra hereditarie confirmasse dilecto nostro Johanni Lesly de Warderis omnes et singulas terras nostras de Garviauche subscriptas videlicet terras de Duncanstoune Gillanderistoune cum molendino eiusdem Donydure cum molendino eiusdem Rochmuriell *le Davech* de Ardvne cum molendino eiusdem Warthill Dornoch et *le Mylnetoun* earundem molendinum de Dornoche Hairlaw Inuerowry Cum *le Daw* et molendino eiusdem Tullifoure Torreis Knokinbarde cum molendino earundem et Knokmorgin cum omnibus *le outsettis* . . . extendentes nunc in integro in rentali nostro ante presentem nostram assedacionem feudifirme ad summam centum quinquaginta vnius librarum vsualis monete regni nostri in pecuniis vndecim martas sex duodenas caponum et quatuordecim duodenas pultrearum jacentes infra vicecomitatum de Abirden in excambium et permutacionem pro terris suis de Balcomy cum manerio et cuniculariis earundem et suis pertinenciis jacentibus infra vicecomitatum nostrum de Fiffe per dictum Johannen nunc in manibus nostris resignatis et sursum redditis nobiscum et cum

APPENDIX XXXIX.

successoribus nostris in proprietate permansuris imperpetuum Tenendas et habendas . . . de nobis et successoribus nostris in feodifirma et hereditate ac libera baronia et libera foresta imperpetuum . . . adeo libere . . . sicut Comites de Mar possessores dictarum terrarum easdem aliquibus retroactis temporibus liberius possidebant . . . Reddendo inde . . . annuatim . . . nobis et successoribus nostris summam centum quinquaginta vnius librarum vsualis monete predicte . . . vndecim martas sex duodenas pultriarum . . . secundum tenorem rentalis nostri antedicti nomine feodifirme tantum in augmentacionem rentalis nostri . . . ad valorem dictarum terrarum de Balcomy nunc sursum reditarum . . . In cuius rei testimonium presenti carte nostre magnum sigillum nostrum apponi precepimus . . . apud Edinburgh vicesimo-
1510. septimo die mensis Marcii anno Domini millesimo quingentesimo decimo et regni nostri vicesimo tercio.

Antiquities of Shires of Aberdeen and Banff, vol. iv. p. 522. From the *Registrum Magni Sigilli*, lib. xvi. No. 59.

Appendix XL.

APPENDIX No. XL.

John Leslie, Second Baron of Wardis.

Charter by King James V. to John Leslie of Wardis, and Annabella Chalmer, his wife, of the Lands of Tulifour, Tavelte, and the Mill and the Milltown of
1525. Durrnoy, in the regality of the Garioch—A.D. 1525.

Jacobus Dei gracia Rex Scotorum . . . Sciatis nos cum . . . consensu Dominorum Consilii nostri ad hoc per tres regni nostri status in Parliamenti nostri electorum . . . confirmasse dilectis nostris Johanni Lesly de Warderis et Anabelle Chalmer sponse sue et ipsorum alteri diucius viuenti in coniuncta infeodacione pro tota tempore vite sue totas et integras terras de Tilifour Tavelte molendinum et *le Myltoun* de Durrnoy cum suis pertinenciis jacentes in regalitate de Gariauch infra vicecomitatum nostrum de

Abirdene Quequidem terre . . . fuerunt dicti Johannis hereditarie et quas idem . . . in manibus nostris apud Edinburgh . . . simpliciter resignauit . . . Tenendas et habendas . . . dictis Johanni Lesly et Anabelle ejus sponse ac eorum alteri diucius viuenti in coniuncta infeodacione ac legitimis et propinquioribus heredibus dicti Johannis quibuscunque de nobis et successoribus nostris in feodo et hereditate imperpetuum . . . Faciendo inde annuatim . . . jura et seruicia . . . debita et consueta In cuius rei testimonium huic presenti carte nostre magnum sigillum nostrum apponi precepimus . . . Apud Edinburgh vicesimo die mensis Januarii anno Domini millesimo quingentesimo vicesimo quarto et regni nostri duodecimo.

APPENDIX XL. — 1524-5.

Antiquities of Shires of Aberdeen and Banff, vol. iv. p. 523. From the *Registrum Magni Sigilli*, lib. xxi. No. 102.

APPENDIX No. XLI.

Appendix XLI.

Alexander Leslie, Third Baron of Wardis.

Charter by Queen Mary to Alexander Leslie of Wardis, and Margaret Forbes, his Spouse, of the Lands of Taviltye—A.D. 1546.

1546.

Maria Dei gracia Regina Scotorum . . . Sciatis nos confirmasse hereditarie dilectis nostris Alexandro Leslie de Warderis et Margarete Forbes eius coniugi et eorum alteri diucius viuenti in coniuncta infeodacione . . . totas et integras terras de Taviltye cum suis pertinenciis jacentes infra vicecomitatum nostrum de Abirdene Quequidem terre . . . pertinuerunt hereditarie dicto Alexandro perprius hereditarie et quas idem simpliciter resignauit . . . Tenendas et habendas . . . dictis Alexandro Leslie et Margarete eius coniugi ac eorum alteri diucius viuenti in coniuncta infeodacione et heredibus masculis inter ipsos legitime procreatis seu procreandis quibus deficientibus heredibus masculis dicti Alexandri quibuscunque de nobis et successoribus nostris in feodo et hereditate imperpetuum . Faciendo inde annuatim . . jura

APPENDIX XLI. et seruicia . . . debita et consueta In cuius rei testimonium huic presenti carte nostre magnum sigillum nostrum apponi precepimus . . . Apud Sanctandrois decimotercio die mensis
1546. Octobris anno Domini millesimo quingentesimo quadragesimo sexto et regni nostri anno quarto.

Antiquities of Aberdeen and Banff, vol. iv. p. 524. From the *Registrum Magni Sigilli*, lib. xxxi. No. 409.

Appendix XLII.

APPENDIX No. XLII.

Alexander Leslie, Third Baron of Wardis.

1585. Charter by King James VI., a.d. 1585, confirming a Charter of Feuferme by George, Earl of Huntly, Lord Gordon and Badenoch, to Alexander Leslie, third Son of Alexander Leslie, third Baron of Wardis, of the Kirklands of the Kirk Town of Dyce in the Barony of Monymusk and Regality of St.
1554. Andrews—a.d. 1554.

Jacobus Dei gratia Rex Scotorum . . . Sciatis nos quandam cartam feudifirme et locationis factam per quondam Georgium Comitem de Huntly dominum Gordoun et Badyenoch etc . . . . ad plenum intellexisse sub hac forma Omnibus hanc cartam visuris vel audituris Georgius Comes de Huntly dominus Gordoun et Badyenoch etc. Salutem in Domino sempiternam Noueritis nos . . .locasse et ad feudifirmam ac perpetuam emphiteosin dimisisse . . . Alexandro Leslie filio tertio genito dilecti nostri Alexandri Leslie de Wardres . . . omnes et singulas terras ecclesiasticas nostras de Kirtoun Dyss . . . jacentes in baronia nostra de Monymusk infra regalitatem Sanctiandree et vicecomitatum de Abirdene Tenendas et habendas . . . prefato Alexandro Leslie filio tertio genito prenominati Alexandri Leslie de Wardres et heredibus suis masculis Quibus deficientibus Patricio Leslie fratri germano prefati Alexandri Leslie junioris et heredibus suis masculis de nobis et heredibus nostris masculis in feodifirma . . . ac

hereditate imperpetuum Reddendo inde annuatim . . . summam trium librarum tresdecim solidorum et quatuor denariorum . . . tanquam pro firmis . . . ab antiquo annuatim persolui solitis Necnon etiam viginti nouem solidorum et quatuor denariorum . . . summam annuatim in solutionem et contentationem gressume . . . ad ratam firmarum duorum annorum pro omni quinquennali locatione . . . necnon et soluendo et reddendo summam triginta solidorum et octo denariorum . . . pro annua augmentatione rentalis nostri et reuerendissimi in Christo Patris Archiepiscopi Sanctiandree . . . per nos . . . secundum tenorem carte nostri soluendi . . . Extendendo in integro . . . ad summam sex librarum tresdecim solidorum et quatuor denariorum . . . Ac faciendo tres sectas ad tria nostra placita capitalia regalitatis annuatim apud Monymusk tenenda Necnon . . . duplicando dictam feudifirmam vnius anni in primo introitu cuiuslibet heredis . . . In cuius rei testimonium huic nostre carte manu nostra propria subscripte nostrum sigillum est appensum Apud Huntly vigesimo primo die mensis Nouembris anno Domini millesimo quingentesimo quinquagesimo quarto coram his 1554.
testibus reuerendissimo in Christo Patre Willelmo episcopo Abirdonensi Georgio domino Gordoun Johanne Gordoun de Finletter filiis nostris carissimis Willelmo Leslie de Kirkhill Magistro Joanne Leslie cum diuersis aliis Quamquidem cartam . . . pro perpetuo confirmamus . . . In cuius rei testimonium huic presenti carte nostre confirmationis magnum sigillum nostrum apponi precepimus . . . Apud Falkland octauo die mensis Julii anno Domini millesimo quingen- 1585.
tesimo octuagesimo quinto et regni nostri decimo octauo.

Antiquities of Shires of Aberdeen and Banff, vol. iv. p. 526. From the *Registrum Magni Sigilli*, lib. xxxvii. No. 136.

APPENDIX.

Appendix XLIII.

APPENDIX No. XLIII.

William Leslie, Fourth Baron of Wardis.

1557. Charter by Queen Mary, A.D. 1557, confirming a Charter by Alexander Leslie, third Baron of Wardis, to William Leslie, his Son and Heir-apparent, of the Lands of the Garioch underwritten—that is to say, Duncanstoun, Gillanderstoun with the Mill, Dunnydure with the Mill, Rochmureill, the Davach of Ardune with the Mill, Warthill, Dornocht with the Mill, Harlaw, Inverurie with the Davach and Mill, Tullifour, Torreis, Knokinbarde with the Mill, and Knokmorgowne with the Foggage and Fogmaill of the Kirktoun of Une and West Hall, with the Tolbeir of Auchlevin and Bourtie; and of the Lands of the Thanedom of Kintore underwritten—that is to say, the Over Davach and Nether Davach with the Mill, the Fermes and the Tolbeir of Kintore, the Lands of Creyche, Taviltie, Mekill Kynnaldie with the Mill, Little Kynnaldie, Petmeddene, Nether Dyce, with the Yearly Rents, the Fishings on the Don, and the Lochs and Bogs—A.D.
1551. 1551.

Maria Dei gratia Regina Scotorum . . . Sciatis nos quamdam cartam concessionis factam per Alexandrum Leslie de Wardres suo charissimo filio et heredi apparenti Willelmo Leslie . . . ad plenum intellexisse sub hac forma Omnibus hanc cartam visuris vel audituris Alexander Leslie de Wardres in Domino Salutem Noueritis me . . . ob filialem affectionem quam gero et habeo erga charissimum filium et heredem apparentem Willelmum Leslie . . . dedisse . . . prefato Willelmo Leslie suis heredibus et assignatis omnes et singulas terras de Gareauch subscriptas videlicet Terras de Duncanstoun Gillandirstoun cum molendino earundem

APPENDIX XLIII.

Terras de Dunnydure cum ipsarum molendino Terras de Rochmuriell davatam de Ardwne cum molendino earundem Terras de Warthill et Dornocht et molendinum earundem molendinum de Dornocht Terras de Harlaw Terras de Inuerrowrie cum dauata et molendino earundem Terras de Tullifour Torreis Knokinbarde cum molendino earundem et Knokmorgowne cum *lie outsettis* dependenciis et pertinentiis *foggage fogmaill* de Kirktoun de Vne et West Hall cum *lie Tolbeir* de Auchlevin et Bourtie Acetiam totas et integras terras de Thanydoune de Kintor subscriptas videlicet Terras de Ovir Daacht et Nethir Daacht cum molendino earundem firmis et *lie tolbeir* de Kintor Terras de Creyche Taviltie Mekill Kynnaldie cum molendino earundem Terras de Litill Kynnaldy Petmeddene Nethir Dyce et Annuos redditus earundem cum piscariis super aqua de Dovne infra limites predictarum terrarum cum lacubus et paludibus earundem et omnibus pertinentiis earundem jacentes infra vicecomitatum de Abirdene Tenendas et habendas . . . de suprema domina nostra Regina et suis successoribus . . . in feudifirma et hereditate ac libera baronia atque libera foresta vt prius imperpetuum . . . Reddendo inde annuatim . . . Supreme Domine nostre Regine et suis successoribus . . . pro . . . predictis terris de Garviaucht summam centum quinquaginta vnius librarum vsualis monete regni Scotie . . . vndecim martas sex caponum duodenas et quatuordecim pultriarum duodenas . . . Ac pro . . . terris thanatus de Kintor suprascriptis . . . summam quinquaginta vnius librarum duorum solidorum et octo denariorum . . . ac reuerendo in Christo patri Willelmo Aberdonensi episcopo et suis successoribus Abirdonensibus episcopis summam quatuor librarum et quatuor solidorum pro decimis denariis thanatus antedicti . . . ac vicecomiti vicecomitatus de Forfar suisque successoribus et heredibus quondam Alexandri Ogiluy de Ouchterhous quibuscunque summam trium librarum monete antedicte . . . secundum formam et tenorem cartarum per quondam illustrissimos et inuictissimos Jacobum quartum et Jacobum quintum Scotorum Reges bone memorie quorum animabus propicietur misericors

APPENDIX XLIII.

et omnipotens Deus mihi et predecessoribus meis desuper concessarum . . . Reseruando tamen . . . liberum tenementum proficuum et vsum fructuum . . . predictarum terrarum de Garviaucht . . . terrarumque thanatus de Kintor . . . mihi dicto Alexandro pro toto tempore vite mee necnon reseruando racionabilem terciam partem . . . terrarum supraspecificatarum . . . Margarete Forbes sponse mee pro toto tempore vite sue . . . In cuius rei testimonium huic presenti carte mee subscriptione manuali mea vt infra subscripte sigillum meum proprium est appensum Apud Abirdene vicesimoprimo die mensis Julij Anno Domini
1551. millesimo quingentesimo quinquagesimo primo coram testibus honorabilibus viris Thoma Menzes de Petfoddellis preposito burgi de Abirdene Magistro Roberto Lummisdene de Cloway Andrea Leslie in Dyce Dauide Mar Georgio Creichtoun de Conze Alexandro Leslie in Creiche Domino Willelmo Thomsoun Magistro Thoma Fynny et Magistro Johanne Kennedy notariis publicis cum diuersis aliis. Quamquidem cartam . . . pro perpetuo confirmamus . . . In cuius rei testimonium huic presenti carte nostre confirmationis magnum sigillum nostrum apponi precepimus . . . Apud Newbottill vigesimoquarto die mensis Julij Anno Domini
1557. Millesimo quingentesimo quinquagesimoseptimo et regni nostri decimo quinto.

Antiquities of Shires of Aberdeen and Banff, vol. iv. p. 525. From the *Registrum Magni Sigilli*, lib. xxxi. No. 409.

APPENDIX.

Appendix XLIV.

APPENDIX No. XLIV.

WILLIAM LESLIE, FOURTH BARON OF WARDIS.

LICENSE, King JAMES VI. to JOHN ERSKINE of Balhagardie to pursue WILLIAM LESLIE of Wardis, and JOHN LESLIE, his Son, notwithstanding the Proclamation regarding the Pest—1589. 1589.

REX,

WE and the lordis of our secreit Counsale vnderstanding that our louit Johne Erskene of Balhagarte hes actioun intentit and dependand at his instans before the lordis of our Counsale agains William Lesle of Wardres and Johnne Lesle his sone and appeirand Air ffor the wrongus molestatioun and troubling of him in his possessioun of his landis of Bennoquhie and wodis of Ardellochie within certaine boundis methis and merchis of the samen as at mair lenth is contenit in his libellit summondis rasit thairuponne In the quhilk actioun process is stayit be ressoun of our lait proclamatioun maid discharging proces in all actionis on the north syde of Forth albeit it be of veriti that the saidis personis persewar and defenderis duellis in the Partis of our realme frie of all suspetion of the Pest. Thairfore we be the tennour heirof grant and geve licence to the saidis persewar and defenderis to persew and defend in the said actioun nochtwithstanding quhatsumever our proclamatioun charge or lettre direct or to be direct in the contrar. Chairgeing heirfore the lordis of our Counsale and Sessioun to proceid and do justice in the said mater nochtwithstanding our said proclamatioun maid as said is or quhatsumeuir vther lettre charge or proclamatioun direct or to be direct proclamit in the contrar, Anent the quhilkis and all pains contenit therein we dispence be thir presentis, Subscriuit be our said Souerane Lord at Haliruidhouse the elevint day of Marche 1589. JAMES R. 1589.

HUNTLYE.

THYRLSTANE.

Pittodrie Papers; *Spalding Club Miscellany*, vol. ii. p. 205.

APPENDIX.

Appendix XLV

APPENDIX No. XLV.

John Leslie, Fifth Baron of Wardis.

1609. Bond be the Laird of Wardes, 1609.

Be it Kend till all men be thir present lettres, me Johnne Leslie of Wardes, ffor the singular love, fauor, and affectioun borne be me to ane noble and potent lord, George Marqueis of Huntlie, Erle of Engzie, lord Gordoun and Badzenoch, and for his lordschippis mantenance of me, my aires and successouris, in all our iust and lauchfull caussis, to be bund and obleist, lykeas I be the tenour heirof bindis and obleississ me, my aires and successouris, in all tyme cuming, to concur, fortifie, serve, and assist, the said noble and potent lord, his aires and successouris, in our awin propper persones, in all and quhatsumeuir actiones, caussis, quarrellis, contrauerseis, and debaites &c. in witnes of the quhilk thing to thir presentis, subscryuit witht my hand, and wretin be Alexander Barclay, notar, my propper seill is to hung, at Striuling, the xiii day of Maii, the yeir of
1609. God M.VI$^{c.}$ and nine yeirs, befoir thir witnessis, Johne Gordoun, seruitour to the said noble lord, George Chalmer of Noth, Normand Arbuthnott, my seruitour, and the said Alexander Barclay.

Jhone Leslie of Vardes.

Gordon Papers; *Spalding Club Miscellany*, vol. iv. p. 257.

Appendix XLVI.

APPENDIX No. XLVI.

Sir John Leslie, Sixth Baron of Wardis, First Baronet.

Process by the Presbytery of Aberdeen against Sir John Leslie, First Baronet of Wardis, and Elspet Gordon, his Wife, for having failed to subscribe the Covenant, and to communicate at the Lord's Table—1601. 1601.

2nd January 1601.

Anent the actioun of nocht subscryving to the religioun, and nocht communicating, persewit agains Johnn Leslie of Wardes, being citat to this day as for the 3 time, onder the pane of excommunicatioun, comperit the said Johnn, and excusit him selff that he cam nocht at first citatioun as being up in the cuntreytht; and forder, offerit to satisfie the Kirkis desyre in all things, nocht onlie to subscryve, but to sweir to the religioun and to communicate at his awin Kirk, at sic tyme as thair wisdomes wald appoinct; and thairfoir the presbyterie thocht it maist meit that he suld communicat at the Lord's tabell on Sunday the (   ) day of this instant, quhairunto the laird descendit and promisit to keip: as also, being desyrit that he wald causs his ladie be present with him, and to subscryve as he did; ansuirit, in thingis concerning hir saull and conscience, he had na power to command her, bot suld do all he docht to move hir thairto, let the ministeris deall with hir utherwayes according to the discipline of the Kirk. The moderator, in name of the rest, ordenit him his ladie to be present and satisfie the Kirk as said is, the said daye, onder pain of excommunicatioun.

And quha sall gang thair and receave his confessioun and ministrat the Communioun, quhither the moderatour, the bischope, or Mr. David Rait, in the nixt exercise it salbe

APPENDIX XLVI.

concludit; because the bischope being south, sall, God willing, returne betwixt this and thair, that he may occupie the Pulpet that day ather in Aberdene or Dyce.

1601.

6th February 1601.

1578-1603.

The quhilk day, the bischope (David Cunningham, Bishop of Aberdeen, 1578-1603) declarit passing to Dyce, and thair was reddie to have ministrat the Communioun to the Larde of Wardes and his ladie efter the subscryving the Confessioun of Faith, quhilk he had reddie ther to present to thame, and nane compeirit thair, but send a lettre to him excusing him selff that it ves a wechtie mater, and he wes a young man, and nocht weill resolued in the heidis of his faith, and thairfoir desyrit that the Kirk wald continew till that he were better informit, and he suld satisfie the Kirkis desyre: as the bischope declarit this daye at gryte lenthe: quhairupone the presbyterie, fynding that he hed mockit baith God and his Kirk, and violat his promeis maid to thame, orderit Mr. Williame Neilsone to summond him to the xx of this instant, to heir and he himselff onderlye the censuris of the Kirk thairfoir, according to justice.

1601.

20th February 1601.

The said day being assignit to Johnn Leslie of Wardes, and Elspet Gordoun, his spous, till haue ansuerit and giffin a sufficient reason of his nocht communicating with his wyf at the Kyrk of Dyce, and for the nocht subscrywing and swering to the true religioun, according as wes mowit to him witht his awin consent and faithfull promeiss, maid to the Kirk as the act beris . Comperit Mr. Williame Nelsone, and producit ane summondis dewlie execut againis the said Johnn and Elspet Gordoun, his spous, as in the summondis at mair lenth is contenit: nochtwithstanding being oft tymes callit, did nocht compeir, The Presbyterie, in respect of their willfull contumacie, being oft tymes citat and disobeyand, ordenit the said Mr. Williame Neilson to proceid with the censuris of the Kirk agains thame:

always for the mair abundance, let them haue ane intimatioun befoir he proceid to prayer or admonitioun. APPENDIX XLVI.

27th February 1601. 1601.

The quhilk day, being assynit to Mr. Williame Neilsone to produce a lauchfull intimatioun maid to the Larde of Wardes and his ladye, comperit the said Mr. Williame, and producit ane summondis, quhairbe he intimeit and chargeit thame at thair duelling places, and publiclie at thair paroche kirk of Dyce, deulie execute and indorsit, desyrand thame as of befoir, to subscryve and communicatt, conforme to the order, onder the pane of excommunication, quha being obstinat and nocht comperand, being oft tymes callit, lauchfull time of day abiddin, the presbyterie ordenit thame to be excommunicat efter admonitioun and prayers, and that the said Mr. Williame giff thame the first admonitioun at the Kirk of Dyce on Sonday nixt: and Robert Forbes to gang to Fintray to supplie his absence.

13th March 1601. 1601.

The quhilk day, Mr. Williame Neilsone being inquerit on his diligence anent the Larde of Wardess and his ladie, that becauss the ladie had offerit to subscryve and communicatt within fourtie dayes, he desistit and gave nocht the admonitioun. This wes his ansuir and excuse: the Presbyterie offerris yet, as of befoir, this courtasie, that, giff he will find sufficient caution, under the pane of tua thousand markis to satisfie within fourtie dayes, they will continew him and thair censuris, utherwayis, ordenit the said Mr. Williame to go forwart to the finall pronounciatioun of the sentence of excommunicatioun.

10th April 1601. 1601.

The quhilk day, Mr. Williame Neilson reported he gave the last admonitioun to the Larde of Wardes and his ladie on Sondaye last, the fyift of this instant, at the kirk, to subscryve the articulis of faith and to communicatt at the Lordis (tabell), conforme as wes decernit to thame to do,

APPENDIX XLVI.

onder the pane of excommunicatioun: in respect of thair obstinacie and admonitionis alreddie past, the said Mr. Williame wes orderit, onder the pane of deprivatioune, to pass to the said kirk of Dyce, and thair proceid aganis theme with the first prayer for thame; and Mr. Robert Mercere to pass thair on Sondaye, cum aucht (dayes) and proceid to the second prayer.

Selections from the Ecclesiastical Records of Aberdeen, pp. 173-175; Spalding Club.

Appendix XLVII.

APPENDIX No. XLVII.

Sir John Leslie, First Knight Baronet of Wardis.

PRECEPT by King CHARLES I., for a Charter to Sir JOHN LESLIE of Wardis, Knight Baronet, and to his Heirs-male whomsoever, of the Barony of Leslie in Nova
1625. Scotia,—A.D. 1625.

PRECEPTUM carte facte Johanni Leslie de Wardes heredibus suis masculis et assignatis quibuscunque hereditarie super tota et integra illa parte et portione terrarum regionis et dominii Nove Scotie vti sequitur particulariter bondata et limitata videlicet Incipiendo super maris littus per sex miliari ex occidente ostii illius fluvii nunc Clyde prius vero Sancti Johannis appellati Et inde pergendo occidentaliter per tria miliaria continue per maris littus ac inde pergendo borealiter in continentem comprehendendo omnimodo tria miliaria in latitudine adversum tria miliaria super maris littore donec ad quantitatem et numerum sexdecim millium acrarum terrarum extenditur cum castris turribus fortaliciis etc. Quequidem terre aliaque in dicta carta ad Dominum Gulielmum Alexander de Menstrie heredtairie pertinuerunt et resignate fuerunt per ipsum in manibus supremi domini nostri Regis pro hac nova carta et infeodatione hereditarie prefato Johanni Leslie de Wardes desuper conficienda etc. Preterea cum clausula vnionis in vnam integram et liberam baroniam ac regalitatem omni tempore affuturo Baroniam de Leslie nuncupandam Tenendam de dicto supremo domino nostro Rege et successoribus suis de corona et regno Scotie in libera alba firma pro annua solutione vnius denarii vsualis monete dicti regni Scotie super solum et fundum dictarum terrarum nomine albe firme si petatur tantum vel alicujus earundem partis in die festo Nativitatis nostri Salvatoris etc . Et quod vnica sasina apud Castellum de Edinburgh capienda erit sufficiens pro omnibus et singulis terris aliisque particulariter et generaliter suprascriptis etc . Et quod dictus Johannes Leslie suique heredes masculi et assignati antedicti habebunt insignia procedentia e manu armata et nuda conjunctis cum hoc dicto . MUNIT HEC ET ALTERA VICIT et cetera in communi forma cartarum Baronettis concessarum etc . Apud Edinburgh primo die mensis Septembris Anno Domini Millesimo sexcentesimo vigesimo quinto et regni nostri anno primo.

APPENDIX XLVII. 1625.

per signetum.

Antiquities of Shires of Aberdeen and Banff, vol. iv. p. 528. From the *Registrum Preceptorum Cartarum pro Baronettis Nove Scotie.*

APPENDIX No. XLVIII.

Appendix XLVIII.

STEPHEN LESLIE, SECOND LAIRD OF WARTHILL.

INSTRUMENT of SASINE in favour of STEPHEN LESLIE of Little Warthill—1582.

1582.

IN Dei nomine Amen... Cunctis pateat ... quod anno incarnationis Dominice millesimo quingentesimo octuagesimo primo mensis vero Martii die vigesimo . . . In mei notarii publici et testium subscriptorum presentia personaliter constitutus discretus vir Stephanus Leslie de Litill Warthill habens... suis in manibus quandam assedationem preceptum sasine in se continentem subscriptam per honorabilem virum Wilhelmum Leslie de Warderes necnon per Wilhelmum Leslie eius filium legitumum in signum sui consensus ... ad infrascripta prefato Stephano Leslie suis heredibus assignatis subtenentibus et coadiutoribus pluribus aut uni

APPENDIX XLVIII. — 1582.

de totis et integris terris crofti vulgo vocati *the Long Croft* of Mekil Warthill cum suis . . . pertinentiis et cum decimis garbalibus et fructibus vicarie eiusdem pro spatio novemdecim annorum Festum Pentecostes in anno 1582 proxime . . . sequentium per dictum Wilhelmum Leslie de Warders factam et concessam Quamquidem assedationem . . . modesto viro Johanni Mvrray in Auldrayn balliuo in hac parte dicti Domini de Warderss . . . presentauit . . . Quiquidem balliuus eandem assedationem . . . mihi notario publico subscripto ad perlegendum tradidit et preceptum in fine dicte assedationis . . . Cuius tenor sequitur . . . Attour be thir presentis . . . ordains my louitis Johnne Mvrray in Auldrayn and ilk ane of thame . . . my . . . balyeis in that pairt . . . to pass efter the sicht of thir presentis to the landis of the saide Lang Croft and gif . . . stait and seasing to the saide Stevin his airs and assignais or thair lauchtfull procuratouris of . . . the saidis landis of Lang Croft of Mekill Warthill . . . for all the . . . termis of the saidis nyntene yeris aboue mentionat, aftir the tennour of this present assedatioun in all poyntis . . . seillit and subscriuit be me and my said sone William Leslie in signe of his consent to the premises as is vnder wreittin at Durnocht the first day of Marche yeir of God ane thousand fiwe hundretht four scoir ane yeir befoir thir witnes George Leslie my sone William Leslie in Durnocht Alexander Keillo Patrick Leslie and Maister Andro Thomsone notar publict, *Et sic subscribitur* Wm. Leslie of Warderss witht my hand Wm. Leslie witht my hand Wm. Leslie in Durnocht witnes Patrick Leslie in Tullefour witnes Alexander Keillo witnes Mr. Androw Thomsone notar and witnes in the premisses witht my hand Ita est Andreas Kyng notarius publicus ac testis in premissis rogatus et requisitus manu propria Post Huiusmodi precepti sasine . . . publicationem . . . prefatus balliuus . . . sasinam . . . Crofte antedicte cum pertinenciis prefato Stephano Leslie personaliter acceptanti . . . deliberauit super quibus omnibus . . . predictus Stephanus Leslie a me notario publico subscripto sibi fieri petiit instrumentum Acta erant hec super solum et fundum dicti *Lang*

Croft. . . presentibus ibidem Georgeo Lamb de Custestoun Andrea Edward in Auldrayne Andrea Mann apud molendinum de Bonytoun Joanne Walcar et Jacobo Spence testibus ad premissa vocatis atque rogatis. APPENDIX XLVIII.

Et Ego Andreas Thomsone artium professor Clericus Abirdonensis diocesis publicusque authoritate apostolica notarius (*etc. in forma communi*).

Antiquities of Shires of Aberdeen and Banff, vol. iii. p. 439; Spalding Club. From original in Warthill Charter-chest.

APPENDIX No. XLIX.

Appendix XLIX.

ALEXANDER LESLIE, THIRD LAIRD OF KINCRAIGIE.

ATTESTATION by a NOTARY PUBLIC that ALEXANDER LESLIE of Kincraigie presented himself at the Pier of Loch Canmor (in Cromar), to have presence of the Earl of Huntly, that he might ask Release of his Lands of Kincraigie, recognosced in the Earl's hands; that the Earl sent Master John Irwing to the said Alexander Leslie, saying that he could not have presence of the Earl at that time, but that the Earl would give an answer to the Notary; that the Notary, being admitted to the Earl's presence, asked Release of the said Lands of Kincraigie, in name and behalf of the said Alexander Leslie, offering to do Homage in his name; that the Earl appointed the said Alexander Leslie to show the Charters by which he claimed the said Lands at a Court to be holden at Cluny on the 27th November, when justice should to be done him—7th November 1529. 1529.

SEPTIMO Novembris anno ($j^m v^c$) xxix° Eodem die personaliter constitutus honorabilis vir Alexander Leslie de Kincraigie apud *lie Peir* de Lochtcanmor ad habendum presentiam Comitis de Huntlie et ab eo ad petendum terras suas de

APPENDIX XLIX.

Kincragy tanquam a domino suo superiore ad plegium sibi dimitti et ad offerendum ei pro relaxatione earundem terrarum per antedictum recognitarum quod de jure domino suo superiori facere tenetur Nichilominus dictus Comes quemdam nuncium misit dicto Alexandro dicendo et allegando dictum Comitem presenciam dicti Alexandri minime pro presenti habere sed dictus nuncius Magister Johannes Irwing asseruit dictum dominum Comitem responsum michi notario dare Ego vero notarius accessi ad presentiam personalem dicti domini Comitis petendo ab eodem nomine et ex parte dicti Alexandri terras suas antedictas de Kincragy ad plegium sibi dimitti et homagium nomine dicti Alexandri dicendo eundem sibi facere Quiquidem dominus Comes antedictus antedicto Alexandro curiam apud Clwne tenendam xxvij^{o} Nouembris instantis assignauit ibidem ad presentandum et demonstrandum euidencias et cartas suas et jura si que habet pro terris antedictis et ad faciendum in dicta assignata curia quod de jure facere tenetur Super quibus hincinde petierunt instrumenta Acta apud Lochtcanmor presentibus ibidem Magistro Johanne Irwing Domino Nicholayo Patersoune Magistro Johanne Brovne Capellanis Willelmo Gordoun de Auchindoir et Alexandro Irwing.

Antiquities of Shires of Aberdeen and Banff, vol. iv. p. 343. From the original in the General Register House, Edinburgh.

Appendix L.

APPENDIX No. L.

Alexander Leslie, Third Laird of Kincraigie.

Attestation by a Notary-Public, that, in the Court of the Earl of Huntly, held at Cluny by Thomas Davidson, his Bailie, Alexander Leslie of Kincraigie asked Release, as from his Overlord of his Lands of Kincraigie, offering the Homage used and wont, but that the Earl's
1530. Bailie refused the Release so sought—20th January 1530.

1529-30. Vigesimo Januarii anno (j^{m}v^{c}) xxix Eodem die personaliter constitutus Alexander Leslie de Kincragy in curia prepotentis domini Comitis de Huntlie tenta per honorabilem virum Thomam Dauidsonne balliuum pro tempore apud Clvne ad petendum terras suas antedictas de Kincragy tanquam a domino suo superiore ad plegium sibi dimitti offerendo dicto balliuo nomine dicti Comitis homagium quod de dictis terris de jure et consuetudine Scotie facere tenetur quod si secus facerit sibi et heredibus suis minime preiudicaret in futurum Quiquidem balliuus dictam requisitionem et antedictarum terrarum relaxationem et ad plegium dimitti refutauit et recusauit super quibus et de remedio juris idem Alexander protestatur et petiit instrumentum Acta apud Clvne hora ante meridiem undecima presentibus Domino Andrea Clark Curato Johanne Forbes Johanne Toucht et Villelmo Crauford. APPENDIX L.

Antiquities of Shires of Aberdeen and Banff, vol. iv. p. 344. From the original in the General Register House, Edinburgh.

APPENDIX No. LI. *Appendix LI.*

George Leslie, Fourth Laird of Kincraigie.

Grant by Queen Mary to George Leslie, Son and Heir-apparent of Alexander Leslie of Kincraigie, of the Goods of John Strachan in Kincraigie, forfeited by his absenting himself from the Queen's Host at Roslin Muir, at the first Siege of St. Andrews, at the Raid of Langholm, and at the Siege of Haddington—18th July 1548. 1548.

Ane lettre maid to George Leslie sone and apperand air to Alexander Leslie of Kincragy . . . of the gift of all gudis . . . quhilkis pertenit to Jhone Strathauchin in Kincragy and now perteining . . . to our Souerane Lady be resoun of eschete throw the said Jhonis tressonable byding at hame fra hir Hienes oistis raidis and armys following or fra ony of thame that is to say . . . the oist raid and army conuenit with hir Tutour on Rosling Mure in the moneth of August the yeir of God $j^{m}v^{c}$xlv yeris quhilk thareafter past to 1545.

APPENDIX LI.

1546. Birgem for resisting of our auld inymeis of Ingland . . . the first sege of Sanctandrois convenit with hir Gouernour in the monetht of October the yeir of God j^{m}v^{c}xlvj yeiris for assegeing and recouering of the Castell thairof fra the withhalderis of the samyn agains hir auctorite togidder with hir Gouernouris sone being thairin . . . the raid of Langholme convenit with hir said Tutour in the monetht

1547 of Julij the yeir of God etc . xlvij yeris for assegeing the Castell thairof and recouering of the samyn fra our auld inymeis of Ingland than presentlie within the said Castell and . . . hir Hienes oist raid and army convenit with the said Lord Gouernour on Gladismure besyde Hadingtoun the x day of Julij instant for assegeing of the burght of Hadingtoun and expelling of our saidis auld inymeis furtht of the samyn . . . At Lethingtoun the xviij day of

1548. Julij the yeir of God j^{m}v^{c}xlviij yeirs.

Per Signaturam.

Antiquities of Shires of Aberdeen and Banff, vol. iv. p. 345. From the *Registrum Secreti Sigilli*, vol. xxii. fol. 20.

Appendix LII.

APPENDIX No. LII.

George Leslie, Fourth Laird of Kincraigie.

1594. Charter by King James VI., a.d. 1594, confirming a Charter by George, Earl of Huntly, Lord Gordon and Badenoch, Chancellor of the whole Realm of Scotland, and Lieutenant of the North, to George Leslie, Son and Heir-apparent to Alexander Leslie of Kincraigie, of the

1549. Lands of Kincraigie, in the Lordship of Tough—1549.

Jacobus Dei gratia Rex Scotorum . . . Sciatis nos quandam cartam . . . factam per quondam Georgium Comitem de Huntlie . . . quondam Georgio Leslie filio et heredi apparenti quondam Alexandri Leslie de Kincragye . . . ad plenum intellexisse sub hac forma Omnibus hanc cartam visuris vel audituris Georgius Comes de Huntlie dominus Gordoun

APPENDIX LII.

et Badyenoch cancellarius totius regni Scotie ac Locumtenens infra partes boreales ejusdem etc. Noueritis nos dedisse... et ... confirmasse ... dilecto nostro seruitori Georgio Leslie filio et heredi apparenti Alexandri Leslie de Kincragye omnes et singulas terras de Kincragy cum suis pertinentiis jacentes in dominio de Touch et infra vicecomitatum de Abirdene pro suo fideli seruicio nobis gratuiter impenso Quequidem terre prius fruerunt dicti Alexandri Leslie hereditarie et quas idem Alexander in manibus nostris tanquam in manibus domini superioris earundem ... simpliciter resignauit, Tenendas et habendas ... dicto Georgio Leslie suis heredibus et assignatis de nobis et successoribus nostris dominis de Huntlie etc. in feodo et hereditate imperpetuum ... cum curiis et earum exitibus amerchiamentis eschaetis herezeldis bludewitis et mulierum merchetis aueragiis carragiis et bondagiis ... saluis nobis et heredibus nostris et assignatis wardis et releuiis et aliis seruiciis debitis et consuetis Reseruato tamen liberotenemento et vsu fructu ... dicto Alexandro Leslie patri prefati Georgii pro toto tempore vite sue ... In cuius rei testimonium sigillum nostrum huic presenti carte nostre manu nostra subscripte est appensum Apud Abirdene decimo quarto die Mensis Aprilis anno Domini millesimo quingentesimo quadragesimo nono 1549.
coram his testibus nobili et potente domino Joanne Comite Atholie Jacobo Betoun commendatario de Abirbrothok Georgio Meldrum de Fyvie milite Thoma Menzeis de Petfoddellis Jacobo Gordoun de Medlok Joanne Betoun de Balfoure et Jacobo Murray de Cowbairdy cum diuersis aliis etc. Quamquidem cartam ... pro perpetuo confirmamus ... In cuius rei testimonium huic presenti carte nostre confirmacionis magnum sigillum nostrum apponi precepimus ... Apud Striuiling vicesimo sexto die mensis Februarii Anno Domini millesimo quingentesimo nonagesimo tercio et regni 1593-4.
nostri vicesimo septimo.

Antiquities of Shires of Aberdeen and Banff, vol. iv. p. 345. From the *Registrum Magni Sigilli*, lib. xxxix. No. 109.

APPENDIX.

Appendix LIII.

APPENDIX No. LIII.

David Leslie, First Baron of Pitcaple.

Charter by David Leslie, Dominus de Pitcaple, to Robert Culan, Burgess of Aberdeen, of an Annual Rent of Four Merks Scots, from the half of the Lands of Crechtmonde, with the Mill, in the Regality of the
1472. Garioch—1472.

Omnibus hanc cartam visuris . . . Dauid Leslie dominus de Petcapill salutem . . . Noueritis me . . . concessisse ac omnino vendidisse . . . honorabili viro Roberto Culan burgensi burgi de Abirdene unum annuum redditum quatuor marcarum usualis monete Scotie exeuntem annuatim . . . de terris meis dimidietatis de Crechtmonde cum parte mea molendini earundem cum suis pertinentiis jacentibus in regalitate de Garyouch infra vicecomitatum de Abirdene . . . Tenendum . . . dictum annuum redditum . . . in feodo et hereditate imperpetuum . . . Reddendo inde mihi et heredibus meis et meis assignatis . . . unum denarium argenti annuatim . . . Et si contingat me heredes meos aut assignatos . . . perturbare . . . dictum Robertum heredes suos et suos assignatos in dicto annuo redditu . . . quod absit obligo me et heredes meos et assignatos ad persoluendum dicto Roberto Culan heredibus suis aut suis assignatis summam centum librarum monete Scotie . . . antequam audiamur in judicio . . . In cuius rei testimonium huic presenti carte mee sigillum meum est appensum apud Abirdene decimo sexto die mensis
1472. Aprilis Anno Domini millesimo quadringentesimo septuagesimo secundo testibus honorabilibus viris Alexandro Menzes burgensi de Abirdene Magistro Alexandro Culan rectore de Ovin Johanne Ramsay Johanne Celle et Domino Roberto Leis notario publico cum multis aliis.

Dauide Lesly manu propria subscribo et approbo.

1510. Note.—In the year 1510, John Cullane of Knawane, burgess of Aberdeen, conveyed the above annual rent to William Elphin-
1512. stoun, rector of Clat, who again, in the year 1512, granted it to

the chaplain of the choir of the church of the New College of the University of Aberdeen, stipulating for the performance of certain religious services for the souls of himself, of his father and mother, of William Elphinstoun, Bishop of Aberdeen, of John Elphinstoun of that Ilk, and of Alexander, Lord Elphinstoun, his son. APPENDIX LIII.

Antiquities of Shires of Aberdeen and Banff, vol. iii. p. 419.

APPENDIX No. LIV

Appendix LIV

David Leslie, Third Baron of Pitcaple.

Service of David Leslie as heir of James Leslie, second of Pitcaple, his Father, in the Lands of Pitcaple and the Mill, in twenty-two Bovates of the Lands of Rosseviot, in the half of the Lands and Mill of Crechmond in an eighth part of the Lands of Ardwne, a third part of the Lands of Harlaw, three-quarters of the Lands of Alehouse of Legatsden, excepting the sixteenth part of these Lands, and in an Annual Rent of Four Merks Scots from the Lands of Crechmond, in the Regality of the Garioch—A.D. 1506. 1506.

Inquisicio facta apud burgum de Abirdene coram honorabili viro Alexandro Bannerman de Wattertone vicecomitis deputato de Abirdene in pretorio burgi eiusdem in curia vicecomitatus ejusdem pro tribunali sedente vicesimo septimo die mensis Octobris Anno Domini millesimo quin- 1506.
gentesimo sexto per subscriptos videlicet Thomam Fraser de Stanyood Willelmum Craufurd de Federay Johannem Mowat de Loscragy Willelmum Turing de Foverne Alexandrum Skene de eodem Jacobum Cheyne de Straloche Johannem Ross de Auchlossin Alexandrum Tulloche de Moncoffir Robertum Burnat de Balmad Johannem Forbes de Echt Alexandrum Johnstone de eodem Johannem Gardin de Latheris Ranaldum Oudny filium et heredem apparentem Willelmi Oudny de eodem Andream Crag de Cragesfintra et Alexandrum Caldour de Sonnaherd Qui

APPENDIX LIV.

juranti dicunt quod quondam Jacobus Leslie de Petcapile Pater Dauid Leslie latoris presencium obijt vltimo . . . sasitus vt de feodo ad pacem et fidem domini nostri Regis de terris de Petcapile et molendino earundem de viginti duabus bouatis terrarum de Rosseuiot de dimidietate terrarum de Crechmond et de dimidietate molendini de Crechmond de octaua parte terrarum de Ardwne de tercia parte terrarum de Herlawe de tribus quartariis terrarum de Ailhouss de Legatisdend excepta decima sexta parte huiusmodi terrarum de Legatisdend et de vno annuo redditu quatuor marcarum vsualis monete Scotie de terris de Crechmond cum suis pertinenciis jacentibus in regalitate de Gareauch infra dictum vicecomitatum . Et quod dictus Dauid est legitimus et propinquior heres dicti quondam Jacobi patris sui de dictis terris molendino dimidietate molendini et annuo redditu cum suis pertinenciis Et quod est legitime estatis Et quod dicte terre molendinum dimidietas molendini et annuus redditus cum suis pertinenciis valent nunc per annum triginta nouem marcas sex solidos et octo denarios et valuerunt xviij marcas tempore pacis Et quod tenentur in capite de supremo domino nostro Rege per seruicium varde et releuij debitum et consuetum Et nunc existunt in manibus domini nostri Regis et prius in manibus comitis de Gareauch legitime per seipsum per decessum dicti quondam patris sui per spacium sexdecem annorum aut eocirca racione varde.

Antiquities of Shires of Aberdeen and Banff, vol. iii. p. 384. From the *Libri Actorum Curiae Vicecomitatus de Aberdeen,* vol. i. MS. in archivis ejusdem.

Appendix LV.

APPENDIX No. LV.

David Leslie, Third Baron of Pitcaple.

Confirmation by King James IV. to David Leslie, third of Pitcaple, and his Heirs, under the Charter in favour of the deceased David Leslie, of the Lands of Pitcaple, and the Mill, with the Patronage of the Chaplainry of Pitcaple at the Altar of the Blessed Virgin Mary, in the Chapel of Garioch, twenty-two Bovates of the Lands of Rosseviot, the half of the Lands and Mill of Crechmond, an eighth part of the Lands of Ardune, a third part of the Lands of Harlaw, three-quarters of the Lands of Alehouse of Legatsden, excepting the sixteenth part of these Lands, and an Annual Rent of Four Merks from the Lands of Crechmond—A.D. 1511. 1511.

Apud Edinburghe . xiv Augusti. $j^{m}v^{c}xi$. Rex confirmavit David Leslie de Petcaple et heredibus suis secundum tenorem antique infeodationis et carte quondam David Leslie terras de Petcaple et molendinum earundem cum donacione et jure Patronatus Capellanie de Petcaple ad altare Beate Marie Virginis infra Capellam de Gariauch viginti duas bovatas terrarum de Rothsyviot dimidietatem terrarum de Crechmond ac dimidietatem molendini de Creichmond octavam partem terrarum de Ardune terciam partem terrarum de Hairlaw tria quarteria terrarum de *le Alehouse* de Legatisdene (excepta decima sexta parte earundem terrarum) ac annuum redditum quatuor mercarum de terris de Creichmond unacum dependenciis *le owtsettis* etc . in regalitate de Gariauch infra vicecomitatum de Abirdene quas idem David resignavit Insuper Rex dictas terras etc . in unam liberam baroniam de Petcaple creavit et incorporavit . Reddendo annuatim Regi unam sectam.

Antiquities of Shires of Aberdeen and Banff, vol. iii. p. 385. From the *Abbreviatio Registri Magni Sigilli*, lib. xvii. No. 3.

APPENDIX.

Appendix LVI.

APPENDIX No. LVI.

Alexander Leslie, Fourth Baron of Pitcaple.

Instrument upon the Sasine given to Alexander Leslie, fourth of Pitcaple, in the Barony of Pitcaple, with the Mills, etc., Four Merks of Annual Rent from the Lands of Crechmond, and the right of Patronage of the Chaplainry of Pitcaple—A.D. 1534.

1534.

Decimo nono Januarii anno etc . xxxiij . Eodem die personaliter constitutus Alexander Leslie de Petcapil super solum et fundum predictarum terrarum suis in manibus tenens quasdam literas papiro scriptas formam sasine hereditarie terrarum baronie de Petcapil cum molendinis outsettis et pendiculis et quatuor mercatis annui redditus terrarum de Crechtmont et cum jure Patronatus Capellanie de Petcapil cum pertinenciis a potenti domino Jacobo Styvart Comite Murrauie ac vicecomite Abirdonensi formam prescriptam sasine hereditarie a capella Regia de dictis terris et pertinentiis sibi directam eius sigillo officii sigillatas honorabili viro Johanni Bissait Mauro in eisdem nominato vigore quarum ipse requisiuit quatenus sibi possessionem hereditariam predictarum terrarum daret . . . Post quarum quidem literarum lecturam dictus Maurus . . . ipsum Alexandrum Leslie in realem actualem et corporalem possessionem predictarum terrarum cum pertinentiis et donatione capellanie predicte induxit et investiuit . . . Super quibus idem inuestitus petiit instrumentum Acta vt supra hora quasi pomeridiana vndecima presentibus Jacobo Leslie in Rosevait Willelmo Mauro Johanne Dauidsone Henrico Meyrnis Alexandro Valentyne et Alexandro Cuyk cum diuersis aliis.

Antiquities of Shires of Aberdeen and Banff, vol. iii. p. 386. From the original in General Register House, Edinburgh.

APPENDIX No. LVII.

Appendix LVII.

John Leslie, Sixth Baron of Pitcaple.

Precept of Clare Constat by George Leslie of that Ilk, in favour of John Leslie, Sixth of Pitcaple, as Heir of Duncan Leslie of Pitcaple, his Father, in the shady half of the Town and Lands of Auquhorsk, lying in the Barony of Leslie, and Parishes of Logydurno and Oyne —A.D. 1627. 1627.

Georgius Leslie de Eodem superior terrarum subscriptarum . . . ballivis meis in hac parte . . . Quia mihi per autentica documenta . . . clare constat . . . quod quondam Duncanus Leslie de Pitcapill pater Johannis Leslie nunc de Pitcapill latoris presentium obijt ultimo . . . sasitus vt de feodo ad pacem et fidem S.D.N. Regis in . . . vmbrali dimidietate totius et integre ville et terrarum de Auquhorsk cum . . . pertinentiis jacentibus in baronia de Leslie infra Parochias de Logydurno et Oyne respectiue et infra vicecomitatum de Abirdene . Et quod dictus Johannes Leslie nunc de Pitcapill est legittimus et propinquior heres dicti quondam Duncani Leslie de Pitcapill sui patris . . . Et quod est legittime etatis . Et quod dicta vmbralis dimidietas totarum et integrarum dictarum terrarum de Auquhorsk cum pertinentiis de me tenentur in capite in feodo et hereditate pro servitiis warde et relevii tantum . . . Vobis igitur precipio . . . quatenus . . . sasinam hereditariam . . . dicte vmbralis dimidietatis . . . dictarum ville et terrarum . . . prefato Johanni Leslie de Pitcapill . . . vel suo certo attornato . . . tradatis . . . In cuius rei testimonium presentibus (manu Joannis Baird scribe signeto Regio scriptis) manuque mea subscriptis sigillum meum est appensum apud Edinburgum decimo die mensis Julij anno Domini Millesimo sexcentesimo vigesimo 1627. septimo coram his testibus Thoma Crombie de Kemnay et Dauide Andersone scribis signeto Regio et Magistro Alex-

APPENDIX LVII.

andro Forbes seruitore dicti Joannis Baird presentium scriba et dicto Johanne Baird.

GEORGE LESLIE of that Ilk.

Antiquities of Shires of Aberdeen and Banff, vol. iii. p. 387. From the original in the possession of the late Patrick Rose, Esq., Sheriff-Clerk of Banffshire.

Appendix LVIII.

APPENDIX No. LVIII.

ROBERT DUGUID, SECOND BAROÑ OF AUCHINHOVE.

CHARTER of the Lands of Auchinhove, Warthill, and Blalok, granted by King JAMES III. to ROBERT DUGUID, Son and Heir of Elizabeth, Heiress of Balcarne—5th March 1470.

1470.

JACOBUS Dei gracia Rex Scotorum omnibus probis hominibus tocius terre sue clericis et laicis salutem Sciatis nos dedisse concessisse et hac presenti carta nostra confirmasse dilecto nostro Roberto Dugude filio et heredi apparenti Elizabeth de Balcarne omnes et singulas terras de Auchinhufe, Warthill et Blalok cum pertinenciis jacentes infra vicecomitatum nostrum de Abirdene Quequidem terre cum pertinenciis fuerunt dicte Elizabeth hereditarie et quas eadem Elizabeth non vi aut metu ducta nec errore lapsa sed sua mera et spontanea voluntate in manus nostras apud Edinburgh per fustem et baculum ac suos procuratores ad hoc legittime constitutos coram subscriptis testibus sursum reddidit pureque simpliciter resignauit ac totum jus et clameum que in dictis terris cum pertinenciis habuit seu habere potuit pro se et heredibus suis omnino quitteclamuit imperpetuum Tenendas et habendas omnes et singulas predictas teras de Auchinhufe Warthill et Blalok cum pertinenciis dicto Roberto et heredibus suis de nobis heredibus et successoribus nostris in feodo et hereditate imperpetuum per omnes rectas metas suas antiquas et divisas prout jacent in longitudine et latitudine cum omnibus et

APPENDIX LVIII.

singulis libertatibus commoditatibus et asiamentis ac justis pertinenciis quibuscunque tam non nominatis quam nominatis ad dictas terras cum pertinenciis spectantibus seu quovis modo juste spectare valentibus in futurum Et adeo libere quiete plenarie integre honorifice bene et in pace in omnibus et per omnia sicut dicta Elizabeth aut predecessores sui predictas terras cum pertinenciis de nobis aut predecessoribus nostris ante dictam resignacionem nobis inde factam liberius tenuit seu possedit tenuerunt seu possiderunt Faciendo inde annuatim dictus Robertus et heredes sui nobis heredibus et successoribus nostris jura et seruicia de dictis terris debita et consueta In cuius rei testimonium presenti carte nostre magnum sigillum nostrum apponi precepimus Testibus reverendis in Christo patribus Andrea Episcopo Glasguensi Willelmo Episcopo Orchadensi dilectis consanguineis nostris Andrea domino Avandale cancellario nostro Colino Comite de Ergile domino Cambel magistris hospitii nostri Davide Comite de Craufurde domino Lindesay Johanne de Culquhoune de eodem milite Jacobo Schaw de Saulchy nostrorum Computorum rotulatore Magistris Archibaldo de Quhitelaw decano de Dunbar Secretario nostro et Johanne Layng rectore de Tannades nostro thesaurario Apud Edinburgh quinto die mensis Marcii Anno Domini millesimo quadringentesimo septuagesimo et regni nostri undecimo. 1470.

Registrum Magni Sigilli, vol. iii. p. 177.

APPENDIX No. LIX.

Appendix LIX

Robert Duguid, Second Baron of Auchinhove.

Deed relating to the Lands of Balcairne, produced by Alexander Seton of Meldrum, and Robert Duguid of Auchinhove—25th August 1478. 1478.

Curia burgi de Abirden tenta in pretorio coram balliuis ejusdem xxv die Augusti anno etc. lxxviii° Quo die comparen . in judicio nobilo viro Alexandro Setoune de Meldrum ex una et Roberto Dogude de Achnahufe ex altera partibus que quidem partes ostenderunt unum publicum instrumen-

APPENDIX LIX.

tum signo et subscriptione Willelmi Keir presbitri Brechinen. dioceseos notarii publici una cum sigillo prouidi viri Johannis Scrymgeour dicti Jak roboratum et sigillatum de et super terris de Balkairne cum pertinen. ac aliis terris in eodem instrumento expressatis de quibus Elizabeth de Balkairne mater dicti Roberti Dogude ipsum infeodauit tam in feodo quam in libero tenemento earundem quam infeodationem Alex[r] Hay sponsus dicte Elizabeth approbauit ratificauit et confirmauit in plena curia coram balliuis burgi de Dunde mediante magno juramento quod nunquam deueniret contra huiusmodo infeodationem et resignationem dicto Roberto factas ut in huiusmodi instrumento plenius continetur. Quod quidem instrumentum dictus Alexander Seton petiit a dictis balliuis transumi ac transumptum sibi desuper distinctum super quibus dicti balliui mature auisati eorum decreto interposito transumptum eidem decreuerunt sub forma publica eorum sigillis sigillatum. Testibus Alexandro Gordon de Megmar Patricio Gordon de Meithlick Roberto Blindsel uno balliuorum Willelmo Blindsel seniore Magistro Johanne Hay Rectore de Crowdane et domino Roberto Leis notario publico cum multis aliis.

Extracts from the Burgh Records of Aberdeen, vol. i. p. 409; Spalding Club.

Appendix LX.

APPENDIX No. LX.

Robert Duguid, Third Baron of Auchinhove.

Achynhufis Band—1536.

1536.

Be it kend till all men be thir present lettres, me Robert Dugoude of Auchinhuif to be bund and oblist, and be the tenour heirof byndis and oblissis me be the faith and treuth in my body, to ane noble and mychty lord George erle of Huntlie, Lord Gordoun, that I sall fore all the dayis of the saidis erlis liftyme and myne, be trest, trow, faithfull, and afald seruand to the said erle and do him seruice, and tak afaild pairt with him in all and sundry his actionis and querelis, agains quhatsumeuir persoun, state, or dignate within the realme of Scotland or vithuth, our souerane lordis hienes allanerly beying exceppit, and that seruice being on the said erleis expenssis in all materis that I serf or ryde in his seruice, except in ostyng and huntyne, etc., in witnes hereof I haue subscriuit this my present obligatioun with my hand, at Edinburgh the first day of Nouember the yere of God M.V^c^xxxvi yeris, befor thir witnes, Nycholl Ross of Achlossin, Walter Berclay of Grantullie, Jhone Gordon, broder to the lard of Geich, and master Villem Gordone witht my hand, vitht utheris diuerss. 1536.

ROBERT DUGUD, Achinhuf.

Gordon Papers ; *Spalding Club Miscellany*, vol. iv. p. 199.

APPENDIX LX.

APPENDIX No. LXI.

Appendix LXI.

ROBERT DUGUID, FIFTH BARON OF AUCHINHOVE.

BIRTH-BRIEF of ROBERT DUGUID, Son of ROBERT DUGUID, Portioner of Ruthven, and Grandson of ROBERT DUGUID, Fifth Baron of Auchinhove.

ATT Aberdein, the sextent day of Junij, 1669 yeirs, in presens of Gilbert Mollisone, ane of the baillies of the said burgh (Aberdeen). 1669.

It wes judicially verefied and prowine, be the depositions of Duncan Forbes of Campbell, Mr. Alex^r.^ Forbes, advocat, and Mr. William Aidy, that Robert Dugat, now reportit to be in , in the Kingdome of Polland, and quho went from this about thretie yeirs agoe, is the eldest laufull sone of the deceast Robert Dugat, portioner of Ruthven, in the schirrefdome of Aberdein, procreat betuix him and Marie Forbes, his spous, in the laufull band of matrimony: and that the said deceast Robert Dugat is the laufull sone of the deceast Robert Dugat of Auchinhove, procreat betuixt him and the deceast Marjorie Gordone, dauchter to the Laird of Aberzeldy, within the

APPENDIX LXI.

said shirrefdom; and that the said Marie Forbes is the laufull dauchter of the deceast Mr. Robert Forbes of Finersie, procreat betuixt him and vmquhill Elizabeth Arbuthnot, his spous, in the laufull band of matrimony: and that the said Elizabeth Arbuthnot is the laufull dauchter of vmquhill Alex$^{r.}$ Arbuthnot, burges of Edinburgh, procreat betuixt him and vmquhill Learmont, his spouse, in the laufull band of matrimony: and that the said vmquhill Mr. Robert Forbes is the laufull sone of the deceast James Forbes of Tillyboy, procreat betuixt him and vmquhill Beatrix Skene, his spous, quho wes dauchter laufull to the Laird of Skene of that ilk: all quhilk they deponit to be of trueth, be wertue of their gret oaths suorne. Wherevpon the baillie ordanit ane testificat to be extendit in ample forme.

Birth-Brieves from the Registers of the Burgh of Aberdeen, 1637-1705; *Spalding Club Miscellany*, vol. v. p. 346.

Appendix LXII.

APPENDIX No. LXII.

William Duguid, Sixth Baron of Auchinhove.

Trial of Gilderoy and his "Complices."

Gilderoy, or, as the word may be translated, "the red lad," has been celebrated in the plaintive ballad which takes its name from the hero of it; but, notwithstanding the romance which has thus been thrown about him, he appears to have been a mere robber and cattle-lifter. A wonderful account of his adventures is given in the "Lives and Exploits of English Highwaymen, Pirates, and Robbers," by Captain Charles Johnson, p. 56.

1636. At Edinburgh, 7th June, 1636. Forsameikle as Archibald, Lord Lorne, heritable justiciar of the south and north Ylleis, and of the shrefdome of Argyle, out of the zeal and affectioun to his Maiesteis service and Peace of the Cuntrey, hes carefully bestirred himselff, and now in end successively takin the arch rebell Patrick McGregour, alias Gilroy, with some of his Complices, be quhome his Maiesteis guid subiectis in the hielandis and north pairtis of this Kingdome hes bene this lang tyme bygane heavielie infested in thair persones and guidis, which being ane service considerable, and quhilk in the consequence thairof will greitlie conduce to the peace and quyet of the countrey, thairfore the lordis of Secreit Counsall findis and declares that the said Lord Lorne hes behaved himself as ane generous and loyall subject, and that he has done guid, reall, and acceptable service to his Maiestie and the estait, and accordingly approves the said Lorde of Lorne his haill proceidings in this matter, ordaining remonstrance to be made to his Maiestie of the said service and merit of the same; Lykas, the saidis Lordis declares that the said Lord of Lorne his taking of the said Gilroy and his complices within the bounds of his justiciarie, and exhibitioun of thame before his Maiesteis Counsall heir, to underly thair tryell and puneishment, sall at na tyme be obtrudet agains the said Lord Lorne, nor sall impoirt any preiudice or derogatioun to the right and Priviledge of the said Lord of Lorne his justiciarie, bot that the same sall stand in full force unpreiudget or impaired be the exhibitioun foresaid; for quhilk purpose, and for preservatioun of the liberteis of his office, ordanis the Lorde Lorne to sit with and be assessor to his Maiesteis justice and his deputies in the trying and censureing of the said Gilroy and such of his complices as ar apprehendit be the said Lord Lorne. Extractum de libris actorum secreti concilii S. D. N. regis per me M. Gilbertum Prymrose clericum eiusdem sub meis signo et subscriptione manualibus. *Sic subscribitur*, Mr. Gilbert Prymrose.

INTRANTES.

Patrick McGregour, alias Gilroy.

Johne Forbes, sone to umquhile James Forbes in Strathdone.

George Grant, sone naturall to James Grant the notorious rebell, callit of Carroun.

APPENDIX LXII.

Allaster Forbes, brother to the said John Forbes.
John McColme, alias Stewart.
Callum Forbes.
John McGregor McEane.
Gillespic McFarlane.
Allaster McInneir.
Ewin McGregor, alias Accawisch.

Dilaitit of the severall and perticuler crymes of slauchters, thiftis, reiffis, depredationes, and oppressiones respective following, viz. the said Patrik Gilroy McGregor, for the tressonable usurpatioun of our Souerane Lordis royal power and authoritie upone him, in cuming to the dwelling-hous of Alexander Hay in Cairnecowlie, and thair, with his complices, breking up the durris thairof, pat violent handes in the persones of the said Alexander and his wyfe, tuik thame captives and prissoneris, caryeid thame as captives tua myles fra thair awin hous under silence of nycht, quhair they keipit the said Alexander and his wife captives the space of twa houris, and wald nocht set thame free quhill they promeist thame ane sowme of money for thair ransome and libertie. Lykas, they staw, reft, and away tuik fra the said Alexander the haill guides and geir being within his houss, countit in wynter last, confessit be the said Patrik Gilroy in his depositiones. Item, for soirning and oppression committit upone the tenents of Sir Robert Innes of Balvanie, knycht, lying upone thame dyverse dayis and nychtis, and violentlie taking of meit, drink, and uther furnitour, without payment of money thairfoir, confessit lykwayis be the said Gilroy, and committit within thir tua zeir. Item, for airt and pairt of the thiftuous steilling of foure hens about
1635. Lambes 1635, pertening to the guidman of Culquharnie, committit be him and be John Dow Gar, and utheris thair complices. Item, for airt and pairt, and being in companie with Donald McConochie, with Robert John McInstalker, Neill McAirthour, Donald McAllaster, with Ewin Neill McPhadrik, Patrik Glas, Duncane Roy Darg, Callum Forbes, John M'Comie, and utheris brokin men at Candilmas

last; and for the tressonable taking of William Dougat of Auchihove, and certane of his servandis, captiues and prissoneris, caryeit thame away and keipit thame prissoneris, and nawayis wald suffer thame to go frie, quhill they gat band and promeis maid of twa hundreth merkis for thair ransome. Item, for airt and pairt, with his complices, of the thiftuous steilling and away taking, in somer last, 1635 yeirs, of fyftene nolt, furth of the landis of Glenprossin, quhilk pertenit to the laird of Fintreyis tennentis. Item, for being airt and pairt, and in companie with John Dow Roy, his brother, John Grahame, his half brother, and utheris thevis and soirneris, and for breking of William Stewartis hous in the Ile of Inchecalzicoth in the Lennox, steilling and away taking furth thairof of his haill insight plenishing, guidis, geir, writtis, and evidentis pertening to him, committit in the moneth of May last. Item, for the crewall slauchter of Chamrone, in anno 1634 yeiris. Item, for soirning with your complice thir thre yeiris bygane, throw the haill boundis of Strathspay, Braemar, Cromar, and countreyis thairabout, oppressing the haill commoun and puir people, violentlie taking and reifing from thame of thair meit, drink, and all provision, with thair haill guidis, gif he and his complices had bene resisted, and for commoun thift and reset of thift.

1635.

1634.

The said John Forbes being dilaittit for airt and pairt, and being the speciall brokin man quha accumpaneit James Grant, callit of Charrone, in all his tressonable and abhominable deidis this fyve yeir bigane, speciallie at the tressonable taking of John Grant, fiear of Ballindalloche, cayreing him from his awin hous to ane killogie, quhairin he wes detenit captiue and prissoner the space of twentie dayis. Item, for being in companie with the said James Grant, rebell, and airt and pairt with him in the crewall murthour and slauchter of umquhile Thomas and John Grantis, callit of Culquoche. Item, for being in companie with the said James Grant, and airt and pairt with him upone the nynt day of Apryle last, of the tressonable resisting with schottis of hagbutis and airrowis, of the bailzie of Strathbogie, quha

APPENDIX LXII.

with ane grit number of the cuntrie people persewit the said James and his associattis within the house of James Anderson, hangman of Strathbogie, to haif apprehendit him and presentit him to justice, and for airt and pairt of the slaughter of umquhile Adame Rynd, sone to the gairdner of Strathbogie, and umquhile Black, quha war baithe schote and slane furth of the said hangman's house, and ane thrid man was schote in the bodie and deidlie hurt. Item, for common thift, soirning, and oppressioun, etc.

The said Allaster Forbes being dilaittit for being in companie, and airt and pairt, with the said James Grant and John Forbes at the slauchter of the said Adame Rynd and Blak, and hunting and wounding of the thrid man furth of James Anderson, hangman of Strathbogie, his house, upone the nynt of Apryle last. Item, for airt and pairt, and being in cumpanie with the said James Grant and Johnne Forbes at the tressonabill taking of Johnne Grant of Ballindalloche, and keiping him prissoner within the killogie of Knockallie the space of xx dayis togidder, and last, for commoun thift and oppressioun, etc.

The said Johne McColmie, alias Stewart, being indytit for airt and pairt, and being in company with the said Patrik Gilroy, Patrik Glas, and thair complices, at the heirschip, reif, and oppressioun committit be thame upon the laird of Cors his tennentis, steilling, reveing, and away taking fra thame of thair haill guidis, geir, insicht pleinsing committit a tua zeir syne or thairby. Item, for being in companie with the said Gilroy and his rebellious associattis at the tressonable taking of William Dougat of Auchinhove, and keiping thame captiues and prissoners, him and his servandis, the space of tua houris, nocht suffering him and his servandis to go frie quhill thay promeist and gave band of tua hundreth merkis, and for being airt and pairt with Gilroy of that tressonable cryme.

The said Callum Forbes for being airt and pairt with the said Gilroy and his complices of the heirschip above written, committit be thame against the tennentis of Corss, and for

APPENDIX LXII.

being airt and pairt with thame at the tressonable takeing and ransomeing of the said laird of Auchinhove. Item, for being airt and pairt, and being in companie with umquhile Patrik Glas at the breking of the duelling house of the minister of the kirk of Birss, steilling and away taking of his haill guidis and geir furth thairof. Item, for airt and pairt, and being in company with the said Patrik Gilroy, John Dow, his brother, and thair complices at the spuillzie, reiffing, and thiftuous steilling at yule last, of the haill guidis, geir, insicht, and plenissing, pertening to Alexander Couttis in Davach in Cromar; and last, for airt and pairt and being in companie with the said Patrik Gilroy McGregour and his complices at the breking of Williame Mitchellis house in Auchintoule, steilling and away taking furth thairof of his haill guidis and geir, insicht and plennissing, apparell and utheris pertening to him, being thairintill comittit about St. Laurence day last.

The said George Grant, base sone to the said James Grant, indytit for being airt and pairt with James Grant, rebell, his father, and in company with him at the breking, under nycht, a sax yeir syne or thairby, of Mr. Robert Udny of Straloche, of his dwelling place, steilling and away taking furth thairof of aucht thousand merkis in rex dollars. Item, for attending the said James, his father, at his tressonabill breking of waird, and escaping furth of the Castell of Edinburgh, and keiping companie with him, be convyoing him fra the said Castell in October, 1632 yeiris, and passing with him to Bigger, and thaireftir to the Falkirk, and 1632.
thairfra to the woid of Harbertschyre, quhair he stayit lying seik nyne dayis, and thairfra convoying him thoro Menteith and Stratherne to the watter of Tay, and thairfra northwardis to Spayside, and keeping companie with him in all his wickit deidis sensyne; speciallie for being airt and pairt, and in companie with the said James his father at the tressonable taking of the said Johne Grant fiear of Ballindalloche, and detening him captive within the Killogie of Knockalie the space of twenty dayis. Item, for airt and pairt, and being in companie with the said James upone

APPENDIX LXII.

the nynt of Apryle last, within the house of James Anderson, hangman of Strathbogie, at quhilk tyme the bailzie of Strathbogie, with ane number of the countrie people, assemblit and convenit about the said hous for apprehending of the said James and his rebellious associattis, and presenting thame to justice, was resistet with schottis of hagbuttis, and Adame Rynd, sone to the gairdner of Strathbogie, William Williamsone, war baith slane out of the said hous, and ane third man named Patrik Anderson was deidlie hurt with ane schot, and sua for airt and pairt of the saidis crymes, &c.

The saidis Johnne McGregour McEane and Allaster McInneir being indytit for airt and pairt, and being in companie with the said Patrik Gilroy McGregor, in the moneth of May last, at the thiftuous breking up of William Stewartis hous in the Ile of Inchcalzeoch in the Lennox, steilling and away taking of the haill guidis, geir, insicht, plenissing, airmour, writtis and utheris pertening to the said William Stewartt, than being within his said hous. Item, for being in companie with the said Patrick Gilroy, John Dow McGregour, his brother, and thair complices, and for being airt and pairt with thame of the thiftuous steilling, be away of maisterfull thift and stouthreif fra the tennentis of James Duik of Lennox, duelland upon his graces landis of Aber, of thair haill guidis, bestiall, and plenissing; as also, for airt and pairt of the hurting and wounding of the saidis tennentis, awneris of the saidis guidis, in defending thairof.

The said Gillespic McFarlane being indytit for being in companie with the said Patrik Gilroy McGregour, that notorious and avowit rebell, and manifest oppressour, dyuerse days and nichts togidder, befoir the said Gilroy his taking, expres agains the actis of Parliament and proclamatioun of his Majesteis lettres, inhibiteing all maner of persones to intercomoun or keip companie with the said Patrik Gilroy, rebill, under the pane of deid.

The said Ewin McGregour, alias Accawisch, being indytit for the thiftuous breking of Patrik Andersones hous in

Aber of Kilmarannach in Junij last, under nycht, steilling and away taking of ane brown horse furth thairof, pertening to the said Patrik. Item, for the breaking of Allaster Dow Stewart his dwelling house in Gartnaforrow, steilling and away taking certane lynning clothes, with certane cheise and uther commoditeis furth thairof. Item, for airt and pairt of thair steilling out of Bartie Mylleris house in Junij last, under nycht, of ane pan with certane stuff for wemenis clothes, togidder with certane pastmentis, raffis, and uther commoditeis than being within the said house. Item, for steilling of ane lynning web pertening to Andro Dyn in the Roiss, in August, 1635, with the said Andro 1635.
his haill abuilzementis. Item, for steilling of ane plaid and certane lyning claith pertening to Walter Brichane, alias McAndro, in Blair, in somer last, 1635, togidder with ane dollour and ane half in moneyis. Item, fra William Kynros in Menteith of ane plaid and ane sword, committit in the moneth of Junij last. Item, for steilling of certane cheis, with ane half dollar in money, fra Walter McAndro in anno 1635. Item, for breking of Thomas Mylleris house in Arochiebeg, at that tyme steilling, and away taking fra him of certane apparrell and silver, with some tobacco, furth thairof. And last, for breking of Margaret Buchananes house in Arochiemoir, and steilling of certane cheise furth thairof, in somer, 1634, under silence of nycht. 1634.

PERSEWAR—

Sir Thomas Hope of Craighall, knycht baronet, advocat to our Soverane Lord for his Hienes intreis.

Archibald Lord of Lorne takis instrumentis of the productioun, and reiding of the foirsaid act of Counsall, quhairby the lordis of Secreit Counsall hes, for preservatioun of the liberties of his office of justice generall within the boundis contenit in his infeftment of justiciarie, hes ordanit his lordship to sit as assessour to the justice deputis sitand in judgement. Lykas, according to the said act of counsall

APPENDIX LXII.

the saidis justice deputis ratifeis his lordship's haill liberteis and privilegis sett doun in the said act, and quhairupone the said noble lord lykwayis askit instrumentis.

The haill persones on pannell being accuset be dittay of the seuerall and perticuler crymes *respective* foirsaidis, mentionit in thair severall dittayis and dispositiones tane be the lordis of Secreit Counsall, and Mr. Alexander Coluile of Blair, his Maiesteis justice deputis, confessit the samyn crymes judiciallie, eftir reiding of thair dittayis, to be verritie, Quhairupone my lord advocat askit instrumentis.

ASSISA—

James Stewart of Ardvorlich.
Mr. Johnne Murray, tutour of Strowane.
Alexander Monteith of Ballieholecht.
John Lennox of Barnchogle.
Archibald Edmesoun in Duntraith.
Robert Stewart of Kilbeg.
John Grahame of Blaircesnok.
Walter McFarlane of Gartavertane.
Archibald Davidson, merchand.
William Blaitheman, flesehour.
Walter McFarlane, fiear of Arrochar.
John Kneilland, servand to Kilsythe.
John Byrnie, merchand, burges of Edinburgh.
Johnne Reid Smyt, in the Cannogait.
Thomas Wilsone, saddler, burges of Edinburgh.

My Lord Aduocat takis instrumentis of the sweiring of the assise, and for verificatioun of the pannellis guiltiness of the severall crymes above written, sett down in thair dittayis, produces thair severall depositiones maid in presens of the lordis of Secreit Counsall and justice depute, and repeittis thair judiciall confessioun of the saidis crymes, speciallie the confessioun of Allaster Forbes judiciallie of the crymes contenit in his dittay, maid in presence of the justice and assyse, and in respect thairof protestit for wilfull error agains the assyse gif thay acquit.

APPENDIX LXII.

Quhilkis persones of assyse being ressauit, sworne, and admittit, eftir accusatioun of the saidis persones, on pannell, of the haill crymes above written, mentionet in thair severall dittayis, thay removet altogidder furth of court to the assyse hous, quhair thay electit and choset, be pluralitie of voittis, the said Mr. John Murray, tutour of Strowane, in chanceller, thaireftir ressonet and voittit upone the severall dittayis above writtin, and the haill crymes thairin contenit, and being ryplie and at length advyset thairwith, re-enterit agane in court, quhair they all in ane voce, be the repoirt and judiciall declaratioun of the said chancellar, fand, pronuncet, and declaret the haill foirnamet ten persones upon pannell to be fylet culpable and convict of the severall and perticuler crymes contenit in thair dittayis, in respect of thair judiciall confession maid be thame thairof, be the interpretatioun and expositioun of the said James Stewart of Ardvorlich, and of the said assyse, and quha was judiciallie sworne in presens of the pannell to be ane trew and faithful interpreter of thair confessiones and declaratioun, and as concerning the puneishment to be inflicted upone Allaster Forbes and Callum Forbes for thair former crymes, for the quhilk thay ar convict in respect of thair confessioun, remittis their puneishment to the justice to consider of thair minoritie, quhairupone my lord aduocat askit instrumentis, and desyret dome to be pronuncet upone thair former convictiones. For the quhilk caus, the justice, with advyce of the lords of Secreit Counsall, and of the said Archibald Lord Lorne, assessor constitute in this criminall process, be the mouth of James Grant, dempster of Court, decernit and adjudget the saidis Patrik McGregour, alias Gilroy, Johnne Forbes, George Grant, John Malcolmie, Johnne Makgregour McEane, Allaster McInneir, and Ewin McGregour, alias Accawisch, to be drawn bakwardis upone ane cairt or hurle, fra the tolbuth or wairdhous, to the mercat croce of Edinburgh, and thair to be hangit quhill thay be deid; and that the said Patrik Gilroy and Johnne Forbes sall be hangit upone ane gibbet quhill thay be deid, quhilk gibbet sall be advancet ane grit degrie heicher nor

APPENDIX LXII.

the gibbet quhairupone the rest sall suffer; and thaireftir the saidis Patrik Gilroy and Johnne Forbes thair heidis be strukin af from thair bodies, with their richt handis, and the said Gilroy his heid and richt hand to be affixit on the eist or netherbow poirt of Edinburgh, and the said John Forbes his heid and richt hand to be put upone the wast poirt thairof, and that this dome and sentence sall be put in executioun upone Friday next, the xxix of Julij, instant, at the ordiner tyme of day, to be appointed be the magistrattis of the said burgh; and as concerning the saidis Allaster and Callum Forbes, and Gillespik McFarlane, continewis the pronunceing of dome agains thame to Fryday next, unto the tyme that the justice be advyset with the lordis of Secreit Counsall thairanent. . . . The quhilk day,
1636. xxix Julij, 1636, dome and sentence agains Allaster and Callum Forbes, and Gillespic McFarlane was pronuncit, ordaining thame to be hangit to the daith, and for that effect to be drawin bakwards to the place of executioun the morne, in the eftirnoone, with the rest of James Grant and Gilroyis complices.

Spalding's *Memorialls of the Trubles in Scotland*, pp. 437-442.

Appendix LXIII.

APPENDIX No. LXIII.

Duguid of Auchinhove.

Epitaph on the Laird of Auchinhove, his Mother, and Chaplain.

In twice three days all under one same roof—
Priest, Laird, Old Lady, died at Auchinhuif.
Three such distinguished worthies death has snatched,
As in their stations rarely could be matched.
Of Seaton's noble blood the Priest was come,
Who long the world had left ere it left him;
On orbs above his mind was fixed, and free
From earthly ties, so heavenly aye was he.
His life was chaste—religious—full of zeal,

APPENDIX LXIII.

Great pity 'twas he died, he lived so well.
Brave Auchinhuif, the Laird, lived wond'rous fast,
So next the Priest, he was the next that passed.
I'll style him man—man every inch—was man
For strength and manhood—match him if you can—
Man, both of head and heart and hand together—
Man, who feared God, and feared no other.
His faith called for the Priest before he dee ;
Priest came in time, then stepped into eternity.
Such blessed example of his dying Priest,
Revived his soul with hopes to be the next,
And follow him who bravely led the way.
To eternal bliss—so just next very day
At self same hour, the Priest had then expired,
Brave Auchinhuif got what he most desired.
The Virtuous Lady spun out her vital thread
Eighty one years, she, saint-like lived and died.
She wished no longer to outlive her son,
So got her wish five short days after him.
Thus buried lie those worthies three together—
The Priest, the Laird, and Lady, the Laird's mother.
May those they've left to fill the vacant stage
Such worthies prove, and thus decore our age.

APPENDIX No. LXIV.

Appendix LXIV.

Hassop Hall.

Hassop Hall, Derbyshire, the seat of Colonel Charles Leslie, K.H., of Balquhain, is a handsome mansion, situated on a fine acclivity, in a well-wooded domain, which rises to a considerable elevation to the west. The hall is closely embowered with luxuriant park-trees, surrounded with tasteful pleasure-grounds and beautiful terraces, adorned with choice flowers and valuable shrubs. The conservatories and vineries, which are arranged on terraces, from their elevated position have a pleasing effect. Near the

APPENDIX LXIV.

entrance to the hall a handsome Catholic chapel was erected in 1816 by the Earl of Newburgh. It is a substantial stone building in the Grecian style of architecture. The interior fittings are of the most chaste and costly description. The altar is composed of various marbles, elaborately worked with foliage and scrolls brought from Naples, and the altar-piece is adorned with an exquisite painting of the Crucifixion by Caracci. There is a good organ erected by Lincoln of London; also a handsome marble monument to the memory of John Thomas, seventh Earl of Newburgh,
1833. who died 22d May 1833, and another to the memory of Dorothy, ninth Countess of Newburgh. In the mansion-house are many fine paintings by the first masters, including works of Caracci, Domenichino, Raffael, Guido, Sacchi, Guercino, Canaletti, Watteau, and Snyders, one of the latter being his finest work in England; also many family portraits, including that of Colonel Eyre, who garrisoned
1643. Hassop Hall for the king in 1643; of Edward Stafford, Duke of Buckingham; and of James, last Earl of Derwentwater, by Sir Godfrey Kneller.

The manor of Hassop formerly belonged to the Foljambes. The heiress of Sir Godfrey Foljambe brought it in the fourteenth century to Sir Robert Plumpton of York-
1498. shire. His grandson, Sir Robert, sold Hassop in 1498 to Catherine, widow of Stephen Eyre, a younger son of Eyre of Padley. Francis Eyre, the direct descendant of Stephen Eyre, succeeded as Earl of Newburgh on the death of An-
1814. thony James, fifth Earl, without issue, in 1814. He died
1827. 23d October 1827, and was succeeded by his eldest son, John Thomas, seventh Earl, who died without issue 22d
1833. May 1833, and was succeeded by his only brother, Francis, eighth Earl. Francis, eighth Earl of Newburgh, died with-
1852. out issue 15th October 1852, and was succeeded in his titles and estates by his sister Dorothy, ninth Countess of
1788. Newburgh, who was born 13th July 1788, and married
1836. 21st July 1836, Colonel Charles Leslie, K.H., of Balquhain.
1853. She died without issue 22d November 1853, and left all

APPENDIX LXIV.

her estates in Derbyshire, Northumberland, Gloucester, and Sussex, to her husband, Colonel Charles Leslie. She was buried in the Leslie family vault, in the chapel of St. Ninian at Fetternear, where a handsome marble monumental tomb was erected to her memory by Colonel Leslie.

APPENDIX No. LXV.

Appendix LXV.

Slindon Hall.

Slindon Hall, Sussex, is the seat of Colonel Charles Leslie, K.H., of Balquhain, who succeeded to it in right of his late wife, Dorothy Eyre, Countess of Newburgh, who was the last heir remaining to her cousin, Anthony James, Earl of Newburgh. The manor-house is delightfully situated upon a commanding eminence in a finely-wooded park, commanding magnificent views of the sea, as well as a large track of fertile country, extending as far as the Isle of Wight to the west, and Worthing to the east. The pleasure-grounds are extensive, and are laid out with great taste, and kept in the highest order. The beech-groves in the park are singularly beautiful, producing trees of great height and dimensions. In the manor-house is a splendid hall, in various parts of which are emblazoned the arms of the Kempes, the Derwentwaters, and the Newburghs. In the public rooms are many fine paintings, including the celebrated one of the Beggar of Antwerp, besides numerous family portraits by eminent artists.

The lands of Slyndon were given by King Henry I. to St. Anselm, Archbishop of Canterbury. The manor-place was first erected in the middle of the thirteenth century by an Archbishop of Canterbury as a summer residence, and was till lately a "peculiar" of the See of Canterbury. Cardinal Stephen Langton, Archbishop of Canterbury, died at
Slindon in 1228. The estate of Slindon was alienated to 1228.
King Henry VIII. by Cranmer in 1543, and was granted 1543.
by King Edward IV. to Sir Thomas Palmer in 1553. It 1553.
was resumed by Queen Mary, and was then granted, and

APPENDIX LXV. confirmed by her and the constituted authorities, to Anthony Kempe, third son of Sir William Kempe of Ollantigh,
1555. Kent, in the second year of her reign, 1555. The estate of Slindon remained in the Kempe family till the death of
1753. Anthony Kempe in 1753, who settled it upon his eldest daughter Barbara, the wife of James Bartholomew, Earl of Newburgh, the son of Charlotte, Countess of Newburgh, and Charles Radcliffe, brother of the Earl of Derwentwater, who was beheaded for his ill-fated attachment to the cause of the Stuarts. The Kempes almost entirely rebuilt the mansion-house of Slindon, accommodating the interior arrangements to the taste of their different ages. The family always remained faithful to the Catholic religion, and they had a Catholic chapel fitted up in the upper part of the house, where mass was celebrated secretly during the
1865. times of persecution. In 1865 a Catholic church was erected in the village of Slindon.

Appendix LXVI.

APPENDIX No. LXVI.

Entail of the Balquhain Estates.

John Edward, Count Leslie, twenty-fourth Baron of Balquhain, incurred a large amount of debt to various creditors. These creditors called in question the validity of the entails of the estates made by Patrick, Count Leslie,
1692-1700. fifteenth Baron, in 1692 and 1700. They commenced legal proceedings against Count John Edward Leslie for the reduction of the entails. To avoid the necessity of each creditor making his claim separately, and to avoid details, all the creditors agreed that one of their number, Mr. Henry Patterson, manager of the North of Scotland Bank, Aberdeen, should act as pursuer in their behalf, and Count John Edward Leslie became the defender.

A summons of adjudication against John Edward, Count Leslie, was issued, dated Outer House, November
1843. 18th, 1843, at the instance of the said Henry Patterson,

APPENDIX LXVI.

for the nominal sum of £1000. By this summons Henry Patterson sought to have the estate of Balquhain adjudged from Count John Edward Leslie, the defender, and all others having or pretending to have right thereto, and decerned and declared to pertain and belong to the pursuer. Count Leslie pleaded in defence that the deed of tailzie of 1700, in connection with the deed of tailzie of 1692, was a strict and complete entail according to the provisions of the Act of 1685, chap. 22, by which act a tailzie executed in obedience to its provisions is declared to be real and effectual not only against the contraveners and their heirs, but also against their creditors, comprisers, adjudgers, and other singular successors whatsomever; and that therefore the estate so entailed was not liable to be adjudged, and could not be affected or carried off by the debt or deed of any of the heirs succeeding thereto, in prejudice of the substitutes.

1700.
1692.
1685.

To these defences the pursuer replied that the deed of 1700 executed by Count Patrick Leslie, whereby he revoked the tailzied destination in the deed of 1692, and introduced a new order of succession, under which the defender took as heir, containing no fetters or restrictions of entail, nor clauses irritant or resolutive, was insufficient of itself to create any valid or effectual entail in terms of the statute of 1685; that the obligation to make resignation in favour of the heirs called by the deed of 1700, as well as the procuratory of resignation itself in that deed, being unqualified by reference to any fetters or limitations of entail, authorised a resignation in fee-simple in favour of the heirs called by the new destination, and consequently there was no warrant for introducing into the title subsequently made up, any such fetters or limitations, and that the same were ineffectual at least against creditors onerously contracting with the heir in possession; that even if the procuratory of resignation in the deed of 1700 were held to import that resignation was to be made under a reference to the fetters of the old entail, so far as not altered by the new deed, such a reference would not constitute an effectual entail

1700.
1692.
1685.
1700.

APPENDIX LXVI.

against creditors, inasmuch as the prohibitions and restrictions of entail, and clauses irritant and resolutive, were not inserted in the procuratory of resignation, nor in any part of the deed, in terms of the statute of 1685; and that more particularly is such an entail by reference ineffectual where the deed of 1700, and the subsequent and relative deed of 1707, not only introduce a new destination, but also alter to a certain extent the conditions and limitations of the tailzie of 1692, to which the reference was supposed to be made.

1700. Count Leslie replied that the deed of tailzie of 1700 was, according to its terms, and in connection with and by
1692. reference to the deed of tailzie of 1692, a strict and complete entail, and was not rendered invalid or ineffectual even against onerous creditors by the introduction of a new destination of heirs, or by the alteration of the conditions or limitations of the tailzie of 1692, as these new destinations or alterations were introduced and made in virtue of
1692. a reserved power in the deed of 1692, which deed, except in so far as it was altered or qualified by the deed of 1700, was incorporated with, and with all its fetters made part of the entail of 1700.

1843. The Lord Ordinary, Lord Wood, 5th December 1843, appointed intimation of this summons of adjudication to be made to all the other creditors of John Edward, Count
1844. Leslie. On the 13th February 1844, the Lord Ordinary, with the consent of the counsel for the parties, held the record closed.

1844. John Edward, Count Leslie, died 19th August 1844, and Henry Patterson obtained a summons of transference against James Michael Leslie, Count John Edward Leslie's successor, 10th December 1844. James Michael Leslie, 8th
1845. January 1845, objected that he was not personally liable to the pursuer for any debt incurred by the late Count Leslie, as he did not represent the said Count in any other character than that of heir of tailzie and provision under the fetters of a strict entail. On the 18th February 1845, the Lord Ordinary having considered the closed records in

the original action of adjudication, and the action of transference thereof, with the revised cases for the parties, transferred the original action of adjudication against the said James Michael Leslie, and decerned. He conjoined the said two actions, and in the conjoined actions, he repelled the defences stated in the action of adjudication, and adjudged, decerned, and declared, in terms of the summons of adjudication, reserving to the said James Michael Leslie all objections to his not being liable for the debts of the late John Edward, Count Leslie, beyond the value of the estate of Balquhain; and he found the pursuer entitled to expenses. APPENDIX LXVI.

James Michael Leslie reclaimed against this interlocutor, 20th February 1845, and on the 1st July 1845 the following decision was pronounced :—

INTERLOCUTOR of the FIRST DIVISION—In Adjudication, Patterson *v.* Leslie.

1*st July* 1845.—The Lords, having considered the reclaiming note for James Michael Leslie, Esq., with the revised cases, and whole conjoined processes—Refuse the prayer of the said reclaiming note, and adhere to the interlocutor of the Lord Ordinary reclaimed against : Find the pursuer entitled to additional expenses : Appoint an account of expenses to be lodged, and remit to the auditor to tax the same and to report : And of new adjudge, decern, and declare, in terms of the conclusions of the summons of adjudication. D. BOYLE, *I.P.D.* 1845.

Sig[d] 2 July.

In consequence of this decision the entails were found to be invalid and ineffectual, and James Michael Leslie became liable for the debts of John Edward, Count Leslie, as burdens on the Balquhain estates, which he could have sold to pay those debts.

NOTE.

Note. THE three ancient charters given in the first volume of this work, Appendix, Nos. I. III. and VI., are important documents, which prove the first four generations of the
1067. original family of Leslie from 1067. These charters are written in black letter, each on a small piece of parchment, and they are now in the possession of the Countess of Rothes. I was anxious to get facsimile copies of these charters for this work, and I was promised photographed copies of them, but I regret to say that this promise has been retracted. However, as I had access to these charters some years ago, I trust that the text given will be found correct. C. L.

Colonel Leslie's manuscripts of this work were most carefully transcribed and prepared for publication by the Rev. Mr. Wilson, Catholic clergyman at Fetternear, who afterwards revised the proof-sheets for the printer.

GENERAL INDEX.

NOTE.

Note.

Commonty of Bennachie.

John Leslie, eighth Baron of Balquhain, granted a charter of alienation in favour of his son, William Leslie, 10th September 1560, of the Barony of Balquhain, and among 1560.
the liberties and privileges of the said barony is enumerated the right of commonty in the whole forest of Bennachie, "cum communitate in tota foresta de Bannoquhye." A precept of sasine was granted by the said John Leslie for infefting the said William Leslie in the said barony, 10th September 1560, and in the enumeration of the privileges of the same, the following words occur :—" Una cum communitate in tota foresta de Bannoquhye." An instrument of sasine, following on the said precept, 11th October 1560, contains the following words :—" Una cum communitate in tota foresta de Bannoquheye." A precept under the Privy Seal was issued, 19th September 1561, for expeding a 1561.
charter of confirmation in favour of the said William Leslie, in which the following words occur :—"Una cum communitate in integra foresta de Bannoquhy." In the retour of the special service of John Leslie, tenth Baron of Balquhain, as heir to his father, William Leslie, 17th October 1573, are 1573.
the following words :—" Una cum communitate in tota et integra foresta de Banochie." A charter of confirmation under the Great Seal, 9th November 1600, confirming a charter 1600.
granted by John Leslie, tenth Baron of Balquhain, in favour of his son, John Leslie, 26th September 1597, contains the 1597.
following :—" Cum communi pastura infra forestam de Bennaquhy et locis solitis et consuetis." A charter of resignation under the Great Seal, 30th August 1610, in favour of John 1610.
Leslie, younger of Balquhain, contains the following :— " Cum communi pastura infra forestam magnam de Bennaquhy et locis solitis et consuetis."

THE END.

Printed by R. CLARK, *Edinburgh.*

Printed in Great Britain
by Amazon

36051383R00416